| DATE DUE | | | |
|---|---|---|---|
| Oct 30 '74 | | | |
| | | | |
| | | | |
| | | | |
| | | | |
| | | | |
| | | | |
| | | | |
| | | | |
| | | | |
| | | | |
| | | | |
| | | | |

# RELIGIOUS LANGUAGE AND THE

# PROBLEM OF RELIGIOUS KNOWLEDGE

# RELIGIOUS LANGUAGE AND THE PROBLEM OF RELIGIOUS KNOWLEDGE

*Edited with an introduction by Ronald E. Santoni*

*Indiana University Press*

*Bloomington & London*

# CONTENTS

5

# PREFACE

The idea for this book developed from a sensed need in the field of contemporary philosophy of religion. There is no question that, given the challenge of logical empiricism and increasing attraction to logical analysis as a method of philosophizing, the claims and language of religion have come under closer empirical and logical scrutiny, and concern about the logical status of religious language and the possibility at all of religious "knowledge" has become one of the most gruelling issues in the field of philosophy of religion today. Irrespective of whether the issue is wrong-headed or misdirected, a growing number of philosophers, analytic and nonanalytic alike, have responded to the challenge which it presents and have sought to include it among the basic questions of the philosophy of religion. Widespread interest in matters relating to religious language and religious knowledge has added new dimensions to traditional philosophy of religion courses and has provided the impetus for new, more specialized courses in the field.

In my introduction, I shall speak briefly to the issue of the relationship between the question of the status of religious language and the question regarding the possibility of religious knowledge. In the meantime, I wish to say that as editor I should be the first to acknowledge the arbitrariness involved in my choice of divisions for this book. In respect to the book's order, my task, plainly, has been one of organizing a considerable amount of relevant material around a small number of recurring themes and concerns which permeate the exciting contemporary discussion of the basic problem of the cognitivity of religious language. Although I am neither arrogant about nor wedded to my choice of divisions, I feel that it does provide a reasonably intelligent grouping of the dominant concerns in the selections, and an adequate framework within which to consider systematically the major aspects of the central problem. That the divisions sometimes overlap seems to me unavoidable, given the intimately related facets of the problem.

Further, although I have attempted to represent fairly the main sides of the dialogue on religious language and religious knowledge, I realize that the conservative religious traditionalist might accuse me of slighting the more traditional view of religious language. But I must remind such a critic, as well as the general reader, that this book is attempting to depict the problem of the cognitivity of religious language in its contemporary context, and that this novel setting seems to force a new perspective on the usual distinction between the liberal and conservative positions. For, in part, the contemporary frustration and concern with religious language has developed as a reaction against the more traditional view of religious language. Hence, to cite but one example, the position of I. M. Crombie, represented here by the longest single selection in the entire book, may well appear liberal alongside the traditionalist position, even though, within the framework of recent discussion of religious language, it is regarded as a "right-wing" response to the problem.* Yet, it should also be noted that with the inclusion in this book of a relatively long selection from E. L. Mascall's important work on analogy, as well as Demos' contribution to a symposium on religious cognitivity, the more conservative and traditional view of religious language can hardly be said to be ignored.

Finally, I wish to acknowledge my indebtedness to the many people who have helped make this book a reality. In particular, I should like to express my gratitude to the following people: the authors and publishers of the materials included in this volume, for the kindness and, often, generosity they have shown in permitting the reproduction of these materials; the publisher, for advice and encouragement in respect to the present project; the Church Society for College Work, whose postdoctoral faculty fellowship in 1961-1962 helped to provide the conditions within which I could pursue interests pertaining to the relation between philosophy and religion; William Christian of Yale University, whose incisive thinking and quiet insights during a seminar on "Meaning and Truth in Religion" both stimulated and challenged me to do considerably more inquiry in this area; to my department

---

* See, for example, William T. Blackstone, *The Problem of Religious Knowledge* (Englewood Cliffs: Prentice-Hall, 1963), p. 116ff. The influence of Blackstone's book will be apparent elsewhere, and I wish to express my gratitude for it.

chairman, Maylon H. Hepp, and Blair Knapp and Parker Lichtenstein of the administration of Denison University, whose understanding has contributed significantly to the satisfactions of my work; Mrs. Quentin Kraft, who, as part-time department secretary, has served efficiently and pleasantly to prevent many a headache for me; Mrs. Louis Brakeman for performing the courageous task of turning my handwriting into typescript; my parents, without whose foresight and self-sacrifice this book and my present career would be but a wishful thought; and finally, my wife Margo and our four young daughters (Christina, Marcia, Andrea, and Juanita), who, subjected to the idiosyncrasies of the academic life, have responded with scarcely believable patience, love, consideration, and selflessness. To all of these, to my students, and to many more, I am deeply indebted, yet I alone assume responsibility for the inadequacies and shortcomings of this work.

RONALD E. SANTONI

*Denison University*

# INTRODUCTION

## Ronald E. Santoni

A crisis in respect to the understanding of religious language has been proclaimed in our time by both philosophy and theology. Not only have self-confident, outspoken philosophers like A. J. Ayer, employing the tools of logical analysis and adopting scientific criteria and principles of investigation, relegated religious discourse to the realm of nonsense or the cognitively meaningless,[1] but a considerable number of exploring and insightful religious thinkers, sensing either the challenge of logical empiricism or disenchantment with conventional religious terminology, have called for and participated in a radical reexamination of religious language. Paul Tillich has told us that "we are in a confusion of language in theology and philosophy and related subjects which has hardly been surpassed in any time in history."[2] He has informed us, further, that words no longer communicate to us what they initially did and what they were intended to communicate;[3] that, in fact, "we no longer have words in which the powerfulness of the word pulsates."[4] Rudolf Bultmann, disturbed by the mythological conceptions still attached to Christian language, has called for a "demythologizing" of the mythology involved in the language of Christianity.[5] Paul van Buren, whose analysis and reconstruction of theological statements was initially associated with the baffling "Death of God" thinking, has affirmed that "Today, we cannot even understand the Nietzschean cry that 'God is dead!' for if it were so, how could we know?" "The problem now," he has maintained, "is that the word 'God' is dead."[6]

All of these statements, by suggesting that religious or theological language today cannot be taken at face value, contribute to a formulation of the contemporary problem to which this book is addressed. Whatever our religious orientation, we are urged to

11

think anew about the nature of religious language, to ask again the question of what religious language is all about. In opening selections in the present book, slightly different versions of this question frame the general issue sharply and succinctly. At the end of his contribution, entitled "Is Religious Language so Idiosyncratic that We Can Hope for No Philosophical Account of It?,"* Alasdair MacIntyre asks specifically: "If talk about God is not to be construed at its face value, how is it to be construed?" And in "Positivism and Religion," Thomas McPherson, looking at pairs of statements like "I and my father are one" and "My father is greater than I," helps us to see other dimensions of the question when, concerning such statements, he asks: "How are we to understand them? Or is it wrong to try to understand them? *Are* they absurd or nonsensical? If they are not, then why not? If they are, then *how* exactly is it that they are absurd or nonsensical?

Of course, as the foregoing van Buren quotation implies, the queries and concerns regarding the nature of religious language drives one to a consideration of epistemological questions. For whatever answer is proposed concerning the status of religious language, one is always entitled to ask the proponent of the given answer how he "knows" what constitutes the nature of religious language, and how he would go about "justifying" or "verifying" his claim. Moreover, one may legitimately ask the user of religious language how he knows that his language refers or applies to the referent or content to which he is claiming reference or application, on what grounds he can claim such knowledge, what he means by "knowledge," and whether, indeed, his language can be, or can be shown to be, true or false. E. L. Mascall gives testimony to the intimacy of this relation between the issue of "religious language" and the issue of "religious knowledge" when he asserts that "The word 'God' must have some content if our statements about God are to be intelligible at all; and if we say what the content is we are inevitably saying things about him."[7] Certainly, the title and contents of the present volume testify to my belief that the nature of religious language and the possibility or meaning of religious knowledge are intimately related facets of the larger problem of

---

* Please note that when, in this introduction, references are to materials included in selections in the present volume, there will be no footnote documentation.

the cognitivity of religious language, and that the separation of the issue of religious language from the issue of religious knowledge is, in the words of Mascall again, "quite impossible."[8]

My joining of these two issues and sets of questions within the basic problem of the cognitivity of religious language calls for at least a working notion of how I conceive of this underlying problem. Briefly stated, by the "problem of the cognitivity of religious language," I mean the fundamental problem, with all of its related issues, of whether religious language (e.g., prayers, confessions, creeds, theological assertions, etc.), either whole or in part, is capable of being true or false. It seems to me that this is the root issue from which emerge concerns as to the very nature of religious language, the literalness of religious language, the possibility of religious knowledge, the justification and verification of religious language, etc. Certainly, insofar as the contemporary discussion of religious language arises, in part, as a reaction against the positivist's criteria for cognitively meaningful language (i.e., language which, for him, can be true or false), my judgment can be supported. My point of view seems to be shared by William T. Blackstone, who argues that the question of "whether religious sentences are cognitive" is "logically prior to the question of whether religious sentences or claims constitute knowledge."[9] But although I am inclined to accept the logical priority of the issue of the cognitivity of religious language to the issue of religious knowledge, it is important to see that my position here does not, as far as I know, entail a commitment to that priority, but simply to the view that the cognitivity of religious language issue is the basic and permeating problem from which the religious knowledge question and other issues stem. Of course, my position does not logically preclude the possibility that the solution of the cognitivity question may be logically dependent on the solution to the religious knowledge question. Because (by seeing the religious knowledge question as an aspect of the more basic and more comprehensive cognitivity of religious language problem) I take a different approach from Blackstone, and because I am not aware fully of the intentions of Blackstone's statement, I can sympathize with, but not endorse, his contention.

Having attempted to delineate the basic problem, issues, and framework in relation to which the selected materials of this book are to be considered and openly confronted, I intend now to make some scattered comments regarding the specific contents of this book. Some of these comments will be brief and sketchy; others will be more detailed and will attempt to formulate serious difficulties within certain readings. Some will endeavor to justify the choice of a given selection; others will attempt to interrelate two or more of the chosen materials. All of them will pay deference to the general order of materials inside the book and, as suggested in my preface, will take for granted an element of the arbitrary in my choice of divisions for the book.

I. *The Logical Status of Religious Language.* I have already pointed out that introductory articles by Alasdair MacIntyre and Thomas McPherson contribute significantly to posing the basic issue to which, assuming a contemporary context, this book is directed. For, clearly, in one way or another, the writings in the present collection are speaking to the question of how we are to understand religious language and what, if any, are its idiosyncrasies. However, before any comment on any answer to this general question is undertaken, it is important to note that William Christian's article, "Truth-Claims in Religion," adds an early dimension of refinement to the general question. By making it clear that he is discussing the "possibility of significant truth-claims in religion" and that he is looking for "some necessary conditions of making truth-claims in religion," he brings out the essential ingredient of what I have called the problem of the cognitivity (i.e., possibility of truth or falsity) of religious language. And the distinction which he draws between "deciding whether some religious proposal makes a truth-claim" and deciding whether such a proposal "is true" is an important one to remember in this whole discussion of religious language. Yet despite this contribution and the incisive way in which Christian presents and lists the conditions essential to any "significant truth-claim" in religion, I must reiterate here my disappointment with his failure to offer one definite example of a religious proposal which meets all of his proposed conditions for a genuine truth-claim.[10] His suggestion of the possibility of significant truth-claims in religion would have been strengthened, it seems to me, by such an illustration.

McPherson's reply to his own questions about the nature of religious language, although conciliatory in spirit, is not likely to satisfy those who are concerned about the logical status or cognitivity of religious utterances. For there is a sense in which McPherson answers the question of religious language by inviting a moratorium on religious language. Adopting a view which combines the positivism of Wittgenstein and that of the Vienna Circle with Otto's emphasis on the non-conceptualizable or non-rational "core" of religion, he appears to endorse the "positivistic way" which suggests that religious utterances are attempts to express what cannot be said. On this interpretation, he is not surprised to find theologians uttering what is " 'literally' absurd" or the Vienna Circle contending that theological propositions are "non-sense," i.e., not open to verification in sense-experience. By pointing out the absurdity (again, in the sense of non-amenability to sense-verification) of the utterances of theologians, the positivist, says McPherson, has "helped to show that religion belongs to the sphere of the unutterable," and that the way out of this absurdity—whether it be the "literally absurd" or empirical "non-sense"—is by retreating into silence. In relegating religion to the domain of silence, McPherson and (on his interpretation) the positivist seem, then, to be answering the question of the status of religious language by suggesting that there shouldn't be any such language. But it is to be noted that this way out, if taken seriously by religious people, not only eliminates the problem of the cognitivity of religious language, but also the possibility of any truth-claim in religion; for, presumably, such a claim would, itself, be either an utterance within religious language or a claim about an utterance in religious language. Moreover, as a number of contemporary writers have either pointed out or implied,[11] McPherson's position seems to suggest a doing away with religious organizations, or, indeed, even a community of believers (for could there be any beliefs to communicate; and if so, how?), and a reduction of religion to feelings and emotions. McPherson's answer, though challenging, is not likely to satisfy, for it neither accepts the framework within which the problem develops nor reflects a careful "listening" to people who consider themselves religious. The latter point is substantiated by his failure to examine seriously the possibility of symbolism, metaphor, or analogy as forms which religious communication might take. He does little more than to mention the theory of analogical predication and then, by suggestion, to dismiss it.

If McPherson lacks sensitivity in respect to the way in which religious people qua religious use their language, I. M. Crombie and Father Joseph Bochenski take pains to listen to, understand, and differentiate religious language. I allow a substantial portion of Crombie's "The Possibility of Theological Statements" to constitute the longest single selection in this book because of my impression that, within the contemporary philosophical effort to analyze and ascertain the logical status of religious language, Crombie's article represents one of the most penetrating, discerning, painstaking, and yet sympathetic, works to appear. I do not believe that either the severest debunker or the most enthusiastic defender of the meaningfulness of religious language can speak either convincingly or decisively about the present problem without taking stock of many of the issues and suggestions brought out by Crombie's essay. Crombie's careful delineation of the logical idiosyncrasies or anomalous formal properties of theological language,[12] his insistence that, far from establishing the meaninglessness of theological statements, these "paradoxical features" contribute to "a grasp of their meaning," his conscientious attempt to delimit the "reference-range" of theological statements and to indicate how this reference-range is fixed, are but a few of the many contributions and counter-challenges which he offers to the contemporary discussion of religious language. Surely, to move beyond both the material and main theme of this section, Crombie here succeeds at least in holding "at bay the wolf who would devour, as meaningless, all theological statements in one meal."[13]

As already indicated, J. M. Bochenski is also keenly open to the peculiarities of religious language. Yet it is to be noted that although he argues that the structure of RD (i.e., religious discourse) differs from that of the discourse of science to the extent that authority assumes an important role in it, he also suggests that from the logical perspective, the situation in RD closely resembles the situation which we find in the discourse of natural sciences. His consideration of the "general structure of RD" in the light of his delineation of the elements in "modern axiomatic systems," his contention that religious discourse is very closely associated with the total discourse (TD) of those who use it, together with his statement (in a later part of the book from which our selection is taken) that, as discourse, RD "is subject to the general laws of formal logic,"[14] provide a basis for an interesting contrast between his analysis and Crombie's equally sympathetic treatment of the logical status of religious language. Moreover, the reader who wishes to pursue Crombie's notion of the relationship between theological language and mystery would be well-advised to turn to Bochenski's full and important book, *The Logic of Religion*, where he will not only find Bochenski's confrontation with the word "mystery" but, among other contributions, Bochenski's earnest scrutiny of how people have tried to justify "basic dogma" in RD, and a pioneering attempt to examine and delineate the formal structure of justification by authority.

II. *The Question of the "Literalness" of Religious Language.* Any conscientious attempt to understand religious language or to come to grips with the question of its cognitivity leads inevitably to the question of whether it is to be taken literally, whether it is to be regarded as univocal, or whether, instead, it is to be understood according to some other mode of interpretation. Indeed, the answer to the question of whether religious sentences can be said to be capable of truth or falsity is often contingent on one's answer to this question of the "literalness" of religious language. An interesting case in point occurs in the first selection, in which A. J. Ayer argues that "transcendent truths of religion" are not possible because the sentences which the religionist employs to express such "truths" have no literal significance. For Ayer, religious sentences belong to the class of metaphysical sentences, and a metaphysical sentence is one which intends to express a genuine proposition, but, in fact, fails to express either a tautology or an empirical hypothesis.[15] Because, for him, "tautologies and empirical hypotheses form the entire class of significant propositions," he feels justified in concluding that all metaphysical assertions—religious utterances included—lack literal significance and are, hence, cognitively meaningless (i.e., in the positivist sense of the word, are "nonsense").[16] But even though such assertions have no literal meaning and are not amenable to any criteria of truth or falsity, Ayer is willing to allow that "they may still serve to express, or arouse, emotion. . . ."[17] Ayer's answer, then, to the question of literalness, though brash and arbitrary, not only illustrates the importance of the question in relation to the larger problem of the cognitivity of religious language, but provides a kind of challenge and pole in respect to which other answers to the question may be considered.

The selection from Paul Tillich's work, "Symbols of Faith," offers one of the most influential and philosophically stimulating views of religious language of our age. In brief, his position is that the language of faith is a symbolic language and that "everything religion has to say about God . . . has a symbolic character."[18] So much is Tillich committed to a view of religious language as symbolic, rather than literal, that he feels that the very meaning of "God" is "completely missed,"[19] and that faith becomes idolatrous, if one takes religious language literally. Moreover, he states emphatically that the distinction between symbolic and non-symbolic speech is of such basic importance that "if we are not able to make understandable to our contemporaries that we speak symbolically when we use such [religious] language, they will rightly turn away from us, as from people who live still in absurdities and superstitions."[20]

The reader must come to grips with the details of Tillich's characterization of the symbol and thereby sense the power which Tillich ascribes to the symbol. Yet before considering any perplexing difficulties in Tillich, we may simply note that Tillich, the theologian, shares with Ayer, the extreme logical empiricist, the position that religious language, if viewed literally, is absurd in some sense of that word. Referring to illustrations of religious language, Tillich says: "Now all this, if taken literally, is absurd." But in radical contrast to Ayer, he does not go on to deny all cognitive meaningfulness to religious language, but, on the contrary, argues that if religious language is taken symbolically, it is a profound—indeed, the ultimate—Christian expression of "the relationship between God and man in the Christian experience."[21] Tillich's rather painstaking efforts to understand and reinterpret religious language makes Ayer's treatment of it appear all the more hasty and cavalier.

For the sake of educational dialectic, Paul Edwards' "Being-itself and Irreducible Metaphors," constituting a section of a longer article entitled "Professor Tillich's Confusions," is presented next. This selection represents a vigorous, provocative, and sharply critical response to Tillich's view of the symbolic nature of religious discourse. The crux of Edwards' objection seems to reside both in his allegation that Tillich's metaphors are "irreducible," that is to say, their truth-claims cannot be "reproduced by one or more sentences all of whose components are used in literal senses," and in his contention that Tillich had failed in his attempts to translate or "reduce" his symbolic statements about God. Given the former contention, the second comes hardly as a surprise. Yet in view of Tillich's insistence that all language about God is to be regarded as symbolic,[22] it *is* surprising to find Edwards asking Tillich to produce literal "reductions" or translations of statements which for Tillich are not to be understood literally. It is equally surprising, given Tillich's characterization of the symbol as participating in the reality to which it points and as opening up new levels of reality, to note Edwards arguing that, because of their "irreducibility" to literalness, Tillich's symbolic sentences must be said to be "unintelligible" and (hence) "meaningless," "devoid of cognitive content," "failing to make an assertion" and "lacking referential meaning."[23] Edwards seems either to have forgotten or to have refused to take seriously Tillich's statement that, with but one exception, "nothing else can be said about God as God which is not symbolic." And he seems to have relegated religious statements to meaninglessness and cognitive vacuousness without coming to grips with Tillich's contentions, for example, that the truth and power of religious symbols reside in "their symbolic character," that "the truth of a religious symbol has nothing to do with the truth of the empirical assertions involved in it," and that "A religious symbol *is* true if it adequately expresses the correlation of some person with final revelation."[24] In short, Edwards, though openly challenging, appears less than sensitive to what Tillich is trying to say, and, thus, his equating of "irreducibility" of metaphors with their "unintelligibility" seems questionable and arbitrary.

My reservations and expression of surprise concerning aspects of Edwards' handling of Tillich's view on religious language must not be taken to suggest that I regard Tillich's position as having no difficulty. In fact, I wish now to delineate what I take to be a serious problem connected with his view of the symbolic nature of "the language of faith."[25] As I believe the problem develops when his view of religious language is seen alongside his analysis of faith, I shall first present a very brief summary of that analysis, and then turn to Tillich's discussion of the symbol "personal God" in Volume 1 of his *Systematic*.

Tillich depicts faith as "the state of being grasped by an ultimate concern,"[26] as "the ultimate concern . . . about what is experienced as ultimate,"[27] as a "total and centered act of the personal self,"[28] and as "a concern of the whole person."[29] Moreover, in a passage which is of crucial relevance to my present intention, Tillich maintains that "nothing that is less than we, nothing that encounters less than the center of our personality, can be of ultimate concern for us."[30] And in the selection from the *Dynamics of Faith*, Tillich states characteristically that "Nothing less than symbols and myths can express our ultimate concern."

To turn again to Tillich's discussion of symbolism in religious language, in Volume 1 of the *Systematic Theology*, we may note his statement that "the symbol 'personal God' is absolutely fundamental because an existential relation is a person-to-person relation"; and also his statement that "Man cannot be ultimately concerned about anything *less than personal*. . . ."[31] Further, in a difficult passage which troubles Edwards, Tillich indicates that " 'Personal God' does not mean that God is *a* person." Rather, it means, Tillich submits, that he is "the ground of everything personal and that he carries within himself the ontological power of personality. He is not a person, *but he is not less than personal*."[32]

The implication, it would seem, of the above statements is that for Tillich it can be said *literally*, i.e., *non-symbolically*, that God is not less than personal. In other words, Tillich seems to be saying that because God is the object of our ultimate concern and we cannot be ultimately concerned with anything less than personal, then it follows that God cannot be less than what literally it is for us to be personal. To express the matter somewhat differently, Tillich's analysis of faith appears to suggest that God must at least be personal in the non-symbolic, literal, univocal sense in which human beings are said to be personal. For it would make little sense for him to argue that we cannot be ultimately concerned with anything less than personal unless he means that our object of ultimate concern must at least be personal in the sense that we are personal. And certainly statements like his affirmation in the *Systematic* that "man is radically concerned only about that which can encounter him on equal terms,"[33] or his contention in *The Courage To Be* that "acceptance by something which is less than personal could never overcome personal self-rejection,"[34] corroborate this meaning.

Now, if my preceding interpretation is sound, a serious difficulty is posed concerning Tillich's position. For if the object of faith or ultimate concern can be said to be personal (i.e., at least personal) in a non-symbolic, univocal sense, as his analysis of faith appears to imply, then the possibility of this literal statement about the object of ultimate concern is in flagrant opposition to Tillich's insistence that "whatever we say about that which concerns us ultimately . . . has a symbolic meaning," or that "the language of faith is the language of symbols." In short, it would seem that Tillich's analysis of faith can be maintained only at the price of sacrificing his basic contention about the symbolic nature of the discourse of faith, and that his view of religious language precludes at least part of what he wants to say about the object of faith. If this problem is to be eliminated, it seems to me that either my interpretation here must be shown to be incorrect, or conceptual revision needs to be undertaken in behalf of one or both of the two fundamental Tillichian hypotheses just considered. And, in passing, it may simply be suggested that the dogmatism which Edwards claims to locate in Tillich's treatment of Being-itself may well stem from the present problem and reflect Tillich's inclination (on the basis of his conception of faith) to make some literal statements about God, even though his view of religious language prohibits that possibility. Moreover, I submit that this problem is part of what James L. Adams has, implicitly, in mind when, in a searching book on the early Tillich, he maintains that Tillich "has inadequately dealt with the question of the character of God." For having examined Tillich's symbology, Adams suggests that Tillich's discussion of symbolism in relation to God does not enable the reader to see what, for Tillich, the character of God is. And Adams appears sympathetic with the questions posed by Wilbur M. Urban as to whether, for Tillich, God is only a symbol and whether God is literally the Unconditioned.[35]

Another manner, often associated with Tillich's way[36] of meet-

ing the question of literalness as to religious language, takes the
form of the doctrine of analogy. This doctrine is generally regarded
as an attempt to escape from the pitfalls involved in viewing religious language either strictly univocally or equivocally,[37] and as
a kind of *via media* by which to avoid both the anthropomorphism
of univocal language about God and the alleged agnosticism implicit in complete equivocity.[38] One of the most succinct and most
discerning formulations of the doctrine of analogical predication
has been offered by E. L. Mascall in his now older but noteworthy
book, *Existence and Analogy*. I am glad to be able to include in
these pages the bulk of his important chapter on analogy. It should
be noted that for Mascall the purpose of the doctrine of analogy
is not to determine whether it is possible to speak intelligibly
about God, but, rather, to explain "how it is that we have been
able to talk about him all along"[39] and to offer an analysis of what,
in fact, we have been doing. His thesis seems to be that by a union
of "analogy of attribution" and "analogy of proportionality" the
cognitive, though not literal, significance of religious language can
be maintained. Although the human mind cannot conceptualize
God's essence, essence, in God, is identical with existence, and
thus an implicit "existential element in all affirmations about God"
allows the possibility of cognitive, non-literal, analogical discourse
about God.

Surely, among other criticisms, the usual kind of objection to
analogy can be raised concerning Mascall's concluding statement
that all our statements regarding God are greatly inadequate insofar as they involve the application of concepts to him, but "they
are thoroughly adequate in so far as they affirm perfections of him."
For, as Blackstone has asked, what would it mean to ascribe perfections to God if we are not able to have a concept of what these
might be? How much does it help to say, for example, that God's
goodness is to God as man's goodness is to man? Doesn't our understanding of analogical knowledge depend on and require having at
least some "nonanalogical" or "literal" knowledge of God? Otherwise, how would we know which analogies are, and which are not,
appropriate to God?[40] Indeed, what is the relation between cognitive significance and the literalness or non-literalness of language?
Can we make the a priori assumption that cognitive significance

necessitates literal language? Mascall's discriminating treatment of analogy provides an occasion for raising and confronting such basic questions as these.

Although the final two selections in this section do not speak directly to the question of literalness in respect to religious language, they present another perspective from which one may attempt to understand religious language and, taken jointly, they appear to have implications for the issue of literalness. Both the short selection from Buber and the longer article by Bultmann point to the need of understanding religious utterances in terms of an existential relationship, a "concrete situation," a living interpersonal "engagement," a "lived concreteness." For Buber, "meaning is to be experienced in living action and suffering itself, in the unreduced immediacy of the moment," and "religious expression is bound to the concrete situation." For Bultmann, every "talking *about*" takes for granted "a standpoint apart from that which is being talked about." And because it is not possible to adopt a standpoint independent of God, God does not allow himself to be spoken about in "general propositions" or "universal truths" which are true without relation to the concrete life-situation of the one who is speaking. Any attempt to do so, according to Bultmann, is not only "error" and "foolishness," but also "sin." Moreover, for Buber, "The religious reality of the meeting with the Meeter . . . knows no image of Him, nothing comprehensible as object." Although Buber surmises that God does not "despise" the "necessarily untrue images" but allows that they be media by which we may look at Him, he points out that, by making themselves more than "pointers to Him," these images impede the way to Him. For Bultmann (to further our comparison), it is only by speaking of ourselves that it is at all possible to speak of God. And even to talk about God as the "wholly other" has sense only when one realizes that the actual situation of man is of a sinner—a sinner who wishes to speak of God and can't, who wishes to speak of himself but can't, for even that would involve speaking of his existence as determined by God. But Bultmann makes it clear, it should be noted, that the consequence is not a "Quietism." "And in fact this is the only answer to the question if and when we can talk of God: when we *must*." This contention, I submit, is in marked contrast to Mc-

Pherson's position (considered in section I) which, by regarding the positivist's way out of the worry about religious language as an important contribution to the discussion, suggests that we should not try to express the ineffable. Bultmann adds that, hypothetically, "we have the possibility to speak and act in God *if* it is given us as necessity." We can understand Him and speak of Him only insofar as He directs his word to us and acts on us. And, adding another idiosyncrasy to this perspective on religious utterance, Bultmann concludes that all that we do or say has meaning only by the gift of "forgiveness of sins," and that it is a matter in which we can only have faith, not control.

III. *Cognitivity and the Possibility of Religious Knowledge.* In an early part of this introduction, I have already tried to show what I take to be the relation between the issue of religious knowledge and the more permeating and more comprehensive problem of the cognitivity of religious language. In brief, my stand has been that the question of whether or not religious sentences or religious claims can ever constitute knowledge emerges from and is a part of the larger and more basic problem of whether religious language is ever capable of being either true or false. The selections offered in the third section of this book are intended to speak to the issue of the possibility of religious knowledge and to bring together this issue with the underlying concern about the cognitivity of religious language. Sensitivity to the way or ways in which the various writers use the word "knowledge," or understand cognitivity, would seem to be imperative as the reader confronts these materials.

In "Ontology and the Possibility of Religious Knowledge," Calvin Schrag poses a question central to the religious knowledge issue when he asks whether knowledge grounded on logical or empirical propositions "exhausts the web of human experience," or whether there is an awareness of non-scientific or non-empirical reality which requires for its illumination "a broader interpretation of history." Employing the phenomenological method of trying to describe and analyze the data of experience as they offer themselves to the subject in his "existential immediacy," he is searching for those structural determinants of human experience which would allow religious knowledge to become an "ontic possibility." Religious knowledge becomes possible, Schrag suggests, "primarily in historical consciousness." It develops out of "a personal and social memory of God's decisive action which fuses the moment with existential import and makes of the future a living reality." It is a knowledge of "divine purpose" as it is manifested in a self's concrete existential encounters. Religious "truth" is to be understood as a "disclosure" which happens within the context of a person's "historical becoming."

As penetrating and insightful as Schrag's article may appear to be, its contribution seems limited by a consideration of which Schrag himself seems to be aware. "Phenomenology *as* phenomenology cannot proceed beyond a description of the various modes of consciousness to a unifying perspective. . . ." But mustn't the issue of religious knowledge, the question of the possibility, conditions, nature, and justification of religious knowledge, penetrate beyond the matter of *describing* the data of experience and the "modes of consciousness"? Is it not the case that the problem of the cognitivity of religious language requires not simply a description of immediate data of experience and modes of consciousness, but an attempt to justify one's interpretation or "reading" of these data and modes? To use more conventional terminology, it would seem that the question of religious knowledge to which we are speaking demands, at its root, not just a delineation of knowledge-claims but a warrant for those claims. To describe human knowledge-claims, or to describe religious consciousness as involving truth-claims, even if the description is accurate, does not *ipso facto* authenticate, justify, or establish the soundness of the claims. Hence, in spite of its contribution to the task of formulating issues pertinent to the question of religious knowledge, the procedure of Schrag's article seems to call into question the efficacy of the phenomenological method as a way of dealing with the problem before us.

Without asking Schrag's question as to whether logical-empirical knowledge "exhausts the web of human experience," the selection from Paul Schmidt's book on religious knowledge mainly raises the issue of whether religious claims can be instances of "empirical knowledge" or what he refers to as "the second type of knowledge by description." In the preceding chapter of his book, he has tried to show the incompatibility of religious statements with what he calls "the first type of knowledge by description"—namely, the formal knowledge of logic, mathematics, and games. After delineating the characteristics of "empirical knowledge" (which he also uses interchangeably with "factual knowledge"), and relating these characteristics to religious claims, he concludes that religious claims do not constitute "factual knowledge" either. But it is to be noted that what Schmidt means by "empirical" or "factual" knowledge presupposes scientific scrutiny, public testing, and continued openness to the same. This suggests that even religious claims that are based on unusual private experiences are not entitled to the label of "empirical knowledge" unless, for instance, they are amenable to public procedures of testing. Schmidt simply rules religious claims out of the sphere of "empirical knowledge" by appeal to an arbitrary, though very common, characterization of "empirical knowledge." It is true that Schmidt regards his move as a "tremendous step forward in the understanding of religion." And he also tells us that the failure of religious claims to have the characteristics of either formal or empirical knowledge is "no reason to disapprove of religion." Yet one wonders to what extent, if, indeed, at all, Schmidt advances the understanding of religion or religious language when he later submits a rather familiar positivist and non-cognitivist position that, religion being a "way of life," "the purpose of religious statements is to express attitudes that lead to a way of life." The reader will have occasion to consider some of the roots of this view of religious language, as well as the basis for Schmidt's comments regarding Hick, in the Braithwaite and Hick selections, respectively, which appear in the final section of this book.[41]

The short selection from Kierkegaard's *Concluding Unscientific Postscript* offers an approach to the question of religious knowledge and religious truth which is in marked contrast to Schmidt's scientific or objective approach. For Kierkegaard, the existing subject who chooses to follow the "objective way" is embarking upon an "approximation process" by which it is impossible to disclose God, because "God is a subject, and therefore exists only for subjectivity in inwardness." One does not have God "by virtue of objective deliberation, but by virtue of the infinite passion of inwardness." This "infinite passion" is the "truth" for Kierkegaard, and because "the passion of the infinite is precisely subjectivity," then "subjectivity becomes the truth."[42] Hence, it is to be noted that the kind of truth which Kierkegaard claims in respect to the "knowledge of God" is not a truth based on procedures of public observation and testing or ascertained by an appeal to objective criteria of certainty. In fact, "the truth is precisely the venture which chooses an objective uncertainty with the passion of the infinite." And, indeed, it is this "objective uncertainty" which augments the tension of one's "infinite passion" or "inwardness." So, although Kierkegaard cannot be included among our contemporary thinkers, his thought, as represented in this book, helps to break the contemporary bondage of truth or knowledge to the scientific and the objective, and introduces an important dialectical pole into the recent discussion of religious cognitivity and knowledge. Moreover, his idiosyncratic approach to truth not only reminds the discussant of the possible inappropriateness of objective models of inquiry when dealing with "infinite passion" or one's "passion for the infinite," but that, in respect to fundamental questions of one's individual existence, "subjectivity" and "inwardness" must be taken seriously as a possible route to truth and cognitive meaningfulness.

Paul Holmer's article, "The Nature of Religious Propositions," serves both to delineate some of the possible sources of confusion in respect to the question of the cognition of religious language and to widen the focus of the discussion. Observing that contemporary philosophy can no longer simply assume the cognitivity of religious language, he yet combines the central question of today's discussion —namely, "Are religious sentences cognitive?"—with the earlier traditional question, "Of what are they cognitive?" This combining of questions adds clarity as well as breadth to the main issue of this section. Holmer diagnoses the confusion regarding religious discourse in the following way: Because religious faith insists on the importance of what he calls a "religious possibility," it frequently is confused with cognitive belief; and because religious sentences insist on the non-cognitive element of faith, they are erroneously taken to be non-cognitive. And he proceeds to offer a distinction which, on his terms, will allow both cognition and faith to be delineated in reference to the same sentences. His answer to the question, Of what are religious propositions cognitive? is that they are cognitive of "historical events" and are also "the occasion for the cognition of a possibly new and definitive mode of life." But he is quick to add that "the religious *act of faith* is not to believe the truth of the description of the possibility nor even the historical claims" (italics mine). Hence, it is to be noted that although Holmer's views bear resemblance, at points, to those of Schmidt, his position, recognizing the non-cognitive element of faith, is yet a cognitivist alternative to Schmidt's narrow non-cognitivism regarding religious language, and one which seems to reflect at times the influence of Kierkegaard's existential and dialectical conception of faith and truth.

The symposium by H. D. Lewis and C. H. Whiteley on "The Cognitive Factor in Religious Experience" focuses on the "religious experience" as a basis for truth-claims and knowledge in religion. Although Lewis believes that the cognitive factor in religious experience is "peculiarly elusive," in the sense of being difficult to describe or to display its content, he is willing to speak cautiously of an "intuition of the being of God," and contends that such an intuition is not elusive in the sense of being restricted either to a few or to extremely rare occasions of illumination or insight. For Lewis, knowledge of God is not a consequent of our speculations about our secular experiences, but involves, rather, an "intrusion" into these experiences. And it is by associating this "intuition of the being of God" with the prominent secular characteristics of the situations in which it happens to a person that form is given to certain religious experiences.

Whiteley proceeds on the assumption that there are specific experiences taking place in religious contexts which are of an extraordinary character and these are to be distinguished from "all secular experiences." He makes a distinctive contribution to the symposium, as well as to this book's dialogue, by attempting to delineate the characteristics peculiar to the religious experience. One of the features which he ascribes to the religious experience, as Lewis also seems to suggest, is "a conviction that something or other is true." But much more than Lewis, Whiteley is profoundly concerned with the wide variation in the reports of what is revealed in the course of a religious experience. For Whiteley, the reports, not being mutually consistent, cannot all be true; and, thus, their diversity would seem to imply that their alleged "cognitive factor" must not be taken at "face-value." His concern, then, is not with whether the language associated with religious experience is intended, or appears, to be cognitive, but whether the language which so appears, or is so intended, really is cognitive.[43] The man who claims that his religious experiences are from God, or that God is apprehended through them, is offering "an explanation of their extraordinary nature." But, for Whiteley, we are not bound to his explanation, but rather to doing justice to "the features of his experience which make his explanation plausible."

In passing, two other points are to be noted briefly regarding Whiteley's offering. First, one may observe that he relates the issue of religious knowledge to the question of whether men ever have a sufficient evidential basis for ascribing an infinite cause to any part of finite human experience. Second, one may note that although Whiteley allows for "ostensible knowing of truths and ostensible awareness of supernatural beings" in religious experience, he regards the "affective and conative elements," not the "cognitive" elements, as the "most striking and most distinctive" factors of that total experience. Both of these are significant issues for the "man of faith" who makes knowledge claims; and together they impel him to examine anew what he means by "faith" and "knowledge" and how he conceives the relation between the two.

The symposium by Raphael Demos and C. J. Ducasse, entitled "Are Religious Dogmas Cognitive and Meaningful?" not only speaks further to this issue of faith and knowledge but also reconsiders the relation between religion and science and affords another look at analogy. To turn to this last consideration first, it is to be noted that, although Demos shares Whiteley's view that language about God appears to contain mutual inconsistencies, he does not draw the same conclusions as Whiteley. For Demos, the situation calls for an understanding of religious language as analogical. Such an understanding, he submits, enables one to see that apparent inconsistency in language about God is only apparent; for, to cite one example, the senses in which, on the one hand, time is affirmed of God, and, on the other hand, it is denied of God, are neither the same nor different: they are *analogical*. Moreover, it might be of interest to the reader to consider whether Demos' view of religious language as analogical, and specifically his treatment of the statement, "God is a person," could provide for Tillich a way out of the kind of difficulty in his position that I attempted to demonstrate in my discussion in section II.

In respect to the science versus religion issue, Demos and Ducasse are clearly in marked disagreement. For Demos, on the one hand, both science and religion are "systems of belief" which float "on the infirm waters of faith" and "rest on ultimate commitments." This does not mean that Demos refuses to recognize any basic differences in the procedures of religion and science—for he de-lineates the "vital differences" between scientific and religious "cognition"—but, rather, that, in his judgment, these two systems of belief are "not known to be knowledge." Both systems, Demos contends, involve acts of faith which not only go beyond available evidence but also go against it. For Ducasse, on the other hand, science and religion are systems of belief which differ radically one from the other. Whereas science is a "system of knowledge" which adheres to "The Rules of Evidence," religion, for him, is a system "only of faith" which (accepting Demos' terms) "rests on no evi-dence whatever." To put the matter another way, while the beliefs of religion are, for Ducasse, "overbeliefs" for which there is no evidence, scientific beliefs are the products of a strict methodological inquiry involving observation, experimentation, and verification, and do not go beyond "what the evidence possessed, if any, ra-tionally warrants."[44] And we learn elsewhere that for Ducasse, to speak of "religious knowledge" is to mean "knowledge only of the fact that faith sometimes can 'move mountains;' and religious faith is belief in the power to do so."[45]

A number of additional observations may now be formulated concerning the symposium. First, it may be noted that Ducasse's approach here is reminiscent, in places, of Schmidt's rigid em-piricism, and, by appearing to restrict knowledge to the observa-tional, experimental, and scientific, seems to be open to the charge of adopting an arbitrary view of knowledge. And Ducasse's arbi-trariness seems to get out of hand (and for him, out of philosophical character) when he asserts that the person who flouts "The Rules of [experimental] Evidence" and continues to use such words as "true" or "false" is playing the game of "*cheating* at the pursuit of knowledge." Second, I should suggest that insofar as both writers allow a view of faith as resting "on no evidence whatever" they are dealing not with faith but with a caricature of faith. Surely, few reflective believers or men of religious faith would endorse such an analysis. Ducasse's inclination, in other writings,[46] to see faith as belief which exceeds the available evidence would, it seems to me, be considerably more acceptable, although it, too, raises the question of the meaning of "evidence" and of how Ducasse would deal with an alleged man-God "encounter" or "confrontation" not open to scientific or objective scrutiny. Third, I wish to mention that for Ducasse, as for Whiteley, it is clearly not the cognitive factor which distinguishes or differentiates religion. Religion, for Ducasse, can function not only to inspire what Whiteley called "peace" and "serenity of mind" in the believer, but to induce him to subordinate his self-interest to the interest of society's welfare, when the two are in conflict.[47] Though noble, these functions hardly represent a viable alternative to a believer's claims to knowledge and cognitivity.

IV. *Justification, Verification, and Falsifiability*. At the end of the selection from *Language, Truth and Logic*, which we considered earlier, A. J. Ayer contends that although the theist "may believe that his experiences are cognitive experiences," we can be certain that he is deceiving himself, unless he is able to "formulate his 'knowledge' in propositions that are empirically verifiable." And he adds that claims to "intuitive" knowledge and religious "truths" are but "material for the psycho-analyst," for acts of intuition can never be said to disclose any truth about any matter of fact unless they issue in verifiable propositions. The precise senses of "verifiability" demanded of non-analytic, literally meaningful statements by the "verification principle" are stipulated carefully by Ayer in his introduction to the second edition of *Language, Truth and Logic*.[48]

Ayer's position, restricting the class of meaningful propositions to empirical hypotheses and tautologies, represents a brash challenge to truth-claims and knowledge-claims made within the framework of religious language. And his stand not only invites counter-instances of meaningful language which, in Ferré's words, are "outside the logical scope of the verification principle of meaning,"[49] but raises the question of how such claims to "meaningfulness," "truth" or "knowledge" can be justified. Yet this call represents only one of the main aspects of the contemporary challenge to the warrantability of religious claims.

John Wisdom's important and frequently reprinted essay entitled "Gods" serves both to present a searching analysis of the logic of religious language and to provide a background from which to trace and view another strand in the recent challenge to the justifiability of religious assertions. Wisdom feels convinced that things are revealed to us by poets, prophets, and artists, as well as by "scientists with their microscopes." And what is so revealed is not simply a matter of "the facts." Indeed, central to his position is his contention, reminiscent of Ian Ramsey's distinction between "the eye for detail" and "the eye of faith" or "disclosure,"[50] that it is possible to have in front of one all the details of a pattern and still fail to see the pattern. Yet it is clear that Wisdom does not reduce religious utterances to mere expressions of attitude, and that he is opposed to the non-cognitivism of Ayer and Stevenson. Although, he says, " 'There is a God' evinces an attitude to the familiar, . . . it also evinces some recognition of patterns in time easily missed," and, hence, the "difference as to there being any gods is in part a difference as to what is so and therefore as to the facts, though not in the simple ways which first occurred to us."

It is this type of consideration which gives rise to Wisdom's well-known parable about two men's response to a "long neglected garden," and, in turn, becomes a kind of starting-place for Antony Flew's "falsifiability" challenge. In Wisdom's parable, the two men appear not to disagree concerning the "facts" about the garden. Yet after they have examined the garden carefully, have studied what happens to unattended gardens, and have shared their findings with one another, they are in fundamental disagreement as to whether "a gardener comes." At this point the "gardener hypothesis" appears not to be an "experimental" issue and, in terms of the parable, the allegation that there is an invisible gardener does not seem to be open to falsification.

It is precisely this issue of the falsifiability of religious statements which becomes the crucial concern of Flew's adaptation of Wisdom's parable, and the central question to which the entire symposium on "Theology and Falsification" is addressed. Flew's challenge is initially put in the words of the "Sceptic" in his parable: "Just how does what you call an invisible, intangible, eternally elusive gardener differ from an imaginary gardener or even from no gardener at all?" And a little later in the symposium, Flew formulates the challenge more directly: In order for an assertion to be a genuine assertion, "it must claim that things stand thus and thus; *and not* otherwise." So if a supposed assertion does not deny anything, then it does not assert anything either: and hence it is not a genuine assertion. Yet "many sophisticated religious people" refuse to admit either that anything does occur or that anything could conceivably occur to count against their theological contentions. Insofar as this is the case, their assertions are "vacuous" and, presumably, without cognitive meaning.

The essence of Flew's challenge, then, is that religious statements are compatible with all evidence, do not allow any evidence to count against them, and are, thus, unfalsifiable pseudo-statements. This contesting of religious claims is often regarded as one of the most formidable contemporary challenges, outside of positivism or radical logical empiricism, to the possibility of justifying religious language.

The remainder of this symposium includes a diversity of responses to Flew's challenge. R. M. Hare, believing that Flew is completely successful on his own ground, shifts ground and offers his much publicized view of religion as *blik*. By *blik* Hare seems to mean a fundamental attitude (to the world) that is presupposed by any explanation but which does not involve any cosmological assertion or group of such assertions. For the persons holding them, *bliks* are not open to the possibility of disproof or falsification. Although Hare makes an interesting association between his *bliks* and Hume's "natural beliefs," and seems to want to emphasize the existential involvement of the believer, he appears to have difficulty, as Blackstone has pointed out, in distinguishing between "right" and "wrong," "sane" and "insane," *bliks*.[51] For such a distinction (as in the case of the lunatic's versus the sane man's *blik* about dons) seems to involve an appeal to evidence, and such an appeal would seem to allow a *blik* to be an assertion by permitting evidence, for example, to count against it. Basil Mitchell makes a contribution to the symposium by distinguishing between the recognition of evidence as counting against an assertion and the recognition of evidence as counting *decisively* against an assertion. His parable seems to suggest that religious assertions allow the former but not the latter. Moreover, his comment regarding the partisan's belief about the Stranger also appears to suggest that religious beliefs can function as "explanation." Finally, I. M. Crombie, reflecting the same sensitivity to religion and religious language as I have noted in section I, attempts to answer the charge that religious statements are not conclusively falsifiable and are, hence, meaningless. His response includes not only the insight that something could count decisively against the assertion (for example) that God is merciful, but also the attempt to show that the demand for "a statement of fact" to be verifiable or falsifiable is "a conflation of two demands." It is important to note that, for Crombie, religious utterances do not fare poorly in relation to the demands for "testing," and Christ is seen as the Christian's "verification, and to some extent also the specification, of the divine love." His reminder, moreover, that although religion has its problems, it is pointless to examine them apart from their religious context, is one which merits continued repetition in the discussion of the cognitivity and verifiability of religious language.

In Braithwaite's lecture, "An Empiricist's View of the Nature of Religious Belief," we are able to observe another response (to Flew's challenge) which endeavors to rescue the significance of religious statements on grounds other than empirical verifiability or falsifiability. Braithwaite offers what he himself labels a "conative" view of religious assertions. Against Ayer and the positivists he is unwilling to accept the view that because religious statements are not either analytic or empirical propositions they simply express emotion and fail to make any genuine assertion. In a Wittgensteinian manner, he regards the meaning of a statement as "being given by the way it is used." A religious assertion for him is a "declaration of an intention" to pursue a specific moral policy, "together with the implicit or explicit statement, but not the assertion, of certain stories." Braithwaite makes it clear that the intention of a Christian, for example, to pursue a Christian (agapeistic) way of life, is the criterion for both the genuineness of his belief in Christianity's assertions and for the meaningfulness of his assertions.

Although Braithwaite believes that his position does justice to both the empiricist's requirement that meaning be confined to empirical use and the religionist's demand that his religious beliefs be taken seriously, it is unlikely that religious believers would find Braithwaite's analysis acceptable. Granted that religious belief and religious assertion may often reflect, involve, or even entail, commitments to a specific moral policy, yet it is highly doubtful whether a believer would allow his religion or his religious discourse to be seen essentially in terms of moral policies or the announcement of allegiance to them.

This misgiving is surely part of what Mascall has in mind when, in response to Braithwaite, he affirms that "Christianity demands personal commitment not to a personal way of life . . . but to the concrete historical person Jesus of Nazareth."[52] Of course, Braithwaite tries to make it clear that religious assertions are not simply moral assertions, but are moral resolves which refer to or "are associated with thinking of different *stories* (or sets of stories)." Yet this point, too, is not without problems, as Mascall, again, attempts to show.[53] For if, as Braithwaite suggests, it is possible for a Christian and a Jew and a Buddhist all to recommend the same "way of life," and if the person making a "religious assertion" need not believe the truth of the stories or that "the empirical propositions presented by the stories correspond to empirical fact," then what is to prevent him from being both a Jew and a Buddhist as well as a Christian, for example? If the truth consideration is irrelevant, as Braithwaite seems to suggest, then nothing would seem to preclude this *multi-faith*, and, in the words of Mascall, "whether I am to be a Christian or a Buddhist or a Marxist" ultimately becomes "a matter of pure personal taste."[54] Yet, in practice, the believer hardly rests his case on personal taste alone. The Christian, for example, refrains from adding Judaism and Buddhism to his religious beliefs because, while believing Christian doctrine to be true, he regards the other doctrines to be false, at least in certain respects.[55] Hence, Braithwaite's lecture, though attempting to circumvent some of the "justifiability" problems related to religion, seems, by its own difficulties, to lead us right back to the question of how to justify truth-claims in religion.

In the selections from his discerning article entitled "Motives, Rationales, and Religious Beliefs," Diogenes Allen makes one of the most thought-provoking and religiously sensitive contributions to the recent discussion of this issue of justifying religious truth-claims. In an admirably forthright manner, Allen tries to show that the "response of faith" may itself be an adequate reason or basis for holding on to truth-claims, and that the truth-claims of religion do not need any other logically different type of reason as a basis for their being adhered to. Allen argues that the "response of faith," as "one's *source* for believing," can also be "one's *ground* for believing truth-claims" because one may receive "satisfaction of certain needs from what the truth-claim says is the case." That is to say, on the condition that there are not "specific reasons which count decisively against" their truth, religious truth-claims may be adhered to and asserted insofar as they "awaken faith" and "nourish or fulfill needs." To put the matter in a somewhat different way, "motives" can be a "sufficient reason" for both making and holding on to religious truth-claims. And, for Allen, there are no reasons which are more fundamental than these biographical ones. Yet it is to be noted that not all motives can, for him, serve as grounds for legitimate truth-claims, but only those "for whose satisfaction" the truth of the truth-claims does in fact matter. To believe on the basis of such grounds, for Allen, is not to act arbitrarily or blindly, but to act on the kind of reasons or basis appropriate to religious beliefs.

Allen's article offers a significant challenge both to those who subject religious claims to a scientific model of inquiry and to those who, by shifting ground, choose to view religious language emotively, conatively, or attitudinally. Alert to the peculiarities of religious claims, Allen is not embarrassed by the idiosyncrasies involved in the justification of these claims. And these idiosyncrasies do not, in his judgment, hamper the cognitivity of religious belief. It should be noted, moreover, that, though not empirical in the positivist's sense of the word, Allen's manner of justifying religious beliefs is indeed related to the experience of needs and the fulfillment thereof. By way of criticism, it must be said, however, that two of Allen's key notions—the notion of the "response of faith" and that of "reasons which count decisively against"—remain undefined and badly in need of clarification in his article.

Finally, in "Theology and Verification," John Hick attempts to speak to both the verifiability and the falsifiability challenges to religious claims. Although he acknowledges an important element of truth in the verification principle of the logical positivist,[56] he seeks to clarify the notion of verification. And although aware of Flew's falsifiability challenge, he is quick to point out that verification and falsification are not always related in a symmetrical fashion. Viewing verification as "the exclusion of grounds for rational doubt concerning the truth of some proposition," he defends the possibility of "eschatological verification" and argues that it is possible to conceive of after-life experiences which would verify theism and thus make theistic assertions cognitively meaningful. Our experience, for instance, "of the fulfillment of God's purpose for ourselves," in combination with "an experience of communion with God," each conforming to Christian revelation, would exclude grounds for our rational doubt of the reality of God. And, in following Hick's argument, it is important to observe that the view of verification which he submits does not demand that this verification of the existence of the Christian God be to *everybody*.

Hick's basic contentions, here, have aroused considerable controversy and counter-claims. For example in "Factual Knowledge and Religious Claims," Paul Schmidt affirms that Hick "fails to show how this private experience [of verification] could be made public," and, in view of this failure, charges Hick of misleadingly departing from the "current use" of "verification."[57] And William Blackstone, in *The Problem of Religious Knowledge*, accuses Hick of begging the question by assuming "the assertion-status of several religious beliefs [e.g., of "after-life"] . . . in the process of arguing for the assertion-status of other religious beliefs [e.g., the "reality of God"]."[58] Schmidt's criticism, it seems to me, is premised on a narrow, arbitrarily restricting view of empirical verifiability which even forgets the notion of "logical verifiability" or "verifiability in principle" as understood by such avowed empiricists as C. I. Lewis and Morris Schlick. And insofar as "afterlife" or "Beatific Vision" or the "Kingdom of God" are hypotheses which are themselves subject to Hick's "removal of grounds for rational doubt" (as his test for verifiability) I do not sense any decisive force in Blackstone's objection. However, without suggesting that I have eliminated either of the above criticisms, I should like to submit, in ending, that the following concluding remark by McPherson concerning the relation between positivism and theology may well be more apropos and merit more prolonged scrutiny and consideration on the part of the reader:

> The proper linkage [of positivism and theology] consists in an accommodation of positivism to theology, *not of theology to positivism*. Theology does not gain by being reduced to the terms of any school of philosophy. (italics mine)

I do not pretend that the above commentary has solved either the problem of the cognitivity of religious language or any of the major questions subsumed under it. Indeed, that has not been my intention. Nonetheless, I hope that my remarks, together with the materials to which they are related, have at least served to represent different models of inquiry concerning the issues at hand, and to enable the reader to observe that a narrow and rigid logico-empirical approach has no a priori warrant for making any definitive statements about the nature or truth-status of religious discourse and beliefs. My further hope is that my commentary and selections have helped to convey a sense of the problem's complexity, and have given the reader better equipment to enter the religious dialogue of our time with a heightened sensitivity as to what religious people are trying to say and claim. Hence, if the foregoing comments have served to raise relevant questions, to represent, compare, and interrelate diverse expressions of the book's central problem, and to induce the reader to confront the issues and source-materials seriously and searchingly, they have been worthwhile.

NOTES

1. See e.g., A. J. Ayer, *Language, Truth and Logic* (New York: Dover Publications, 1956), p. 115.

2. Paul Tillich, "Religious Symbols and Our Knowledge of God," *The Christian Scholar*, 38 (1955), p. 189.

3. Ibid.

4. Quoted by James L. Adams in Paul Tillich's *Philosophy of Culture, Science, and Religion* (New York: Harper & Row, 1965), p. 2.

5. See Rudolf Bultmann, *Jesus Christ and Mythology* (London: SCM Press Ltd., 1960), especially pp. 17, 67.

6. Paul M. van Buren, *The Secular Meaning of the Gospel* (New York: Macmillan, 1965), p. 103.

7. E. L. Mascall, *Words and Images* (London: Longmans, Green, 1957), p. 2.

8. Ibid., p. 1.

9. William T. Blackstone, *The Problem of Religious Knowledge* (Englewood Cliffs: Prentice-Hall, 1963), p. 47.

10. For an elaboration of this point, within a larger context, see my feature review of Christian's *Meaning and Truth in Religion* in *International Philosophical Quarterly*, V, 1 (February, 1965).

11. See, for example, Blackstone, *The Problem of Religious Knowl-*

*edge*, pp. 88-89, and F. Ferré, *Language, Logic and God* (New York: Harper & Row, 1961), pp. 36-37. I wish here to note my appreciation of Ferré's book, as I have of Blackstone's.

12. I employ the expression "theological language" here instead of "religious language" in deference to Crombie's usage. I have been using "religious language" as a more general term, which certainly includes "theological language" but which might cover more than "theological language," depending on what is meant by "theological language." Sometimes, for example, theological language is restricted to statements about God.

13. I. M. Crombie, "Possibility of Theological Statements" in B. Mitchell, ed., *Faith and Logic* (Boston: The Beacon Press, 1957), p. 77.

14. J. M. Bochenski, *The Logic of Religion* (New York: New York University Press, 1965), p. 83.

15. Ayer, *Language, Truth and Logic*, p. 41.

16. Ibid.

17. Ibid., p. 44.

18. Paul Tillich, *Systematic Theology*, 2 (Chicago: The University of Chicago Press, 1957), p. 9.

19. Ibid.

20. Tillich, "Religious Symbols and Our Knowledge of God," p. 194.

21. Ibid., for both quotes in this paragraph.

22. I am aware of the fact that in both Volume 1 and Volume 2 of *Systematic Theology*, Tillich makes a single exception (a different one in each volume) to this general view. See *Systematic Theology*, 1 (Chicago: The University of Chicago Press, 1951), p. 239. The one exception here is the statement that "God is being-itself or the absolute." In Volume 2, it seems to be the statement "that everything we say about God is symbolic." (p. 9)

23. See Edwards' identification of these expressions in part 2 of the article from which this selection is chosen. *Mind*, 74 (1955), p. 195.

24. Tillich, *Systematic Theology*, 1, p. 240, for this quote and the immediately preceding one.

25. In what follows regarding Tillich, I have drawn heavily on my article, "Symbolism and Ultimate Concern—A Problem," published in *Anglican Theological Review*, 49 (1967), pp. 90-94.

26. Paul Tillich, *Biblical Religion and the Search for Ultimate Reality* (Chicago: University of Chicago Press, 1955), p. 51.

27. Paul Tillich, *Dynamics of Faith* (New York: Harper Torchbook, 1958), p. 9.

28. Tillich, *Dynamics of Faith*, p. 8.

29. Tillich, *Biblical Religion and the Search for Ultimate Reality*, p. 51.

30. Ibid., p. 24.

31. Tillich, *Systematic Theology*, 1, p. 244. Italics mine.

32. Ibid., p. 245. Italics mine.

33. Tillich, *Systematic Theology*, 1, p. 223.

34. Paul Tillich, *The Courage To Be* (New Haven: Yale University Press, 1952), p. 166.

35. Quotation and references here are from Adams, op. cit., pp. 270-71. I recommend Adams' entire book as an important study of Tillich's thought preceding 1945.

36. For example, Blackstone, op. cit., p. 68, or George F. Thomas, *Religious Philosophies of the West* (New York: Scribner's, 1965), p. 421.

37. For the sake of this discussion, let us understand that a term is said to be predicated univocally in respect to x and y if its meaning is exactly the same in both cases; equivocally, if the term is used in two different senses.

38. For example, Ferré, op. cit., pp. 67-69, or Lewis S. Ford, "The Three Strands of Tillich's Theory of Religious Symbols," *The Journal of Religion*, 46 (1966) No. 1, part 2, pp. 105-106. See also p. 113 of the book from which the Mascall selection is taken.

39. Eric L. Mascall, *Existence and Analogy* (London: Longmans, Green, 1949), p. 94. Republished by the Shoe String Press, Hamden, Connecticut, in 1967. He also repeats this sentiment at the end of the selection.

40. Blackstone, op. cit., pp. 65-66.

41. Paul F. Schmidt, *Religious Knowledge* (Glencoe: The Free Press of Glencoe, 1961), p. 111.

42. See Schmidt's attack on Kierkegaard's view of truth, op. cit., pp. 119-21.

43. Blackstone has the same kind of concern in op. cit., pp. 48-51, for example.

44. C. J. Ducasse, "Christianity, Rationality and Faith," *Review of Religion*, March (1958), pp. 132, 133. See also C. J. Ducasse, "What Has Science Done to Religion?" *The Centennial Review*, 3 (1960), 115-25, and *A Philosophical Scrutiny of Religion* (New York: The Ronald Press Co., 1953), e.g., pp. 148-49, 417.

45. Ducasse, *A Philosophical Scrutiny of Religion*, p. 148.

46. See, for instance, the two preceding footnotes.

47. See, for example, Chapter 8 and p. 415 of *A Philosophical Scrutiny of Religion*.

48. See Ayer, op. cit., p. 13, especially.

49. Ferré, op. cit., p. 56.

50. See Ramsey's recent formulation of this distinction in *Christian Discourse: Some Logical Explorations* (London & New York: Oxford University Press, 1965), pp. 2-5, for example.

51. Blackstone, op. cit., p. 77.

52. Eric L. Mascall, *Words and Images* (London: Longmans, Green, 1957), p. 60.

53. Ibid., pp. 58-59.

54. Ibid., p. 61.
55. Ibid., p. 59.
56. See footnote 1 of his article.
57. See, again, the last few paragraphs of the Schmidt selection.
58. Blackstone, op. cit., p. 114.

# Religious language and the problem of religious knowledge

# I. The Logical Status of Religious Language

# 1. IS RELIGIOUS LANGUAGE SO IDIOSYNCRATIC THAT WE CAN HOPE FOR NO PHILOSOPHICAL ACCOUNT OF IT?

*Alasdair MacIntyre*

*Alasdair MacIntyre is Prelector in Philosophy at University College, Oxford University. He is editor (with Antony Flew) of* New Essays in Philosophical Theology, *and author of* A Short History of Ethics.

It would be odd if the answer to this question were 'Yes.' For a great many of the expressions which find a place in religious utterance, in fact the vast majority of such expressions, derive their sense from their use in other and nonreligious contexts. To praise, to love, to recount great deeds, to express awe: all these employ expressions which find their place in the fabric of everyday language. Nor does religion confer on such expressions a new and esoteric meaning. That this is so is shown by the insistence of theologians that certain particular expressions should be used in religious utterance, and not others. God is our Father, but not our Mother; loves us, but does not hate us; we are bound to obey him, not defy him; and so on. Father-Mother, love-hate, obey-defy: these conceptual contrasts are transferred with all their familiar meaning into our speech about God. This rather obvious fact at once renders untenable three views of religious utterances which have found favour with certain schools of theologians.

Reprinted by permission of SCM Press Ltd. from *Metaphysical Beliefs* (1957), pp. 175-79.

There has been a consistent strain in Protestant theology which has held that meaning is conferred on religious assertions by a special illumination of the believing mind. Certain statements of Karl Barth, for example, seem to suggest that the assertions of the Bible are meaningless to anyone who has not received a special miracle of grace. But to suggest this is to use the word 'meaningless' meaninglessly. For what would it be to confer meaning on an otherwise meaningless expression? Suppose the form of words: 'Mountain neither fire red here.' The syntactical rules of English render this meaningless. To make it meaningful one would have to provide a set of rules whereby such an expression could be decoded, could be translated into a syntactically recognizable expression. Unless the expression could be decoded it would be meaningless for anyone, whatever their special inner graces; if the expression could be decoded it would be meaningful for anyone, provided only that there was access to the code, to the rules of translation. But for most theological and biblical expressions there is not even a problem of decoding. Because most religious language utilizes familiar words with familiar meanings their sense is equally apparent to believer and unbeliever. Talk about 'the language of the Bible' or 'religious language' must not conceal from us that such language is nothing more nor less than Hebrew or English or what you will, put to a special use. As Sir Edwyn Hoskyns put it, the language of the Holy Spirit is New Testament Greek. So that a special miracle of grace might be bound up with finding the biblical assertions acceptable or important (and *via* 'significant' we sometimes use 'meaningful' to mean 'important') but could not be involved in finding them meaningful.

A variant on this orthodox Protestant view is the liberal Protestant view that religious expressions do indeed have to be decoded since they refer to inner experiences which only some people enjoy, or at least only some people recognize. And on this view only those who have these crucial experiences could hope to decode them. But to say this is simply to commit a mistake that is obvious the moment that one tries to vindicate this view-point by an example. Schleiermacher, for instance, suggests that when we say that God created the world we are really saying something about our inner experience of absolute dependence. But if we use the words 'God created the world' in their ordinary sense then the rules of meaning and syntax in English preclude us from referring by them to any inner experience. We could of course recommend that this expression should be construed in a new way; and no doubt this is what Schleiermacher is in fact doing. But if one wishes to mean something other than what the words mean, taken as they stand, it would seem misleading to use this form of words. Theologians do want to insist on this form of words—for example, in the creeds. Hence it is misleading to suggest that Schleiermacher and orthodox theologians disagree about the meaning of the assertion 'God created the world'; what they really disagree about is whether to say this at all.

The root of the matter is, however, deeper than this. For the suggestion of the liberal theologian that theological expressions have private meaning by referring to private experiences is ruled out by the fact that no expressions can derive their meaning in this way. To have shown this is one of the central achievements of Wittgenstein.[1] For to name our private experiences in such a way that they can be recognized, identified and, if you like, dated is to introduce words which are used according to rules. And a rule is something essentially public, something which can be taught and learned. So words like 'pain' and 'sensation' which refer to private experience, if any words do, are words in public language. It is not that we have private experiences and invent words for them. But we learn the words and find their application in our experience. The language is in a sense prior to—and even, although this could be misleading, in a sense formative of—the experience. This is as true of religious language as of any other. In so far as it refers to private experience, we learn that it does so because the meaning of the expressions can be taught publicly. This is why two believers can discuss their common experiences. If indeed religious expressions referred to private experiences and their meaning was exhausted by such a reference, then no two believers would use the same language—for the experience and the language of each would be private to each—and two believers could never know that their experiences were the same. In fact, believers are able to talk with one another on religious matters—they do so at length; and this is because religious language is no private code, but is at once public and familiar.

There is yet another third way of ignoring this familiar content of religious language. Sceptics sometimes say that religious utterances are nonsensical. Some believers meet this charge by not only admitting, but welcoming it. Religion, they argue, deals essentially with 'what cannot be said.' Writers on mysticism are apt to stress this and some theological writers have suggested a link here between Wittgenstein's aphoristic utterances at the end of the *Tractatus*, such as, 'There is indeed the inexpressible. This *shows* itself; it is the mystical' and what mystics have said about how to experience the divine is to experience something that cannot be put into words. Two points at once suggest themselves. The first is Dr. Johnson's on Boehme, 'If Jacob saw the unutterable, Jacob should not have tried to utter it.' Mystical writers tend to say what cannot be said at somewhat inordinate length and it is clear that for them such expressions as 'the unutterable' take on an idiomatic sense in which they are of great use in describing and naming what they have experienced. A sceptic and a mystic who unite in saying, 'To try to speak on these topics is to go beyond the limits of what can be said' mean different things by what they say. But this leads us to another and more important point. Most religious language, as I have already reiterated, is of a thoroughly familiar kind. And, as I have also insisted already, theologians and believers generally want to assert some things, to deny others. But where everything is nonsense, there can be neither assertion nor denial. Where everything is nonsense, one kind of nonsense is as good as another. It is precisely because the theologian must, to preserve his theology, use familiar terms in familiar ways to assert and to deny that he cannot accept any overall classification of his kind of talk as 'nonsense.'

These theological views of the meaning of religious utterances have been overthrown by considering the large degree of resemblance between religious language and everyday speech. The real difficulties arise when we consider both the resemblances and the differences together. In the Bible men go on journeys, suffer greatly, marry, have children, die, and so on. So far no difficulty. But they go their journeys because God calls them, suffer in spite of God's care, receive their brides and their children at the hand of God, and at death pass in a special sense into God's realm. So with Abraham, with Job, with Jacob and the Maccabean dead. This reference to God introduces all the difficulty. What is said of God is again familiar enough. God calls, God hears, God provides. But these verbs appear to lack the application which is their justification in non-religious contexts. The name 'Abraham' is used as ordinary proper names are used, and when as subject it is conjoined to descriptive verbs these two are used ordinarily. But the name 'God' is not used to refer to someone who can be seen and heard, as the name 'Abraham' is, and when descriptive verbs are used to state that God's call is heard, it is not ordinary hearing that is meant. Hence all the puzzles. If talk about God is not to be construed at its face value, how is it to be construed?

NOTES

1. *Philosophical Investigations* (Blackwell 1953), *passim,* esp. § 256-317.

# 2. POSITIVISM AND RELIGION

## Thomas McPherson

*Thomas McPherson is Senior Lecturer in Philosophy at University College of South Wales and Monmouthshire. He is author of* The Philosophy of Religion *and articles in scholarly journals.*

I

People sometimes say that certain Christian beliefs are nonsensical. How, for example, can God be One Person yet Three Persons? Or Three Persons *in* One Person? Is God One Person yet Three Persons in the way that an actress playing Miss Hardcastle in *She Stoops to Conquer* is one person (herself) yet three persons (herself, Miss Hardcastle, and Miss Hardcastle pretending to be the barmaid)? Or in the way in which I may simultaneously be one (affectionate) person to my wife and children, a "totally different" (bad-tempered) person to my subordinates in the office, and all the time a third person as well (the "real me" whom nobody understands—the person I think I am when I am "dramatizing myself" as we say, or "being inscrutable" as James Thurber says, or being Existentialist)? Or in the way in which a man may be three different persons in succession: in early youth a profligate, in late youth reformed and a leader of men, in middle age dully respectable and unadventurous? And is God Three Persons *in* One Person in the way that Pooh Bah was a great many persons in one, or the editor of a very small country newspaper may be three persons in one (reporter, editor and sub-editor)? Or is he Three Persons in One in the way that Siamese triplets would be three persons in one?

God is "wholly other" yet God is "in us." Christ died yet lives. Man is made in the image of God, yet God has no *form* that any

Reprinted by permission of the author and editor from *Philosophy and Phenomenological Research*, Volume 14 (1953-1954), pp. 319-30.

mirror could image. Christ said both "I and my father are one" and "My father is greater than I." Christ is the Son of God and God is his Father, and God is also the Father of all of us, yet not in the same way. We are commanded to work out our *own* salvation *for* it is God which worketh in us. The service of God is perfect freedom. These are the kinds of things that are pointed to as hardly good sense.

Now what do such beliefs *mean?* How are we to understand them? Or is it wrong to try to "understand" them? *Are* they absurd or nonsensical? If they are not, then why not? If they are, then *how* exactly is it that they are absurd or nonsensical? Is it because they do not make "literal" sense? But do they then have some "deeper meaning" which is not their literal meaning; do they make sense on a different "level" from that of literal meaning? And, if so, what is this level, and *how* is it different from the level of literal meaning?

All these questions indicate a *worry*—a worry that we may feel not only with theological statements but with other sorts of statements as well, but we feel it particularly with theological statements because they are (rightly) thought to be asserting something very important. Not everyone has this worry over theological statements, but some do. Of those who have it, some are not Christians mainly because they have it. Others who have it and who *are* Christians, are not altogether sure whether their worry needs to be reconciled with their Christianity, and if it does how they are to accomplish this. There is a difference between "direct" statements of religious belief (some quotations from the Bible are clearly of this kind) and propositions of a more sophisticated sort constructed by theologians. Sometimes the latter are not so much expressions of the worry as themselves attempts to settle it. But for our purposes we can ignore this distinction.

Christian theologians today who themselves have this worry, or can see that others have it and consider that they ought to say something to help them, react to the worry in varying ways.

There are those who glory in the fact that there are absurdities among Christian beliefs. They are pleased that Christianity is full of nonsense, only do not say "nonsense;" they say "paradox." (Commonly they say it in English with a Scottish, or—I write as an Englishman—an American, accent, or in German with a Swiss accent.) Language is just not designed to deal with certain things, they would say. The truths of Christianity are too difficult to be expressed in simple language. Some things are easy to say, and ordinary people succeed in saying them easily. Other things are hard to say, and theologians say these with an effort. Theologians use language, which is the only tool they have, but a poor one for their purposes, to express things which look "on the surface" absurd (paradoxes) but which have a "deeper" meaning.

Other theologians dislike the appearance of absurdity of some Christian doctrines, and would ignore it if they could. They say that the doctrines may appear to be absurd, but that we ought not to let that worry us. We are all sensible men together—believers and non-believers. Let us put first things first. What is important is to live a Christian life. Let us not be too narrowly "logical" about Christian doctrines. Let us be as little children; let us catch the "spirit" of doctrine as we catch the "spirit" of Christ's parables. This is said in all sorts of accents.

Again, some deny that Christian doctrine contains absurdity or nonsense. Difficulties, yes; plenty of difficulties; but not nonsense. They ask us to be *rational* about it. It is sense because sense can be made of it in terms of Aristotle's logic. (Not quite as Aristotle left it, but refined and improved; in particular, with a developed section labelled "Analogy.") This is said in English or French and supported by quotations in Latin.

There is a fourth way out of the worry. It is this: There are some things that just cannot be *said*. As long as no one tries to say them, there is no trouble. But if anyone *does* try to say them he must take the consequences. We ought not to try to express the inexpressible. Now the things that theologians try to say (or some of them) belong to the class of things that cannot *be* said. The way out of the worry is retreat into silence. This is said not usually by theologians (though it is, of course, said by some important religious persons who are not theologians) but by philosophers—and philosophers of a kind that theologians commonly regard as their enemies.

The situation, then, is this. We have a certain set of statements that look absurd or nonsensical. What are we to do about them? Well, we can invent a special kind of logic where words mean what we want them to mean; where, for example, God can properly be called a "person" yet can be described as having attributes that no person has, or where God can be one and many at the same time (or neither one nor many);[1] and we can justify ourselves in this by saying that the "ordinary" use of words will not do for *this* subject-matter. That is the first way out of the worry. Or we can shut our eyes to the whole difficulty. That is the second way. Or we can account for it all by a theory of analogical predication. That is the third way.

Or we can go to the source of the worry; admit it to be a reasonable worry; and draw this conclusion from it: We can agree that some things cannot be *said*, and that if we try to say them we are bound to talk nonsense. Christian theologians have tried to say some things that cannot be said. They have succeeded, as might have been expected, only in saying nonsense. They ought not to have tried to say these things. This is the fourth way.

There is much that needs to be made clearer in this account. But before I go on there is this to be said. It may be felt that the worry I am writing about is one that no sensible person ought to have. In particular, persons who have had a training in theology may feel that the worry arises from altogether too naïve a way of looking at things. *Of course*, it will be said, there are Christian beliefs which, when written down in cold ink, look nonsensical if judged by ordinary tests of sense and nonsense. But that is just where we can easily go wrong. The tests by which these statements look nonsensical are all very well when applied to some other statements, but such tests are out of place here. The statements of Christian theologians are not intended to be statements like these others. So we cannot try them by such tests.

Now it is true that there are different kinds of nonsense. To see this we need only compare, " 'Twas brillig, and the slithy toves Did gyre and gimble in the wabe," and "This book is red and green all over," and "All only every but," and "Socrates is numerous." (And there are more kinds of nonsense than these.)

It is also true that the tests for one kind of nonsense will not be the tests for another. A single test for nonsense applied indiscriminately to all propositions will result in some propositions being classed as nonsense-propositions where without such single-mindedness we might prefer to call them, for example, "strikingly-expressed." But sometimes people *do* want to say: "God *is* both One Person and Three Persons, and this is not just a way of speaking; I mean that he *really* is both One Person and Three Persons."

Then we have to ask, What exactly *does* this mean?, and we are
surely entitled to begin by taking it perfectly literally.

To make the same objection again. The worry is thought to be
silly in that it arises from overliteralness. *Of course*, it will be said,
"God is One Person yet Three Persons" looks nonsense; but only
because you are assuming as your model for sense and nonsense
something like "The cat sat on the mat." But what about poetry?
"Tyger, tyger, burning bright." What does *that* mean? How can a
tiger burn? Is the tiger "literally" in flames? Yet you know perfectly
well what it means, and you do not call it nonsense.

But, we must point out in answer to the objection that the whole
point of the worry lies in this: How, if at all, are theological propositions different from other kinds of propositions? *Are* theological
statements to be interpreted like statements in poems?—like "Tyger,
tyger, burning bright"? (Like these in some ways, that is; but
naturally not *completely* like them.) That is just what the worry
is about. Are theological statements sense or are they nonsense:
and what kind of sense, and what kind of nonsense? If they are
nonsense are they to be classed with some other common kind of
nonsense, or are they their own kind of nonsense?

The word "nonsense" here has a question-begging look, and, for
a reason we shall note later, tends rather to put one off. But if one
is to find out what these theological statements really amount to it
is best to begin by being naïve and literal-minded. Perhaps they are
to be assimilated to the model of sentences in poems, or to the
model of sentences in books of metaphysics, but this is what has
to be found out. This (or something like it) cannot be simply
assumed so as to dispose of the worry; for the worry itself is about
what *sort* of sense or nonsense these propositions are.

Now this is something that I cannot discuss fully here. What I
have to say is really preliminary to any such discussion. But I can at
least indicate that I think the best answer to the question "What
sort of meaning do theological propositions have?" is that they have
their own kind of meaning. They have not the same sort of meaning as the poet's, the metaphysician's, or the scientist's statements.
Indeed, why should it be thought that they have? Of course, they are
similar to each of these in some ways, but they are not the *same*.
It is the liking of philosophers for neatness—a liking shared with
other sorts of people—that makes them want to put all statements

into a very small number of boxes (significant and meaningless, analytic and synthetic, a priori and empirical).

It is the last of the four ways out of the worry that I wish to discuss: and we can call it the positivistic way. I have expressed it above in a very general manner. Variations and refinements we need not take into account.

The other three ways have been discussed frequently enough. The fourth is often rejected without examination. Theologians do not see it as an admissible answer to the worry. (Occasionally the philosophical view from which it springs is picked upon by some theologian with philosophical training but developed in an unwise and mistaken manner. I shall return to this at the end.) I am not arguing *for* anything. All I want to do is to clear the ground and show what is involved in the fourth way. I am neither adopting nor rejecting it: I want to see what it *is*. What to the Jews was a stumbling block and to the Greeks foolishness is to logical positivists nonsense. There is more to be learnt from this than has yet been realised by most theologians.

## II

Rudolf Otto can take us some distance towards an understanding of the fourth way. Otto holds[2] that what is most distinctive in religion cannot be put into words. This is the "non-rational" part of religion; "non-rational" he equates with "not capable of being conceptualized." The distinctive (non-rational) thing in religion is a certain sort of experience—the numinous experience; and this is partly a feeling—a feeling of creatureliness or creaturehood—and partly consciousness of "something outside" us, consciousness of the Numen (or the Numinous), the Wholly Other.

Christianity is a highly conceptualized religion, Otto says. He means by this that Christianity is full of words: hymns, sermons, theological books, the Bible itself. The conceptualized part of religion—the part that is put into words—is very important. But we, with our highly conceptualized religion, must not forget that there is something else which *cannot* be put into words; there is a non-rational element in religion, and this is the experience of the numinous.

This is one interpretation of what Otto means, and on the whole

I think it is the right one, but there are passages which suggest a different, milder, view.

Otto shifts between two uses of "concept" and "conceptualize." Sometimes he seems to mean by "concept" something like the concepts of spirit, reason, purpose,[3] and by "conceptualize" something like "express in terms of such concepts." So to say that Christianity is a conceptualized (or a *highly* conceptualized) religion is like saying that Christianity is expressed in rather an "abstract" way; it uses too many hard words, is not expressed in "concrete" terms, is too "philosophical." But Otto at other times seems to mean something much wider than this by "concept." He says: "*All* language, in so far as it consists of words, purports to convey ideas or concepts;—that is what language *means*;—and the more clearly and unequivocally it does so, the better the language. And hence expositions of religious truth in language *inevitably* tend to stress the 'rational' attributes of God."[4]

According to this wider interpretation, religion is conceptualized merely by being put into words—*any* words. It is not conceptualized only because it is put into hard words or "abstract" words. And it is this wider view that I think Otto on the whole wants to hold.

Now, Otto is writing about the non-rational element in religion, but he writes about it very rationally. His approach is thoroughly matter-of-fact and reasoned. He is writing about a special sort of *feeling* which he says cannot be clearly and accurately described, yet it is obvious that the aim of his book is clarity and accuracy. His English translator—Professor Harvey—renders Otto's title *Das Heilige* as *The Idea of the Holy*. It is indeed the *idea*—or *concept*— of "the holy" (whose essence is the numinous) that Otto is writing about; even though the point that he most wants to make about it is that the essence of the holy is not capable of *being* conceptualized. Otto is writing about that part of religion that cannot, he thinks, be reduced to language, but naturally he has to use language in order to write about it, and it is noticeable how *well* he uses language; and, furthermore, it is noticeable that he uses language *descriptively*. In writing of emotions he does not use language in the way that itself arouses emotion: he writes in an objective, "scientific" way.

Indeed, Otto's rationality is such that he seems hardly aware that language can be used for *expressing* feelings and not just for *talking about* feelings. He commonly interprets the quotations that he himself gives to illustrate "expression" of the numinous as if they were dispassionate scientific accounts of what it is like to have a numinous experience, and not (as some of them are) themselves really *expressions of* that experience. Language, as has often been pointed out recently, is not used only for conveying information; it is used also for expressing emotions and attitudes and for evoking them in others: Otto seems not clearly to realize this, or at least he does not stress it. He says that something *can* be "asserted" of "the object of the religious consciousness,"[5] but, if we are to judge by his general argument in the book,[6] he can hardly mean "asserted"; I interpret him as meaning something like "shown" (in Wittgenstein's sense[7]). Otto was not clear about the uses of language, but he is not to be expected to be familiar with distinctions that philosophers have seen fit to draw. What is important to see is that Otto can be interpreted in terms of modern discussions about the uses of language, and that such an interpretation gives his work an interesting new significance.

Otto, then, uses language in order to explain what cannot be said in language. You cannot define the concept of the holy in a completely satisfactory way: you cannot satisfactorily tell others in words what it is: but what you can do in words is tell them about, or remind them of, feelings which are *like* the numinous feeling (but different from it, too, for the numinous feeling is a unique feeling, and not to be confused with any other no matter how similar to it it may be). You can talk round and round the subject, never quite hitting it exactly (for it is impossible to hit it with words), until you bring your hearer or reader to the point where he *sees for himself* what the numinous experience is.

Otto, in fact, is writing about the non-rational in a supremely rational way. But he thinks that rationality is *not good enough* for religion; and it takes a very rational man to see that. He does not want to say that it is *wrong* for a religion to be highly rational (highly conceptualized). What he wants to say is that we must not be bewitched into overlooking the fact that at the core of religion is a non-rational element—a part that eludes conceptualization.

Now what would Otto say about our worry? Otto, I imagine, would not be at all attracted to the *first* way out. He would not say, "Ah! these are great mysteries," and happily go on talking nonsense, interlarding it with cries of, "This is a paradox." And Otto is too rational to be satisfied to turn his back on the whole problem: so the *second* way is not for him. He is too sturdily a Kantian and a Protestant to take the *third* way.

I think he would take the *fourth way*. Otto's reaction to the worry might be expressed, for him, like this: "I agree with you that there is much nonsense in Christian doctrine." And he would not content himself with agreeing; he would produce illustrations of his own[8] to show just *how* much nonsense there is in Christian doctrine. Then he would say: "There are some things that *cannot* be said; so let us not try to say them. If we would understand religion we must not forget this."

Some of what I have just put into Otto's mouth is invention or embroidery. What Otto explicitly says cannot be conceptualized is the numinous experience.[9] As I have just interpreted him I have made him say more than this. But from what he says about "concept" and "conceptualize" (on the wider view) this is not an unreasonable interpretation. (Perhaps if Otto had realised that he had laid himself open to be interpreted in this way he would have wished to retreat to his narrower use of "concept" and "conceptualize.")

But we need not press Otto too far. It is enough if we interpret him as saying only that the numinous experience is what cannot be put into words: for this is, in Otto's view, the distinctive thing in religion. We can find out what more we need to know about the fourth way from others. Let us try Ludwig Wittgenstein.

It is interesting to compare with Otto's *The Idea of the Holy* the closing pages of Wittgenstein's *Tractatus Logico-Philosophicus*. Wittgenstein speaks there of "the mystical" (das Mystische). For example, he says: "The feeling of the world as a limited whole is the mystical feeling."[10] This has clear affinities with Otto's "creature-feeling."[11] The interesting thing in this part of the *Tractatus*, for our purposes, is the view there put forward of religion ("the mystical"). The sort of questions about the world that can be asked and answered, according to the *Tractatus*, are questions about *how* the world is. (That is, roughly, questions about "how the world *works*.") And these are questions of natural science. But the sort of questions that religious people ask are questions about the fact that there is a world at all. ("Why is there a world anyway?")

As Wittgenstein says: "Not *how* the world is, is the mystical, but *that* it is."[12]

But the trouble about this sort of question, he holds, is that it cannot be answered. (At the least, we may say, if it appears to be answered, there will not be agreement that any suggested answer is the *right* answer.) Questions about how the world works can be asked, and answered. But questions about why there is a world at all are quite different: they cannot be answered; that is to say, their answer cannot be an answer *in words*. Because they cannot be answered in words neither can they be *asked* in words. "For an answer which cannot be expressed the question too cannot be expressed."[13] (It follows, Wittgenstein holds, that scepticism about religious matters is senseless. The questions and answers of religion are not capable of being expressed, and it is absurd to have doubts about the answer to a question that is not capable of being expressed. "For doubt can only exist where there is a question; a question only where there is an answer, and this only where something *can* be *said*."[14])

Men cannot help feeling that even if all the "how" questions had been answered the "that" question would remain. The problems of life ("the riddle") men feel are not touched on in the answers to the "how" questions. The way out of this, Wittgenstein says, is found when we see that our feeling that the problems of life have not been touched on comes from the desire to ask questions that cannot *be* significantly asked. If *all* "how" questions *are* answered there are no other questions left that *can* be answered (and therefore none that can properly be asked).

It is at this point that Wittgenstein and Otto would part company. Wittgenstein goes on to say that the "solution" of "the problem of life" (the desire to ask "that" questions) comes when it is seen that such questions cannot (sensibly) be asked; the solution takes the form of a vanishing of the sense that there *is* a problem of life. Otto's direction from this point would be different. Where Wittgenstein ends he begins. For Wittgenstein, perhaps, to see that in religion we are asking questions that cannot be answered is, in a way, to see the pointlessness of religion. For Otto, to see that in religion we are asking questions that cannot be answered is to see its point; we do not lose the sense that there is a problem of life, or a "meaning" to life; but we perhaps realize that the question, "What is the meaning of life?" is not one that can be clearly answered *in words*, and so not one that can be properly asked.

## III

Now positivistic philosophy is commonly held to be an enemy of religion. But a branding of religious assertions as "nonsense" need not be anti-religious. It can be interpreted as an attack on those who in the name of religion are perverting religion. It can be interpreted as a return to the truth about religion. Otto conceived himself in *The Idea of the Holy* to be recovering the *essential* element in religion—which had been in danger of being lost under a cloud of rationalizing. What is essential about religion is its *nonrational* side, the part that cannot be "conceptualized"—that is, the part that cannot be put into words. Otto travels the same road as Wittgenstein. Are we to call Otto an enemy of religion? Why not call Wittgenstein its friend?

Modern positivistic philosophy has been developed by men of a scientific and not a religious turn of mind. (Perhaps this is not true of Wittgenstein himself.) The interest of the members of the Vienna Circle was mainly in science, and for them the use of philosophers was as the helpers of scientists. The observation statements of science were their model for sense,[15] and because scientists' observation statements are empirically verifiable the test for sense becomes "amenability to verification by sense experience," and whatever is not so verifiable accordingly is "non-sense." (An exception is made of "analytic" propositions, which are also found in science in the form of mathematical propositions; but the only *theological* proposition that has any obvious claim to be regarded as analytic is "God exists," and the grave difficulties that arise if one *does* regard this as analytic have been pointed out by both St. Thomas Aquinas and Kant.) Theological propositions are not (most of them, anyway) verifiable by sense experience, so *they* are nonsense. "Nonsense" is a pejorative word, and people do not like being told that they are talking nonsense.[16] Theologians like it as little as anyone else. People who insult one are one's enemies. So the positivists are enemies of religion.

I want to say that this opinion *may* be a mistaken one. Positivistic philosophers have certainly not thought of themselves as supporters of religion. But that could be because they have mistaken what is important about religion. Theologians have thought of positivistic philosophers as the enemies of religion. But that could be because theologians have mistakenly thought that what the positivists very properly pointed out strikes at what is most important in religion, whereas what it strikes at is what is least important—something concentration on which has led to a mistaken emphasis in accounts of what religion is. Perhaps positivistic philosophy has done a service to religion. By showing, in their own way, the absurdity of what theologians try to utter, positivists have helped to show that religion belongs to the sphere of the unutterable. And this may be true. And it is what Otto, too, in *his* way, wanted to point out.[17] Positivists may be the enemies of theology, but the friends of religion.

I have in the preceding paragraph been trying to make a point in a very general way. But it will be obvious that there is an ambiguity in what I have been saying. There is, as I pointed out earlier, more than one kind of nonsense. I have myself been using "nonsense" in two ways. There is nonsense in the usual sense in which the theological propositions I began by listing have been held to be nonsense—i.e., perhaps, "literally" absurd. And there is nonsense in the positivists' sense—i.e. where "nonsensical" means "not verifiable by sense experience." And surely these are different senses of "nonsense." And if they *are* different senses of "nonsense" then to praise the positivists for pointing out that theological propositions are "nonsensical" (in *their* sense) is not to have said anything that bears on the opening part of this article; for there it was pointed out that people may have a certain worry because they feel some theological propositions to be nonsensical—but "nonsensical" in a *different* sense of "nonsensical."

But there is an important connection. That theological propositions are nonsense in one sense of "nonsense" gives rise to a worry. One way out of the worry (the fourth way mentioned above, or the positivistic way) can be found when it is seen that theological propositions are nonsense in *another* sense of "nonsense." Put Wittgenstein and the Vienna Circle together, and join both with Otto, and we have the fourth way out of the worry: a way that is not a turning of one's back on the worry, not a "resolving" of it (in the sense of overcoming a neurotic feeling, though Wittgenstein taken alone might to some suggest something of this sort), not an anti-religious reaction (for we have Otto to give it religious respectability).

Religion belongs to the sphere of the unsayable, so it is not to be wondered at that in theology there is much nonsense (i.e., many absurdities); this is the natural result of trying to put into words—and to discuss—various kinds of inexpressible "experiences," and of trying to say things about God. Also, theological propositions are held to be non-sense (i.e., not amenable to verification by sense experience) by the Vienna Circle; and the *reason why* they are non-sense is that they are attempts to say the unsayable. It is not to be expected that the results of attempts to say the unsayable should be propositions that are amenable to verification by sense experience. (Notice that this is the *reason why* and not just another way of saying the same thing.)

I have discussed the positivistic way out of the worry as a serious contribution to philosophy of religion because that is what I think it is. To regard it as anti-religious is wrong; to think of it as by-passing the worry is wrong; not to take the worry itself seriously is wrong. The positivistic way is important both because it helps to pinpoint the worry and because it shows a way out of it.

Is it the *right* way? There is no answer to this question, for there is no one right way out of the worry. Worries are not like that. But the positivistic way is *an* answer; and an answer that is so often not seen, or rather not seen for what it is, that it deserves to be looked at. There certainly seems to be this wrong with it, that it may exclude too much: in throwing out the water of theology we may be also throwing out the baby of "direct," "first-order" religious assertions; and this we may well not want to do.

Perhaps something should be said about the relation of the positivistic way to mysticism, but I have no qualifications to say anything about this, and shall not try. Also, but this is too long a story to attempt here, something needs to be said about the relation between religion and theology.

One point to end. If it is foolish for theologians to refuse to learn from positivistic philosophy it is disastrous for them to mistake the lesson. Another, and a preposterous, kind of linking of positivism and theology is possible, and has even been tried.[18] This linking takes the form of an acceptance of the verification principle of the

Vienna Circle—that a proposition (unless it is analytic) "has sense," "is significant," "is meaningful," only if it is amenable to verification by sense experience—and issues in an attempt to bludgeon theological propositions to make them meet this prescription. This is a forlorn hope, and it is a dangerous thing to do. The proper linkage consists in an accommodation of positivism to theology, not of theology to positivism. Theology does not gain by being reduced to the terms of any school of philosophy.

NOTES

1. See R. Otto, *The Idea of the Holy*, p. 205, and *Religious Essays*, pp. 85-6 and 97.
   The Christian use of "person" in "God is Three Persons in One" is not to be dismissed as easily as I have dismissed it above in taking it as an example of "nonsense." If this were a serious discussion of that proposition we should need to consider it as "God is three *personae* in one *substantia*."
2. R. Otto, *The Idea of the Holy*.
3. Op. cit., p. 1.
4. Ibid., p. 2. My italics.
5. Ibid., p. 2.
6. See, e.g., p. 7.
7. Something *like*, indeed, but not, I think, quite the same. What exactly Wittgenstein *did* mean by "show" is not clear. He uses "zeigen," so did he mean something like "point at" or "indicate"? However, *Tractatus* exegesis aside, we may put the matter thus: Just as a statement does not say what the logical form of reality is but nevertheless somehow shows it, so when we make "statements" about God we may not succeed in saying anything (anything significant, that is) but for all that we may show something, even if it is only the "senselessness" of what we are saying. On the interpretation of the *Tractatus* see D. A. T. Gasking, "Anderson and the Tractatus Logico-Philosophicus," *Australasian Journal of Philosophy*, May, 1949. The interpretation adopted in the present paper differs from Gasking's in certain respects.
8. See, again, *The Idea of the Holy*, p. 205, on the Christian use of "person."
9. In so far as the numinous experience is an emotion it is no different from other emotions in this. No emotion can be defined in words, or even described—"directly" described—in words.
10. *Tractatus Logico-Philosophicus*, 6.45.
11. *The Idea of the Holy*, pp. 10, 52. It has even more affinities with current interpretations of the Cosmological Argument; see, e.g., E. L. Mascall, *Existence and Analogy*.
12. Op. cit., 6.44.

13. Ibid., 6.5. Cf. Otto, *Religious Essays*, pp. 90-91: "For the unspeakable is unspeakably beatifying, it is *fascinans*. So rich is its content of blessedness that all other values are shed. But the nature of its content can only be felt, not expressed: therefore 'let him who is wise attempt to add no word.'" And Wittgenstein again: "There is indeed the inexpressible. This *shows* itself; it is the mystical" (*Tractatus*, 6.522).

14. Ibid., 6.51.

15. Scientific *laws* should be held to be "nonsense" as much as theological statements, for they are not verifiable by sense experience.

16. Nor do they like being told that what they are saying is "non-significant," which suggests that it is *in*significant, i.e. unimportant. But "non-significant," and "nonsensical," mean for the positivist only "not amenable to verification by sense experience."

17. In M. Buber's *I and Thou* there is a similar view. Buber wants to say that the distinctive thing in religion is the "I-Thou relation." But if you try to analyze this relation, or to talk about it, it will vanish, and you will find yourself talking about *I* and *It*. It follows that theologians are bound to fail should they seek to say what religion is.

18. See on this my "The Existence of God" (*Mind*, October, 1950).

# 3. TRUTH-CLAIMS IN RELIGION

## William A. Christian

*William A. Christian is Professor of Religion at Yale University. In addition to his contributions to scholarly journals, he is author of* An Interpretation of Whitehead's Metaphysics *and* Meaning and Truth in Religion.

I want to discuss the possibility of significant truth-claims in religion. This is not the same as discussing criteria for truth-judgments. Deciding whether some religious proposal makes a truth-claim is different from deciding whether it is true. In the former case we are deciding only whether a truth judgment is *in order*. In truth-judgments themselves we decide whether or not truth-claims are valid, whether proposals are true or untrue. I want to consider some necessary conditions of making truth-claims in religion.

First I should explain what I mean by proposals. I mean utterances addressed to other human beings in which something is proposed (recommended). So this rules out *prayers*, which are not addressed to other human beings. It also rules out *meditative utterances*, like:

> The Lord is my shepherd.
> The Jewel in the Heart of the Lotus.

For these utterances are not addressed at all. They present something to be entertained and contemplated by those who utter them.

This also rules out *confessions*, like:

> I believe in God.
> I take refuge in the Buddha.
> I take refuge in the Dharma,
> I take refuge in the Sangha.

Reprinted from *Journal of Religion*, Volume 42 (1962), pp. 52-62, by permission of the University of Chicago Press. Copyright 1962 by the University of Chicago.

But it rules them out in another way. For while some confessions are prayers and some are meditative utterances, others are addressed to other human beings, as when we "bear testimony." But even so they are not proposals, at least not explicitly, though testimonial confessions are used to *convey* proposals. For example, if I say to someone that I believe in God, I may mean to suggest to him that he should believe in God too.[1] But I am not making an explicit proposal.

Proposals are of different sorts. Some are injunctions to act in certain ways, outwardly or inwardly, for example:

> Remember the Sabbath day to keep it holy.
> Perform every action with your heart fixed on the Supreme Lord. Renounce attachment of the fruits.
> Therefore, O Ananda, be ye lamps unto yourselves,
> Rely on yourselves, and do not rely on external help.

Closely related to injunctions are suggestions of patterns of conduct, paradigms conveyed through narratives and other devices, like:

> Ye are the light of the world.
> A skillful soldier is not violent;
> An able fighter does not rage;
> A mighty conqueror does not give battle.
> A great commander is an humble man.
> Him I call a brahmana whose path the gods do not know, nor spirits, nor men, whose passions are extinct, and who is an arhat.

These proposals I have just mentioned are different from those I shall be discussing. For in the case of these proposals we are not tempted to say that they are true or to say that they are untrue. They ask us to do something or to be something. They are proposals for action; the proposals I want to discuss are proposals for belief. But it is well that we keep other types of religious utterances in mind—prayers, meditations, confessions, and injunctions—and remember the complexities of patterns of meaning in religious discourse.

So another way of putting my question is: Under what conditions is a religious proposal a proposal for belief? For I suppose that if (and only if) a proposal asks us to believe something, a significant truth-claim is being made. I suggest four such conditions:

1. The proposal must be capable of self-consistent formulation.
2. The proposal must be liable to significant disagreement.
3. The proposal must permit a reference to its logical subject.
4. The proposal must permit some support for the assignment of its predicate to its subject.

I shall state the first condition very briefly, passing over the problem of paradoxes, and spend more time discussing the other three.

1. Suppose we are trying to formulate some proposal. And suppose, every time we try to express it, it comes out in pairs of contradictory statements. Then we might comfort ourselves by saying, "Nevertheless, there is something *in* it." Still, we might agree that what we have to offer is, at best, only a suggestion. (At worst, we are simply confused.) We do not yet have something which might be judged to be true or untrue. We might hope that the person addressed could say, "I think I see what you mean." But we would hardly expect him to say, "Yes, that is true." So it seems that we cannot make a significant truth-claim unless the proposal permits of self-consistent formulation.

2. The reason for the second condition is as follows. If something cannot be negated consistently, then it has no significant consequences. Therefore, it seems, nothing can count for or against its being true. And if this is the case, then it seems that no significant truth-claim is being made.

For example, suppose "God is the ground of being" is construed in such a way that (i) it makes no sense (since it would involve a self-contradiction) to say that God is not the *ground of being* (adding perhaps that God is an illusion and therefore not the ground of being), *and* (ii) it makes no sense to say it is not *God* that is the ground of being (adding perhaps that it is Nature or the Absolute that is the ground of being). Then the proposal, construed in this way, would exclude the possibility of any consistent alternative.

In this case it seems that "God is the ground of being" is being construed as a tautology. It would still be possible to claim that it is logically true. But I suppose we want to know whether religious proposals make claims to truth in some more important sense. This is what I have meant by a significant truth-claim, a claim to other-than-logical truth. So, to count as a truth-claim of this latter sort, the proposal would have to be construed in such a way that it would make sense to insert before it the words, "It is not the case that. . . ."

This negation might then be developed in either of the two ways mentioned above. However it is developed, the proposal would mean that this negation is untrue.

Let us take another example. Suppose "Nirvana is the supreme goal of life" were construed in such a way that (i) it is not logically possible to say that Nirvana is not the supreme goal of life (adding perhaps that it is irrelevant to moral values), *and* (ii) it is not logically possible to say that it is not Nirvana (but, say, the vision of God) that is the supreme goal of life.

Then the proposal would have no consistent alternative. An apparent disagreement with it would be an infallible sign that it has not been understood. Further, it would have no significant logical consequences. This can be shown by considering the following sentences:

    P. Nirvana is the supreme goal of life.
    Q. Existence is unhappiness.
    Q'. Existence is not unhappiness.
    P'. Nirvana is not the supreme goal of life.

Now suppose that P is so construed that it *does* have a significant logical consequence. Suppose that Q follows from it (i.e., that if P is true then Q is also true). And suppose that Q' is logically possible, so Q is a genuine assertion and not itself a tautology. Then P' is logically possible, since if Q' is true, then P' is true. Thus if P has some significant consequence, then it has some consistent alternative. It is not being construed as a tautology.

But if a proposal has no significant consequences, because it is construed as a tautology, then we would have no way of telling what *might* count for or against its being true. Then it would become very doubtful, to say the least, whether any significant truth-claim is being made.

I conceive this second requirement for truth-claims as a very weak one. Its weakness can be illustrated by reference to Anselm's ontological argument. If the argument is a significant argument (i.e., if it establishes something that was not previously established), then a negation of its conclusion must be logically possible in the sense of "logically possible" I have in mind.

And, if I understand Anselm correctly, this is the case. He did not really think he was wrestling with a shadow. He thought he had a real opponent, against whom an argument was needed. (Though at the end of chapter iii of the *Proslogium* he seems *tempted* to think of the fool not in the biblical sense of "fool" but as a stupid person.) He did not suppose that "There is no God" is senseless. If it were senseless, then an argument against it would have been out of order.

So, to make a significant truth-claim, one condition his conclusion ("God exists both in the understanding and in reality") must satisfy is that a negation of it (e.g., "God exists only in the understanding") should be logically possible. I take it that Anselm grants this possibility.[2] He admits a sense in which it can be conceived that God does not exist, and he explains this sense as follows: "In one sense, an object is conceived, when the word signifying it is conceived."[3] This means, I suppose, having *some* conception of the object, if the word is *taken as* signifying the object, though not perhaps a complete and adequate conception of the object. (For if the word were *not* taken as signifying the object—as if, for example, someone should utter a word from a foreign language without knowing in the least what it meant, then an argument would not be in order. What would be in order in that case would be instruction in the use of the word.) We may well ask, "When is a conception (relatively) complete and adequate?" But this is different from asking whether or not a statement makes *some* sense.

With this requirement for making truth-claims in mind, let us consider the possibility of disagreements among different religions. In this way we can learn something about the range and scope of truth-claims in religion. Also, this will lead us to an important distinction between different sorts of religious propositions.

Ordinarily we suppose that proponents of different religious systems like Hinduism, Buddhism, Judaism, Christianity, and Islam disagree with one another. Of course there can be differences without disagreements, and many of the differences between religious systems are differences of style, like differences between styles of painting. But certainly some of the differences appear to be real disagreements. Let us consider two ways in which this might be the case.

Let us begin with what we might call proposals of doctrines (doctrinal propositions) and take for example:

A. Jesus is the Messiah.

Other examples of doctrinal propositions would be:

> Israel is the Chosen People.
> Allah is merciful.
> Atman is Brahman.
> All the buddhas are one.

Now it might be argued that when Jews say that Jesus is not the Messiah and Christians say Jesus is the Messiah, this is not a full-fledged disagreement. Because, we might say, even though the same term is being used by both, they do not mean the same thing by it. Jews mean by the Messiah a non-divine being who will restore Israel as an earthly community and usher in the consummation of history. Christians mean a promised savior of mankind from sin. Two different Messiah-concepts are being expressed; two different propositions are being asserted.

If we think along this line about doctrinal disagreements, we might come to Schleiermacher's conclusion that Christian dogmatics is only for Christians. And, going beyond Schleiermacher's conclusion, we might argue more generally for the logical isolation of doctrinal systems from one another. We might say that argument about some doctrine can go on significantly only within the community whose faith the doctrine expresses. Within the community there are common concepts, so that rules of relevance in doctrinal arguments are possible. Also, the community has rules of judgment to appeal to, for instance "What does the Bible say?" But, we might argue, no two doctrinal systems have enough common concepts to make significant disagreements between them possible. No common rules of relevance, much less common rules of judgment, can be formulated. How could a Christian and a Taoist significantly disagree about whether the Holy Spirit proceeds from the Father and from the Son, or only from the Father?

Indeed, it would seem that on this view there would be no doctrinal proposition about which Christians and non-Christians, for example, could really disagree. In cases of apparent disagreement, like the apparent disagreement between Jews and Christians about A, it would turn out that the parties to the apparent disagreement are not really considering the same proposition.

It seems to me highly implausible to explain all religious doctrines in this way. So let us reconsider the apparent disagreement about A. We might say that, though Jews and Christians have different concepts of the Messiah, we can reformulate the proposal so that significant disagreement is possible, as follows:

B. Jesus is the one God promised to send to redeem Israel.

We could grant that Jews and Christians have different concepts of Israel, and even different concepts of God perhaps. But these concepts might overlap enough to allow B to be significant for both. Then we could say that Jews and Christians consider the same proposition but judge it differently. Jews judge it is untrue; Christians judge it to be true. Thus there could be a real disagreement, not merely an apparent one.

May we go further? Might there have been a genuine disagreement about B not only between, say, Paul the Apostle and Rabbi Gamaliel, but also between Paul and a Stoic philosopher, for example Seneca? Now we might conceive that if Seneca were confronted with B, he might be perplexed, because he thinks God does not act in history as this seems to suppose. *God* does not "promise" anything in this way, and he does not "send" anyone in this way. So, Seneca might think, the proposal as it stands does not really make good sense. So a negation of it would not make good sense either.

In this case Seneca is denying one of the presuppositions of B if (but only if) there is some overlapping between his concept of God and Paul's concept of God. And this might be the case. We might say that for Paul (and Gamaliel) *the being who rules the world* acts in history and that for Seneca this being does not do so (at least not in the same way). So in this case a disagreement about B, if there is one, would derive from a disagreement about:

C. The being who rules the world acts in history.

Here we have extended the range of possible disagreements, and we have done it by finding a common reference ("the being who rules the world"), and constructing a proposition implied by the one we began with. Beginning with an apparent disagreement, we locate a real one. *In* the two concepts, Paul's conception of God and Seneca's conception of God, we find a common reference. So Seneca might even be said to disagree with Paul about A, in an indirect way. "If that is what you mean by the Messiah (someone promised and sent by the being who rules the world)," he might say, "I do not believe that is true."

Might we go still further in this manner? Might there be a real disagreement about A in some such indirect way between a Christian and a Neoplatonist like Plotinus? We might conceive that the Neoplatonist, confronted with C, might be perplexed in the way the Stoic was perplexed about B. And he might express his perplexity by saying, "But the source of all being (which I suppose you are referring to) does not rule the world in any way at all, much less by acting in history in the way you say. So what you are saying does not seem to make good sense."

Again we might look for overlapping concepts to use in constructing a proposition about which real disagreement would be possible. And we might construct the proposition:

D. The source of all being rules the world.

About this there might be real disagreement. The Christian (and the Jew and the Stoic) might say it is true; the Neoplatonist might say it is untrue. Again we have found a common reference. And this reference gives us a logical subject of which some predicate might be said to be true or untrue.

In this manner we might go a long way. We might continue to extend the range of religious disagreements by looking for common references and then formulating predicates which bring out points of direct disagreement. The aim is to find something which both parties to the apparent disagreement can say something *about*, some common logical subject, and then find some predicate which one party means to affirm of this subject and the other party means to deny of it. This would be a general rule for formulating what I have called doctrinal disagreements.

Now let us see whether we might extend the range of religious disagreements—and thereby the range of significant truth-claims in religion—in another way. We might look for some common predicate, some predicate both parties mean to assign to some subject or other, and for different logical subjects to which this predicate might be assigned by the two parties, respectively.

These would be disagreements of a different logical sort from doctrinal disagreements. Doctrinal disagreements are of the form:

$$Fm \ / \ Gm$$
For example: Jesus is the Messiah. / Jesus is a teacher.

These disagreements would be of the form:

$$Fm \ / \ Fn$$
For example: God is the ground of being. / Nature is the ground of being.

To distinguish these disagreements from those we have been considering, let us call them basic religious disagreements. And let us say that, as doctrinal disagreements are about doctrinal proposals, basic religious disagreements are about basic religious proposals. So we have two sorts of religious proposals in which significant truth-claims might be made.

As examples of predicates that might be useful in formulating basic religious proposals we might take the following:

"the ground of being"
"the supreme goal of life"
"that on which we unconditionally depend"
"more important than anything else"
"ultimate"
"holy"

One feature of these predicates needs to be noticed. The predicate cannot be true of *both* the logical subjects involved in a basic religious disagreement. So, if "God is holy" is a formulation of a basic religious proposal, "holy" is being used in an eminent sense and not in the sense in which a mountain *and* an altar *and* a book might be said to be holy. In this eminent sense, it would not be consistent to say that God is holy *and* nature is holy. We might still say, of course, that nature gets its (relative) holiness from its relation to God.

One reason why the formulation of basic religious disagreements is important is that we might have a better chance, in this way, of formulating significant disagreements between religions which have little or no obvious point of contact in their doctrines. For sometimes it is difficult to find a common logical subject to which different doctrines seem to be referring.

For example, in the course of the transition above from A to D, it becomes somewhat less convincing to treat "the source of all being" as a *reference* common to Christians and Neoplatonists than to treat "Jesus" as a reference common to Jews and Christians. "The source of all being" begins to look more like a predicate expression than like a reference to a logical subject. And we begin to see, beyond any doctrinal disagreement that could be formulated in this way, another sort of disagreement that is more fundamental, a disagreement about what it is that is "the source of all being." This would be a basic religious disagreement. Christians say that God (as explained in the creeds and doctrines of the church) is the source of all being. Neoplatonists say that the One is the source of all being.

This limitation on the range of doctrinal disagreements becomes even clearer if we take two religions that have even less of a common heritage than Christianity and Neoplatonism do, for example Theravada Buddhism and Islam. Taking Nirvana and Allah as their central concepts, respectively, it does not seem very promising to try to find a common reference in these concepts and thus formulate a doctrinal disagreement. But it might be possible to find some predicate which, we might say, Theravada Buddhists mean to assign to Nirvana and Moslems mean to assign to Allah. In this way we might formulate a basic religious disagreement.

Why is it important to extend the range of religious disagreements? The reason is that in doing so we are extending the range of possible truth-claims, since one condition of making a significant truth-claim, in some religious proposal, is that the proposal should be liable to disagreement. Some negation of the proposal must be logically possible in the sense of "logically possible" I have tried to explain.

3. The third condition of making a significant truth-claim is that it must be possible to make a reference to the logical subject of the proposal. The term used for the logical subject must mean something and it must mean something in a certain way. It must mean something not only in the sense that the proposer knows what he is talking about but also in the sense that others might (a logical "might") be able to learn what he is talking about. Making a reference consists in putting others in mind of what is being talked about. So this condition is that others might be led to understand what the proposer is talking about.[4] Some answer to the question, "What is it that you are referring to?" must be possible. Otherwise, it seems, a significant truth-claim is not being made.

Suppose, for example, it is proposed that "JHWH is the lord of

life." Then it would be in order to ask, "What do you mean by
JHWH?"—meaning "What is it that you are referring to?" The
proposer might well respond by saying, "JHWH is the one who led
Israel out of Egypt." Similarly, for other proposals references might
be made as follows:

> Zeus is the hurler of thunderbolts.
> Nature is the whole of which all other things are parts.[5]
> God is the first cause of all particular effects.
> Nirvana is the state in which no craving remains.

This condition requires of a proposal of the form "*m* is *F*" that
there should be additional information about *m*, beyond saying it
is *F*. Further, this additional information must be of a certain kind.
For example, in answer to the question about JHWH it would not
be relevant to say "JHWH is powerful." This would not tell the
questioner what he wants to know. A reference is being asked for.
And I suppose this means that the proposer must do two things:
(i) he must adduce some fact or other as a starting point for his
reference; and (ii) he must, by employing some interpretative
category, connect this fact with the logical subject of this proposal.

Thus in the examples of references given above, the exodus from
Egypt, thunderbolts, particular things and states (effects) in general, and cravings are the facts used as starting points. And, to be
used in this way, a fact must be independent of the proposal. It
must be logically possible to accept the fact without accepting the
proposal. Then in each case the proposer aims to lead someone from
this factual starting point to the logical subject of the proposal,
which is the goal of the reference. He does this by making use of
some interpretative category or other, for example "the hurler of,"
"whole," "cause," or the notion of a limiting state.

Why is it that the possibility of making a reference is a condition
of making a significant truth-claim? This can be seen by considering
some cases in which it is not possible to make a reference.

Suppose someone who, we might say, does not know what he is
talking about—suppose he has something in mind (or feels he has
something in mind) that he means to designate by the subject term
of his proposal. But what he has in mind is so extremely unclear
that he could not know how to begin or proceed in making a reference to it.

Or suppose the proposer has something in mind with reasonable clearness. Still it might happen that no facts are available as starting points for references to it. This might be so for a fantasy which, we would say, is quite out of touch with reality. In such a case the object mentioned is useful only as a symptom of a state of mind. That, we say, is all we can make of it.

It is different with the imaginary objects mentioned in fairy tales, myths, and other literary works. Bluebeard, the Augean stables, and Falstaff are more important than purely artistic fantasies. There is truth, we say, in these fictions. But, though they are vehicles of poetic truth, it is neither appropriate nor logically possible to make a reference to one of them, except in a peculiar sense which we need not explore. They are not meant to be referred to.

I suppose that the logical subjects of basic religious proposals are meant to be referred to. They are not proposed as things are proposed in fairy tales, myths, and poetry. It is true indeed that myths often bear a religious meaning and that in religious literature symbols abound. The difference is that the myths and symbols, when used in serious religious discourse, are meant to point to something. So the important question is whether in religious discourse truth-claims of another sort than claims to poetic truth are possible, truth-claims of which one necessary condition is the possibility of making references.

Let us take an extreme case. Suppose the subject term of a proposal has no connotation for someone. Suppose he has never heard of Ahura Mazda, but the expression sounds to him like a proper name. So he says, "Will you please tell me what you are referring to when you speak of Ahura Mazda?" Clearly it will not do to give him another proper name (e.g., Ormazd) which is equally without sense for him. This would not help. What is needed is either some synonym which would have both a sense and a reference (which would amount to giving an implicit reference) or some description which contains an explicit reference, for example "the source of light and goodness."

Now suppose that in this case the proposer literally has nothing to say. (Which is not at all the same thing as saying nothing. There can be meaningful silences.) Suppose the subject term cannot be explained by any reference, implicit or explicit. Then the term is only a name. (Or, we might say, it is a word that only sounds like a name. We are misled by its position in the sentence.) Then *would* it seem that a significant truth-claim is being made?

4. The fourth condition of making a significant truth-claim is that it must be possible to give some support to the predication made in the proposal. It must be possible to give some reason for saying that $m$ is $F$. And giving a reason means bringing up some fact or other according to some rule of judgment. So we need to consider how there can be rules of judgment for religious proposals.

Here again it is helpful to distinguish between doctrinal proposals and basic religious proposals. Let us consider how it might be possible to formulate some rules of judgment for a basic religious proposal. Since these rules would have to be formulated "in the frame of" some particular predicate, let us consider proposals of the form "$m$ is holy" (in an eminent sense of "holy"). And let us construe "holy" after the manner of Rudolf Otto as a complex category having both rational and non-rational elements. Whatever is holy is numinous; it is *mysterium tremendum et fascinans*. This is the non-rational element in the category of the holy. But in an experience of something holy, the numinous is schematized by rational concepts. That is, when we say of something holy that it is powerful, we are using the concept of power as a schema for apprehending the numinous object we are referring to. We are not using the concept in the way we apply it to "natural" objects. We are using it as an open pattern, so to speak, through which the numinous character of the object can shine.

Now suppose that some proposal of the form "$m$ is holy" (reading, for $m$, Allah or Nature or Mankind or the One or the sun, for example) has met the first three conditions we have discussed. Suppose it can be explicated with reasonable consistency, that it is liable to disagreement in the way explained, and that a reference to $m$ is possible. Then it is being claimed that, for *any* $n$, $m$ is holier than $n$. So, for some $n$, we need rules to guide us in deciding whether or not $m$ is holier than $n$.

Then we might say that $m$ is holier than $n$: if (i) $m$ is more numinous than $n$, and if (ii) $m$ is more susceptible of rational schematization than $n$. Thus $n$ might fail to be as holy as $m$ in either of two ways, or in both. (i) It might be less numinous than $m$. The feelings appropriate to it are less sharply in contrast with the feelings appropriate to other objects. It is deficient in "otherness," in being other than "natural" things (i.e., the rest of the universe relative to it). This might count against $n$, for example, if $n$ is a mountain, an emperor, or (in the modern world) the sun.

(ii) It might be less susceptible of rational schematization. This might count against Caliban's god, for example, or against the "momentary gods" who appear in primitive religion, and more generally against anything which lacks consistency of character or endurance in being.

It is important to notice that the rules I have just formulated are in the frame of a particular predicate. They are not rules for judging any and every religious proposal. For proposals using other predicates, other rules of judgment would have to be formulated. It may turn out to be the case that all predicates used in basic religious proposals have certain functions in common. But we do not need to reduce all basic predicates to some one. Just as various general theories of religion are possible and useful, so various predicates derived from these general theories are possible and useful.

It may be easier to formulate rules of judgment in the frame of one predicate than in the frame of another. One set of rules may give more guidance to judgments than another set does. In this way some predicates may give more significance to truth-claims than others do.

My main point is that unless it is possible to give some support to a religious predication, it seems that a significant truth-claim is not being made. And it is possible to support a predication only if some rules of judgment, in the frame of the predicate in question, can be formulated.

Clearly we cannot expect, in judging religious proposals, to find quasi-mechanical decision procedures, as in some parts of logic and mathematics. Nor do we have the highly quantifiable public data that are available for deciding questions in the natural sciences. Religious questions are obviously of another sort, and agreements are far more difficult to arrive at.

Let me return briefly to the point I began with. Deciding whether religious proposals make truth-claims is different from making religious judgments and arguing for them. Suppose we should take some proposal as making a truth-claim, and suppose we should want to know whether we should accept, or reject, or suspend judgment on this claim. Then, along with many other considerations, we would need to see whether (i) an adequate reference (i.e., one whose factual starting point is firm enough and whose interpretative categories are sufficiently perspicuous) to its logical subject and (ii) adequate support for the predication are available. I have not tried to say how such decisions might be made. I have been asking: Under what conditions would it be appropriate to take some religious proposal as making a significant truth-claim?

Of course, if we can answer this question, we know something about religious judgments and something about the form religious arguments would have to take. But on these latter topics much more would need to be said.

Indeed, much more needs to be said about the narrower topic I have been considering. I would mention two questions which (especially the second) need much more attention than I can give them here:

1. Are there any basic religious proposals to which the second condition above (that they be liable to significant disagreement) somehow fails to apply, perhaps because they express "necessary truths" or in some other way?[6]

2. Does the third condition (that the proposal permit a reference to its logical subject) conflict with a generally accepted norm, namely, that religion ought not to be obsessive (in religious terms, idolatrous)? Are there ways of referring to logical subjects of basic religious proposals (e.g., to God, or to Nirvana, or to Nature, or to Humanity) which do not commit us to treating them as things in some *bad* sense of "thing"? Answers to this question would have far-reaching consequences.

NOTES

1. He might understand this quite well and might respond by saying, "But how *can* you, in view of . . . ?" His "can" is a logical "can" and is a sign that he is replying to an implicit proposal for belief.

2. If Anselm's argument were aimed at an intelligent atheist, its first premise would have to be something like "We conceive a being than which nothing greater can be conceived" instead of "We believe that thou art a being. . . ." And, for his conclusion to make a significant truth-claim, a negation of this reformulated first premise would have to be logically possible also. Would Anselm have granted this?

3. *Proslogium* iv (Deane trans.)

4. It is important to notice that the logical subject of a basic religious proposal does not have to be a single entity. "The gods" would be a

proper subject term in a polytheistic proposal. And this is of more than antiquarian interest.

5. Or, in a Comtean proposal, Humanity is the whole of which human beings are members.

6. It may be worth noticing that "God exists" is not an explicit statement of a basic religious proposal, though someone might mean by it more than he says.

# 4. THE POSSIBILITY OF

# THEOLOGICAL STATEMENTS

## I. M. Crombie

*I. M. Crombie is Lecturer in Philosophy and Webster Fellow at Wadham College, Oxford University. His published works include* An Examination of Plato's Doctrines *and* Plato, the Midwife's Apprentice, *among others.*

## 1. INTRODUCTION

Christianity, as a human activity, involves much more than simply believing certain propositions about matters of fact, such as that there is a God, that He created this world, that He is our judge. But it does involve believing these things, and this believing is, in a sense, fundamental; not that it matters more than the other things that a Christian does, but that it is presupposed in the other things that he does, or in the manner in which he does them. This is a fact, but it is in some ways an awkward fact, and for many years some theologians have tried to sidestep it. It is an awkward fact because, for example, if one professes certain beliefs, it seems that one ought to be willing to offer some kind of grounds for them. Yet we all know that it is difficult, and some think it is impious, to offer adequate grounds for the faith. Again—a requirement which has become more prominent with recent developments in philosophy—if one professes certain beliefs it seems that one ought to be willing to map out, roughly at any rate, the extent of the claims one is making by saying what is compatible and what is incompatible with them; and that again, in the case of religious beliefs, is something which is difficult

Reprinted by permission of George Allen and Unwin Ltd. from *Faith and Logic* (1958), pp. 31-67.

to do, for reasons which will be considered in this chapter. Therefore some theologians have tried to sidestep these problems by denying that the Christian religion involves anything that may fairly be called factual beliefs about a transcendent being. That, it is said, is metaphysics, and religion has no interest in metaphysics. A simple-minded move, that has had its devotees, consists in saying that we do not believe that there is a God; we believe in God. More sophisticated apologists have urged that credal affirmations may, without significant loss, be treated as equivalent to recommendations of the behaviour and attitudes that are agreed on all hands to be their proper corollaries. 'There is a God' thus becomes equivalent, or nearly equivalent, to something like: 'Treat all men as brothers, and revere the mystery of the universe.' Beliefs are said to be merely the expression—the somewhat misleading expression—of an attitude of worship.

But, in spite of the piety and wisdom of those who have been seduced by them, these expedients must be denounced as evasions. The distinction between *believing that* and *believing in* is, of course, valid; but it does not help us, for *believing in* is logically subsequent to *believing that*. I cannot believe in Dr. Jones if I do not first believe that there is such a person. Nor is the reduction of credal affirmations to the behaviour of worship and general charitable conduct that ought to follow from them of any avail. For Christian worship cannot be exhaustively described in terms of how the worshipper feels, of what he says and does; it retains an irreducible element of belief. Christian worship is neither a kind of poetry nor a kind of *ascesis*, neither a giving vent to feelings of awe and reverence, nor a cultivation of the soul. Fundamentally it is thought of by the Christian as an entry into relationship with a transcendent being, whom non-Christians do not believe to be there to enter into relationship with. Christian worship, therefore, is not only something which the non-Christian *does* not do, it is something which, by virtue of the difference of his beliefs, the non-Christian *cannot* do, though he can, of course, do something which, in externals, is as closely similar as you please. What the non-Christian does, whether in church or out of it, may be better or it may be worse than what the Christian does, but it cannot be the same, because it cannot share the same credal basis.

There are then certain factual beliefs which are fundamental to

Christianity, in the sense that they underlie all Christian activity, and give it its specifically Christian character. The expression of such beliefs I shall refer to as the making of *theological statements*.[1]

## The problem stated

Our problem in this chapter, then, is: how are theological statements possible? For it is a fairly common philosophical position today to say that there can be no meaningful theological statements. This view may be loosely put by saying that theological statements are unverifiable, and therefore meaningless; or it may be more carefully put by attending to the rules which Christians appear to lay down for the interpretation of theological statements, and contending that these rules conflict with each other in such a way that no meaningful statements could possibly be governed by such rules. For, it is said, the statements purport to be about a quasi-personal subject, and in that way to be parallel to statements about, say, Julius Caesar; and yet if we proceed to draw conclusions from them, to bring arguments against them, in general to test them as if they were parallel to statements about Julius Caesar, we are told that we have failed to grasp their function. They have, apparently, some kind of special exemption from empirical testing; and yet if one attempts, for this reason, to assimilate them to other kinds of utterances (moral judgments for example, or mathematical formulae) which enjoy similar exemption, one is at once forbidden to do so. How paradoxical this is; and how much easier it makes it to believe that the making of theological statements rests on some kind of confusion than to accept them at their face-value!

My procedure will be to ignore the loose statement of the case (the doctrine that unverifiable statements are meaningless is like the doctrine that cars are fast; not entirely false, but blanketing so many important distinctions as to be useless), and attend to the more careful one. Here I shall not dispute that theological statements have the paradoxical features attributed to them by their opponents, but I shall argue that these paradoxical features need not be regarded as demonstrating the impossibility of meaningful theological statements, but rather as contributing to a grasp of their meaning by giving a partial characterization of their subject. For, I shall argue, their paradoxical features make it clear that these statements are made about no object which falls within our normal experience, or any imaginable extension of our normal experience; and to learn this is to learn something about the nature of religion. Something, but not much. To know that God may not be identified with anything that can be indicated is only the first step in theology. I shall therefore go on to try to define the extent to which we can claim to have any positive grasp of what we are talking about when we make theological statements, and thus to elucidate the sense in which they are meaningful. Very briefly, my argument will be: the inquirer may learn from the paradoxical features of theological statements, that, if they are about anything, they are about a mystery. If he requires further specification ( and he is right to ask for some, though if he is wise he will not demand that those who believe in a mystery should offer him a detailed anatomy of it ) he must seek it from two sources. Firstly from the affinities and relationships which exist between theological statements and utterances of other kinds (for example moral judgments; to do the will of God is our supreme duty); and secondly by considering whether a sense of mystery seems to be the appropriate response to any part of our experience. If this enables him to see not only what theological statements are not about, but also, so to speak, in what region the mystery that they are about is located, then he may feel that he understands what it is that Christians are talking about, but not why they talk about it; for surely it is self-stultifying both to say that something is a mystery, and also to make 'statements' about it. To this I shall reply that, if we claim to know something of the mystery, we do so because we believe ourselves to possess a revelation, that is to say a communication made in terms that we can understand; and I shall argue that if we reflect on the kind of thing such a communication would have to be, we shall see why theological statements have the characteristics that they have, and how they are to be taken. That is to say, I shall attempt to show that theological statements are meaningful by showing what they are about, and how they offer information about it. For, after all, all that is necessary for an utterance to be a meaningful statement is that it should be governed by rules which specify what it is about, and what it asserts about it. The problem about theological statements is simply that there is a sense in which we cannot know what they are about (a sense in which we cannot know God) nor what it is that they assert. The solution of the problem must consist in defining the sense in which, on the other hand, we can know enough of these things for our speech about them to have an intelligible use.

## The critic's case

So much by way of preliminary sketch. Let us begin our argument by considering the case advanced by the critic, as I shall call the man who denies the meaningfulness of theological statements.

He knows of course, that theological statements have many of the characteristics of meaningful statements, in particular that they form a system, within which inferences may be drawn, incompatibility relations obtain, and so forth; and that they command a response, both emotional and moral, in those who accept their validity. What he suspects, however, is that although they form a system, it is a system without reference to anything in the real world. The system maintains itself, not because it is seen to report the truth about certain objects, but because it is causally connected with a set of images and practices which are valued for their own sake, and in particular because it can be thought of in mythological terms. That is to say, one can think of divine judgment in terms of the pictures on mediæval chancel arches; of beings with wings weighing souls in balances or driving them into a fish's mouth with pitchforks; and one may be moved, poetically and morally, by such pictorial representations. Because one is moved by the picture, one wants to believe that it is a representation of something which will really happen at the last day; because one has the picture, one is able to imagine that one is believing in something when one says that 'he shall come again with glory to judge both the quick and the dead.' Now the Christian is perfectly willing to admit that he does not expect at the last day any event having any resemblance, in any literal sense, to the events depicted in mediæval dooms. Whenever a trumpet sounds he knows it is not the last trump because, whatever the last trump will be, it will not be the sound of a trumpet. But he maintains that he believes in something, of which the mediæval doom is a pictorial representation. It is here that the critic dissents. He can understand why the Christian wants to believe that he believes in something underlying his mythology; but, in his judgment, there is nothing there. This judgment he bases on the peculiar elusiveness of theological statements, once they are stripped of mythological form.

In its most general terms, this elusiveness takes the following form: on the one hand the Christian claims that his statements are concerned with a particular being, God, with particular kinds of events, such as the creation, the last judgment, the operation of the Holy Ghost. Yet if you try to pin him down by asking such questions as 'Which person? Where is He? What events are you talking about?' he protests that such questions display crude misunderstanding of the nature of theological language. Yet if he uses words which appear to be proper names, or which appear to refer to cosmological happenings, or to occurrences in human personalities, surely such questions are perfectly proper ones to ask. It is, of course, true that anybody who knows anything about the more abstract intellectual disciplines is familiar with many words and phrases whose use is logically much more complex, whose relationship to their subject-matter is much more devious, than that of words like 'axe' or 'butterfly'; and the critic is quite prepared to believe that the words (like 'God' and 'grace') whose use is peculiar to theological statements may be of this kind, and also that when ordinary words (such as 'loves' and 'made') are put to theological use, they also are made to work under similar conditions. But if we consider words of this kind from other spheres, such as 'electron' or 'Œdipus complex,' we see that we can gather what they are about by observing how they are used, by noticing what kind of observations are held to substantiate a statement about an electron, what kind require that it be withdrawn. There are specific laboratory or clinical conditions with which these words are fairly tightly connected. But let us take a word like 'grace,' and begin by observing that it appears to be used about certain happenings in human personalities. Now let us go on to try to discover which happenings these are; let us ask such questions as: 'If a man decides to go to church, is that an example of what you call "the effects of grace"?' Always we seem to get an ambiguous answer: 'It might be or it might not. It would be if it were the result of divine influence; it would not be if the decision proceeded from some other cause.' But this will not help us much; it tells us that grace is what God does to a man; but unless we know what God is and what form His action takes, we are no further forward. We tried to break our way into the system of theological statements by taking a concept—grace— which appears to refer to events in human beings in the hope that these parts of the system might be familiar to us and so enable us to understand the rest of it. But when we try to isolate the events in question, in order to discover what is being talked about, we are offered no characterization of them except that they are the results of divine influence. It would appear then that we must begin at the difficult end; if we are ever to discover what theological statements are about, we must tackle the concept of God. But if we ask what the word 'God' refers to, we are likely to be told that God is a transcendent being who cannot be known to us except in his effects.

It appears then that we are imprisoned in a circular maze. Grace is what God does, and God is the being whose action in human souls is grace. How, asks the critic, is anybody supposed to discover what this circular system of concepts is about? Is it not much easier to believe that the system is nothing but the relic of pre-scientific mythology in which God was an almost human being and grace was something concrete, like the prosperity of the law-abiding; that with growth in scientific knowledge and moral sensitivity, theological concepts have been progressively detached from the fictitious celestial being, and real, but insufficiently edifying, terrestrial events, with which they were once identified; and that the whole system has been preserved, beyond the point at which it was evacuated of all content, only for what one may brusquely call sentimental reasons?

## Ambiguity of the critic's case

That, or something like it, is the case for the meaninglessness of theological statements. It is a case which I do not propose to dispute. The premises are sound enough, though the circle is not so complete as I have let it appear (it is true that the Christian will never assert positively that this or that thought or action could only have flowed from divine grace;[2] but he will claim that faith, hope and charity are supernaturally infused virtues, and he is prepared to offer, not exactly criteria for the infallible recognition of these gifts, but some account of what he takes genuine faith, hope or charity to be). But it is indisputable that there is no region of experience which one can point to and say: 'That is what theological statements are about.' If you care to conclude from that that there is no way of discovering what theological statements are about, then that, too, is indisputable if your meaning is that one can never know what it is like to be, for example, divinely inspired, in the way in which one can know what it is like to have a cold, or even, perhaps, an Œdipus complex. What I do wish to maintain, however, is that this does not show that theological statements have no legitimate use; it is simply a partial definition of the use that they have. For the elusiveness we are considering is a consequence, indeed an expression, of the fact that all theological statements are about God, and that God is not part of the spatio-temporal world, but is in intimate relation with it.

To maintain this contention, it will be necessary to look rather more closely at this characteristic of elusiveness. It derives, we must begin by insisting, not from the natural shiftiness of persons who make theological statements, but from the uses for which such statements are devised. If one is to talk about these matters, one has to do so by making use of statements governed by apparently conflicting rules. The formal properties of theological statements (that is to say, the rules determining how they are to be taken and how they are supposed to be related to statements of other kinds) have to be, at first sight, mutually contradictory if they are to do their proper work. We must turn to a more detailed consideration of these antinomies.

## 2. THE ANOMALIES OF THE FORMAL PROPERTIES OF THEOLOGICAL STATEMENTS

### The first anomaly

Since all theological statements are, by definition, about God, then however they are worded, we may say that God is the subject of them all (statements about grace, for example, are not about a commodity which is dispensed from heaven, but about what God does to men). Therefore we may describe the first antinomy in the following terms: theological statements are to be interpreted as if their subject was a particular individual, and yet differ in logical character from all other statements about particular individuals. Let us put it in the following way.

If I say that Tom loves Mary, you can ask me who Tom is, and it is at least logically possible for me to point him out to you. But if I say that the average man falls in love at least once between the ages of 18 and 27, you display that you do not understand the expression 'the average man' if you ask me who he is. I shall put this by saying that while 'Tom' is a *proper proper name*, statements about the average man *have to be reduced*; the first statement, I shall say is *directly* about Tom; the second is *obliquely* about people in general. Now what about the statement 'God loves mankind'? On the one hand the question 'Who is God?' is proper, and on that account the statement appears to be direct and does not have to be reduced; and yet although the question is proper, there is an important sense in which it cannot be answered. There is such an operation as introducing somebody to Tom, but there is no such operation as introducing somebody to God; or rather if there are operations which may, from the standpoint of faith, be so described, it is so only from that standpoint, and they differ vitally from ordinary introductions. If a child asks 'Who is God?' he can only be given statements (such as 'He made us') by way of answer. He can never be brought into a situation in which it is proper to say 'That is God.' The symbol 'God' might therefore be described as an *improper proper name*. It resembles a proper name like 'Tom' in that we are told that statements about God are direct statements about God and not oblique statements about something else, and yet it differs from ordinary proper names in that its use is not based fundamentally, as theirs is, on acquaintance with the being it denotes. It is not easy to see how such a symbol could have a valid use.

There are however other symbols in somewhat similar case; and it may illustrate and sharpen the point to consider some of them. Take first the expression 'point.' The rules governing the use of this expression in geometry require (1) that points be in space, but also (2) that they be not even tiny volumes. Now, one might say, I can understand that something can be sizeless; a thought, for example, has no size. But then it is also not in space. How can anything be both sizeless and also somewhere? Being somewhere is occupying space, and to occupy space one must have size. The expression 'point,' therefore, like the expression 'God,' seems to be governed by contradictory rules. Or take proper names for fictitious characters. 'Titania' is a proper name, and to ask 'Who is Titania?' is to ask a proper question. And yet it can only be answered by statements (such as 'She is the wife of Oberon'); there can never be a situation in which 'That is Titania' is the right thing to say, and that not because one cannot get to fairyland, but because the idea of a journey to fairyland is a logically incoherent idea. 'Titania,' too, is an improper proper name.

In other words, the expression 'God' in some ways resembles words which stand for fictions. Titania is certainly a fiction, and Plato called points geometers' fictions. But the religious man will of course insist that this comparison in no way illuminates the nature of theological statements. He obviously does not want to give God the status of Titania, and it is equally fatal to give theological statements the status of geometrical statements. For geometry is about spatial relationships; and we tolerate the expression 'point,' although in a sense there could not be such a thing as a point (nothing could conform to the definition), because we know clearly enough how talk about points is useful in talk about spatial relationships. If then one appeals to statements about points (admittedly respectable) in support of statements about God, one will be told that statements about points are valuable because one knows how to translate them into statements about sets of volumes; into what are statements about God to be translated? Here of course the religious man must reply that they are not to be translated, and so the point of the comparison is lost.

This comparison having failed us, we are back where we were, forced to admit that the expression 'God,' being an improper proper name which is devised for non-fictional discourse, is in a logically anomalous position. On the one hand statements about God are not reducible, and in that they are like statements about Tom as opposed to statements about the average man. On the other hand, although they are not reducible, but have their own distinct subject, in the manner of 'Tom loves Mary,' that subject is not an ordinary subject. And yet in saying that God is not an ordinary subject, we do not mean that he is a peculiar or extraordinary subject, like Diogenes, who lived in a tub; we mean to assert something like a logical difference, while at the same time we deny that it is any ordinary difference, like that between Tom and the average man. When we say that Tom is not the same kind of being as the average man, we mean something different from what we mean when we make the same statement about Tom and God; and yet we mean more by saying that God is not the same kind of being as Tom, than we mean by saying that my brother is not the same kind of being as my dog. The difference between God and Tom is in some ways like a logical difference, and yet it is not a logical difference. Or, to put the same point rather differently, the impossibility of going to heaven and seeing God is not a technical impossibility, like the impossibility of going to Neptune, and yet it is not a logical impossibility, like the impossibility of going to a state of perfect competition and seeing the economic man. A claim to have seen God is outrageous, without being exactly logically outrageous. The statement to a child 'You can't see God' is not like 'You can't see a virus,' nor like 'You can't see the average man.' The difference between God and other subjects is neither precisely a logical, nor precisely a physical difference. The religious man may claim that the difference is a metaphysical difference, that the point is that God is a transcendent being; but the critic will reply that he could only understand the meaning of these phrases—'metaphysical difference' and 'transcendent being'—in the light of an example, and that the example offered is of no use to him because he cannot understand what statements about God are supposed to be about. As far as he can see, he will say, the expression 'God' purports to stand for an individual; now some expressions ('the average man' again for example) which purport to stand for individuals do not in fact do so; they are on a different logical level from that on which they purport to be; they are used in speech about classes from a particular aspect, or something of the kind. But this kind of treatment of the expression 'God' is not permitted: 'God' is not allowed to stand collectively for human benevolent impulses or anything of the kind. But if it is claimed that it stands for an individual, what can be made of this claim, when all the normal criteria of individuality are held not to apply in this case? There are no doubt innumerable individuals (perhaps 'the oldest male on Mars' may describe one of them) of which we know nothing, but of these we do not seriously speak. Individuals about whom we do speak seriously are either known to us, or have been known to somebody (Tom, Tom's wife, or Julius Caesar), or else are uniquely characterized as satisfying some comprehensible description (the man who invented writing, the largest oak in Hampshire). God is not known to anybody, and these descriptions which are sometimes offered as uniquely characterizing Him ('the first cause,' 'the necessary being') are such that nobody can say what it would be like to

conform to one of them (if one knew what it would be like for
something to be a necessary being, then one could say that 'God'
stood for whatever satisfies these conditions; but one does not),
and therefore have no identifying force. How then can the reference
of the expression 'God' be fixed? And if it cannot be, how can this
expression be treated as a proper name?

## The second anomaly

This then is the first perplexity: it concerns the reference of
theological statements—what they are made about. The second
perplexity concerns their content—what they say about whatever
it is they are about. This perplexity can be divided into two parts.
We are now considering the predicates of theological statements,
and, generally speaking, these predicates are or can be expressed in
everyday words: '. . . loves us,' '. . . made the world.' Now it is fairly
obvious that these everyday words are not being used in their everyday senses. When I make a table I take some tools and some materials, but Creation is *ex nihilo*. Therefore the words which express
the predicates of theological statements are presumably being used
in an unusual sense, and one may want to know what that sense is.
Now the second perplexity, which, as I said, can be divided into
two parts, concerns the fact that nothing which happens is allowed
to necessitate the withdrawal of theological statements; they are
allowed to overrule all factual objections.[3] The first part of the
perplexity derives from noticing this fact (and not making any
difficulties about the meaning of the words in the predicate-
expression), and consists in asking how, in that case, it can be
claimed that theological statements can be regarded as factual
statements, which can be true or false. The second part derives from
noticing the irrefutability of theological statements, and asking how,
in that case, we can ever learn what meaning to attach to the words
in the predicate-expression, when theologically employed. The two
parts are no doubt facets of the same point, but it will be convenient to consider them separately, taking the first one first.

( 1 ) Those who believe that God loves us, or that He created the
world, believe that these are factual statements. That is, they are
comparable to 'Tom loves Mary' or to 'John made a model boat'
and not to the large and heterogenous class of familiar utterances
which are not to be regarded as factual statements. For example, 'I

promise . . .' does not report my promising; it is my promising: 'Shut the door' is a request: '2 + 2 = 4' is a correct arithmetical formula and not an observation about the habits of pairs. None of these can ever be false because, by virtue of being the kind of utterances they are, they are logically incapable of colliding with the facts. They are preserved from falsity, not in the way in which 'John made a model boat' is preserved from falsity when John made a model boat, not by the existence of a fact for them to correspond to or agree with, but by their logical incapacity to agree or disagree with any facts. Now the theist wants to say that God really does love us, that He really did make the world; and he wants to say that these are not edifying stories, or expression of pious attitudes, but statements of fact. But, says the critic, what can be meant by 'fact' in this context? When we say, of an ordinary factual statement, that it accords with the facts, we mean something like this: a statement like: 'The cat is on the mat' delimits a range. There can be very different kinds of cats, very differently disposed on very different kinds of mats. 'The cat is on the mat' therefore does not indicate just one quite specific kind of situation, but delimits a range. There are situations which cannot count as the cat's being on the mat, and situations which can; and learning to draw the line between them is learning the meaning of the sentence. When there exists a situation which falls within the range delimited by 'the cat is on the mat,' then a statement to that effect will be true; when there does not, it will be false. Now, normally, to say that a statement is factual is to claim that, by virtue of its meaning, it selects in this manner between possible situations; it has a range, such that some possible situations fall outside it, and its truth is the existence of a situation which falls within its range. But, in the case of theological statements, the theist denies that there are any situations which fall outside the range of 'God loves us' or 'God created the world,' and he denies this without claiming an exhaustive knowledge of all the situations which there are. 'God loves us,' he says, is not an empirical hypothesis about the pious prospering; he is quite content to leave it to historians and others to find out what happens to people in the world; 'God created the world' is not meant to prejudge the deliberations of astronomers; the theist does not pretend to know how the world began; he only claims to know that, however it began, God created it. In other words, says the critic, the theist says what he says, not because he has discovered that there are in fact no situations incompatible with his assertions, but because, in his opinion, there could be none. If you ask him how God's loving us differs from the hypothetical case of God's not loving us, he denounces the second alternative as unreal, because it assumes a modification in the divine nature, whose fixity is the foundation of everything. But then, if no possible situations could fall outside the range of 'God loves us,' that must surely mean that this formula is such that, by virtue of its meaning, it is incapable of choosing between situations; that is, that it is a request, performatory utterance, tautology or something of the kind, and in no sense a factual statement.

Here again, it may be worth observing in passing, fictional statements are in somewhat the same boat with theological ones. It is entirely to misunderstand 'Holmes sprang into a passing hansom' to treat it as a request, tautology or performatory utterance, and yet nothing whatsoever can offer the slightest ground for supposing that Holmes did not spring into a passing hansom. And yet once more the comparison is embarrassing rather than helpful to the theist; for the statement about Holmes is preserved from the possibility of a collision with the facts by belonging to a world of make-believe; and the theist does not want to take that way out. But how, in that case, are the theist's statements preserved from the possibility of collision with facts? And if they are not so preserved, how can he assert them without exhaustive knowledge of all the relevant facts? Since he makes no claim to possess this knowledge, surely he must judge it unnecessary, and surely it can only be unnecessary if his 'statements' are not intended as statements of fact, but as recommendations of attitudes, or something of the kind.

(2) So much for the first part of the second perplexity. The second part draws attention to the difficulty of learning what particular theological statements can be supposed to mean. Taking for our example the statement 'God created the world,' we can put the difficulty in the form of a dilemma: either this assertion selects from among conceivable alternatives, and as such is a cosmological hypothesis subject to scientific refutation; or it does not select, and in that case it is impossible to say what it means.

For, says the critic, it is agreed that the theist is not alleging any ordinary making when he talks about creation. What he is alleging, then, remains to be discovered. How are we to discover it? Well, the statement is supposed to tell us something about the world—that it was created by God. Let us then take the propositional function 'X was created by God.' Now if we are allowed to suppose that this function delimits a range of possible situations, such that some situations fall outside this range, then the statement about any given thing that it was created by God would convey information to anybody who was apprised of the boundaries of the range. But how can we become apprised of the boundaries of the range? We need to be capable of envisaging specimen situations which fall within the range, and specimen situations which fall outside it. Since, *ex hypothesi*, there can be no actual examples of these latter in this case, the specimen situations from outside the range of 'God created the world' will have to be imaginary ones. Since I have got to be able to envisage these situations, they must consist of familiar elements rearranged. But in that case, what 'God created the world' excludes is a set of possible situations which can be fancifully constructed by taking actual objects or properties, and supposing them arranged otherwise than as they are. 'The cat is on the mat' gives me information, not simply because it is incompatible with 'The cat is somewhere other than on the mat' (one does not know what a sentence means by knowing that it is incompatible with its own negation), but because I can easily envisage situations which agree with the one and disagree with the other. Supposing I have never seen that cat anywhere but on that mat, then I have never encountered any situation excluded by 'the cat is on the mat'; and indeed perhaps there has never been one. But because cats can be in all kinds of places, the class of excluded situations may be said to exist, and I can easily envisage specimens, for example by combining the familiar elements: the cat, being on, and the sideboard. Because I know that being on the sideboard or under the sofa would not be a case of being on the mat, I know what is claimed by 'the cat is on the mat' (the non-existence of all the incompatible situations) and thus what it means. But in the case of 'God created the world,' if I am to know what this means, I must have some idea of the incompatible situations, and if I am to be able in this way to envisage them, they must be situations which can be constructed by rearranging familiar elements, and in that case what the assertion we are considering rules out must be something which logically might be the case. But if something is such that it logically might be the case, then it is always possible that some observation, some day, will show that it is the case. Therefore on this view 'God created the world,' if we are ever to discover what it means, must be a scientific hypothesis, subject to scientific refutation. Consider, as a fair parallel, 'the universe is expanding.' This is a fair parallel because it is, like the creation statement, completely general. If it is true, then there are no cases of a non-expanding universe, ever, anywhere. Nothing actual is excluded by the statement. When, then, an astronomer makes it, how do we discover what he means? By looking to see what evidence he brings in support of the view, what observations he admits would refute it. Perhaps the spectra of the heavenly bodies are such as they would be if observer and observed were moving rapidly away from each other; if this were not so he would withdraw his claim. We thus know what his claim amounts to. If 'God created the world' is allowed to be in similar case, then we can know what it means, and what it means must be something empirical. If it is not, then we cannot discover what it means, because it cannot literally mean anything, and we must conclude that its efficacy in discourse is not that of an ordinary factual statement. Perhaps it is a myth that we tell in order to inculate an attitude of reverence.

So much for the philosopher's perplexities about theological statements. To summarize them, the first is that these statements purport to be about a particular object, which it is in principle impossible to 'indicate' in any non-linguistic way, and which is thus different from all other particular objects in whose existence we have any ground for believing; the second that while it is claimed that these statements are true, and have determinate meaning, none the less the theist seems not to regard himself as embroiled in scientific dispute; he claims an immunity which belongs properly to persons who do not make statements of fact. In themselves, his sentences are perfectly intelligible. We all know what '. . . loves us' means, and 'God' is a proper name. Anybody, therefore, can understand the assertion 'God loves us' on its own. But as used in theological discourse it acquires formal properties which render it utterly baffling to the critic; the rules laid down about how such utterances are to be taken (e.g. that 'God' is indeed a proper name, but that it is in principle impossible to see God) are such that he cannot see either what its reference can be (the first perplexity) or what its content (the second).

### 3. WHAT FOLLOWS FROM THE FACT OF THESE ANOMALIES?

*The anomalous formal properties of theological statements help to fix the reference of these statements*

We must now turn to see what we can do about these perplexities. Let us begin by considering what a theist might reply to such a critic. Might he not say something like this: None of the above arguments are compelling. You show that God is unlike all other individuals and expect us to conclude that therefore there is no such individual. You show that statements about Him are not like ordinary contingent truths and so invite us to class them with tautologies and requests. Admittedly we might do these things, but we do not have to. Is it not clear, from the formal properties of our statements alone, that we believe in the existence of a being different in kind from all ordinary beings, and in some way detached from the events of the spatio-temporal universe; and that, therefore, we shall inevitably make statements having the *prima facie* peculiar, formal properties outlined above? Surely the formal properties of our statements delineate the object of our belief rather than furnish evidence that there is no such object.

For the formal properties of theological statements can themselves be expressed in higher-level statements having God as their subject, just as the formal properties of ordinary statements about triangles (such as that their interior angles total 180 degrees) can be expressed in higher-level statements having triangles as their subject (such as that triangles are not physical objects, but a shape). Thus we can express some of the formal properties of theological statements in the higher-level statement 'God is a transcendent, infinite and incomprehensible being, in incomprehensible relationship with the familiar universe.' Now is not this a tolerable statement of vague undifferentiated theism, not far from the kind of belief in God which we find, for example, in Aristotle? Too vague, indeed, for the needs of religion, but still the essential foundation on which religion must be built?

Up to a point this reply is justified, but we must tread carefully here. If some such higher-level statement is to be regarded as simply recording the formal properties of theological statements, then the words occurring in it must bear no sense beyond what is necessary to express these properties. 'God is a transcendent being' becomes something like 'There exists an object of discourse which is particular but not indicable.' But of course when stated thus, there is nothing religious about the formula. So the position is something like this: the theist may claim that if he wants to talk about a transcendent being, his statements will have to have the formal properties of theological statements, and that, therefore, there is nothing scandalous about their possession of such properties. The critic may reply that he still cannot see what talk about a transcendent being is talk about, and therefore the theist cannot claim that the formal properties of his statements are sufficient to delineate the object of his belief. The most the theist can claim for the consideration of the formal properties alone (or, if you prefer, the higher-level theological statements in which they are expressed) is that it diverts attention away from all irrelevant subject-matters; that it makes clear that all non-theological subject-matters are irrelevant—theology is not to be assimilated to anything else; and that, therefore, if anybody is to understand what religion is about, he must be willing to conceive the possibility of an object which is neither similar to, nor in any normal relation with, any spatio-temporal object.

What the argument so far has shown is that there is no direct inference from the paradoxicality of the formal properties of theological statements to their meaninglessness. The critic's case is a *probable* case, and the theist has a probable case on the other side. The critic, feeling no impulsion to talk about anything which would have to be talked about in such a fashion, judges it probable that such talk only occurs because theologians, valuing for various reasons the simple piety of simple people with their anthropomorphic God and geomorphic heaven, but aware that they cannot defend these beings against the advance of knowledge, protect them from scientific criticism by the assertion that they are beings of a peculiar order. The theist, on the contrary, believing in a mystery beyond experience, traces of which he claims to detect in experience, contends that he is obliged to use, for the expression of his beliefs, language governed by paradoxical rules.

## The 'affinities' of theological statements help to fix their reference

But the theist cannot really rest there. The critic is open to be convinced of the validity of theological language, if someone can show him what such language is used about, and how it succeeds in communicating truth about it. Let us then continue with the argument and see how much further we can get towards meeting the first of these requirements; that is, how much further we can fix the reference of theological statements.

First we might ask the critic to bear in mind the formal properties of theological statements, as an essential negative clue, and then listen to people making use of theological statements. For, we may say, an important hint concerning their reference may be derived from observing the relationships which appear to obtain between theological statements and statements of other kinds. For although we do not regard the divine love as identical in kind with human love, divine creation as identical with human making, none the less the words which are chosen for use in theological predicates are chosen for some kind of appropriateness. Again, although we do not identify the divine activity with any set of finite events, and for that reason refuse to let statements about providence or grace be strictly equivalent to empirical generalizations of history or psychology, none the less we do maintain that statements about grace are about a subject-matter which overlaps at least with the subject matter of psychology.[4] We do not regard the doctrine of divine love as a doctrine of exemption from suffering, and for that reason evidence to the effect that people suffer is not allowed to over-rule the doctrine that God loves them. Yet the theist must be intellectually sensitive to the existence of suffering; if for example somebody said that our life was one of unalleviated misery the theist would be committed by doctrine as well as by common sense to disagree with him. Against the rule that theological statements, not being empirical generalizations, cannot come into logical conflict with empirical generalizations, not being moral judgments, cannot come into logical conflict with moral judgments, and so on, you must set the rule that, since the subject-matter of theological statements overlaps with the subject-matters about which empirical generalizations and moral judgments are made, theological statements are sensitive to, and have affinities and relationships with statements of other kinds.

Listen, then, we say to religious discussion. You will find that religion is connected, in this loose way, with ethics, cosmology, history, psychology; that it has nothing very direct to contribute to mathematics, literary criticism or marine biology. Surely, if you do not pitch your demands too high, this will begin to fix for you the reference of theological statements? But first let us amplify the caution against pitching your demands too high. Imagine a game: one player leaves the room, and the rest select an object. On the return of the first player, the others utter the predicates only of true statements about the chosen object, and the first player must guess the object. Thus the players say '. . . invaded Britain,' '. . . kept a log,' '. . . required his wife to be above reproach'; and the first player guesses 'Julius Caesar.' Theists are not playing a game of that kind; God is not a familiar object cryptically named, as anti-fascist Italians used to speak of Mussolini as 'Mr. Smith.' God is a mystery, and therefore you cannot expect that knowing what statements about God are about will involve anything like having a precise conception of their subject. The most that can be hoped for is something much vaguer, of which the following may serve as an example.

I do not know what a quaternion is; for all I know it may be a measure of time, like a quinquennium, a dance, like a quadrille, a kind of lizard, a poem, an elementary particle, or anything whatsoever. But now suppose I listen (as we are advising the critic to listen) to people talking about quaternions. Fairly quickly I shall discover that they are not dances or lizards, and they hardly seem to be periods of time. Gradually they will place themselves for me somewhere in the region of the mathematical sciences. I shall still be very ignorant indeed of what they are; but I shall know what section of the library to go to to look for a book about them. If you like, we might mark the extreme vagueness of my grasp of quaternions at this stage, by saying that, while my listening has not fixed the reference of 'quaternion' for me (for I do not know what they are), it has fixed the reference-range (for I know what kind of thing they are). Surely, then, we may say to the critic, if you listen attentively to theological discourse, you will come to discover its reference-range?

Now the critic must, I think, concede that negatively such listening may be of considerable assistance. It is at least as useful as attending to the formal properties of theological statements for seeing what theological talk is not a contribution to. But for providing positive identification, it is a very different matter. Crudely put, identification by negation is only positive identification if one has a list and eliminates all the items but one. But the trouble is that God is not on the critic's list and therefore he cannot be enlightened by elimination. Let him put the point thus: the man who, from listening to talk about quaternions, comes to place them in the region of the mathematical sciences, only does so because he knows at least something among these latter, or at least can envisage their possibility. A child or a primitive, who had not yet abstracted the idea of number, could not place quaternions in the region of the mathematical sciences, because he would be absolutely without a notion of them. But, says the critic, with respect to God he is himself in the position of the unmathematical child with respect to quaternions. Nobody has ever taught him how to abstract the idea of God. Furthermore, he suspects that his listening has now made him unteachable; for it has shown him that religion is closely connected with such subjects as history, psychology, ethics, and cosmology. Theological vocabulary draws upon words commonly used in these subjects, innovations in these subjects are apt to upset theists and so forth. But if he is asked to find room for a further subject, related to these subjects as theology is apparently supposed to be related to them he simply cannot do it. How can anything underlie moral obligation as the divine will is supposed to do? How can grace be something which occurs in human souls and yet something which the psychologists can manage without? Again, he may say, it is no good saying that the reference-range of theological language is fixed by the language itself. For it is precisely fictions which are created by talking, and theology is not, apparently, a multi-volume novel. The reference-range of 'quaternion' may be fixed for me by listening to mathematics talking, but it is fixed for mathematicians by the existence of the appropriate mathematical problems. If there were no such problems, there would be no talk about them. Theists cannot therefore content themselves with telling us to listen to them if we want to find out what they are talking about, for if they are talking about anything, then it must be possible to indicate what it is, or talk about it would never have begun. Unless they can indicate what their subject is, it is fair to ask them why they ever started uttering, and how it would matter if they stopped.

To some extent this reply is, certainly, justified. If theological talk has any valid use, then it must be possible to show in what kind of context one becomes conscious of the need to talk in this way; and this demonstration cannot be sufficiently given by disclosing that theological statements cannot be identified with statements of any other kinds, but have affinities and relationships with some of them. In so far as the critic believes that he can show that there could be no other subject-matter related to history, psychology and the rest, in the way in which theology is supposed to be related to them, there is no reason why we should agree with him. But in so far as he merely confesses a personal incapacity to see what this further subject is, he is, of course, perfectly justified. He is also perfectly justified if he stresses once more that the reference-range of theological statements is supposed to be fixed, and yet is not fixed by any normal kind of indication or conceptual description, that this is logically anomalous, and that he has a right to be given some account of it.

What is it that impels people to make theological statements? The short answer is, a conception of the divine. But what, asks the critic, is that? Is it not the remains of primitive myth, adorned by the feeling of awe in the face of natural phenomena? What are we to answer him? As we have seen above, a conception of the divine must be a conception of a being outside space and time, on whom the spatio-temporal universe is in some sense dependent. Given such a being, talk about him will have the formal properties theological talk has been found to have. It will not be possible, in any ordinary way, to indicate such a being, for indicating is selecting a region of space-time in which certain qualities are manifested. Again, it is natural to suppose that if the universe is dependent on

God, then what is true of Him will be, not exactly necessarily true (certainly not tautological) but, so to speak, less contingently true than truths about the dependent universe. It also seems natural to suppose that if God is conceived as the source of the space-time universe, Himself outside space and time, His activity will not be manifested (at least normally) here rather than there (for then He would *be* here rather than there) and hence that statements about His relation to the created universe will not take the form of cosmological hypotheses, verifiable by observing the contents of particular spatio-temporal regions. So far, so good; given a conception of the divine it looks as if we might be able to smooth away the apparent logical anomalies of theological language; to show them to be necessary consequences of the purpose for which it is intended. But are we given such a conception?

We must acknowledge at once that in the ordinary sense we have no conception of the divine nature. We do not know God, and it would be absurd to claim that we know what kind of being He is. In so far as we use adjectives about Him ('omniscient,' 'eternal' and so on) they do not enable us to conceive what it is like to be God. Omniscience is not infinite erudition, and what it is must be beyond our comprehension. And yet people, whether they be theists, atheists, or agnostics do normally suppose themselves to know what people are talking about when they talk about God. The critic, of course, has his own explanation of this fact. According to him, what makes people suppose that they can grasp the reference of talk about God is nothing more than the old anthropomorphic conception of a superhuman being somewhere above the sky. No civilized person believes there to be such a being, but the picture serves, in unsophisticated minds, to conceal from us that we do not know what we are talking about.

This is certainly a possible account of how the reference-range of theological language is fixed for most people; whether it is, for you, a plausible account, will depend on your opinion of the critical powers of those who use such language. But our business, if we want to convince ourselves of the validity of theological language, is to show that the widespread readiness to attach sense to the notion of a being outside space and time has a more fundamental and more respectable origin than that.

## 4. THE REFERENCE OF THEOLOGICAL STATEMENTS

*A 'conception of the divine' being necessary
to fix their reference, what is this?*

Can we, then, find a more fundamental and more respectable origin for our readiness to attach sense to the notion of a being outside space and time, a being whose nature would explain the anomalies of theological statements? To this we must now turn. What I propose to argue could be put like this: the conception of the divine is indeed in one sense an empty notion; but it is the notion of a complement which could fill in certain deficiencies in our experience, that could not be filled in by further experience or scientific theory-making; and its positive content is simply the idea of something (we know not what) which might supply those deficiencies. This bald account I must try to supplement, but not without a warning that what follows will be extremely sketchy and inadequate. The business of explaining the origin of the conception of God has provoked a very considerable literature, which passes under the name of natural theology. Often it has been held to be the task of natural theology to prove the existence of God. This seems to me to be a task which cannot, in any strict sense of 'prove' be accomplished. What however the arguments of the natural theologians do do is reveal the intellectual pressures which lead people to talk about God; and, in so doing, they illuminate the meaning of such talk. This being so, I must ask the reader to turn to the classical works on natural theology if he wants a more adequate treatment of the subject with which the following paragraphs are concerned.[5]

Our willingness to entertain the notion of a being outside space and time (of what I shall call a 'spirit') is perhaps most fundamentally based on our inability to accept with complete contentment the idea that we are ourselves normal spatio-temporal objects.[6] No doubt the point has often been put in extremely misleading ways, and many quite untenable claims have been made; but it remains true that you cannot adequately describe a human person with the range of concepts which is adequate for the description of a chair, a cabbage or even an electronic calculating machine. And the additional concepts which are needed for the adequate description of human experience—*loving, feeling, hoping,* even *seeing* are obvious examples—all have a relative independence of space, not in the sense that we can think of a loving being that is not somewhere, but in the sense that if you try to anatomize his loving you cannot think of it as rest or motion of parts, while you can think of his walking or digesting in such terms. One can of course think of the organic correlates of loving or hoping in physical, and therefore spatial terms; but while few would wish to distinguish the organic correlates of a psychical state, and the state itself, as two separate things, it remains true that we most of us feel uncomfortable about completely identifying them; not that we suppose that we are here dealing with two distinct, but accidentally conjoined, things, but that a full description of this one thing in terms of adrenalin glands, or whatever it may be, does not begin to do justice to the thing as it is known in experience, and has no logical connexion with an adequate description of the latter. Much, that is, of what goes on in us is describable from two standpoints: the standpoint of the observer, who can see our muscles twitch, observe our brain-pulsations in an encephalograph; and the standpoint of the agent who is directly aware of himself; and what is described from this latter standpoint demands a distinct set of concepts. I would agree with the tradition from Aristotle to Professor Ryle which does not see in this duality of the human person any warrant for describing a man as a committee of two distinct entities, body and soul; but the duality remains, and is, as far as we know, a distinctive characteristic of our experience. We are not, nor is any part of ourselves, beings outside space and time, or spirits, but part of our experience of ourselves is only describable with the aid of concepts of a non-physical kind. What we should derive from this is not the grandiose view that we are spirits, but the ability to conceive the notion of a being independent of space, that is a being whose activity is not at all to be thought of in terms of colliding with this, or exercising a gravitational pull on that. We cannot of course form any kind of a lively idea of what it would be like to be such a being; but this is not the positive inability with which we are unable to conceive of a being corresponding to a self-contradictory or meaningless description. In the case of 'spirit' we do not know that there could not be a being like that, as we know that nothing could correspond to the description 'round square' or 'asymptotically democratic potato.'

'Spirit' is not an expression which affronts our logical conscience or leaves us with no clue at all. There are many different grades of 'not knowing what is meant by . . .' and our ignorance of the meaning of 'spirit' (that is, of what something would have to be like to conform to the requirements of this word) is not absolute. To say, then, that we conceive of God as a spirit, is to pitch our claims rather high; for the suggestion is of something parallel to conceiving of Tom as a sergeant-major, where there is some body to the conception. But because of the duality of our own nature, and of the applicability to ourselves of concepts which are not needed for the description of the material world, the formal properties of theological statements, requiring as they do that God be a spirit, leave us unable to conceive what it would be like to be God, but do not leave us without any inkling of the reference-range of such statements. It is not a conception, but a hint of the possibility of something we cannot conceive, but which lies outside the range of possible conception *in a determinate direction.*

But the duality of our human nature is of course a freakish characteristic in the world of space and time. If the world of common experience is all there is, then its purely 'material' contents form a sufficiently complete system on their own, with human spirituality a kind of alien intruder like the ornamentation on Victorian furniture. The pressure of this 'sense of alienation,' this sense that we are strangers and sojourners upon earth, has led men for centuries to posit, what they cannot imagine, a spiritual world, to which we really belong; so that we are no longer bits of irrelevant ornament upon an independent structure, but the meeting point of two 'worlds,' or interconnected systems of beings, to each of which we belong in one of our dual aspects.[7] Or, if you like, our limited and imperfect spirituality—the fact that we are not spirits, but beings with a spiritual aspect—leads us to think of beings who are perfectly what we are imperfectly; not that we can properly conceive of such beings, but that we are forced to frame the abstract notion of them, by the feeling that the smattering of spirit which we find in ourselves must be a pointer to a pool from which it comes.

But, the reader may complain, I am talking of all this in terms appropriate to explaining the genesis of an illusion. I ought to be anatomizing the meaning of the word 'spirit,' and that ought to mean listing those experienceable characteristics which we refer to in using the word. Instead of this I am apparently conceding that the word has no meaning (is used of something we cannot conceive of), and trying to explain why people use it as if it had. This I am doing because, in a sense, the notion of spirit is, not exactly an illusion, but an illegitimate notion; illegitimate because it is a kind of reified abstraction. For the words 'spirit,' 'spiritual,' and so forth, come to have specific meaning for us by being connected with particular characteristics of, or events in, human beings. We distinguish 'spirit' from 'influenza' or 'digestion' by showing to which aspects of men these words severally refer. 'Spirit' derives from 'spiritual' and 'spiritual' acquires specific meaning by correlation with thinking and other activities which only occur, in our experience, as activities of human beings. 'Spirit,' then, is not a common noun like 'mouse,' because it is not the name of a distinct kind of being; it follows from the way the specific meaning of the word is learnt that it is an abstract noun like 'digestion,' because it stands for activities of beings called men. We should all regard it absurd to speak of beings which were pure digestions; not the digestings of animals, but just digestings. Is it not equally absurd to speak of things which are pure spirits; not the spiritualizing of animate physical objects, but just spirits? Surely it must be a category mistake to use the word 'spirit' as anything but an abstract noun, or aspect-word?

Now, against a claim that we know what we mean by 'spirit' in the way in which we know what we mean by 'digestion' or 'smile,' such an objection would be decisive. In the sense of 'meaning' in which the meaning of a word is those experienceable characteristics to which it refers, anybody who knows the meaning of 'spirit' can infer that, just as smiles can only be arrangements of features, so spirits can only be characteristics and activities of men. But I am not claiming that we 'know the meaning' of 'spirit' (in the theological use) in this sense. In Berkeley's words, I admit that we have no idea of spirit, and claim only that it is extravagant to say that we have no notion whatsoever of how the word is used. How the word is used (and this, of course, defines such meaning as it has for us) in the theological context is by the deliberate commission of a category-mistake under the pressure of convictions which require us to depart from normal language-practice in this way. For if a man believes that there are beings, or one being, who are comparable to us only in so far as we are spiritual, then the following two things would appear inescapable: (1) that he cannot have any clear and distinct conception of the object of his belief; and (2) that, to express it, he will require some such noun as 'spirit' which will (a) retain specific meaning by connexion with 'spirituality' as the name of a human aspect, but (b) be governed by a rule declaring that this noun is not to be taken as an abstract noun like 'smile' or 'bad temper,' but as a concrete noun like 'man.' If you are prepared to accept the view that belief in the existence of purely spiritual beings is simply the result of logical illusion (like the belief in universals as independent entities), that theism is simply a category-mistake, then you need not sully your tongue with a word whose syntactical behaviour is incompatible with the way in which its meaning is learnt; but if you feel that you might entertain the view that there are purely spiritual beings, then you have to have the word. It does not seem to me at all plausible to regard theism as a category-mistake, for it is not pressures derived from logical theory that make people theists. People do not believe in *greenness*, existing independently of green things, until they have been subjected to philosophical reasoning, and told that, if A and B are both green, then there must be a common something in each of them, viz. the universal *greenness*. This is a pressure derived from (mistaken) logical theory. But theism has a quite different origin; we do not believe in God as a pure spirit because we are told that if Smith and Brown are spiritual beings, pure spirituality must exist—or anything of the kind. The notion of God as a spirit is indeed a category-mistake, or category-transgression, but one deliberately committed to express what we antecedently feel; and, if we antecedently feel something, the category-transgression we deliberately commit to express that feeling has some meaning—that, namely, which it is designed to express. Disagreement with this conclusion must rest, I believe, on one or other of two general principles, for neither of which can I see any compelling argument: (1) that there can never be good grounds for committing category-transgressions; and (2) that there can be no 'meanings' which do not correspond to clear and distinct ideas.

Let me add, as a pendant to this discussion of 'spirit,' that the sense that, in one aspect of our being, we belong to a country in which what is imperfectly realized in us is fully and perfectly realized, is not, of course, a compelling argument for the existence of such a country. I claim only two things; the first, that it does not rest solely on inadvertence to logical grammar, but can even survive a clear realization of the logical anomalies of such a belief; the second, that it is this belief or feeling which fixes for us the reference-range of 'spirit' and related expressions as they occur in theological language.

But God is not only a spirit, but also Infinite Spirit. We have so far been discussing the noun; what of the adjective?

Here again an adequate discussion would be equally beyond my space and my powers. But by way of further illustration of the way in which the reference-range of theological language is fixed for us, I shall again venture something.

When we speak of God as an infinite being we are not, of course, using the word 'infinite' in its strict mathematical sense. We mean, negatively that He is unlimited; or, more positively, that, being the source of all limitation, there is nothing whatsoever to which He is conformed, or to which He must conform Himself. 'Infinite,' therefore, comes to very much the same thing as 'necessary,' 'omnipotent,' 'creator of all things,' and other words of the same kind which we use about God. Now it is characteristic of all these words, that, in so far as they have any precise sense, they cannot be used about God. For, since we do not know God, they cannot acquire a precise sense by reference to His properties; if then they have a precise sense they must acquire it from reference to the properties of something else; and, since nothing else can be an adequate model for God, in so far as they have a precise sense, it cannot be applied to Him. Suppose we say, then, that what we mean is something rather loose and vague, loosely and vaguely connected with the normal uses of these words (or, in the case of a word like 'omnipotent,' with the result of combining the normal forces of their components). Even so, we have many difficulties to face. Take, for example, the formula I used above, that God is 'the source of all limitation,' and that, therefore, 'there is nothing whatsoever to which He is conformed, or to which He must conform Himself.' Now even supposing it is admitted on all hands that we cannot expect to have any idea of what it would be like to be, or encounter, such a being, we may still be asked to provide *some* sense for the phrase 'source of all limitation.' What can we say?

Limitations are due to natural laws, natural laws to the natures, behaviour patterns, or whatnot which things have. If then God is the source of all limitations, He gave things their natures, or created them. But although we can push the counters about in this way, and travel by 'bastard inference' from *infinite* to *creator*, where have we got to go when we arrive? What does a doctrine of creation amount to? If you think of God anthropomorphically, creation is all very well. He took some raw material, and by compounding and arranging it, gave it the properties we see around us; He now sustains it, and will one day put it on the bonfire. But if you think of God anthropomorphically, who made God?

So far are we, in fact, from being able to argue from the contingency of the world to the necessary being of God, that we cannot see how to attach a clear sense to the claim that the world is contingent. The logical sense of the word will not do: in that sense parts of the world may be said to exist contingently—that only means that if x exists, it might not have done so, and that only means that from what we know of the rest of the world we cannot strictly deduce that x exists. But the world as a whole cannot be contingent in this sense. We cannot sensibly say that, from what we know of the rest, we cannot strictly deduce that the world as a whole exists, for there is no 'rest' for us to have knowledge about—unless indeed the rest be God. Yet although we cannot find a clear sense for 'contingent' 'created' and so forth in this context, the fact remains that people do persist in having beliefs for the expression of which they call upon such terms. To some extent, no doubt, these beliefs rest on theoretical errors. Thus people may hold that there must be a God because, they say, the world can't have come from nothing, for *ex nihilo nihil fit*. If you reply that either it is possible for a thing to 'come from nothing,' or it is not possible, and that in the former case the world may have 'come from nothing,' and in the latter case God cannot have done (so that by parity of reasoning we must ask: 'Who created God?'), you may or you may not dislodge the belief. If it rests merely on the theoretical error of applying the principle *ex nihilo nihil fit* to the entire universe, on the ground that it may be legitimately applied to particular portions of it, then no doubt you will. But in some people on whom you employ this reasoning, you may encounter an obstinate conviction that none the less this is in fact a created universe; a conviction which involves the belief, not that, as a general 'truth of reason,' everything whatsoever must have an origin outside itself (in which case God must, too, *ad infinitum*), but rather that *this* universe is something about which one is prompted to ask where it comes from, with the corollary that there might be something about which one was not prompted to ask this question.

What those features of this universe are which make us feel that it is not its own origin, I am not going to enquire. Many of the classical arguments for the existence of God are designed to draw attention to these features. Nor, of course, am I suggesting that because people feel that there might be a being about which one was not tempted to ask 'What is its origin?', therefore such a being must exist. My claim is only that if you want to know what is meant by such expressions as 'infinite,' 'omnipotent' or 'creator' when applied to God, then the sense that this is a derivative universe, with the corollary that a non-derivative being might exist, is the nearest you can get to an understanding of their meaning.

'Finite' and 'infinite,' 'contingent' and 'necessary,' 'derivative' and 'non-derivative': all these are pairs. When we use either member of any of them in the theological context we cannot anatomize the meaning to be attached to it. When we speak of the world as finite we do not mean that it can be counted, or travelled across; when we speak of it as derivative, we do not think of it as extracted from its origin by any normal kind of derivation. But the meaning to be attached to the second member of each pair is to be got at by seeing what kind of judgment about the world is intended by the use of the first. The kind of judgment intended by the use of such expressions (or by the parallel use of less metaphysical language, such as 'There must be something behind all this passing show') is an intellectual dissatisfaction with the notion of this universe as a complete system, with, as corollary, the notion of a being with which one could not be thus dissatisfied.[8]

That is, you may say, of a being who could claim one's adoration. And many will hold that, to fix the reference-range of theological statements it is better to attend not to what religious people feel or say about the world, but to how they dispose themselves towards God—that is, to learn what worship is. It is the contrast between the attitude of worship, and the attitude which religion commends towards creatures (always to be valued, but never, absolutely, in themselves) which illuminates what religion takes the infinite-finite contrast to be. It was the ban on idolatry which taught the Jews what God is. Indeed, it may be said that the sense of contingency is psychologically a correlative of the attempt to worship; one does not begin to feel a sense of finitude until one has made an effort of self-surrender. I do not want to quarrel with any of this; I have tried a more theoretical approach, because I think one should be possible, and because one ought to be suspicious of the possible abuses of appealing to what a man does for the elucidation of what he believes. But I have no doubt that if any vividness of apprehension of the meaning of such terms as 'infinite' is required, then the activity of religion may best supply it.

Let me try to sum up this part of the argument. We are considering how the reference-range of theological statements is fixed—how we know what statements about God are about. The problem is posed by the fact that we neither know God nor know what kind of a being He is. God is neither 'that being,' nor 'the being such that. . . .' More positively, we want to say that God is a being beyond the reach of our conception. Very well, then: God is inconceivable. But, it may be said, that is only a clumsy and misleading way of saying that the expression 'God' lacks meaning. We cannot *mean* inconceivables, for the meaning of any expression can only be those conceivables by reference to which we use it, by indicating which we could teach its use to others. I have tried to define a sense in which we *can* mean inconceivables, and that is when we use a word to refer to the postulated, though unimaginable, absence of limitations or imperfections of which we are aware. It is a little as if I were dissatisfied with a sentence I have written; it is inelegant, and somehow it does not express my meaning. Now the expression 'the correct version of that sentence' is not entirely without meaning to me, although, alas, I cannot at the moment conceive what it stands for. But I should recognize and welcome it if it came, and it would remove a fairly specific dissatisfaction from which I am suffering, or at least a dissatisfaction about a specific subject. This analogy must not be pressed;[9] but it may shed some little light on the sense in which it may be claimed that such an expression as

'Infinite Spirit' has meaning for us. Such expressions stand for the abstract conception of the possibility of the removal of certain intellectual dissatisfactions which we may feel about the universe of common experience.

The critic complained that he could see neither what theological statements were about—how their reference-range was fixed—nor how they could be regarded as making statements about it—how one could extract their content. I have been trying to deal with the first problem, and must now pass to the second. But before I do so I have a caution to offer. In trying to fix the reference-range of theological statements I am trying to fix it for *the critic*, that is for the man who says that he cannot see what religious people are talking about, and does not believe that there is anything which can be talked about in such a way. It is only to him that one would ever think of answering the question 'What does "God" stand for?' in such a way. To the religious man the natural answer to such a question is ' "God" is the name of the Being who is worthy to be adored.' And, as I have said, that is perhaps the most illuminating answer one can give. The answer I have given is one which would only be given to a man from whom the other answer would provoke the retort that, as he did not know what 'adoration' referred to—certain actions apart—the phrase 'the being worthy to be adored' could serve as no kind of identification for him. I have been trying to offer a neutral account of what 'God' stands for, one which does not employ any notions whose understanding presupposes a religious outlook. To put it another way, I have not been trying to describe what the Christian takes God to be, but merely to answer a logical challenge, to the effect that theological statements cannot be meaningful because they employ a proper name which seems to be such that it is logically impossible to indicate to an inquirer what it stands for.

NOTES

1. This is, of course, a wide use of the word 'theological.' In this use theological statements are the kind of statements ('affirmations,' etc., if you prefer) which all Christians make, not only theologians.
2. On this see Chapter VI [of *Faith and Logic*].

3. As I shall argue later, this is only a half-truth.

4. Again the reader should turn to Chapter VI [of *Faith and Logic*].

5. See for example: Austin Farrer, *Finite and Infinite*; or E. L. Mascall, *Existence and Analogy*.

6. On this I must refer the reader to Chapter V [of *Faith and Logic*].

7. Friendly critics have objected to my use of the word 'aspect' here. While agreeing, more or less, with the arguments of this section, they hold it less misleading to talk, in the traditional way, of spirituality as a 'part' rather than an 'aspect' of men. For, they say, spirituality is at least an essential aspect; we identify ourselves with our spiritual activity in a way in which we do not identify ourselves with such other aspects as our height or weight. I agree that the word 'aspect' could be misleading; I use it for the reasons given below, and I think that if its meaning is confined to that which is required by these reasons it will not seriously mislead. In other contexts, I would quite agree, 'part' is often better.

8. Professor Findlay's article: 'Can God's existence be disproved?' (*Mind*, 1948; reprinted in *New Essays in Philosophical Theology*, ed. Flew and MacIntyre) depends for its disproof of God's existence on taking 'necessary' in 'Necessary Being' in the logician's sense; but seems to me to provide a very fair characterization of the theist's sense, by its characterization of 'the religious attitude.'

9. There is no difficulty about the *sense* of 'the correct version of that sentence'; but only about its *reference*.

# 5. THE STRUCTURE OF

# RELIGIOUS DISCOURSE

## Joseph M. Bochenski, O. P.

*Joseph M. Bochenski, O. P., is President of the University of Fribourg, Switzerland, and a well-known logician of the twentieth century. He has published widely in the areas of formal logic and contemporary philosophy, including the field of Soviet philosophy.*

### 17. On the formal structure of a discourse and its problems

Every propositional discourse (which is, *a fortiori*, a meaningful discourse) is structured in some way. It need not be—and often is not—axiomatized, that is, its different factors are not explicitly stated; but, nevertheless, some structure is always present. If this is often overlooked, it is because we are so accustomed to applying its rules that we do not notice them.

The types of discourse most studied up to now are our modern axiomatic systems. In such a system we usually find the following elements:

1. A class of meta-linguistic rules, indicating which expressions are expressions of the system.

2. A meta-linguistic rule indicating which sentences are to be assumed as valid in the system without proof.

3. A class of meta-linguistic rules indicating how, from a sentence valid in the system, other sentences valid in it can be derived.

4. A class of object-linguistic expressions which, having the characteristics indicated by (1), are well-formed expressions of the system.

Reprinted by permission of New York University Press from *The Logic of Religion* (1956), pp. 53-58, 59-62, 62-68, by Joseph M. Bochenski, O.P.

5. A class of object-linguistic sentences which, having the characteristics indicated by (2), are the axioms of the system.

6. A class of sentences which, having been derived, directly or indirectly, from the axioms (4) by the use of the rules (3) are valid (derived) theorems of the system.

This is the ideal case of a formalized axiomatic system; such types of discourse are rare and it is doubtful if there are many outside pure logic. Nevertheless, the study of such an axiomatized system allows one to see what the structure of each discourse must be. For even if the structure is neither formalized nor even intuitively axiomatized, as is the case in most sciences, it must have at least one characteristic in common with the formalized systems, namely, there must be a distinction in it between a class of object-linguistic expressions and a class of meta-linguistic rules indicating what expressions are meaningful and, in the case of sentences, which are valid in the system.

For our purposes it will be necessary to examine briefly only that part of the above structure which is concerned with sentences. According to what has been said, this consists of a class of meta-linguistic rules indicating which sentences are to be recognized as valid in the system, and of a class of such valid object-linguistic sentences, whether they are axioms or derived theorems.

However, when a system is not studied exclusively for its internal structure—as it is with logicians—that is, when its theorems are recognized (with some interpretation) by a subject as valid, then a third factor is needed, namely, a rule stating that any sentence belonging to the class of axioms or derived theorems of the system is to be accepted as valid. Then we have three factors:

1. The class of valid sentences; this is object-linguistic; it consists, in the case of an axiomatized system, of axioms and derived theorems. It will be called here "objective content."

2. The class of rules determining which sentences belong to the objective content. These rules—which are meta-linguistic—will be called "heuristic rules."

3. The meta-linguistic statement that every sentence designated by the heuristic rule is valid. This statement will be called here the "basic assumption."

Another remark must be added. The objective content of a discourse is usually itself structured, insofar as some of its elements are assumed as axioms and others are derived from them. However, once a certain number of such derived sentences has been obtained, a reorganization of the objective content is often carried out; and now some of the sentences which have been derived are taken as axioms, whereas others—and among them the very axioms of the primitive system—are deduced and become proved theorems.

This may be best seen in the field of physics or of any other sufficiently developed natural science. Here we have, first, a set of axioms designated by the heuristic rule under the basic assumption. These axioms are, obviously, the experimental sentences, that is, the sentences expressing propositions about observed facts. From these sentences, with the use of some previously established theorems and of certain rules of (inductive) derivation, explanatory sentences such as general laws, hypotheses, and so on are obtained. The explanatory sentences are again explained in a similar way by more general sentences. At a given point in time, the mass of sentences making up the objective content of physics is reorganized in such a way that now one or more among the explanatory sentences is taken as an axiom and the remaining sentences are derived from them by means of the rules of deductive logic. An important point is that here the very sentences which played the role of axioms in the primitive system now become derived theorems.

We have, consequently, in every such field a twofold virtual axiomatization. In the first axiomatization, only experimental sentences (along with some mathematical laws) are axioms; in the second, on the contrary, these sentences are derived theorems, whereas some sentences which were derived in the first system are now axioms.

This distinction is often overlooked, especially by those who consider mathematics of a Platonic type as being the paradigm of every axiomatization. In mathematics of this type these two sets of axioms coincide—and this is because all rules used are deductive. But in the empirical sciences a distinction must be drawn in order to avoid misunderstanding.

We shall term the axioms of the first systems—namely, those obtained by means of the heuristic rules—"basic sentences" or alternatively "epistemic axioms"; the axioms of the second system will be called "logical axioms." The expression "logical axioms" is somewhat inadequate, but it will do here for practical reasons.

The main structural problems of a discourse may now be enumerated in the following way:

First, there will be a class of quite generic problems, concerned with the first systems, that is, with the nature of the basic assumption, of the heuristic rules, and of the objective content of the discourse.

Then problems will arise as to the logical structure of the objective content itself, in particular as to the formal logic used in its second axiomatization. It is a well-known fact that, for example, in microphysics, some sort of many-valued logic seems to be necessary.

Third, a number of questions may sometimes arise as to the relations between a given discourse (for example, that of a science) and other discourses (for example, those of other sciences) insofar as the same subject may consider several of them as making up his total discourse.

All these problems are concerned with the sentences of the discourse. But there may also be questions concerned with its terms—above all, if we exclude semantic considerations, the problems of the syntactical status of some among them.

## 18. *On the structural problems of RD*

All the problems enumerated above arise in connection with RD [religious discourse]. However, as was to be expected, here they take a particular form because of the peculiarities of this discourse. The structure of RD is different from that of the discourse of science insofar as authority does play a considerable role in it; as a consequence, the logical nature of the basic assumption is different from that met in the sciences. This is one major difference between the logic of religion and the logic of science.

Another difference is as follows: the discourse of a science, especially when it is highly developed, is constructed, so to speak, autonomously, that is, without taking other discourses into consideration. A physicist, for example, does not need, while constructing his system, to take into consideration the everyday discourse he uses outside science. But the situation in RD is different. For reasons which will be discussed later on, RD is very closely connected with the TD (total discourse) of its users, that is, it cannot be disconnected and considered separately from the PD (profane discourse) of the same subject. Therefore, the problem of the relations between the two discourses, the RD and the PD, is here particularly important. . . .

## 19. *On the general structure of RD*

When we consider RD of the great religions it appears that it is always constructed in the following way:

1. First we find a class of object-linguistic sentences which are about the OR [object of religion]. This we shall call "objective faith," symbolically "$\rho$," and we shall call its elements "$\rho$-sentences." $\rho$-sentences are what the believers directly believe; most of what is found in creeds, catechisms, and so on belongs to this class. "There is a God," "Christ is the Son of God," "Mohammed is the Prophet of Allah," "There is Reincarnation," are instances of such $\rho$-sentences. Objective faith corresponds to what we called in Section 17 "epistemic axioms"; they are sentences which are assumed by the believer without a further object-linguistic proof.

2. Second, there is a heuristic rule indicating which sentences are to be considered as elements of objective faith. It is a meta-linguistic rule and corresponds to the rule by which the axioms are enumerated in logical systems. It must indicate some characteristics of $\rho$-sentences, and, curiously enough, these characteristics are usually found to be syntactical. This certainly is the case in the Catholic religion, where it is possible to formulate the heuristic rule in purely syntactical terms, namely, by describing the form and the context in which elements of objective faith are to be found. In other religions, this rule is perhaps less precise, but there is always at least a tendency toward a syntactical formulation; this appears especially in the fact that in practically all religions there is a rule which says that whatever is contained in the Scriptures or in the creed of that religion belongs to the objective faith. Of course, the Scriptures usually need a lot of interpretation before they may serve as a basis for the use of the heuristic rule; but, this being supposed, the rule can, in principle, be formulated in syntactical terms.

3. Third, there is the basic assumption, called here "basic dogma" ("BD"), a meta-logical rule, according to which every element of objective faith—that is, every sentence designated by the heuristic rule—has to be accepted as true. Thus a Mohammedan would ad-

mit that whatever has been revealed by Mohammed has to be considered as true; and a Catholic catechism says that whatever God revealed and the Church proposes to be believed is true, and so on.

At the same time, the BD also states something which is rarely explicit in it, but is known to be understood by all believers, namely, that all sentences designated by the heuristic rule have to be considered as possessing the probability $1$. In most theologies it is even asserted that the certainty of the $\rho$-sentences is by far greater, indeed belongs to a quite different order, than the certainty of any other sentence. This, however, is a psychological matter; logically there is no probability higher than $1$.

From the logical point of view, the situation in RD is very similar to that which we find in the discourse of natural sciences. The $\rho$-sentences play in RD a role closely similar to that of experimental sentences in those sciences. The only question which may arise in both cases is whether the given sentence really does belong to the class under consideration, that is, whether it really is a $\rho$-sentence, or a duly established protocol sentence. An enquiry concerning this circumstance is always possible and legitimate. But a quite general rule—namely, the basic assumption—provides every sentence which the subject is fully satisfied does belong to the said class with the probability $1. \ldots$

## 20. *On the axiomatization of $\rho$*

We will now proceed to our second problem, namely, that of the nature of the axioms in RD. As far as the epistemic axioms are concerned, the question is exhausted by what has been said in Section 19. However, the heuristic rule which permits selection of all sentences belonging to $\rho$ does not permit the ordering of it. What the believer has as $\rho$ is an unordered class of sentences. He is not bound by his faith to any axiomatization of that class.

But man is constituted in such a way that he always tends to axiomatize his discourse; and the religious man is no exception in this respect. There will be, consequently, a more or less pronounced tendency in believers to order the class $\rho$ by axiomatizing it. Such an axiomatization is the field of what is called "theology" (or "Buddhology") in the strict meaning of the term; theology may, indeed, also have other tasks—for example, it may try to make the heuristic rule more precise, and to apply it to the given sources (Scriptures, and so on). But these are meta-logical tasks of theology and, by their very nature, marginal with regard to the object-linguistic task of axiomatizing the class $\rho$.

How will this axiomatization be accomplished? The theologian might proceed either by ordering the $\rho$-sentences alone, or by adding new sentences to them. Although theoretically the first method is not impossible, it seems often difficult to apply and, anyway, in historical practice the theologians frequently used the second method. This is also recommended by the circumstance that a considerable enrichment of the field may thus be achieved, as in all sciences.

But if this second method is applied, a question arises as to the logical status of the new sentences obtained in the system—logical as opposed to epistemological status, because from the epistemological point of view they will always be derived sentences (theological conclusions). Again there are two possibilities *a priori*: the theological conclusions may be obtained either deductively, or reductively, or in both ways. What the method of existing theologies really is has been little studied; yet the following provisional theorem may be perhaps considered as well established empirically: [20.1] *very few, if any, theological conclusions have been obtained deductively by the use of $\rho$-sentences only and purely logical laws and rules.*

Moreover, most theological conclusions seem to be established reductively. In other words, theology is more like physics than like mathematics. This may be seen in the following comparative table.

| *Physics* | *Theology* |
|---|---|
| Starts (theoretically) with experimental sentences (epistemic axioms) | Starts (theoretically) with $\rho$-sentences |
| Explains the experimental sentences by other sentences from which the former may be deduced | Explains the $\rho$-sentences by theological conclusions which are such that from them the $\rho$-sentences can be deduced |
| Deduces from the explanatory sentences new ones which may be verified by experiment | Deduces from the theological conclusions new sentences, which may be verified by seeing if they do belong to $\rho$ |

| Physics | Theology |
|---|---|
| Explains the first-grade explanatory sentences by further explanatory sentences in the same way | The same |
| Verifies such sentences by examining their consistency with other sentences in the system | The same |
| Introduces new "theoretical" terms not found in protocol sentences | Introduces new "theological" terms not to be found in $p$-sentences |

The above view needs to be substantiated by studies in the logical structure of concrete theological work: such studies are unknown to the present author. The view suggested here assumes that the main task of the theologian is the axiomatization of objective faith and not the deducing of consequences from it.

## 21. *On the logical syntax of "God"*

We have next to consider the problems of the primitive terms of RD. Such terms offer many interesting semantic problems, but these do not belong in the context of this discussion; what is left are the syntactical problems of such terms.

From a grammatical point of view, RD is not unlike PD: it is composed of terms which may be grammatically divided into nouns, adjectives, verbs, and so on. A logical analysis at least of the theistic religions shows that, exactly as in PD, we may classify all terms of RD into arguments and different kinds of functors. These functors do not seem to offer any syntactical particularity. On the contrary, at least one basic argument is of syntactical interest, namely, the term "God" and analogous expressions in other languages and religions. This term plays a considerable role in RD; it has been said, and probably rightly so, that whatever is said in RD is about God in one way or another, that is, that all $p$-sentences assert a property of or a relation of God. Consequently, the syntactical status of "God" is of major interest for our study.

There are two possible hypotheses concerning this term: it may be either a name or a description. The first is possible only if the user of that term has a knowledge of God by acquaintance; if he does not have such knowledge, "God" must be an abbreviation for a description, namely, God is to such a man the subject which has such and such properties. In order to decide whether "God" is a name or a description, we must, therefore, consider the epistemological situation of the users of RD.

The class of those who use the term "God" may be roughly subdivided into two mutually exclusive subclasses: that of prophets who are the authors of the Scriptures and so on, and that of believers who are users of RD but not its authors.

As to the prophets, it is sometimes assumed by the users of RD that they had—at least in most cases—some direct experience of God. This means that they have a knowledge of Him by acquaintance—and that, therefore, for them the term "God" is a name. It must be said that not all users of RD assume that all the prophets of their respective religions had such a knowledge; but at least for a subclass of them this may be admitted.

But as far as the believers are concerned, there are two opposed theories: according to one, every believer "meets" God every day, in every act of worship, and so on. The second contends that there is no such meeting of God by believers at all, and that at least the bulk of them have to "live on faith," "in the darkness of faith," without having any direct experience of God. According to the first theory, the term "God" will be a name for the believers. According to the second, it must be a description, that is, God is known by the believer only by some predicates applied to Him in the Scriptures. The partisans of the second theory would sometimes make some exceptions, for example, for the mystics; but this does not apply to the mass of believers.

The problem at hand has been still further complicated by the introduction of the term "religious experience" and the phenomenological studies of such experiences. It has been shown rather convincingly that, for example, in the act of prayer there is a so-called intentional object, namely, God, as the object of prayer; and the phenomenologists of religion, following Rudolf Otto, often contend that there is a particular type of experience of such an object.

However, in spite of the nearly complete lack of serious empirical studies in this field, it seems that the great majority of believers, as they are now, do not have any real experience of God at all.

They pray and worship Him, but as they know Him, and nothing in their declarations suggests that in an act of prayer or other religious act they know anything more about God than what they learned from their creed. The only new factor seems to be purely subjective. But the creeds always describe God and cannot, by their very nature, convey a knowledge of Him by acquaintance.

On this assumption, we are entitled to state the following: [21.1] the term "God," as used by the bulk of today's believers, is a description.

It is an abbreviation for a substitution in the formula

$$(\imath x) \quad \{\varphi x\}$$

where "$\varphi$" is substituted by the product of the predicates attributed to God by the creeds concerned.

$\chi$)

# II. The Question of the Literalness
## of Religious Language

# 6. ON THE LITERAL SIGNIFICANCE

## OF RELIGIOUS SENTENCES

## Alfred J. Ayer

*Alfred J. Ayer is Wykeham Professor of Logic at Oxford University. In addition to his controversial* Language, Truth and Logic, *he is author of* The Foundations of Empirical Knowledge, The Problem of Knowledge, *and* The Concept of a Person and Other Essays. *He has also written, edited, and contributed to, a number of other philosophical works.*

This mention of God brings us to the question of the possibility of religious knowledge. We shall see that this possibility has already been ruled out by our treatment of metaphysics. But, as this is a point of considerable interest, we may be permitted to discuss it at some length.

It is now generally admitted, at any rate by philosophers, that the existence of a being having the attributes which define the god of any non-animistic religion cannot be demonstratively proved. To see that this is so, we have only to ask ourselves what are the premises from which the existence of such a god could be deduced. If the conclusion that a god exists is to be demonstratively certain, then these premises must be certain; for, as the conclusion of a deductive argument is already contained in the premises, any uncertainty there may be about the truth of the premises is necessarily shared by it. But we know that no empirical proposition can ever be anything more than probable. It is only *a priori* propositions that are logically certain. But we cannot deduce the existence of a god from an *a priori* proposition. For we know that the

Reprinted by permission of Victor Gollancz, Ltd. and Dover Publications from *Language, Truth and Logic,* Second Edition (1946), pp. 114-20. The title is provided by the editor.

reason why *a priori* propositions are certain is that they are tautologies. And from a set of tautologies nothing but a further tautology can be validly deduced. It follows that there is no possibility of demonstrating the existence of a god.

What is not so generally recognised is that there can be no way of proving that the existence of a god, such as the God of Christianity, is even probable. Yet this also is easily shown. For if the existence of such a god were probable, then the proposition that he existed would be an empirical hypothesis. And in that case it would be possible to deduce from it, and other empirical hypotheses, certain experiential propositions which were not deducible from those other hypotheses alone. But in fact this is not possible. It is sometimes claimed, indeed, that the existence of a certain sort of regularity in nature constitutes sufficient evidence for the existence of a god. But if the sentence "God exists" entails no more than that certain types of phenomena occur in certain sequences, then to assert the existence of a god will be simply equivalent to asserting that there is the requisite regularity in nature; and no religious man would admit that this was all he intended to assert in asserting the existence of a god. He would say that in talking about God, he was talking about a transcendent being who might be known through certain empirical manifestations, but certainly could not be defined in terms of those manifestations. But in that case the term "god" is a metaphysical term. And if "god" is a metaphysical term, then it cannot be even probable that a god exists. For to say that "God exists" is to make a metaphysical utterance which cannot be either true or false. And by the same criterion, no sentence which purports to describe the nature of a transcendent god can possess any literal significance.

It is important not to confuse this view of religious assertions with the view that is adopted by atheists, or agnostics.[1] For it is characteristic of an agnostic to hold that the existence of a god is a possibility in which there is no good reason either to believe or disbelieve; and it is characteristic of an atheist to hold that it is at least probable that no god exists. And our view that all utterances about the nature of God are nonsensical, so far from being identical with, or even lending any support to, either of these familiar contentions, is actually incompatible with them. For if the assertion that there is a god is nonsensical, then the atheist's assertion that there is no god is equally nonsensical, since it is only a significant proposition that can be significantly contradicted. As for the agnostic, although he refrains from saying either that there is or that there is not a god, he does not deny that the question whether a transcendent god exists is a genuine question. He does not deny that the two sentences "There is a transcendent god" and "There is no transcendent god" express propositions one of which is actually true and the other false. All he says is that we have no means of telling which of them is true, and therefore ought not to commit ourselves to either. But we have seen that the sentences in question do not express propositions at all. And this means that agnosticism also is ruled out.

Thus we offer the theist the same comfort as we gave to the moralist. His assertions cannot possibly be valid, but they cannot be invalid either. As he says nothing at all about the world, he cannot justly be accused of saying anything false, or anything for which he has insufficient grounds. It is only when the theist claims that in asserting the existence of a transcendent god he is expressing a genuine proposition that we are entitled to disagree with him.

It is to be remarked that in cases where deities are identified with natural objects, assertions concerning them may be allowed to be significant. If, for example, a man tells me that the occurrence of thunder is alone both necessary and sufficient to establish the truth of the proposition that Jehovah is angry, I may conclude that, in his usage of words, the sentence "Jehovah is angry" is equivalent to "It is thundering." But in sophisticated religions, though they may be to some extent based on men's awe of natural process which they cannot sufficiently understand, the "person" who is supposed to control the empirical world is not himself located in it; he is held to be superior to the empirical world, and so outside it; and he is endowed with super-empirical attributes. But the notion of a person whose essential attributes are non-empirical is not an intelligible notion at all. We may have a word which is used as if it named this "person," but, unless the sentences in which it occurs express propositions which are empirically verifiable, it cannot be said to symbolize anything. And this is the case with regard to the word "god," in the usage in which it is intended to refer to a transcendent object. The mere existence of the noun is enough to foster the illusion that there is a real, or at any rate a possible entity corresponding to it. It is only when we enquire what God's attributes are that we discover that "God," in this usage, is not a genuine name.

It is common to find belief in a transcendent god conjoined with belief in an after-life. But, in the form which it usually takes, the content of this belief is not a genuine hypothesis. To say that men do not ever die, or that the state of death is merely a state of prolonged insensibility, is indeed to express a significant proposition, though all the available evidence goes to show that it is false. But to say that there is something imperceptible inside a man, which is his soul or his real self, and that it goes on living after he is dead, is to make a metaphysical assertion which has no more factual content than the assertion that there is a transcendent god.

It is worth mentioning that, according to the account which we have given of religious assertions, there is no logical ground for antagonism between religion and natural science. As far as the question of truth or falsehood is concerned, there is no opposition between the natural scientist and the theist who believes in a transcendent god. For since the religious utterances of the theist are not genuine propositions at all, they cannot stand in any logical relation to the propositions of science. Such antagonism as there is between religion and science appears to consist in the fact that science takes away one of the motives which make men religious. For it is acknowledged that one of the ultimate sources of religious feeling lies in the inability of men to determine their own destiny; and science tends to destroy the feeling of awe with which men regard an alien world, by making them believe that they can understand and anticipate the source of natural phenomena, and even to some extent control it. The fact that it has recently become fashionable for physicists themselves to be sympathetic towards religion is a point in favour of this hypothesis. For this sympathy towards religion marks the physicists' own lack of confidence in the validity of their hypotheses, which is a reaction on their part from the anti-religious dogmatism of nineteenth-century scientists, and a natural outcome of the crisis through which physics has just passed.

It is not within the scope of this enquiry to enter more deeply into the causes of religious feeling, or to discuss the probability of the continuance of religious belief. We are concerned only to answer those questions which arise out of our discussion of the possibility of religious knowledge. The point which we wish to establish is that there cannot be any transcendent truths of religion. For the sentences which the theist uses to express such "truths" are not literally significant.

An interesting feature of this conclusion is that it accords with what many theists are accustomed to say themselves. For we are often told that the nature of God is a mystery which transcends the human understanding. But to say that something transcends the human understanding is to say that it is unintelligible. And what is unintelligible cannot significantly be described. Again, we are told that God is not an object of reason but an object of faith. This may be nothing more than an admission that the existence of God must be taken on trust, since it cannot be proved. But it may also be an assertion that God is the object of a purely mystical intuition, and cannot therefore be defined in terms which are intelligible to the reason. And I think there are many theists who would assert this. But if one allows that it is impossible to define God in intelligible terms, then one is allowing that it is impossible for a sentence both to be significant and to be about God. If a mystic admits that the object of his vision is something which cannot be described, then he must also admit that he is bound to talk nonsense when he describes it.

For his part, the mystic may protest that his intuition does reveal truths to him, even though he cannot explain to others what these truths are; and that we who do not possess this faculty of intuition can have no ground for denying that it is a cognitive faculty. For we can hardly maintain *a priori* that there are no ways of discovering true propositions except those which we ourselves employ. The answer is that we set no limit to the number of ways in which one may come to formulate a true proposition. We do not in any way deny that a synthetic truth may be discovered by purely intuitive methods as well as by the rational method of in- duction. But we do say that every synthetic proposition, however it may have been arrived at, must be subject to the test of actual experience. We do not deny *a priori* that the mystic is able to discover truths by his own special methods. We wait to hear what are the propositions which embody his discoveries, in order to see whether they are verified or confuted by our empirical observations. But the mystic, so far from producing propositions which are empirically verified, is unable to produce any intelligible propositions at all. And therefore we say that his intuition has not revealed to him any facts. It is no use his saying that he has apprehended facts but is unable to express them. For we know that if he really had acquired any information, he would be able to express it. He would be able to indicate in some way or other how the genuineness of his discovery might be empirically determined. The fact that he cannot reveal what he "knows," or even himself devise an empirical test to validate his "knowledge," shows that his state of mystical intuition is not a genuinely cognitive state. So that in describing his vision the mystic does not give us any information about the external world; he merely gives us indirect information about the condition of his own mind.

These considerations dispose of the argument from religious experience, which many philosophers still regard as a valid argument in favour of the existence of a god. They say that it is logically possible for men to be immediately acquainted with God, as they are immediately acquainted with a sense-content, and that there is no reason why one should be prepared to believe a man when he says that he is seeing a yellow patch, and refuse to believe him when he says that he is seeing God. The answer to this is that if the man who asserts that he is seeing God is merely asserting that he is experiencing a peculiar kind of sense-content, then we do not for a moment deny that his assertion may be true. But, ordinarily, the man who says that he is seeing God is saying not merely that he is experiencing a religious emotion, but also that there exists a transcendent being who is the object of this emotion; just as the man who says that he sees a yellow patch is ordinarily saying not merely that his visual sense-field contains a yellow sense-content, but also that there exists a yellow object to which the sense-content belongs. And it is not irrational to be prepared to believe a man when he asserts the existence of a yellow object, and to refuse to believe him when he asserts the existence of a transcendent god. For whereas the sentence "There exists here a yellow-coloured material thing" expresses a genuine synthetic proposition which could be empirically verified, the sentence "There exists a transcendent god" has, as we have seen, no literal significance.

We conclude, therefore, that the argument from religious experience is altogether fallacious. The fact that people have religious experiences is interesting from the psychological point of view, but it does not in any way imply that there is such a thing as religious knowledge, any more than our having moral experiences implies that there is such a thing as moral knowledge. The theist, like the moralist, may believe that his experiences are cognitive experiences, but, unless he can formulate his "knowledge" in propositions that are empirically verifiable, we may be sure that he is deceiving himself. It follows that those philosophers who fill their books with assertions that they intuitively "know" this or that moral or religious "truth" are merely providing material for the psycho-analyst. For no act of intuition can be said to reveal a truth about any matter of fact unless it issues in verifiable propositions. And all such propositions are to be incorporated in the system of empirical propositions which constitutes science.

NOTES

1. This point was suggested to me by Professor H. H. Price.

# 7. SYMBOLS OF FAITH

## Paul Tillich

*Paul Tillich (1886-1965), one of the outstanding and most influential philosophical theologians of our time, has given much attention to the understanding of religious language. His extensive bibliography includes his majestic* Systematic Theology.

## 1. The Meaning of Symbol

Man's ultimate concern must be expressed symbolically, because symbolic language alone is able to express the ultimate. This statement demands explanation in several respects. In spite of the manifold research about the meaning and function of symbols which is going on in contemporary philosophy, every writer who uses the term "symbol" must explain his understanding of it.

Symbols have one characteristic in common with signs; they point beyond themselves to something else. The red sign at the street corner points to the order to stop the movements of cars at certain intervals. A red light and the stopping of cars have essentially no relation to each other, but conventionally they are united as long as the convention lasts. The same is true of letters and numbers and partly even words. They point beyond themselves to sounds and meanings. They are given this special function by convention within a nation or by international conventions, as the mathematical signs. Sometimes such signs are called symbols; but this is unfortunate because it makes the distinction between signs and symbols more difficult. Decisive is the fact that signs do not participate in the reality of that to which they point, while symbols do. Therefore,

Reprinted by permission of Harper & Row, Publishers, Inc. from *Dynamics of Faith* (1957), pp. 41-54, by Paul Tillich. Copyright © 1957 by Paul Tillich.

signs can be replaced for reasons of expediency or convention, while symbols cannot.

This leads to the second characteristic of the symbol: It participates in that to which it points: the flag participates in the power and dignity of the nation for which it stands. Therefore, it cannot be replaced except after an historic catastrophe that changes the reality of the nation which it symbolizes. An attack on the flag is felt as an attack on the majesty of the group in which it is acknowledged. Such an attack is considered blasphemy.

The third characteristic of a symbol is that it opens up levels of reality which otherwise are closed for us. All arts create symbols for a level of reality which cannot be reached in any other way. A picture and a poem reveal elements of reality which cannot be approached scientifically. In the creative work of art we encounter reality in a dimension which is closed for us without such works. The symbol's fourth characteristic not only opens up dimensions and elements of reality which otherwise would remain unapproachable but also unlocks dimensions and elements of our soul which correspond to the dimensions and elements of reality. A great play gives us not only a new vision of the human scene, but it opens up hidden depths of our own being. Thus we are able to receive what the play reveals to us in reality. There are within us dimensions of which we cannot become aware except through symbols, as melodies and rhythms in music.

Symbols cannot be produced intentionally—this is the fifth characteristic. They grow out of the individual or collective unconscious and cannot function without being accepted by the unconscious dimension of our being. Symbols which have an especially social function, as political and religious symbols, are created or at least accepted by the collective unconscious of the group in which they appear.

The sixth and last characteristics of the symbol is a consequence of the fact that symbols cannot be invented. Like living beings, they grow and they die. They grow when the situation is ripe for them, and they die when the situation changes. The symbol of the "king" grew in a special period of history, and it died in most parts of the world in our period. Symbols do not grow because people are longing for them, and they do not die because of scientific or practical criticism. They die because they can no longer produce response in the group where they originally found expression.

These are the main characteristics of every symbol. Genuine symbols are created in several spheres of man's cultural creativity. We have mentioned already the political and the artistic realm. We could add history and, above all, religion, whose symbols will be our particular concern.

## 2. *Religious symbols*

We have discussed the meaning of symbols generally because, as we said, man's ultimate concern must be expressed symbolically! One may ask: Why can it not be expressed directly and properly? If money, success or the nation is someone's ultimate concern, can this not be said in a direct way without symbolic language? Is it not only in those cases in which the content of the ultimate concern is called "God" that we are in the realm of symbols? The answer is that everything which is a matter of unconditional concern is made into a god. If the nation is someone's ultimate concern, the name of the nation becomes a sacred name and the nation receives divine qualities which far surpass the reality of the being and functioning of the nation. The nation then stands for and symbolizes the true ultimate, but in an idolatrous way. Success as ultimate concern is not the national desire of actualizing potentialities, but is readiness to sacrifice all other values of life for the sake of a position of power and social predominance. The anxiety about not being a success is an idolatrous form of the anxiety about divine condemnation. Success is grace; lack of success, ultimate judgment. In this way concepts designating ordinary realities become idolatrous symbols of ultimate concern.

The reason for this transformation of concepts into symbols is the character of ultimacy and the nature of faith. That which is the true ultimate transcends the realm of finite reality infinitely. Therefore, no finite reality can express it directly and properly. Religiously speaking, God transcends his own name. This is why the use of his name easily becomes an abuse or a blasphemy. Whatever we say about that which concerns us ultimately, whether or not we call it God, has a symbolic meaning. It points beyond itself while participating in that to which it points. In no other way can faith express itself adequately. The language of faith is the language of symbols. If faith were what we have shown that it is not, such an assertion could not be made. But faith, understood as the state of being ultimately concerned, has no language other than symbols. When saying this I always expect the question: Only a symbol? He who asks this question shows that he has not understood the difference between signs and symbols nor the power of symbolic language, which surpasses in quality and strength the power of any nonsymbolic language. One should never say "only a symbol," but one should say "not less than a symbol." With this in mind we can now describe the different kinds of symbols of faith.

The fundamental symbol of our ultimate concern is God. It is always present in any act of faith, even if the act of faith includes the denial of God. Where there is ultimate concern, God can be denied only in the name of God. One God can deny the other one. Ultimate concern cannot deny its own character as ultimate. Therefore, it affirms what is meant by the word "God." Atheism, consequently, can only mean the attempt to remove any ultimate concern —to remain unconcerned about the meaning of one's existence. Indifference toward the ultimate question is the only imaginable form of atheism. Whether it is possible is a problem which must remain unsolved at this point. In any case, he who denies God as a matter of ultimate concern affirms God, because he affirms ultimacy in his concern. God is the fundamental symbol for what concerns us ultimately. Again it would be completely wrong to ask: So God is nothing but a symbol? Because the next question has to be: A symbol for what? And then the answer would be: For God! God is symbol for God. This means that in the notion of God we must distinguish two elements: the element of ultimacy, which is a matter of immediate experience and not symbolic in itself, and the element of concreteness, which is taken from our ordinary experience and symbolically applied to God. The man whose ultimate concern is a sacred tree has both the ultimacy of concern and the concreteness of the tree which symbolizes his relation to the ultimate. The man who adores Apollo is ultimately concerned, but not in an abstract way. His ultimate concern is symbolized in the divine figure of Apollo. The man who glorifies Jahweh, the God of the Old Testament, has both an ultimate concern and a concrete image of what concerns him ultimately. This is the meaning of the seemingly cryptic statement that God is the symbol of God. In this qualified sense God is the fundamental and universal content of faith.

It is obvious that such an understanding of the meaning of God makes the discussions about the existence or nonexistence of God meaningless. It is meaningless to question the ultimacy of an ultimate concern. This element in the idea of God is in itself certain. The symbolic expression of this element varies endlessly through the whole history of mankind. Here again it would be meaningless to ask whether one or another of the figures in which an ultimate concern is symbolized does "exist." If "existence" refers to something which can be found within the whole of reality, no divine being exists. The question is not this, but: which of the innumerable symbols of faith is most adequate to the meaning of faith? In other words, which symbol of ultimacy expresses the ultimate without idolatrous elements? This is the problem, and not the so-called "existence of God"—which is in itself an impossible combination of words. God as the ultimate in man's ultimate concern is more certain than any other certainty, even that of oneself. God as symbolized in a divine figure is a matter of daring faith, of courage and risk.

God is the basic symbol of faith, but not the only one. All the qualities we attribute to him, power, love, justice, are taken from finite experiences and applied symbolically to that which is beyond finitude and infinity. If faith calls God "almighty," it uses the human experience of power in order to symbolize the content of its infinite concern, but it does not describe a highest being who can do as he pleases. So it is with all the other qualities and with all the actions, past, present and future, which men attribute to God. They are symbols taken from our daily experience, and not information about what God did once upon a time or will do sometime in the future. Faith is not the belief in such stories, but it is the acceptance of symbols that express our ultimate concern in terms of divine actions.

Another group of symbols of faith are manifestations of the divine in things and events, in persons and communities, in words and documents. This whole realm of sacred objects is a treasure of symbols. Holy things are not holy in themselves, but they point beyond themselves to the source of all holiness, that which is of ultimate concern.

### 3. *Symbols and myths*

The symbols of faith do not appear in isolation. They are united in "stories of the gods," which is the meaning of the Greek word "mythos"—myth. The gods are individualized figures, analogous to human personalities, sexually differentiated, descending from each other, related to each other in love and struggle, producing world and man, acting in time and space. They participate in human greatness and misery, in creative and destructive works. They give to man cultural and religious traditions, and defend these sacred rites. They help and threaten the human race, especially some families, tribes or nations. They appear in epiphanies and incarnations, establish sacred places, rites and persons, and thus create a cult. But they themselves are under the command and threat of a fate which is beyond everything that is. This is mythology as developed most impressively in ancient Greece. But many of these characteristics can be found in every mythology. Usually the mythological gods are not equals. There is a hierarchy, at the top of which is a ruling god, as in Greece; or a trinity of them, as in India; or a duality of them, as in Persia. There are savior-gods who mediate between the highest gods and man, sometimes sharing the suffering and death of man in spite of their essential immortality. This is the world of the myth, great and strange, always changing but fundamentally the same: man's ultimate concern symbolized in divine figures and actions. Myths are symbols of faith combined in stories about divine-human encounters.

Myths are always present in every act of faith, because the language of faith is the symbol. They are also attacked, criticized and transcended in each of the great religions of mankind. The reason for this criticism is the very nature of the myth. It uses material from our ordinary experience. It puts the stories of the gods into the framework of time and space although it belongs to the nature of the ultimate to be beyond time and space. Above all, it divides the divine into several figures, removing ultimacy from each of them without removing their claim to ultimacy. This inescapably leads to conflicts of ultimate claims, able to destroy life, society, and consciousness.

The criticism of the myth first rejects the division of the divine and goes beyond it to one God, although in different ways according to the different types of religion. Even one God is an object of mythological language, and if spoken about is drawn into the framework of time and space. Even he loses his ultimacy if made to be the content of concrete concern. Consequently, the criticism of the myth does not end with the rejection of the polytheistic mythology.

Monotheism also falls under the criticism of the myth. It needs, as one says today, "demythologization." This word has been used in connection with the elaboration of the mythical elements in stories and symbols of the Bible, both of the Old and the New Testaments—stories like those of the Paradise, of the fall of Adam, of the great Flood, of the Exodus from Egypt, of the virgin birth of the Messiah, of many of his miracles, of his resurrection and ascension, of his expected return as the judge of the universe. In short, all the stories in which divine-human interactions are told are considered as mythological in character, and objects of demythologization. What does this negative and artificial term mean? It must be accepted and supported if it points to the necessity of recognizing a symbol as a symbol and a myth as a myth. It must be attacked and rejected if it means the removal of symbols and myths altogether. Such an attempt is the third step in the criticism of the myth. It is an attempt which never can be successful, because symbol and myth are forms of the human consciousness which are always present. One can replace one myth by another, but one .cannot remove the myth from man's spiritual life. For the myth is the combination of symbols of our ultimate concern.

A myth which is understood as a myth, but not removed or replaced, can be called a "broken myth." Christianity denies by its very nature any unbroken myth, because its presupposition is the first commandment: the affirmation of the ultimate as ultimate and the rejection of any kind of idolatry. All mythological elements in the Bible, and doctrine and liturgy should be recognized as mythological, but they should be maintained in their symbolic form and not be replaced by scientific substitutes. For there is no substitute for the use of symbols and myths: they are the language of faith.

The radical criticism of the myth is due to the fact that the primitive mythological consciousness resists the attempt to interpret the myth of myth. It is afraid of every act of demythologization. It believes that the broken myth is deprived of its truth and of its convincing power. Those who live in an unbroken mythological world feel safe and certain. They resist, often fanatically, any attempt to introduce an element of uncertainty by "breaking the myth," namely, by making conscious its symbolic character. Such resistance is supported by authoritarian systems, religious or political, in order to give security to the people under their control and unchallenged power to those who exercise the control. The resistance against demythologization expresses itself in "literalism." The symbols and myths are understood in their immediate meaning. The material, taken from nature and history, is used in its proper sense. The character of the symbol to point beyond itself to something else is disregarded. Creation is taken as a magic act which happened once upon a time. The fall of Adam is localized on a special geographical point and attributed to a human individual. The virgin birth of the Messiah is understood in biological terms, resurrection and ascension as physical events, the second coming of the Christ as a telluric, or cosmic, catastrophe. The presupposition of such literalism is that God is a being, acting in time and space, dwelling in a special place, affecting the course of events and being affected by them like any other being in the universe. Literalism deprives God of his ultimacy and, religiously speaking, of his majesty. It draws him down to the level of that which is not ultimate, the finite and conditional. In the last analysis it is not rational criticism of the myth which is decisive but the inner religious criticism. Faith, if it takes its symbols literally, becomes idolatrous! It calls something ultimate which is less than ultimate. Faith, conscious of the symbolic character of its symbols, gives God the honor which is due him.

One should distinguish two stages of literalism, the natural and the reactive. The natural stage of literalism is that in which the mythical and the literal are indistinguishable. The primitive period of individuals and groups consists in the inability to separate the creations of symbolic imagination from the facts which can be verified through observation and experiment. This stage has a full right of its own and should not be disturbed, either in individuals or in groups, up to the moment when man's questioning mind breaks the natural acceptance of the mythological visions as literal.

If, however, this moment has come, two ways are possible. The one is to replace the unbroken by the broken myth. It is the objectively demanded way, although it is impossible for many people who prefer the repression of their questions to the uncertainty which appears with the breaking of the myth. They are forced into the second stage of literalism, the conscious one, which is aware of the questions but represses them, half consciously, half unconsciously. The tool of repression is usually an acknowledged authority with sacred qualities like the Church or the Bible, to which one owes unconditional surrender. This stage is still justifiable, if the questioning power is very weak and can easily be answered. It is unjustifiable if a mature mind is broken in its personal center by political or psychological methods, split in his unity, and hurt in his integrity. The enemy of a critical theology is not natural literalism but conscious literalism with repression of and aggression toward autonomous thought.

Symbols of faith cannot be replaced by other symbols, such as artistic ones, and they cannot be removed by scientific criticism. They have a genuine standing in the human mind, just as science and art have. Their symbolic character is their truth and their power. Nothing less than symbols and myths can express our ultimate concern.

One more question arises, namely, whether myths are able to express every kind of ultimate concern. For example, Christian theologians argue that the word "myth" should be reserved for natural myths in which repetitive natural processes, such as the seasons, are understood in their ultimate meaning. They believe that if the world is seen as a historical process with beginning, end and center, as in Christianity and Judaism, the term "myth" should not be used. This would radically reduce the realm in which the term would be applicable. Myth could not be understood as the language of our ultimate concern, but only as a discarded idiom of this language. Yet history proves that there are not only natural myths but also historical myths. If the earth is seen as the battleground of two divine powers, as in ancient Persia, this is an historical myth. If the God of creation selects and guides a nation through history toward an end which transcends all history, this is an historical myth. If the Christ—a transcendent, divine being—appears in the fullness of time, lives, dies and is resurrected, this is an historical myth. Christianity is superior to those religions which are bound to a natural myth. But Christianity speaks the mythological language like every other religion. It is a broken myth, but it is a myth; otherwise Christianity would not be an expression of ultimate concern.

# 8. BEING-ITSELF AND

# IRREDUCIBLE METAPHORS

## Paul Edwards

*Paul Edwards is a Professor of Philosophy at New York University. He is author of* The Logic of Moral Discourse *and editor (with Arthur Pap) of* A Modern Introduction to Philosophy. *He is also Editor-in-Chief of* The Encyclopedia of Philosophy.

As we saw, Tillich readily admits that only in the basic statement of his system are all words used in their literal senses. All other statements about Being-itself are "symbolic" or "metaphorical." Tillich not only repeatedly makes general statements to this effect, he also tells us on many, though *not* on all, occasions when he discusses the characteristics of Being-itself that the words he uses in characterizing the Ultimate Reality are not to be understood literally. Thus he writes, "If one is asked how nonbeing is related to being-itself, one can only answer metaphorically: being 'embraces' itself and nonbeing. Being has nonbeing 'within' itself as that which is eternally present and eternally overcome in the process of the divine life" (*CB*, p. 34). Again: "In a metaphorical statement (and every assertion about being-itself is either metaphorical or symbolic) one could say that being includes nonbeing but nonbeing does not prevail against it. 'Including' is a spatial metaphor which indicates that being embraces itself and that which is opposed to it, nonbeing. Nonbeing belongs to being, it cannot be separated from it" (*CB*, p. 179). Again: "The divine life participates in every life as its ground and aim. God participates in everything that is; he has community with it; he shares in its destiny. Certainly such state-

Reprinted by permission of the author and editor from "Professor Tillich's Confusions," *Mind*, Volume 74, Number 294 (April, 1965), pp. 197-206.

ments are highly symbolic. . . . God's participation is not a spatial or temporal presence. It is meant not categorically but symbolically. It is the parousia, the 'being with' of that which is neither here nor there. If applied to God, participation and community are not less symbolic than individualization and personality" (*ST*, p. 245). And again: "But in God as God there is no distinction between potentiality and actuality. Therefore, we cannot speak of God as living in the proper or nonsymbolic sense of the word 'life' " (*ST*, p. 242).

Tillich sees nothing at all wrong in his constant employment of metaphors. On the contrary, he stresses the fact that without employing terms taken from "segments of finite experience," theological sentences would have little or no emotional force. "Anthropomorphic symbols," he writes, "are adequate for speaking of God religiously. Only in this way can he be the living God for man" (*ST*, p. 242). Tillich is indeed aware of the objection of certain philosophers that it is illegitimate to use terms which have a reasonably well-defined meaning in everyday contexts to make assertions about a reality that is infinitely removed from the contexts in which these expressions were originally introduced. He dismisses this objection without much ado. Such "accusations are mistaken," Tillich replies, "they miss the meaning of ontological concepts. . . . It is the function of an ontological concept to use some realm of experience to point to characteristics of being-itself which lie above the split between subjectivity and objectivity and which therefore cannot be expressed literally in terms taken from the subjective or the objective side. They must be understood not literally but analogously." This, however, Tillich insists, "does not mean that they have been produced arbitrarily and can easily be replaced by other concepts. Their choice is a matter of experience and thought, and subject to criteria which determine the adequacy or inadequacy of each of them" (*CB*, p. 25).

The rejoinder that "of course" the terms in question are used "analogously," "symbolically" or "merely as metaphors" exercises the same hypnotic spell over Tillich as it has on metaphysicians in the past. He seems to think that it is a solution of the problem. In fact, however, it is nothing of the sort. It is an implicit admission that a problem exists. The concession by an author that he is using a certain word metaphorically is tantamount to admitting that, in a very important sense and a sense relevant to the questions at issue between metaphysicians and their critics, he does not mean what he says. It does not automatically tell us what he does mean or whether in fact he means anything at all. When Bradley, for example, wrote that "the Absolute enters into . . . evolution and progress," it is clear that the word "enter" is used in a metaphorical and not a literal sense. But realizing this does not at once tell us what, if anything, Bradley asserted.

Often indeed when words are used metaphorically, the context or certain special conventions make it clear what is asserted. Thus, when a certain historian wrote that "the Monroe Doctrine has always rested on the broad back of the British navy," it would have been pedantic and foolish to comment "what on earth does he mean—doesn't he know that navies don't have backs?" Or if a man, who has been involved in a scandal and is advised to flee his country, rejects the advice and says, "No, I think I'll stay and face the music," it would be absurd to object to his statement on the ground that it is not exactly music that he is going to hear. In these cases we know perfectly well what the authors mean although they are using certain words metaphorically. But we know this because we can eliminate the metaphorical expression, because we can specify the content of the assertion in non-metaphorical language, because we can supply the literal equivalent.

The examples just cited are what I shall call "reducible metaphors." I prefer this to the phrase "translatable metaphor" because of certain ambiguities in the use of "translatable." We sometimes say of the English version of a foreign original—e.g. of the Kalisch version of the *Rosenkavalier*—that it is a bad or inadequate translation although it does in fact reproduce all the truth-claims contained in the original. Conversely we sometimes, as in the case of the Blitzstein version of the *Dreigroschenoper*, speak of a magnificent translation although we know that *not* all truth-claims of the original have been reproduced. In the present context, however, we are exclusively concerned with reproduction of truth-claims and in calling a metaphor "reducible" all I mean is that the truth-claims made by the sentence in which it occurs can be reproduced by one or more sentences all of whose components are used in literal senses.

Now, Tillich and many other metaphysicians fail to notice the difference between metaphors which are reducible in the sense just explained and those which are not. When a sentence contains an irreducible metaphor, it follows at once that the sentence is devoid of cognitive meaning, that it is unintelligible, that it fails to make a genuine assertion. For what has happened is that the sentence has been deprived of the referent it would have had, assuming that certain other conditions had also been fulfilled, if the expression in question had been used in its literal sense. To say that the metaphor is irreducible is to say in effect that no new referent can be supplied.

It will be instructive to look at an actual case in which a philosopher gave this very reason for his accusation that certain statements by another philosopher were devoid of meaning. I am referring to Berkeley's attack on Locke's claim that the material substratum "supports" the sense-qualities. Berkeley first pointed to the original context in which the word "support" is introduced, as when we say that pillars support a building. He then pointed out that since, according to Locke, the material substratum is a "something, x, I know not what" whose characteristics are unknown and indeed unknowable, and, since, therefore, it is not known to resemble pillars in any way, Locke could not possibly have been using the word "support" in its "usual or literal sense." "In what sense therefore," Berkeley went on, "must it be taken? . . . What that is they (Locke and those who share his view) do not explain." Berkeley then concluded that the sentences in question have "no distinct meaning annexed"[1] to them.

Let us consider some possible answers to Berkeley's criticism without in any way implying that Locke himself would have approved of any of them. Perhaps the most obvious answer would be that Locke should never have spoken of the material substratum as an unknowable entity. It should really be understood as an aggregate of material particles to which certain adjectives like mass- and velocity-predicates can be applied in their literal senses. Locke's statement that the material substratum supports the sense-qualities can then be translated into some such statement as that the particular "gross" sense-qualities perceived at any moment are, in part, causally dependent on the distribution and velocities of the particles in question. On this view there would be no irreducible metaphors in the original sentence.

A second line of defence would begin by admitting that the

material substratum *would* be completely unknowable, if sensory observation were the only method of becoming acquainted with objective realities. In fact, however, it would be said, we possess a "super-sensuous" faculty with which we "experience" such realities as material and spiritual substances. We could, if we wanted, introduce a set of terms as the symbols literally referring to the data disclosed by this super-sensuous faculty and we could exchange information about these with all who share in the possession of the faculty. If we call this the "intellectual language," then, so this defence of Locke would run, sentences with metaphors, when containing terms from the "sensory level," can be translated into sentences in the intellectual language which will be free from metaphors.

Finally, in view of our later discussion, it is worth looking at a particularly naïve and lame answer to Berkeley. A defender of Locke, when confronted with the question "You do not mean 'support' in its literal sense, what then do you mean?" might say, "I mean that the material substratum holds the sense qualities together." The answer to this is obvious. "Hold together" is no more used in its literal sense than "support" and hence the difficulty has in no way been removed.

Turning now to Tillich's metaphysical theology, it seems perfectly clear from numerous of his general observations that Being-itself is, even in principle, inaccessible to anybody's observation. In this respect it is exactly like Locke's material substratum. We do not and cannot have a stock of literally meaningful statements about it at our disposal which would serve as the equivalents of Tillich's "symbolic" statements. The metaphors in Tillich's sentences are, in other words, irreducible and hence, if my general argument has been correct, the sentences are unintelligible. If Tillich's statements are not to become propositions of physics or psychology or history no way out corresponding to the first of the defences of Locke is feasible. And unlike certain contemporary writers, Tillich does not avail himself of an appeal to mystical experience which would correspond to the second defence. For, if I understand Tillich correctly, he denies that even the mystic experiences Being-itself. The (true) "idea of God," Tillich writes, "transcends both mysticism and the person-to-person encounter."[2] As I shall show in a moment, Tillich does avail himself of a line of defence corresponding to the third of the defences of Locke. We already saw, however, that such a defence is altogether futile.

It may be said that I have not been fair to Tillich and other metaphysicians who defend themselves by insisting that they are using certain expressions metaphorically or analogously. It may be said that I have emphasized the negative implications of this admission—that the words in question are not used in their literal senses—without doing justice to its positive implications. For, it may be argued, when it is said that a certain word is used "analogously," it *is* implied that the term has a referent, namely a referent which is in some important respect similar to the referent it has when used literally.

This objection rests on a confusion. We must here distinguish two possible meanings of the assertion that a certain word is used "analogously." This may, firstly, mean no more than that the word in question is *not used literally*. But it may also amount to the much stronger claim that the word *has a referent* and hence that the sentence in which it occurs is, if certain other conditions are fulfilled, cognitively significant. If "analogously" is used in the former sense, then of course I would not for a moment deny that the relevant words are used analogously in Tillich's sentences and in the sentences of other metaphysicians. But this is an innocuous admission. For to say that the words are used analogously in this sense has no tendency whatever to imply that the sentences in which they occur possess cognitive meaning. If "analogously" is used in the second sense, then, as just observed, it would automatically follow that the sentences are, if other conditions are also fulfilled, cognitively significant; but in that event I would deny that the terms we have discussed are used analogously in Tillich's sentences or in the sentences of other metaphysicians. To put the matter very simply: merely saying that a sentence, or any part of it, has meaning does not by itself give it meaning. Such a claim does not assure us that the sentence is intelligible. Similarly the claim that a sentence has an "analogous" referent is a claim and no more —it may be false. If I say, to use an example given by Sidney Hook,[3] that the sea is angry, the word "angry" really has a referent which is analogous to its referent when used literally. I can in this case specify the features of the sea to which I am referring when I call it angry and I can also specify the similarities between these features and the anger of human beings. If, however, I say that Being-itself is angry, I could not independently identify the features of Being-itself to which I am supposedly referring. Nor of course could I specify the similarities between the anger of human beings and the putative anger of Being-itself. My claim that "angry" is used analogously in this sentence in a sense in which this implies that it has a referent would be false or at any rate baseless.

The narcotic effect of such phrases as "symbolic language" or "analogous sense" is only a partial explanation of Tillich's failure to be clear about the irreducibility of his metaphors. To tell the whole story one has to take notice of an aspect of Tillich's philosophizing which I have so far ignored. What I have so far brought out may be called Tillich's "modest" side—"modest" because he does not in the passages in question claim any literal knowledge about Being-itself. But there is also what may be called Tillich's "dogmatic" side. He then seems to be jotting down in a matter-of-fact way the characteristics of Being-itself, much as a doctor might jot down descriptions of the symptoms displayed by a patient. He then writes as if he had a completely unobstructed view of the Ultimate Reality. Thus we are told as a plain matter of fact and without the use of any quotation marks that "God is infinite because he has the finite (and with it that element of non-being which belongs to finitude) within himself united with his infinity." The expression "divine life," we are told, points to "this *situation*" (*ST*, p. 252, my italics). "The divine life," Tillich admits, "is infinite mystery," but we can nevertheless say that "it is not infinite emptiness. It is the ground of all abundance, and it is abundant itself" (*ST*, p. 251). Again, we are told, without the use of any quotation marks, and I do not think their absence is a mere oversight, that God "is the eternal process in which separation is posited and is overcome by reunion" (*ST*, p. 242). In one place, to give one more illustration of the dogmatic side of his philosophy, Tillich discusses the question of whether will or intellect are dominant "in God." He quotes the rival views of Aquinas and Duns Scotus and he notes that Protestants have tended to favour the latter position which subordinates the intellect. Tillich easily resolves this dispute as if he were reading off the truth by a quick glance at God. "Theology," he writes, "must balance the new with the old (predominantly Catholic) emphasis on the form character of the divine life" (*ST*,

p. 248), *i.e.* it must assign equal rank to will and intellect in God. The divine life, we are assured, "inescapably unites possibility with fulfillment. Neither side threatens the other nor is there a threat of disruption" (*ST*, p. 247).

Tillich, the dogmatist, does not hesitate to offer translations or what I have called reductions of his "symbolic" statements about God. We can also express literally, for example, what we mean "symbolically" when we say that God is living. "God lives," the reduction runs, "insofar as he is the ground of life" (*ST*, p. 242). Again, our symbolic statement that God is personal "does not mean that God is *a* person. It means that God is the ground of everything personal and that he carries within himself the ontological power of personality" (*ST*, p. 245). And if we symbolically say God is "his own destiny" we thereby "point to . . . the participation of God in becoming and in history" (*ST*, p. 249).

I wish to make two observations concerning all this. Firstly, although Tillich gives the impression that the metaphors have been eliminated in these and similar cases, this is not so. He never seems to have noticed that even in his basic statement, when elaborated in terms of "ground" and "structure," these words are used metaphorically and not literally. When Tillich writes that God or Being-itself "is the ground of the ontological structure of being and has the power of determining the structure of everything that has being," the word "ground," for example, is clearly not used in any of its literal senses. Being-itself is surely not claimed to be the ground of the ontological structure in the sense in which the earth is the ground beneath our feet or in the sense in which the premises of a valid argument may be said to be the ground for accepting the conclusion. Similar remarks apply to the use of "structure," "power," and "determine." Hence when we are told that "God lives insofar as he is the ground of life" or that "God is personal" means "God is the ground of everything personal and . . . carries within himself the ontological power of personality," expressions like "ground" and "carry within himself" and even "power" are not used literally. Tillich is here in no better a position than the supporter of Locke who substituted "hold together" for "support." That Tillich does not succeed in breaking through the circle of expressions *lacking* literal significance, *i.e.* lacking referential meaning, is particularly clear in the case of the "translation" of the sentence

"God is his own destiny." By this "symbolic" characterization, as we just saw, we "point" among other things to "the participation of God in becoming and in history." But a little earlier, in a passage which I also reproduced, we were informed that "God's participation is not a spatial or temporal presence" and twice in the same paragraph we were given to understand that when "applied to God," participation "is meant not categorically but symbolically." In other words, one metaphorical statement is replaced by another but literal significance is never achieved.

Tillich constantly engages in "circular" translations of this sort. Again and again he "explains" the meaning of one "symbolically" used expression in terms of another which is really no less symbolic. Thus in a passage reproduced at the beginning of section 3 of this article the sentence "being includes nonbeing" which contains the admittedly symbolic word "include" is translated into "nonbeing belongs to being, it cannot be separated from it." "Belong" and "separate" are no longer put inside quotation marks and one is apt to suppose that some progress has been made. Countless other illustrations of this practice could be given.

Secondly, I have the impression that, in spite of his distaste for "monarchic monotheism," Tillich occasionally relapses into something not too different from it. When offering translations such as those just quoted and generally when assessing the adequacy of certain symbols as "pointers" to the "divine life" Tillich seems to think that he has at his disposal a stock of literal truths about God not too different from those asserted by anthropomorphic believers. There is a remarkable passage in which this is strikingly evident:

> "Religious symbols are double-edged. They are directed toward the infinite which they symbolize *and* toward the finite through which they symbolize it. They force the infinite down to finitude and the finite up to infinity. They open the divine for the human and the human for the divine. For instance, if God is symbolized as 'Father,' he is brought down to the human relationship of father and child. But at the same time this human relationship is consecrated into a pattern of the divine-human relationship. If 'Father' is employed as a symbol for God, fatherhood is seen in its theonomous, sacramental depth. . . . If God is called the 'king,' something is said not only about God but also about the holy character of kinghood. If God's work is called 'making whole' or 'healing,' this not only says something about God but also empha-

sizes the theonomous character of all healing. . . . The list could be continued" (*ST*, pp. 240-241).

Now, if it were known or believed that God is "majestic" in the same sense in which human beings have sometimes been called that, it would make sense to call God a "king" and it would be right to prefer this symbol to symbols like "slave" or "waiter" or "street-cleaner." Similarly, if it were known or believed that God is "concerned with the welfare" of all human beings in the literal sense of this expression, then it would make sense to speak of him as our "father" and it would be right to prefer this symbol to symbols like "daughter" or "soprano" or "carpenter." An anthropomorphic believer has criteria at his disposal in such cases, but Tillich's non-anthropomorphic theology necessarily deprives him of it. Tillich says very correctly that this list of adjectives "could be continued." Since the "comparison" between fathers and kings on the one hand and the infinitely transcending, infinitely mysterious, indescribable Being-itself, on the other, is a bogus comparison, God may no less appropriately be said to be a soprano, a slave, a street-cleaner, a daughter, or even a fascist and a hater than a father or a king.

NOTES

1. *Principles of Human Knowledge*, §§ 16-17.
2. *CB*, p. 178. I am not sure that I have here correctly understood Tillich. He also seems to be saying the opposite at times—that mystics do have "direct access" to Being-itself. If that is Tillich's position then some of the criticisms which follow would not apply, but it would then be open to a number of other objections.
3. "The Quest for Being," *op. cit.* p. 715.

# 9. THE DOCTRINE OF ANALOGY

## Eric L. Mascall

*Eric L. Mascall is Professor of Historical Theology at King's Col-
lege, University of London. His many works include* Existence and
Analogy, Words and Images: A Study in Theological Discourse,
*and* Theology and Images.

Is it possible, we therefore ask, for statements expressed in human
language to mean anything when made about God—that is to say,
are theological statements meaningful or meaningless? (The relevance of this discussion to the questions raised by the logical positivists will be immediately clear to those who have any acquaintance
with their works.) Starting from a famous distinction made by
Aristotle,[1] we remark that, even within the realm of discourse about
finite beings, one and the same word, when applied to two things,
sometimes bears the same sense in both applications and sometimes different ones. In the former case it is used *univocally*
(συνωνύμως), as when Carlo and Fido are both called dogs. Even if
Carlo is a great Dane and Fido a Pomeranian, we mean the same
thing about each of them when we call them both *dogs*; the characteristics in each that distinguish Carlo as a Dane from Fido as a
Pomeranian, while they cannot be found in their totality except in
dogs, are additional to caninity as such. But sometimes we use
words purely equivocally (ὁμωνύμως), as when we apply the word
"mug" both to a drinking utensil and to the victim of a fraud. (The
neglect of this distinction can lead to unfortunate consequences,
as the choirboys found who were starting a cricket team, when they
asked the vicar for one of the bats which the verger had led them
to believe were in the belfry.) But in addition to these two uses, it
is alleged, a word is sometimes applied to two objects in senses that

Reprinted by permission of Longmans, Green, and Co., Ltd. and The Shoe
String Press, Inc. (Archon Books edition, 1967), from *Existence and Analogy*
(1949), pp. 97-121.

are neither wholly different nor yet wholly the same, as when we say that Mr. Jones and Skegness are both healthy, the former because he *enjoys*, and the latter because it *induces*, health; in this case we are said to use the term "healthy" *analogically* (ἀνάλογως).

At first sight the introduction of this mode of predication might seem to be unnecessary and trivial, and certainly Aristotle did not accord to it anything like as much attention as the scholastics do. We might be tempted to suppose that analogy is only a dignified kind of univocity, and that it is quite sufficient to say that the healthiness of Mr. Jones and the healthiness of Skegness are merely two ways of being healthy, just as the Danishness of Carlo and the Pomeranianity of Fido are merely two ways of being canine. Or, alternatively, we might go to the other extreme and say that analogy is only equivocity in sheep's clothing, that to enjoy health and to induce health are two altogether different activities and that only for the sake of economy in words can there be any justification for using the same term "healthy" *tout court* to denote them both. Furthermore, it might be asked, even if we admit this *tertium quid* of analogy, can we ever be quite sure when it applies? When we say that Mr. Jones is alive and that an oyster is alive, is the difference between the life of Mr. Jones and the life of the oyster something additional to a quality, namely life, which is found univocally in both, as the Danishness of Carlo and the Pomeranianity of Fido are additional to their common caninity? Or, on the other hand, is the life which is attributed to Mr. Jones and to the oyster, as the scholastics would say, an analogical perfection, contracted to each subject not by external *differentiae* but by different internal modes of participation? Can one possibly settle this kind of question? Can we even give the distinction any real meaning?

Now, so long as we are merely considering qualities and properties of finite beings, the introduction of analogical discourse, in addition to univocal and equivocal, might well appear to be an unnecessary and artificial complication. There are, however, two instances in which it—or something like it—seems to be unavoidable, namely when we are discussing transcendentals and when we are discussing God. And it is worth noting that, in Christian thought, it is precisely the necessity of talking about God that has given rise to the great development which the doctrine of analogy has undergone. Let us consider these instances in order.

The transcendentals, in scholastic thought, are those six primary

notions—*ens, res, unum, aliquid, verum* and *bonum*—which, because of their very universality, refuse to fall in any of the Aristotelian categories, but cut across them all.[2] The last five ultimately
reduce to the first, so it will be sufficient to consider that. What,
then, is meant by the analogy of being? Why is it denied that being
is univocal? Simply because there is nothing outside being by which
it could be differentiated. When we say that Carlo and Fido are
both dogs, the word "dog" means precisely the same when applied
to each of them; the differences that distinguish them as dogs are,
as we have seen, extrinsic to caninity as such. But when we say that
Carlo and Fido are both *beings*, the differences that distinguish
them as beings cannot be extrinsic to being as such, for being, in its
altogether universal reference, must embrace everything, including
differences; if differences were not instances of being, they would
be non-existent, and then no two things could be distinct from each
other. So the scholastics tell us, being is not a genus,[3] since there is
nothing outside it which could act as a differentia to it, to subdivide
it into species; nevertheless everything is an instance of being, and
being is differentiated by its own inherent analogical variety. To be
is to be in a certain way, and the way is the very heart of the being.
So the whole order of beings, of *entia*, from the triune Deity down
to the speck of dust and the electron, consists of nothing more and
nothing less than analogical instances of being: self-existent being
and dependent being, actual being and possible being, substantial
being and accidental being, real being and notional being, not in
any pantheistic or monistic sense, as if being were some kind of
cosmic material, a metaphysical modelling-clay appearing now in
this shape and now in that, but in the far more profound sense that
every being must *be*, and must be in some determinate way, and—
the theist will add—in the sense that the way in which it has being
depends in the last resort upon its relation to the self-existent Being
which is the prime analogate of all.

Now what is true about beings as such in their relation to one
another must be true *a fortiori* about finite beings in their relation
to the God who is self-existent Being. If being is not a genus, then
the supreme Being transcends all genera, and the principle of
analogy, which we have seen applies even between creatures when
they are considered as they participate in the transcendentals, will
apply with even greater force when creatures are brought into comparison with the altogether transcendent God and when God is

spoken about in words whose meaning is derived from their application to finite things. Here, if anywhere, the distinction between the *perfectio significata* and the *modus significandi* will hold; here, if anywhere, will the classical definition of analogy apply, namely that it is the application of a concept to different beings in ways that are simply diverse from each other and are only the same in a certain respect, *simpliciter diversa et eadem secundum quid.*[4] It is noticeable that St. Thomas does not deny that analogues are equivocal but only that they are purely so.[5]

Let us now proceed to consider in more detail this classical doctrine of analogy. The precise classification of the various types of analogy that can be distinguished is to this day a matter of considerable controversy; the method that I shall adopt will, however, bring out the salient points.

II

In the first place, we may distinguish between analogy *duorum ad tertium* and analogy *unius ad alterum*; this is the fundamental distinction made by St. Thomas in both the *Summa Theologica* and the *Summa contra Gentiles.*[6] Analogy *duorum ad tertium* is the analogy that holds between two beings in consequence of the relation that each of them bears to a third (the analogy considered is, it must be noticed, between the *two*; the *tertium* only comes in as something in the background to which they are both related). For example, if the adjective "healthy" is applied both to Skegness and to the complexion of Mr. Jones who lives there, this double attribution of the adjective can only be seen to be legitimate if it is grasped that in its strict and primary application the adjective applies neither to Skegness nor to the complexion but to Mr. Jones. It is he who is (in the scholastic sense) *formally* healthy and is the *prime analogate*. His complexion is healthy only in the sense that it is a *sign* of health in him, Skegness is healthy only in the sense that it *induces* health in him (or in others like him); we cannot rationally justify the attribution of the same predicate "healthy" to things as diverse as a complexion and a seaside town except by referring them both to human beings to whom the predicate formally and properly belongs.

This type of analogy can, however, have little or no application to the case where we are attributing the same predicate to God and to a creature, for there is no being antecedent to God to whom the predicate can apply more formally and properly than it applies to him. We therefore pass to the other type of analogy, analogy *unius ad alterum*, which is founded not upon diverse relations which each of the analogates bears to a third, but upon a relation which one of them bears to the other. And this type of analogy itself subdivides into two.

The former of these sub-types is that which is known as analogy of *attribution* or of *proportion*, analogy *unius ad alterum* in the strict sense. In this case the predicate belongs formally and properly to one of the analogates (which is thus not merely *an* analogate but is the *prime* analogate), and only relatively and derivatively to the other. Thus it is by an analogy of attribution or proportion that Mr. Jones and his complexion are both described as healthy; health is found formally and properly in Mr. Jones, and his complexion is described as healthy only because it bears a certain relation to his health, namely the relation of being a sign of it. In its theological application, where the analogates concerned are God and a creature, the relation upon which the analogy is based will be that of creative causality; creatures are related to God as his effects, by all those modes of participation by the creature in the perfection of its creator which are indicated, for example, by the Thomist Five Ways. Thus when we say that God and Mr. Jones are both good or that they are both beings, remembering that the content which the word "good" or "being" has for us is derived from our experience of the goodness and the being of creatures, we are, so far as analogy of attribution is concerned, saying no more than that God has goodness or being in whatever way is necessary if he is to be able to produce goodness and being in his creatures. This would not seem necessarily to indicate anything more than that the perfections which are found formally in various finite modes in creatures exist *virtually* in God, that is to say, that he is able to produce them in the creatures; it does not seem to necessitate that God possesses them formally himself. (In the case of Mr. Jones, of course, his complexion did indicate his formal possession of health, but there is, literally, all the difference in the world between the relation between two analogates in the finite realm and that between God and a creature.) Analogy of attribution certainly does not exclude the formal possession of the perfections by God, but it does not itself ascribe it to him. The mode in which the perfection which exists in the secondary analogate also exists in the prime analogate will depend on the relation between them; and if this relation is merely that the latter analogate is the *cause* of the former, the possession by the latter of a perfection that exists formally in the former will not, so far as the present mode of analogy is concerned, be necessarily anything more than a virtual one. Creatures are good (formally but finitely), God is the cause of them and of all that they have, therefore the word "good" applied to God need not mean any more than that he is able to produce goodness.[7] It is at this point that the second sub-type of analogy comes to the rescue.

This is analogy of proportionality, also called analogy *plurium ad plura*. In it there is a direct relation of the mode in which a perfection is participated to the being by which it is participated, independently of any relation to a prime analogate. (There may be a prime analogate, and indeed some would maintain that there must be,[8] but it does not come in at this stage.) A spurious, though sometimes useful, form of this type of analogy is *metaphor*, in which there is not a formal participation of the same characteristic in the different analogates but only a similarity of effects. Thus, to take a classic example, the lion is called the king of the beasts because he bears to savage animals a relation similar to that which a king bears to his subjects, but no one would assert that kingship is to be found formally in the lion. Again, God is described as being angry, because his relation to the punishments which he imposes is similar to that which an angry man has to the injuries which he inflicts, but no one (at least, no scholastic philosopher) would say that anger was to be found formally in God.[9] In the strict sense, an analogy of proportionality implies that the analogue under discussion is found formally in each of the analogates but in a mode that is determined by the nature of the analogate itself. Thus, assuming that life is an analogous and not a univocal concept, it is asserted that cabbages, elephants, men and God each possess life formally (that is each of them is, quite literally and unmetaphorically, *alive*), but that the cabbage possesses life in the mode proper to a cabbage, the elephant in that proper to an elephant, the man in that proper to a man, and finally God in that supreme, and by us unimaginable, mode proper to self-existent Being itself. This is commonly expressed in the following quasi-mathematical form, from which, in fact, the name "analogy of proportionality" is derived:[10]

$$\frac{\text{life of cabbage}}{\text{essence of cabbage}} = \frac{\text{life of elephant}}{\text{essence of elephant}}$$

$$= \frac{\text{life of man}}{\text{essence of man}} = \frac{\text{life of God}}{\text{essence of God}}$$

We must, however, beware of interpreting the equal sign too literally. For the point is not that the life of the cabbage is determined by the essence of the cabbage in the *same* way as that in which the life of the man is determined by the essence of the man, but that the way in which cabbage essence determines cabbage life is proper to cabbagehood, while the way in which the human essence determines human life is proper to manhood. But at this point various objections rapidly spring to the mind.

In the first place, it may be asked, has not the remark just made landed us in an infinite regress? We began by denying the univocity of the identity,

$$\text{life of cabbage} = \text{life of man,}$$

and substituted for it the proportionality:

$$\frac{\text{life of cabbage}}{\text{essence of cabbage}} = \frac{\text{life of man}}{\text{essence of man}}$$

But we now have denied that the equal sign in this latter equation really signifies equality and have substituted for it a proposition which, in quasi-mathematical form, can be written as follows:

$$\frac{\text{way in which life of cabbage is determined by essence of cabbage}}{\text{essence of cabbage}}$$

$$= \frac{\text{way in which life of man is determined by essence of man}}{\text{essence of man}}$$

And again we shall have to remember that the equal sign means not identity but similarity, and shall now have to write:

$$\frac{\text{way in which way-in-which-life-of-cabbage-is-determined-by-essence-of-cabbage is determined by essence of cabbage}}{\text{essence of cabbage}}$$

$$= \frac{\text{way in which way-in-which-life-of-man-is-determined-by-essence-of-man is determined by essence of man}}{\text{essence of man}}$$

and so *ad infinitum*.

To put this more briefly, if we write L for "life of" and E for "essence of," $c$ for "cabbage" and $m$ for "man," and use A/B to signify "determination of A by B," we began by denying $Lc = Lm$, and put in its place

$$Lc/Ec = Lm/Em;$$

then we said that what we really meant was

$$(Lc/Ec)/Ec = (Lm/Em)/Em;$$

then we found that for this we should have to substitute

$$[(Lc/Ec)/Ec]/Ec = [(Lm/Em)/Em]/Em.$$

The next stage will be

$$\{[(Lc/Ec)/Ec]/Ec\}/Ec = \{[(Lm/Em)/Em]/Em\}/Em,$$

and so we shall go on for ever, at each successive stage denying progressively more complicated relationships between cabbages and men, and never managing to assert a relationship which we shall not immediately have to deny. And at the end of it we shall have nothing but a series of negations:

$$Lc \neq Lm,$$
$$Lc/Ec \neq Lm/Em,$$
$$(Lc/Ec)/Ec \neq (Lm/Em)/Em,$$
$$[(Lc/Ec)/Ec]/Ec \neq [(Lm/Em)/Em]/Em, \qquad \text{etc.}$$

Our proportionality has completely collapsed, and all we are left with is the fact that cabbages have nothing in common with men except the fact that, for no valid reason, men have described them both as being alive. In fact, the introduction of analogy as a *via media* between univocity and equivocity has turned out to be nothing more than an imposing piece of mystification. This is the first objection of which we must take account; it is obviously a serious one. It strikes, not in particular at the analogical application of terms to God, but to analogical predication as such. I shall not attempt a full reply until I have stated another objection which is concerned with the specifically theological case, but I shall offer a few observations in passing.

First, then, we may remark that the objection, while on the surface plausible, has something of the appearance of a conjuring trick. It brings to mind two somewhat similar feats of philosophical legerdemain. The first is Lewis Carroll's *What the Tortoise said to Achilles*.[11] In this problem, which its originator did not perhaps intend to be taken as seriously as it really demands, Achilles maintained that, if two premisses A and B logically implied a conclusion Z, then anybody who saw this and also accepted A and B as true would have to accept Z as true also. The tortoise objected that this would only be the case if he accepted a further proposition C, namely that if A and B are true then Z must be true. Achilles was thus forced to modify his original assertion, so that it now took the form "Anyone who accepts A, B and C as true must accept Z as true also." But again the tortoise objected that this involved the acceptance of another proposition D, which was that, if A and B and C are all true, Z must be true as well. And so on for ever! This corresponds, of course, to the well-known fact that the principle of inference is incapable of formal symbolic statement within the logical calculus to which it applies.[12] A logical system cannot, as it were, operate under its own steam, without help from outside; we shall derive from this fact a pointer towards the solution of our present problem. The other puzzle to which I wish to refer is one which its originator took much more seriously: I mean Mr. F. H. Bradley's famous argument that relations are illusions.[13] It is, he urged, of the essence of a relation to unite terms, but how is each term united to the relation? It can only be by another relation, but if so, what unites the term to this? To make the first relation intelligible we have to presuppose an infinite sequence of relations antecedent to it, and none of these is yet intelligible. Hence, Mr. Bradley concluded, relations are mere illusion. Lord Russell has caustically remarked that if Bradley's argument were valid it would prove that chains are impossible—and yet they exist.[14] Dr. C. D. Broad has dealt with Bradley's problem in some detail. He takes as an instance of it the fact that A is father of B. "Here," he writes, "we have a perfectly intelligible statement, involving the non-formal[15] relation of *fatherhood*. At the next stage we get the fact that A is referent to *fatherhood*, and the fact that B is relatum to *fatherhood*. The 'relations' introduced at this stage are purely formal. At the next stage we get the fact that A is referent to *referent to*, that *fatherhood* is relatum to *referent to*, that *fatherhood* is referent to *referent to*, and that B is relatum to *referent to*. Thus no new 'relations' are introduced at this or any subsequent stage. The fact that at every stage after the first the relating relations are purely formal and are merely repeated shows that we are now embarked on the self-evidently impossible task of explaining, by means of particular relational judgments, that general relational form which is presupposed by all relational judgments whatever."[16] We might, in fact, say that, while it is of the essence of relations to unite terms, they are not themselves terms in this context (though, of course, in another context they may become terms, as when we pick out two relations, or a relation and a term, and ask what is the relation between them). Similarly, in the case of analogy of proper proportionality, we might reply to our objector that we are simply concerned with the fact that essences determine their qualities, and that the truth of this is not in the least affected by the fact that they can only do this if they also determine the way in which they determine their qualities, and the way in which they determine the way in which they determine their qualities, and so on to the crack of doom. *Ce n'est que le premier pas qui coûte.*

Such a reply would, I think, go a very long way, though I am doubtful whether it is altogether sufficient. For the fact remains that we have denied that our equal signs really stand for equality and we have not indicated anything definite that they do stand for. Can we in some way re-establish this bond that we have broken? Clearly we cannot by analogy of proportionality, but I shall suggest that we can by analogy of attribution, and that the two types of analogy, while either in separation is insufficient, can in combination do what is required.[17] But this is an anticipation. I will pass on now to consider the second objection, which is specially concerned with analogical discourse about God.

III

Let us therefore see what happens when we attribute life both to a creature and to God; any other perfection which can be formally predicated of God would, of course, do as well. Analogy of proportionality asserts:

$$\frac{\text{life of man}}{\text{essence of man}} = \frac{\text{life of God}}{\text{essence of God}}$$

Now, the objector urges, even if the first objection has been successfully overcome, so that we have no longer to bother about the fact that the equal sign does not indicate an exact identity of relationship, our formula will not in fact tell us in what sense life is to be predicated of God. For the essence of God is as little known to us as is his life; indeed his life is, formally considered, identical with it. Our equation has therefore two unknowns and cannot be solved. Nor can we get out of our difficulty by comparing essence with existence and saying that the essence of a being will correspond to, and be determined by, the act in virtue of which it exists:

$$\frac{\text{essence of man}}{\text{existential act of man}} = \frac{\text{essence of God}}{\text{existential act of God}}$$

Once again, both the terms on the right-hand side are unknown. Sheer agnosticism seems to be the outcome. What reply can we make?

Some scholastic philosophers, of whom Garrigou-Lagrange is one, claim to answer this objection, while remaining in the realm of analogy of proportionality, by denying that there are two unknown terms on the right-hand side. This last-mentioned writer, for example, taking the analogy

$$\frac{\text{creature}}{\text{its being}} = \frac{\text{first cause}}{\text{its being}}$$

asserts that only the fourth term is in fact unknown. "We have," he says, "(1) *the very confused concept of being in general,* which a child possesses from the moment of its first intellectual knowledge, (2) *the concept of finite being,* of which we know positively the finite mode and which is nothing else than the essence of the things that we see, stones, plants, animals, etc., (3) *the concept of analogous being,* imperfectly abstracted from the finite mode . . . ; it is a precision of the first very confused concept possessed by the child, and the metaphysician acquires it by recognizing that the formal notion of being does not in itself include the finite mode which accompanies it in the creature, (4) *the concept of the divine being,* the cause of created beings. These latter," he continues, "not having in their essence the reason of their existence, require a cause which exists of itself. In the concept of the divine being, the divine mode is expressed only in a negative and relative way, e.g. as non-finite or as supreme being. What is positive in this analogical knowledge of God is what God has that is proportionally common to him and the creature."[18] Again, he writes, "*being* designates *that which* has relation to existence; this relation is implied in the very nature of that which exists and it is essentially varied according as it is necessary or contingent. The created essence in its inmost entity is altogether relative to its contingent existence, which it can lose; the uncreated essence is conceived only relatively to that necessary existence with which it is identified. . . . Analogous perfections are thus not pure relations. They are perfections which imply in the creature a composition of two correlative elements, potentiality and act, but which in God are pure act. Our intelligence conceives that they are realized more fully according as they are purified of all potentiality; in God they exist therefore in the pure state. We thus see that there are not two unknowns in the proportionalities set up by theology."[19]

For this distinguished French Dominican, therefore, the third term in the formula is given us as that in which essence and existence are identical, and this gives us a limited and analogical, but nevertheless genuine, knowledge of the fourth term, while remaining within the realm of analogy of proportionality.[20] We can transfer the notion of any perfection from a finite being to God, remembering that the difference of mode is that which corresponds to the difference between a being whose essence involves merely a possibility of existence and one whose essence involves existence of necessity. Of course, we do not know positively what the mode of the perfection in God is; to demand that would be to demand a quidditative knowledge of the divine essence and to abolish analogy altogether in favour of univocity. We are given all that we have a right to ask for; the comparison of the finite and the infinite modes of perfection is based on a comparison of the relations to existence which are proper to finite essence and to the divine essence respectively.

Now all this seems very satisfactory so far as it goes, but does it go far enough? Is it sufficient simply to base the comparison of the finite and infinite modes of a perfection upon a comparison of the finite and infinite modes of the essence-existence relation, without bringing in an explicit reference to the concrete relation which the creature has to God? There are indeed traces in Garrigou-Lagrange's own discussion of an awareness of the need of this further step; the very form in which he writes the formula last quoted suggests this. For he does not describe the finite being as a being in whom essence does not necessarily involve existence, but as a "creature"; and he does not describe God as a being whose essence necessarily involves existence, but as the "first cause." "In these equations," he writes, "two created terms are known directly, one uncreated term is known indirectly *by way of causality* and we infer the fourth term which is known indirectly in a *positive* manner as regards what is analogically common with creatures and in a *negative* and relative manner as regards its proper divine mode."[21] And the first cause and the creature are directly related by the relation of creation, which thus, as it were, cuts horizontally across the analogy of proportionality with an analogy of attribution.[22] The equal sign does not, as we have seen earlier, express a mathematical identity, but, on the other hand, the two sides of the formula are not left in complete separation. They are bound together by an analogy of attribution *unius ad alterum*, of the creature to God in the case which we have just been considering. In the cases considered earlier, where the two sides of the formula both refer to finite beings, the linking analogy is an analogy *duorum ad tertium*, which holds in view of the fact that each of the analogates is in an analogy of attribution *unius ad alterum*, of itself to God. The figure below may help to make this plain.[23]

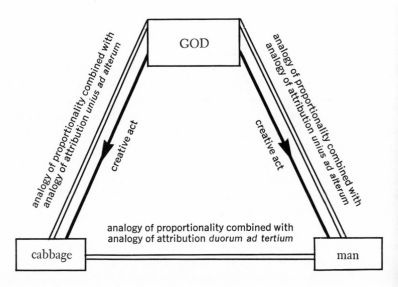

The conclusion would thus seem to be that, in order to make the doctrine of analogy really satisfactory, we must see the analogical relation between God and the world as combining in a tightly interlocked union both analogy of attribution and analogy of proportionality. Without analogy of proportionality it is very doubtful whether the attributes which we predicate of God can be ascribed to him in more than a merely virtual sense; without analogy of attribution it hardly seems possible to avoid agnosticism. Which of the two forms of analogy is prior to the other has been, and still is, a hotly debated question among scholastic philosophers. Sylvester of Ferrara, in his great commentary on the *Summa contra Gentiles*, asserted the primacy of attribution and alleged that in this he was expressing the true thought of St. Thomas,[24] but the "prince of commentators" Cajetan, in his luminous little treatise *De Nominum Analogia*, asserted that only proportionality was analogy in the true and strict sense[25] and the majority of Thomists have followed him, down to Garrigou-Lagrange,[26] Penido,[27] and Maritain[28] at the present day, though Descoqs is a notable exception.[29]

IV

It is perhaps necessary at this point to make a clearer distinction than has yet been made in this discussion between the three orders of thought—the logical, the epistemological, and the ontological[30]—to which the notion of analogy applies. However anxious we are to maintain the realist position that words and concepts are both about things, the fact remains that words, concepts and things are not identical and that at some point the distinction must be made. (Cajetan himself remarks that for the logician analogy of attribution is merely a kind of equivocity, while for the philosopher it is a kind of analogy.[31]) And it is vital to the whole position which I have been maintaining to insist that in natural theology we are not merely instituting comparisons between two orders of concepts but considering created and uncreated being as the former actually exists in dependence on the latter. That is to say, we are not merely concerned with the question "How can an infinite, necessary and immutable Being be described in terms that are derived from the finite, contingent and mutable world?" but with a question that is anterior to this and without which this cannot be properly discussed at all, namely "How is the possibility of our applying to the infinite Being terms that are derived from the finite order conditioned by the fact that the finite order is dependent for its very existence on the fiat of the infinite and self-existent Being?" In the order of predication or of conceptualization it may well be the case that the two types of analogy are disconnected, that proportionality is prior to attribution, or that, as John of St. Thomas suggests,[32] the analogy of attribution between God and the creature is only virtual; but when we are concerned with the affirmation of God as the supreme existent, whose existence can nevertheless only be affirmed by us as a result of our prior recognition of the existence of finite existents, it would seem that our statements about God can hardly exclude all reference to the relation in which he stands to his creatures in existential fact.[33] M. Gilson has developed this line of thought in a most stimulating way in one of the sections which, in accordance with his enhanced recognition of the existentialism of St. Thomas, he has added to the revised edition of his book *Le Thomisme*.[34] He begins by commenting on the contrast between the paucity and restraint of St. Thomas's own treatment of the subject and the immense volume of the discussions that it has provoked among his disciples. He suggests that this is largely due to "a secret desire to rescue from a too glaring lowliness the knowledge of God which St. Thomas Aquinas allows us to have. People thus come," he says, "step by step to speak of analogy as a source of almost positive knowledge which would allow us to conceive more or less confusedly the essence of God. But perhaps," he continues, "it is not necessary to force the Thomist texts in order to obtain from this notion the services desired. It is enough to interpret them, as St. Thomas does himself, not in the order of the concept but in that of the judgment."[35] For M. Gilson, then, the purpose of the doctrine of analogy is not to allow us to form concepts of the divine essence, but to allow us to affirm the divine existence; not to compare God's features with those of finite beings, but to allow us to assert that he exists when we can identify him only by describing him in terms derived from the finite order. As we have seen,[36] the great problem for a radically transcendent theism is how to keep God, as it were, from slipping out of our grasp at the moment in which we affirm his existence. The world requires as its cause a being totally transcending it in every respect; but how can we even affirm the existence of such a being, if our experience of the world gives us no words by which to define him? There is no solution, says Gilson, in terms of essences and concepts. Referring to the perennial controversy between those who stress the element of agnosticism in St. Thomas's theology and those who insist in contrast on the positive value which it guarantees to our knowledge of God, he writes as follows: "On the level of the concept there is no middle way between the univocal and the equivocal. At that point the two interpretations are irreconcilable, but they would surely cease to be so if we transferred them to the level of the judgment. We must observe, in fact, that in the case of God, every judgment, even if it has the appearance of a judgment of attribution, is in reality a judgment of existence. When we speak, with reference to him, of essence or substance or goodness or wisdom, we are doing nothing more than repeating about him: he is *esse*. That is why his name *par excellence* is *Qui est*. If then we take the divine attributes one by one and ask whether each of them is to be found in God, we must reply that it is not there, at least as such and as a distinct reality, and since we can in no way conceive an essence which is nothing but an act of existing, we cannot in any way conceive what God is, even with the help of such attributes. . . . On the other hand," he adds, "St. Thomas undoubtedly does allow us a certain knowledge of God, [and] unless we are to admit that St. Thomas has grossly contradicted himself, we must suppose that the knowledge of God which he grants us does not in any way bear upon his essence.[37] . . . Every effect of God is analogous to its cause. The concept which we form of this effect can in no case be transformed for us into the concept of God which we lack, but we can attribute to God, by our affirmative judgment, the name that denotes the perfection corresponding to this effect. To proceed in this way is not to posit God as similar to the creature, it is to ground oneself on the certitude that, since every effect resembles its cause, the creature from which we start certainly resembles God (*S.c.G.*, I, xxix)."[38]

This point is so important that I will try to make it in a slightly different way. So long as we are talking about finite beings we can make statements about their natures or essences without any assertion about their existence. I can say that a unicorn has a horn on its nose and that a rhinoceros has a horn on its nose without suggesting that any animals with horns on their noses exist; that rhinoceroses do exist and that unicorns do not is a purely empirical fact. But I cannot say that God is good without asserting the existence of a good being; for since God is by definition self-existent being, to affirm that God is good is to speak of self-existent goodness, that is to say of goodness that cannot but exist.[39] Again, in talking about finite beings, we can ascribe to them properties not necessarily included in their essences. If I say that the Cambridge buses are red, I am not asserting that redness is necessarily inherent in the nature of a Cambridge bus; in fact there was a time when the Cambridge buses were green. When, however, I say that God is good or wise or just, I am inevitably asserting that goodness, wisdom and justice are inherent in the nature of God, for in God there are no accidents, no qualities that are not included in his essence.[40] It follows that all our statements about God have a directly existential reference, such as is possessed by none of our statements about finite beings except those in which existence is explicitly asserted. The only way in which I can assert that beings with horns on their noses exist is by affirming existence either of such beings in general or of some such being (for example, a unicorn or a rhinoceros) in particular; but I can assert that a good being exists simply by affirming that God is good. Since in God essence and existence are identical, any assertion about God's essence is at the same time an assertion about existence; anything which is affirmed to be included in God's nature is at the same time affirmed to exist, and indeed to be self-existent.

It is then, I suggest, in virtue of this inherently existential element in all our affirmations about God that the possibility of analogical knowledge of God and of analogical discourse about him can be maintained. If it were possible to make a statement about God that bore exclusively on the essential or conceptual order, that statement would collapse into sheer equivocity and agnosticism, for no concept of the essence of God can be formed by a finite mind.[41] Since, however, God's essence necessarily involves his existence, no statement about him can remain in the essential or conceptual order; it passes over immediately into the order of existence and the judgment. What begins as an attempt to conceive God's goodness—an attempt which is doomed to failure—issues in an affirmation that self-existent goodness exists; but even this last statement needs careful interpretation if it is not to be taken as implying that we form a concept of "self-existent goodness."[42] It would perhaps be better to say that goodness exists self-existingly, for then the fundamental dependence of analogical predication upon the metaphysical analogy of being is made clear. We can then see how we must interpret the formula

$$\frac{\text{goodness of finite being}}{\text{finite being}} = \frac{\text{goodness of God}}{\text{God}}$$

as holding not merely in the order of essence but in that of existence, as expressing not a comparison of concepts but an existential judgment. The second term on the left-hand side of our formula ("finite being") expresses precisely that contingency of existence which arises from the fact that in finite beings essence and existence are really distinct; the second term on the right-hand side ("God") expresses that necessity of existence which arises from the fact that in God essence and existence are really identical. And the two sides of the formula are held together by that analogy of attribution which asserts, not merely in the conceptual but in the existential order, that finite being can exist only in dependence upon God. The goodness of God is thus declared to be self-existent goodness, and, as such, identical not merely with God's essence but with the act by which God exists. Analogy does not enable us to *conceive* God's goodness as identical with his essence but to *affirm* it as identical with his existence. Hence all our assertions about God are grossly inadequate in so far as they apply concepts to him, but they are thoroughly adequate in so far as they affirm perfections of him. Here the relevance of the distinction between the *perfectio significata* and the *modus significandi* can be seen at the full, as can also the reconciliation of the apparent contradition between St. Thomas's "agnosticism" and his conviction that we can make genuine assertions about God. The names which we apply to God, he says, "designate the divine substance and are predicated of God substantially, but they fall short of representing him."[43] We cannot, in short, know God's essence by forming a concept of it, but we can know it analogically in our concepts of finite beings. I shall conclude at this point this already over-long discussion of the scholastic doctrine of analogy, and in doing so I will remind the reader again that its purpose has been, not to discover whether it is possible intelligibly to talk about God, but to explain how it is that we have been able to do so and to analyse what it is that we have in fact been doing. It is too much to hope that the explanation has been entirely adequate; it is perhaps sufficient if it has revealed some intelligibility in what by its very nature must be a mystery.[44]

NOTES

1. *Categories*, I. It is true that in this text Aristotle mentions only univocity and equivocity, though elsewhere he makes considerable use of the notion of analogy. Cajetan remarks *à propos* of this text that logicians (in contrast to philosophers) call analogy of attribution equivocation (*De Nom. Anal.*, cap. ii, no. 19).

2. It should be noted that they are called transcendentals because they transcend the categories. This is not the meaning which the word "transcendent" has when applied to God to indicate that he transcends the realm of finite being. Nor is it the meaning that "transcendental" has for Kant: "I apply," he says, "the term *transcendental* to all knowledge which is not so much occupied with objects as with the mode of our cognition of these objects, so far as this mode of cognition is possible *a priori*" (*Critique of Pure Reason*, Introduction, ch. vii, trans. Meiklejohn). Cf. Garrigou-Lagrange, *Dieu*, p. 200, *n.* 1.

3. R. G. Collingwood surprisingly asserts that for the traditional metaphysics being is the *summum genus* of which the ten Categories are species; in consequence he has little difficulty in arguing that there cannot be a science of pure being (*Essay in Metaphysics*, pp. 9, 10 f). What Aristotle actually thought will be found in *Met.* B., 998b.

4. This is the Thomist definition of analogical discourse. For the Suarezians, however, with their conceptualist bias and the consequent sharp line drawn between thought and the extra-mental thing, an analogical concept applies to different beings in ways *simpliciter eadem et diversa secundum quid*.

5. *Hoc modo aliqua dicuntur de Deo et creaturis analogice, et non aequivoce pure neque univoce* (*S. Theol.*, I, xiii, 5c). We may compare the well-known statement of the Fourth Lateran Council that "between the creator and the creature no likeness can be discerned without a greater unlikeness having to be discerned as well" (*inter creatorem et creaturam non potest tanta similitudo notari quin inter eos major sit dissimilitudo notanda*, cap. ii; Denzinger-Bannwart, *Enchiridion*, 11th ed., no. 432). It is easy to see what this means, but it would be difficult to defend it as a precise philosophical statement, as it appears to assume

that likeness and unlikeness are two different species of a measurable genus. One can validly say that two objects are less alike in one respect than they are in another, but to say that they are less alike in one respect than they are *unlike* in another does not seem to be strictly intelligible.

6. *S. Theol.*, I, xiii, 5c; *S.c.G.*, I, xxxiv.

7. It is important to observe that we are not arguing that the formal possession of goodness by creatures does not *prove* that goodness is formally in God; the argument is not here on the metaphysical but merely on the linguistic and logical plane. All that is asserted is that if the only analogy between God and creatures was analogy of attribution then the word "good" applied to God would not necessarily *mean* any more than that goodness was in God virtually. *In fact* the metaphysical relation of the world to God implies analogy of proportionality as well, and it is at this later stage that the formal attribution of goodness to God becomes clear.

8. Thus Garrigou-Lagrange writes: "It is not necessary here to mention the principal analogate in the definition of the others, but there nevertheless always is a prime analogate. In metaphorical analogy of proportionality, it is the one to which the name of analogue belongs in the strict sense. In strict analogy of proportionality, the principal analogate is that which is the higher cause of the others: the analogical similitude that exists in this latter case is always based on causality; it exists either between the cause and the effect or between the effects of the same cause" (*Dieu*, p. 532, *n.* 3). This last remark seems to imply the assertion that will be made later on: that in its theological application analogy of proportionality needs to be reinforced by analogy of attribution; Garrigou-Lagrange does not, however, explicitly make the assertion. We may add here, as a point of terminology, that the word "analogue" (*analogum*) refers to the common predicate (or common quality or transcendental signified by it), while the word "analogate" (*analogatum*) refers to the various subjects to which it is attributed, or to its diverse modes in them. An alternative nomenclature refers to the analogue as *analogum analogans* and the analogate as *analogum analogatum*.

9. A further example of purely metaphorical proportionality is provided by Canning's celebrated epigram:

"Pitt is to Addington
As London is to Paddington."

10. "Let magnitudes which have the same proportion ($\lambda\acute{o}\gamma o\varsigma$) be called proportional ($\grave{\alpha}\nu\acute{\alpha}\lambda o\gamma o\nu$)" (Euclid V, Def. 6). For the sake of clarity it may be useful to indicate by a diagram the classification of analogy which I have adopted:

I. Analogy *duorum ad tertium.*
II. Analogy *unius ad alterum.*

    (i)  Analogy of attribution or proportion, strictly *unius ad alterum.*

   (ii)  Analogy of proportionality, *plurium ad plura*
      (*a*)  in loose sense (metaphor)
      (*b*)  in strict sense.

Slightly different classifications may be found in Garrigou-Lagrange, *Dieu*, p. 351; Maquart, *Elem. Phil.*, III, ii, p. 36.

   11.  *The Complete Works of Lewis Carroll*, pp. 1104 f.

   12.  Cf. B. Russell, *The Principles of Mathematics*, pp. 16, 35, where explicit reference is made to Lewis Carroll's puzzle.

   13.  *Appearance and Reality*, I, ch. iii.

   14.  *Outline of Philosophy*, p. 263.

   15.  "Formal," for Broad and all the modern logicians, means "purely logical," "having no reference to particular concrete individual entities," This is very different from the scholastic use of the word.

   16.  *Examination of McTaggart's Philosophy*, I, p. 86.

   17.  It may be interesting to see how Dr. A. M. Farrer deals with this difficulty. For him "this proportionality claims to hold between four terms, and not two relations. We are not saying," he continues, " 'The way in which the divine intelligence is related to the divine existence resembles the way in which the creaturely intelligence is related to the creaturely existence' for that is exactly what we have to deny. The way in which the several aspects of the divine being (e.g. intelligence) have their synthesis into one, itself differs from the way in which the several aspects of the creaturely being have their synthesis into one, *as* the divine being itself differs from the creaturely. What we are saying is completely different, viz. 'Divine intelligence is appropriate to divine existence as creaturely to creaturely' " (*Finite and Infinite*, p. 53, italics in original).

Dr. Farrer's first point seems to me to be valuable, at least as denying *equality* of relations; in this respect the older mathematical notation for proportionality, $a : b :: c : d$, might be less misleading than the more modern $\frac{a}{b} = \frac{c}{d}$. But I do not think any scholastic would deny that proportionality was *some* sort of relation between two relations or would reduce it simply to a polyadic relation uniting four terms. Dr. Farrer himself in the quotation above seems, by italicizing the word "*as*," to admit the equal sign at a subsequent stage and, while denying

$$\frac{\text{divine intelligence}}{\text{divine existence}} = \frac{\text{human intelligence}}{\text{human existence}},$$

to be asserting

$$\frac{\text{synthesis of aspects in God}}{\text{being of God}} = \frac{\text{synthesis of aspects in creature}}{\text{being of creature}}$$

but I cannot think that this was his intention. He has previously said that the formula "presupposes that intelligence can be attributed to God, and declares how it is to be understood when it is attributed to him and not to the creature, viz. as differing from its creaturely mode with a difference analogous to that by which the divine existence differs from the creaturely. And so it presupposes also the 'proportion' between the two 'existences.'" He goes on to say: "Proportion logically underlies proportionality, but this need not mean that we originally entertain the notion of the proportion 'divine existence/creaturely existence except as the foundation for a proportionality; the two are distinguished by philosophical analysis only." The proportion now mentioned is, it will be noticed, not either of the proportions that form the two sides of the proportionality, but the proportion between a term on one side and a term on the other. This seems to be in line with my assertion that, in the relation of God to creatures, analogy of proportionality and of attribution (proportion) are interlocked. Dr. Farrer continues: "The natural use of the proportion is inseparable from that of the proportionality, as the apprehension of the very fact of the divine being is inseparable from some apprehension of its mode."

18. *Dieu*, p. 541.

19. Ibid., p. 542.

20. Penido's answer to the objection (*Rôle de l'Analogie*, pp. 136 f.) rests upon his assertion previously noticed (p. 96, *n*. 1, *supra*) that no use of analogy is necessary in the mere demonstration of the *existence* of God. Thus, in the proportionality,

$$\frac{\text{essence of creature}}{\text{existential act of creature}} = \frac{\text{essence of God}}{\text{existential act of God}},$$

the fourth term is not unknown; it is already given to us as self-existence, *ipsum esse subsistens*, existence not really distinct from essence. Thus, whereas for Garrigou-Lagrange the *third* term is given to us *in* and *through* the analogy, for Penido the *fourth* term is given to us *prior to* the analogy; thus he writes, "L'analogie . . . n'apparait pas *explicitement* au début de notre marche vers Dieu, elle ne s'occupe pas de la question 'an sit,' elle n'entre en jeu que lorsqu'il s'agit du 'quomodo sit' " (*Rôle*, p. 138). I cannot help feeling that at this point Penido is nearer the truth.

21. *Dieu*, p. 543 (first set of italics mine).

22. Garrigou-Lagrange himself writes: "If the analogy of being is formally an analogy of proportionality it is virtually an analogy of attribution, in the sense that if, *per impossibile*, being did not belong intrinsically to the creature it could still be extrinsically attributed to it, in so far as the creature is an effect of the prime Being" (*Dieu*, p. 541, note). It is the word "virtually" in this passage from which I am disposed to dissent. Penido lays great stress upon the "mixed" nature of the analogy between God and the world (*Rôle de l'Analogie*, p. 134 *et al.*).

23. It should here be noted that analogy *duorum ad tertium* is itself an instance of analogy of attribution.

24. *Comm. in S.c.G.*, I, xxxiv. In this place in *S.c.G.*, and in *S. Theol.*, I, xiii, 5c, where (with purely verbal differences) he divides analogy into (*a*) *duorum ad tertium,* and (*b*) *unius ad alterum* and asserts that only the latter of these applies when creatures are compared with God, St. Thomas certainly seems to hold this view. However, in *De Veritate*, ii, 11, he writes: "There are two kinds of proportional association and so there are two kinds of community by analogy. For there is a certain association between things which have a proportion between them, because there is a determinate distance or other relation between them, such as 2 has to 1 because it is its double, and there is another association when two things are compared with each other between which there is no proportion but rather a likeness of two proportions to each other, as when 6 associated with 4 because 6 is the double of 3 and 4 is the double of 2. The former is an association of proportion, the latter of proportionality. So by the former mode of association we find something analogously said of two things of which one has a relation to the other, as substance and accident are both called beings because of the relation between them. . . . But sometimes something is said analogically in the latter mode of association, as bodily sight and understanding are both given the name of sight, because as sight is to the eye so is understanding to the mind. Therefore because in things said analogically in the former mode there must be some determinate relation between the things which have something in common analogically, it is impossible for anything to be said in this mode of God and a creature. But in the other mode of analogy no determinate relation holds between the things which have something in common analogically, and so in this mode nothing prevents a name from being analogically spoken of God and a creature. Nevertheless this can happen in two ways: [metaphorically and strictly]." We may note: (i) that the passages can be reconciled if we take proportion (attribution) and proportionality as a subdivision of analogy *unius ad alterum* (as in *n.* 2 on p. 104), and see the passage in *De Ver.* as defining precisely the way in which this type of analogy can validly be given a theological use, (ii) that the rejection of proportion in *De Ver.* is made only on the assumption that proportion and proportionality are mutually exclusive. It would be consistent with the passage in question to hold that, whereas we should have to reject proportion if proportion and proportionality were taken as being mutually exclusive, nevertheless proportionality needs to be combined with proportion (or even to be subordinated to it) if the two are taken as mutually consistent. It must, of course, be admitted that St. Thomas does not actually assert this, and it is in any case possible that he changed his mind when he came to write the *Summae.* Cf. the quotation in the next note from the Commentary on the Sentences, which is a still earlier work than the *De Veritate.*

We may add that Suarez and his followers strongly hold to the primacy of attribution, but in their case the matter is complicated by the conceptualist bias of Suarezian epistemology.

25. *De Nom. Anal.*, cap iii, no. 23. He says that the name of analogy is given only improperly (*abusive*) to that "analogy of inequality" (not mentioned in my discussion) in which the analogue is found in the various analogates in different degrees but in the same precise sense in all, and which is therefore only a form of univocity. St. Thomas makes this threefold distinction in his Commentary on the Sentences of Peter Lombard: "Aliquid dicitur secundum analogiam tripliciter: vel *secundum intentionem* et non secundum esse [*analogy of attribution*], et hoc est quando una intentio refertur ad plura per prius et posterius quae tamen non habet esse nisi in uno . . . ; vel *secundum esse* et non secundum intentionem [*analogy of inequality*]et hoc contingit quando plura parificantur in intentione alicujus communis, sed illud commune non habet esse unius rationis in omnibus . . . ; vel *secundum intentionem et secundum esse* [*analogy of proportionality*], et hoc est quando neque parificantur in intentione communi neque in esse" (*In I Sent.*, d. 19, q. 5 a. 2 *ad* 1).

26. *Dieu*, pp. 530 f.

27. *Le Rôle de l'Analogie en Théol. dogm.*, pp. 46, 145.

28. *Distinguer pour unir*, app. II (not in E.T.). He stresses "the profound remark of John of St. Thomas that, in mixed cases (where analogy of attribution and of proportionality are joined together), the analogy of attribution is only virtual. When from the existence of created being we conclude that of its uncreated Cause, we are in fact (even if unconsciously) using analogy of strict proportionality, for this reasoning implies that the notion of *cause* is itself analogous with strict proportionality and also that the uncreated Being with which it ends and the created being from which it begins are both called by the same name 'being,' not only because the former is the cause of the latter but because what the concept of being signifies is found in both of them according to a similitude of proportions. From the fact that the relation of causality gives rise to an analogy of attribution between the effect and the cause, it does not follow that we formally use analogy of attribution whenever we follow the way of causality to establish the 'existence of the source' of the created perfections" (p. 826).

29. See his *Praelectiones Theologiae Naturalis*, II, pp. 795 f., for his controversy on this point with Penido. Penido himself writes very reasonably: "From a certain point of view, it is perfectly true to say that proportionality is not primary, since it presupposes the causality which gives us the third term of all our proportions. Without the analogy of attribution which establishes the existence of a source, it is clear that proportionality would have no real support; we should remain enclosed in possibilities and conditional propositions. But is such an answer 'equivalent to putting all proportionality out of service'? By no means. It is simply equivalent to putting proportionality in its true place, which is the centre. As our opponent admits, causality demonstrates the *existence* of an X. But what is its *nature*? This is the proper domain of proportionality."

(*Rôle de l'Analogie*, p. 146. Note that what Penido here calls the *third* term is what he has previously called the *fourth*, i.e. the term which stands for the divine *existence*. He is here thinking of the proportion in the form:

$$\frac{\text{finite existence}}{\text{finite essence}} = \frac{\text{divine existence}}{\text{divine essence}}).$$

For my own reflections see the text.

30. See p. 96 *supra*.

31. *De Nom. Anal.*, cap. ii, no. 19, 20.

32. *Cursus Phil.*, q. 14, a. 3. (Cf. Garrigou-Lagrange, *Dieu*, p. 541 *n*.)

33. Thus St. Thomas writes: "We cannot grasp what God is, but only what he is not *and how other things are related to him*" (*Non enim de Deo capere possumus quid est, sed quid non est, et qualiter alia se habeant ad ipsum* (*S.c.G.*, I, xxx.).)

34. Part I, ch. v, sec. ii, "La connaissance de Dieu par voie d'analogie."

35. *Le Thomisme*, 5ᵐᵉ éd., p. 153.

36. See ch. iv *supra*.

37. He is referring, of course, to the knowledge of God that we can have by our natural powers and in this life. But even in the Beatific Vision, although the divine essence is known by the blessed, it is seen *totum sed non totaliter*.

38. Op. cit., pp. 155 f.

39. I am assuming here, of course, that God has been already shown to exist. Until that has been done, to assert that God is good does not ascribe to goodness existence *ut exercita*, but only *ut signata*; to hold otherwise would be to accept the ontological argument.

40. The apparent exceptions to this statement, arising from God's action in the finite realm, are discussed elsewhere in this book. (Ch. vi *infra*.)

41. On this ground one can, I think, justify Sertillanges' description of Thomism as "an agnosticism of definition" (*Le Christianisme et les Philosophies*, I, p. 270), for definition is concerned with the essence and the concept. One could not validly describe Thomism as "an agnosticism of the judgment." It is important to grasp that, whereas in the case of analogy between finite beings, the doctrine of analogy has merely to grapple with the distinction between the *perfectio significata* and the *modus significandi*, in the case of analogy between a finite being and God it has to grapple with the far greater difficulty of the gulf that separates the finite creature from the infinite Creator.

42. The tendency of the human mind to take refuge in concepts is as ineradicable as its tendency to turn to sensible images: *convertit se ad phantasmata*, indeed, but also *ad conceptus!* It is always trying to conceptualize existence instead of affirming it.

43. *Nomina significant substantiam divinam et praedicantur de Deo*

*substantialiter sed deficiunt a repraesentatione ipsius* (*S. Theol.*, I, xiii, 2*c*).

44. I have received much help in writing this chapter from an article on "God and Analogy," by Fr. Columba Ryan, O.P., in *Blackfriars*, April 1944.

# 10. MEANING AND ENCOUNTER

## Martin Buber

*Martin Buber (1878-1965) is an eminent Jewish thinker. I and Thou and other of his writings have had a profound influence on contemporary theological and philosophical thought.*

The religious essence in every religion can be found in its highest certainty. That is the certainty that the meaning of existence is open and accessible in the actual lived concrete, not above the struggle with reality but in it.

That meaning is open and accessible in the actual lived concrete does not mean it is to be won and possessed through any type of analytical or synthetic investigation or through any type of reflection upon the lived concrete. Meaning is to be experienced in living action and suffering itself, in the unreduced immediacy of the moment. Of course, he who aims at the experiencing of experience will necessarily miss the meaning, for he destroys the spontaneity of the mystery. Only he reaches the meaning who stands firm, without holding back or reservation, before the whole might of reality and answers it in a living way. He is ready to confirm with his life the meaning which he has attained.

Every religious utterance is a vain attempt to do justice to the meaning which has been attained. All religious expression is only an intimation of its attainment. The reply of the people of Israel on Sinai, "We will do it, we will hear it," expresses the decisive with naïve and unsurpassable pregnancy. The meaning is found through the engagement of one's own person; it only reveals itself as one takes part in its revelation.

## 6.

All religious reality begins with what Biblical religion calls the "fear of God." It comes when our existence between birth and death becomes incomprehensible and uncanny, when all security is shattered through the mystery. This is not the relative mystery of that which is inaccessible only to the present state of human knowledge and is hence in principle discoverable. It is the essential mystery, the inscrutableness of which belongs to its very nature; it is the unknowable. Through this dark gate (which is only a gate and not, as some theologians believe, a dwelling) the believing man steps forth into the everyday which is henceforth hallowed as the place in which he has to live with the mystery. He steps forth directed and assigned to the concrete, contextual situations of his existence. That he henceforth accepts the situation as given him by the Giver is what Biblical religion calls the "fear of God."

An important philosopher of our day, Whitehead, asks how the Old Testament saying that the fear of God is the beginning of wisdom is to be reconciled with the New Testament saying that God is love. Whitehead has not fully grasped the meaning of the word "beginning." He who begins with the love of God without having previously experienced the fear of God, loves an idol which he himself has made, a god whom it is easy enough to love. He does not love the real God who is, to begin with, dreadful and incomprehensible. Consequently, if he then perceives, as Job and Ivan Karamazov perceive, that God is dreadful and incomprehensible, he is terrified. He despairs of God and the world if God does not take pity on him, as He did on Job, and bring him to love Him Himself. This is presumably what Whitehead meant when he said that religion is the passage from God the void to God the enemy and from Him to God the companion. That the believing man who goes through the gate of dread is directed to the concrete contextual situations of his existence means just this: that he endures in the face of God the reality of lived life, dreadful and incomprehensible though it be. He loves it in the love of God, whom he has learned to love.

For this reason, every genuine religious expression has an open or a hidden personal character, for it is spoken out of a concrete situation in which the person takes part as a person. This is true also in those instances where, out of a noble modesty, the word "I" is in principle avoided. Confucius, who spoke of himself almost as unwillingly as of God, once said: "I do not murmur against God, and I bear no ill will toward men. I search here below, but I penetrate above. He who knows me is God." Religious expression is bound to the concrete situation.

That one accepts the concrete situation as given to him does not, in any way, mean that he must be ready to accept that which meets him as "God-given" in its pure factuality. He may, rather, declare the extremest enmity toward this happening and treat its "givenness" as only intended to draw forth his own opposing force. But he will not remove himself from the concrete situation as it actually is; he will, instead, enter into it, even if in the form of fighting against it. Whether field of work or field of battle, he accepts the place in which he is placed. He knows no floating of the spirit above concrete reality; to him even the sublimest spirituality is an illusion if it is not bound to the situation. Only the spirit which is bound to the situation is prized by him as bound to the *Pneuma*, the spirit of God. . . .

9.

The religious reality of the meeting with the Meeter, who shines through all forms and is Himself formless, knows no image of Him, nothing comprehensible as object. It knows only the presence of the Present One. Symbols of Him, whether images or ideas, always exist first when and insofar as Thou becomes He, and that means It. But the ground of human existence in which it gathers and becomes whole is also the deep abyss out of which images arise. Symbols of God come into being, some which allow themselves to be fixed in lasting visibility even in earthly material and some which tolerate no other sanctuary than that of the soul. Symbols supplement one another, they merge, they are set before the community of believers in plastic or theological forms. And God, so we may surmise, does not despise all these similarly and necessarily untrue images, but rather suffers that one look at Him through them. Yet they always quickly desire to be more than they are, more than signs and pointers toward Him. It finally happens ever again that they swell themselves up and obstruct the way to Him, and He removes Himself from them. Then comes round the hour of the philosopher, who rejects both the image and the God which it symbolizes and opposes to it the pure idea, which he even at times understands as the negation of all metaphysical ideas. This critical "atheism" (*Atheoi* is the name which the Greeks gave to those who denied the traditional gods) is the prayer which is spoken in the third person in the form of speech about an idea. It is the prayer of the philosopher to the again unknown God. It is well suited to arouse religious men and to impel them to set forth right across the God-deprived reality to a new meeting. On their way they destroy the images which manifestly no longer do justice to God. The spirit moves them which moved the philosopher.

# 11. WHAT SENSE IS THERE

# TO SPEAK OF GOD?

## Rudolf Bultmann

*Rudolf Bultmann is Professor of New Testament, Emeritus, at the University of Marburg. He is author of many historical and theological studies of the New Testament, among which are* History and Eschatology *and* Theology of the New Testament. *His essay, "New Testament and Mythology," in which he presents his demythologizing thesis, has caused much ferment in contemporary theology and discussion of religious language. The translator of the following article is Professor Franklin H. Littell.*

I

If by speaking "of God" one understands to *talk* "*about* God," then such style of speaking has no sense at all; for in the moment when it happens the subject *(Gegenstand)*, God, has been lost. For when the thought "God" is thought at all, the implication is that God is the Almighty, i.e., the reality controlling everything. But this thought is not thought at all when I *talk about* God—that is, when I regard God as an object of thought toward which I can take a position; when I adopt a point of view from which I stand indifferent to the problem of God; when I suggest propositions concerning God's way and reality which I can reject or, if they are illuminating, accept. Anyone who is moved by proofs to have faith in God's *reality* can be certain that he has comprehended nothing of the reality *of God*; and whoever thinks to proclaim something of God's reality by means of evidences of God is debating about a mirage. For every "talking *about*" presupposes a standpoint apart from that which is being talked *about*. But there can be no stand-

Reprinted by permission of the author and the National Council of the Churches of Christ from *The Christian Scholar*, Volume 43 (1960), pp. 213-22.

point apart from God, and for that reason God does not permit himself to be spoken of in general propositions, universal truths which are true without reference to the concrete existential situation of the one who is talking.

It makes just as little sense to talk about God as it does to talk about *love*. In fact it is impossible to talk *about* love unless the talking about love be itself an act of love. All other talking about love is no speech of love, for it takes a position outside love. In short a psychology of love would be something quite different from speaking about love. Love is no given situation *(Gegebenheit) for the sake of which (woraufhin)* something done or something spoken, something not done or not spoken, is possible. It comes into being only as a condition of life itself; it only *is* in that I love or am loved, not as something secondary or derivative *(daneben oder dahinter)*. The same is true of the relationship of fatherhood and childhood. Viewed as a natural circumstance—so that one can talk about it— it does not reveal its unique nature at all, but is simply a single incident in a certain natural event which takes place between individuals of a species. Where the relationship really comes into being it cannot be seen from the outside, i.e., it isn't something *for the sake of which* for example a son accepts or even allows this or that, feels himself obligated to this or that. The moment the reflection "for the sake of which" enters the relationship, it is ruined. It only *is* at the point where the father actually lives as father, the son as son.

If this be true, then the possible *atheism* of a science could not assert itself for example in denying the reality of God: it would be just as atheistic if it asserted itself to be a science. For to speak in scientific propositions, i.e., in universal truths, about God means nothing else than to speak in propositions which have their precise meaning in that they are generally applicable, that they are detached from the concrete situation of the speaker. But exactly because the speaker does that, he puts himself outside the actual reality of his existence, therefore apart from God; and he speaks of something quite different from God.

To talk about God in this sense is however not only error and foolishness: it is *sin*. In his *Commentary on Genesis* Luther made the point very clearly that Adam's sin was not the deed itself with which he, eating of the forbidden fruit, broke the commandment.

Rather it was that he entertained the question: Should God have spoken?—the "disputare de deo" that sets itself apart from God and makes of God's claim on men a disputable issue. For if we want to avoid this conclusion and say, this dispute isn't necessarily so badly purposed after all; on the contrary it can be well meant; indeed it can arise from the quest for the true (*Wahrhaftigkeit*), the longing for God—then we show again that we have not comprehended the thought of God. This would be to fall into the old error and put forward the omnipotence of God and our being conditioned by it as a fact which is comprehended as a universal truth, something like the fact that every earthly object is determined by the law of causation. But it is precisely this that would not encompass what the determining of our existence by God means: for it means at the same time the *claim* of God upon us. Thus every standing apart from God is a denial of the claim of God upon us, that is, godlessness, sin. It could be otherwise only if a position of neutrality in relation to God were possible. But in this the thought of God would be sacrificed. Adam thought he could flee from God; but God's claims are not met by flight. Thus talking about God becomes sin.

And the fact remains: it is *sin* even when it comes from an honest search for God. And from this it is only too clear that when we are in such a situation in which we honestly must debate about God, then we are sinners and cannot do anything to get out of sin through our own power. For it wouldn't do us any good at all if, because of a right understanding of the thought of God, we should cease to argue about God (*disputare de deo*). For to speak otherwise of God, namely in God, is something we obviously cannot presume for ourselves. For as *our* effort it would again be sin, precisely because it would be *our* effort in which the thought of God's almighty sway would be sacrificed. To speak of God as being *in* God is obviously something which can only be given by God.

II

It is therefore evident that if one wishes to speak of God he must certainly *speak of himself*. But how? For if I speak of myself am I not speaking of a human being? And is there not likewise in the thought of God most assuredly the thought that *God is the "wholly*

*other*," over and beyond the human *(Aufhebung des Menschen)*?
Then do we not stand between two negative commandments, as
a result of which only the condition of resignation, of silence is
possible? On the one hand there is the definite insight: that every
speech in which we stand apart from our own specific existence is
no speaking of God; that it can only be a statement about our own
existence? On the other hand the equally definite insight: all speaking of ourselves can never be a speaking of God because the speaking
is only of men?

For in fact every confession of faith, every speaking of experience
and inner life, would be to speak of the human. And however enthusiastic the confessions of another might be, these would not help
me with my doubt unless I wish to deceive myself. Yes, even my
own experiences, if I would comfort myself with them or depend
upon them in the situation of doubt, would slip through my fingers.
For who assures me that each personal experience was not an illusion? that I should not move beyond it? that I do not now see reality
more clearly?

Or must we claim that we speak indeed *in* God when we bear witness, when our inner life speaks, when our experience expresses itself? Without doubt that can be the case. But in *that* very moment
when we set up our confession of faith, our inner life, our experiences, as that which brings us to trust God; or which we recommend
to others as that whereby they shall be certain of God—in *that* very
moment we are *talking about* our existence and have by that fact
separated ourselves from it. And that is also the case when we consciously seek after experiences for ourselves: we are then concerned
about ourselves rather than questing for God. When I seek after
myself—looking backwards or forwards—then I have at the same
time split my ego; and the ego which seeks after itself is my existential ego; the other ego after which I seek, which I assume as a
fact, is a mirage without existential reality. And the existential ego
which is concerned about itself, which quests, shows itself in this
very questioning, in this self-concern to be godless. If we wish to
speak of God, we obviously cannot begin as though we would speak
of our experiences and our inner life, which as soon as we objectify
them, have lost their existential character. And over against this
human being, seen as a condition, stands the word that *God is the
wholly other.*

But this word has its meaning only in its strong dependence upon the first word—that God is the reality which determines our existence. Cut loose from that, the phrase can only mean that God is some*thing* quite different from man, a metaphysical being, some kind of an ethereal world, some combination of secret powers, a creative original force (whereby the possible claim that this is meant only figuratively contradicts itself, because in this context God is in fact thought about quite naturalistically), or finally the *irrational*. A piety which wished to base itself on this idea of God would be flight from God, because in it man wishes in fact to escape from the reality in which he stands; he wishes indeed to run away from his concrete existence in which alone he can comprehend the reality of God. In this modern piety it becomes very clear how right Luther was in saying that the natural man flees from God and hates God. He seeks indeed, in wishing to escape from the reality of his concrete existence, to escape that in which alone he can find God. It is of course very understandable that the Pseudo-God of the creative or the irrational can bewitch the human yearning for God; for it promises man that he can get away from himself. But this promise is a misconception and a deception; for because a man wishes *thus* to get away from himself, he runs away from God—provided that God is the power shaping his concrete existence—and runs into his own arms, provided the thoughts of a creative original force and of the irrational are human abstractions and the experiences—in which a man puts his trust in such circumstances—are all too human events. The thought of the "wholly other" cannot be pursued in this way at all. Moreover of course that man does not in truth escape God at all; but while his attitude toward God is that of aversion, his existence is—insofar as it is determined by God—that of the sinner.

The thought of *God as the wholly other* cannot mean therefore, if the talk is to be of God the Almighty, that God were something apart from me which I must first seek, and that I must first flee from myself in order to find. That God, who determines my existence, at the same time is the wholly other, can only mean that he confronts me, the sinner, as *the* wholly other; that, insofar as I am *world*, he confronts me as *the* wholly other. To speak of God as the wholly other only makes sense when I have seen that the actual situation of man is that of the sinner—who wants to speak of God and cannot; who wants to speak of his existence and cannot do that either. He would have to speak of his existence as one determined by God and he can only speak of it as such as a sinner: i.e., as of being in an existence in which *he* cannot see God, in which God is confronted as the wholly other.

## III

The circumstances of our existence are indeed as startling in their own way as the Divine; we cannot really talk about either and we have control of neither. What does that mean?

The *reality* about which we usually speak is the world-image which has dominated our thinking since the Renaissance and Enlightenment—under the influence of the world-view of Greek science. We accept something as real when we can comprehend it in the total unity of this world, whether this relationship is conceived in terms of causal or teleological destiny, whether its elements and powers are conceived as material or spiritual; for the contrast of materialistic and idealistic ideology is, in terms of the issue here at stake, irrelevant.

For this view of the world is conceived without consideration of our own existence; we ourselves are treated rather as an object among other objects and placed in the context of this world-view which is posited quite apart from the question of our own existence. It is customary to call the perfection of such a world-view through the inclusion of the human element, an ideology (*Weltanschauung*), and we are usually longing for it, and if we assume that we have it, we propagate it. That such ideologies are very popular, even if they do not speak of mankind in flattering terms— perhaps as the accidental result of a combination of atoms, as the highest of the vertebrates and cousin of the apes, or as an interesting example of psychic complexes—is easily understood. For they perform for man again the great service that they release him from himself, that they lift from him the problem-complex of his concrete existence, the anxiety about it and the responsibility for it. That is indeed the foundation of the longing of man for such a so-called ideology, that in the face of the enigma of fate and death he can withdraw to it, that precisely in the moment when his existence is shaken and problematical he declines to take this moment seriously, in order to understand it rather as one case among others, to organize it in a relationship, to objectify it—and so to free himself from his own existence. And precisely this is the arch-deception ($\pi\rho\tilde{\omega}\tau\text{ov } \psi\epsilon\tilde{\upsilon}\delta\text{os}$), and it leads necessarily to the erroneous comprehension of our existence, in that we see ourselves from the outside as the object of self-orienting thinking. And that is not improved when, in contrast with the other objects with which we see ourselves in relationship, we put ourselves forward as protagonists. For man seen by himself as a protagonist is still viewed from the outside. In the question of our existence therefore the distinction between subject and object has to be dropped completely. And the case is not improved at all by having a theistic or a Christian ideology, based on the view that our existence is grounded in God —as though an ideology which includes this proposition satisfies the demands and comprehends our existence. For in this too God is viewed as an outside object just as man. Whoever has a modern world-view which is constituted by the concept of law has a godless world-view—even when he thinks of universal laws as a result of the powers and forms of divine action or when he looks at God as the source of this law. For the acts of God cannot be viewed as general events, at which we could look, as in the contemplation of laws, disregarding our own existence, and which we could later incorporate into our own existence—in order to make it intelligible. For thereby we would sacrifice the primary thought of God as the reality which determines our existence. And we concede this unwillingly or unknowingly, in distinguishing ourselves in our individual being quite clearly from the universal laws. For nobody will conceive the life relationships of love, thankfulness, and reverence in which he is tied to others as law; in any event not when he actually lives in these relationships. It is clearly impossible therefore to conceive God as the foundation (*Prinzip*) of the world by which the world and thereby our own existence becomes intelligible. For in this God would be viewed from the outside, and the proposition of his existence would be a universal truth, a truth which would more or less have its proper place in a system of knowledge (of universal truths), in short in a system which sustains itself and our existence too, instead of being an expression of our existence itself. God would then be a given factor, to which a relationship of perception would be possible, a relationship which could be realized according to wish. God, that is, his existence, would then be a

Thing, *toward which (woraufhin)* an attitude—this or that—would be possible for us. And just this is again the arch-deception (πρῶτον ψεῦδος): if the thought of God is taken seriously, then God is nothing *toward which* something or other can be undertaken. He would then be seen from the outside, and just so we would have seen ourselves from the outside. For example we cannot say: because God rules reality he is also my master. Only when man knows himself to be addressed *(angesprochen)* by God in his own life does it make sense to speak of God as the lord of reality. For every talking about reality which ignores the sole moment in which we can have reality, that is, the moment of our own existence, is self deception. God is never something seen from the outside, something over which we have disposition, something "toward which . . ." or "for the sake of which. . . ."

If it be true that the world seen from the outside is godless and that we, in so far as we see ourselves as a part of the world, are godless, then it is again clear that God is not the wholly other in that he is somewhere outside the world but in that this world, being godless, is also sinful. This world seen from the outside, in which we move about as protagonists, is exactly our world—which we take seriously and thereby denote as sinful.

There are in fact only two things clear to us about our existence: (1) that we have the care and responsibility for it; for it signifies indeed, "necessity compels thee" *(tua res agitur)*; (2) that it is absolutely uncertain and we can not make it secure; for to do so we should have to stand outside it and be God himself. We can not talk about our existence because we can not talk about God; and we can not talk about God because we can not talk about our existence. We could only do one if we could do the other. If we could talk of God *in* God, then we could also talk of our existence, and vice versa. In any case a talking about God, *if* it were possible, would have to be at the same time a talking about us. Thus it remains true: if it be asked how it is possible to speak of God, then it must be answered, only by speaking of us.

I V

But doesn't perhaps something quite different follow from the situation described, that as we are sinners, we shouldn't speak at all? That would naturally mean at the same time that we should not act at all! Does not the point of view that God is the wholly other to men, that he is over and beyond the human, lead to *Quietism?* Whoever thought thus would be making the old mistake. He would, that is, be seeing the thought of God as something *toward which* a certain relationship would be possible or proper; the mistake that the thought of God could be calculated at all as a thing given for our relationship over which we have control. If the thoughts of God as the Almighty and the Wholly Other are taken seriously in their close dependence upon each other, then they clearly mean that we are not given authority for such a self-determining question and self-decision based upon reflection, whether we speak or are quiet, act or relax; that the decision in the matter is God's and that for us there is only a *necessity (Müssen)* of speaking or silence, a necessity of acting or not acting. And in fact this is the only answer to the question if and when we can speak of God: when we *must.*

It has meaning for us however to reflect on what this *necessity* actually means. For according to our traditional way of thinking we immediately see this "necessity" as something from the outside again; that is, we see ourselves, the compelled *(Müssenden)*, as object which stands under the causal compulsion of a subject; and in this case we see God, the commander, as the subject. That means: we see this situation of man as conditioned by God—which is implied in the "necessity" mentioned as a natural process—from the outside. But here only a necessity can be intended which is a *free act*; for such only derives from our existential being, *in* such alone *are* we ourselves and are we whole. Such act is obedience; for obedience means: to respond to necessity by a free act. It signifies no work which we had to decide on because of the will of God; for then God would be seen from the outside, and in work which we accomplish and present to God we are not ourselves; rather we stand outside it. Such an act means utter dependence, not as pious feeling but rather precisely as a free act, for only in the act are we ourselves. This necessity signifies therefore obedience.

This means that one can never turn to generalities when this necessity is put to us. One cannot know about this necessity in advance, for then a position outside of the necessity would be required, a position that is outside of our being as those who must, and one would not understand at all the meaning of this existential necessity. The action cannot be taken as something freely intended because a necessity lies at hand but only as something free and *at the same time* as that made necessary. It hardly needs mentioning that this does not mean that the act breaks forth from a necessity of enthusiasm or passion, out of a secret depth of our inner being. For that would be to talk of natural necessity. The much or little of enthusiasm is as unimportant as the much or little of resistance or self-conquest or that the deed can seem to the human eye as a greater or smaller sacrifice. It is not a question of a psychological necessity. The "thou shalt" is spoken by God and is entirely outside our control. Ours is the free act alone. We can only say hypothetically that we have the possibility to speak and act in God *if* it is given us as necessity. But whether such a necessity will become reality for us, we cannot know in advance. We can only make clear to ourselves what this necessity means, namely that it can signify a free act on our part only because otherwise it would not include our existential being. On the question whether this necessity is reality, we can only *have faith*.

v

Now just this and nothing else is the meaning of *faith*. But of course this is not the total of all that it means. For when we said ours was only the free act, then this proposition too, or rather the conviction that something determined is our free act, is only faith. For free act, being the expression of our existence, precisely because only in it and nowhere else do we exist, cannot be known in the sense of something objectively established. It cannot be put forward as an hypothesis supported by evidence. For thereby we would objectify it and put ourselves outside it. Rather it can only be done (and so far as we *speak* of this action its possibility can only be held) by faith.

At last we see ourselves led to the point that even our own existence—for it is based indeed in our act—can never be known by us. Is it illusion? Unreality? Certainly it is nothing of which we know, about which we can talk, and yet it is that alone—when it is real in our speaking and acting—which can give reality to speaking and acting. We can only have it by faith. And does this faith lie in our hand, so that we can decide for it? Obviously this faith must also be free act, the original act *(Urtat)*, in which we become certain of our existence—and yet it should definitely not be an arbitrary assumption, which we make, but obedience, necessity, precisely *faith*.

The question how such a faith is arrived at is insoluble when it is intended as a search for the process which runs its course when we see ourselves from the outside; it makes no difference whether we define the process rationalistically or psychologically, dogmatically or pietistically. The quest only has meaning—and in this sense it is in fact unavoidable—when it asks about the meaning of faith. This faith can only be the affirmation of God's acting upon us, the answer to his word directed to us. For if faith refers to the comprehension of our existence and if our existence is grounded in God— that is, not comprehensible apart from God—then to comprehend our existence is to comprehend God. But if God is not a general law, a foundation, a given factor, then we can comprehend him only in that which he speaks to us, in that he acts upon us. We can only speak of him in so far as we speak of his word directed to us, his acting upon us.

"Of God we can only tell what he does to us."[1]

The meaning of this word of God, this acting of God upon us, would obviously be this, that God, in giving us our existence, changes us from sinners to righteous men, in that he forgives the sins, justifies us. This would not mean that he forgives us this or that, light or serious mistake *(Missgriff)*; rather he gives us the freedom to speak and to act in God. For only in acting as the free expression of a person—nay, rather in that relationship wherein a person exists at all—can a person enter into a relationship with another person; and everything is spoiled right away of course when the acting is determined from the standpoint of a legal event *(gesetzlichen Geschehens)*.

That cannot mean that he inspires us, makes of us ecstatics and doers of wonders, but that he accepts us as justified while we are separated from him and can only talk *about* him, quest for him. It is therefore not as though something extraordinary, recognizable had happened in our life, that extraordinary qualities were channeled into us and we did extraordinary things or spoke extraordinary words which were not human. Think of all that we could do and say that would *not* be human! But *this* has happened—that all of our doing and speaking has been released by the curse—to separate us from God. It always remains sinful so long as it is something undertaken by us. But precisely as something *sinful* it is justified, that is, it is justified by *grace*. We *know* nothing of God; we *know* nothing of our own reality; we have both only in faith in God's grace.

Does this mean that faith is the Archimedean point by which the world is lifted from the corners and changed from a world of sin to the world of God? Yes, that is the message of the faith. But whoever would ask further about the necessity and about the law-fulness, about the ground of faith—he would receive only one answer, in that he would be referred to the message of faith which comes to him with the claim to be believed. He would receive no answer which would give the validation of faith by some final authority *(Instanz)* or other. If this were not so the word would not be *God's* word; but rather God would be called to account; faith would not be obedience. The word enters our world entirely for-tuitously, entirely contingently, entirely as an event. No guarantee is there by means of which faith can be held. No one's summons has a claim *(Platz)* in the faith of others whether it be Paul or Luther. Indeed faith can never be for us a standpoint toward which we take a position but always and ever a new act, new obedience. Always uncertain, as soon as we look about ourselves as men and question; ever uncertain, as soon as we reflect on it, as soon as we talk about it; only certain as deed. Only certain as faith in the grace of God unto the forgiveness of sins which justifies me—when it pleases him —although I have not the capacity to speak in God but can only talk about God. All of our doing and speaking has meaning only by grace of the forgiveness of sins, and over that we do not dispose; we can only have faith in it.

This address also is a talking about God and as such, if God is, it is sinful; and if God is not, it is senseless. Whether it is mean-ingful and whether it is justified rests with no one of us.

NOTES

1. W. Hermann, *Die Wirklichkeit Gottes* (1914), p. 42.

# III. Cognitivity and the Possibility of Religious Knowledge

# 12. ONTOLOGY AND THE

# POSSIBILITY OF

# RELIGIOUS KNOWLEDGE

## Calvin O. Schrag

*Professor Schrag is a member of the Philosophy Department of Purdue University. In addition to having contributed to many scholarly periodicals, he is author of* Existence and Freedom: Towards an Ontology of Human Finitude.

Assuredly one of the central tasks of philosophy of religion is the elucidation of the structure of religious knowledge. In every religious assertion, from the initial statement of faith to the detailed elaboration of the ethical implications of this faith, an ontology of knowledge is presupposed. Our central question can be phrased as follows: What are the structural or ontological determinants of human experience in terms of which religious knowledge (as well as other types of knowledge) can become an ontic possibility? The formulation of our question suggests that the question of knowing is inseparable from the question of being and that any ontic analysis of the sources, methods, and criteria of the special types of knowledge presupposes an ontological understanding of the conditions which make human knowledge possible. Knowledge presupposes being. Cognitive attitudes and methodological procedures, if they are to be anything more than arbitrary constructions, are referential to regions or orders of being and intentional structures within these orders which determine their adequacy or legitimacy of application.

Reprinted from the *Journal of Religion*, Volume 42 (1962), pp. 87-94, by permission of the University of Chicago Press. Copyright 1962 by the University of Chicago.

The order of matter, for example (independent now of the question concerning its nature and status), as circumscribing the province of the physical sciences, has a peculiar propriety for experimental investigation and quantitative analysis. And, strictly defined, the scientific method possesses precisely this character. Logical empiricism, more than any other contemporary philosophical movement, has concerned itself with a clarification of the methods and criteria of meaning which are applicable to scientific knowledge and has emerged with some notable (and probably noteworthy) results. The logical empiricist argues that the meaning and truth of logical statements are rooted in the criterion of rational intelligibility. Logical propositions, or what Hume had already referred to as relations of ideas, are true if their denial entails a contradiction. "A square has four sides" or "all bachelors are males" is a logical truth which carries meaning by virtue of its self-evident character. Empirical statements, having to do with matters of fact rather than relations of ideas, become meaningful not by virtue of their logical self-evidence but by virtue of some kind of experimental verification. The solubility of sugar is not rationally self-evident. The assertion of its opposite does not necessarily involve a contradiction. The validity of the statement rests upon empirical rather than logical validation.

The question which now arises is whether knowledge based upon logical and empirical propositions exhausts the web of human experience or whether there is a consciousness of non-empirical or non-scientific reality which demands for its elucidation a broader interpretation of experience. If it is indeed asserted that scientific empiricism and logical analysis alone constitute the realm of meaningful discourse and knowledge, then we would witness a most violent reduction of knowledge to the logical and the experimental. Knowledge veritably involves the logical and the experimental, but it also veritably involves *more*. It involves knowledge of other selves, knowledge of aesthetic reality, and knowledge of religious truths—knowledge which is experiential rather than experimental and hence remains outside the purview of the strict empiricist's methodology. Furthermore, the positivist's criterion of meaning with respect to logical and empirical statements itself presupposes a view of reality or a theory of being in which logical predication and empirical analysis can become possible modes of experience and can be evaluated on the basis of a metaphysically colored distinction between the "meaningful" and the "meaningless." What is the meaning of meaning? If religious statements are meaningless, for whom are they meaningless? What structure of experience is necessary for such "statement" to be meaningless? These are ontological questions which the positivist cannot avoid. (Now in many positivistic circles, we might add parenthetically that there is an increasing lack of resistance to ontological investigation, provided that ontology always has its epithelial filaments neatly trimmed with Occam's razor.)

An ontological investigation of the nature of human knowledge involves an analysis and description of the structure of experience in which the datum of consciousness appears within one or another of its intentional fields. The proper method for the delineation of this structure of experience is the phenomenological method. Phenomenology is here understood as an attempt to analyze and describe the data of experience as they present themselves in the subject's existential immediacy. If a philosophical method does not permit the data to speak for themselves, it is hardly worthy of serious consideration. The method must be oriented toward the data, and it is the data which constitute the subject matter of philosophy—not the method. Hence any preoccupation with methodological procedures as such—that is, logical and epistemological inquiry—may conceal rather than reveal the data which it seeks to disclose. "The constant sharpening of the knife," writes Lotze in the Introduction to his *Metaphysics*, "is tedious if there is nothing to cut." Phenomenology seeks to overcome the hiatus between methodological analysis and the data of experience. For phenomenology, logical analysis and epistemological construction are derivative rather than primitive philosophical functions. Phenomenological description precludes any a priori delineation of logical or epistemological "rules of the game"; these *follow from* and in *no way precede* the investigation of the data of immediate experience as it presents itself in its concrete immediacy.

The relevant datum for a phenomenology of knowledge is the datum of consciousness, understood in its broadest sense; and the philosophical task involved is that of delineating the structural determinants which account for the differentiation of this consciousness into its various experiential modes. Consciousness is by no means a simple phenomenon. It is experienced in one mode or in a combination of different modes, each of which has a distinguishable reality element or intentional field. Consciousness as it occurs in the horizon of experience exhibits a fivefold modification into sentient consciousness, moral consciousness, historical consciousness, thematic consciousness, and aesthetic consciousness. Each of these modes of consciousness has a quality of intentionality by virtue of which it is vectorially related to its object or to its field in such a way that the structures of the intentional object or field are given in the operational activity of the consciousness itself. A neglect to describe the structures of the intentional act leads inevitably to a psychological reductivism which unwarrantedly restricts, and indeed falsifies, the data of immediate experience. It has become commonplace to point out the tendencies toward such a psychological reductivism in the phenomenologies of Edmund Husserl (*Ideen*) and Rudolph Otto (*Das Heilige*). Although the tendencies undoubtedly are there, the two phenomenologists certainly sought to keep *in mente* the irreducible difference between psychology and logic (Husserl) and psychology and ontology (Otto). If psychologizing tendencies become apparent in Husserl and Otto, it is because language has been unable to express the inseparable connectedness of consciousness with its field. The concern of every future phenomenology must be to seek to avoid these psychologizing tendencies which seem to appear intermittently in the writings of these two phenomenologists.

Sentient consciousness is the consciousness of man's primitive awareness. It arises from a pre-cognitive life-relatedness in which the differentiation between self and other (either as thing or other self) has not yet appeared. It precedes any knowledge of individuated selves as well as knowledge of an external world which unfolds as a quantitatively discrete series of objects and things. It is a consciousness of undifferentiated living relationships in which no *determinate* intentional object is specified. We are here dealing with a level of experience which precedes any split between a *subject* and an *object* of consciousness. The intentionality of sentient consciousness is a pretheoretical and predeterminate intentionality, disclosing a living and vital world in which consciousness simply experiences its presence. The world as disclosed in sentient consciousness is in no sense a thematic determinant; it is rather a field of sentient relationships in which consciousness "feels" presence through various non-determinate moods—such as anxiety, boredom, melancholy, sympathy, love, and hope. These moods are not to be confused with simple psychological states. They may be ontically expressed as such, but this ontic expression in no way exhausts their function. In the sentient consciousness they emerge primarily as *intentional vectors* and as such perform a revealing function. They disclose the world in which consciousness feels presence. Aristotle was aware of the intentional character of mood when he chose to discuss the phenomenon of fear in his *Rhetoric* (B5 1382a 21) rather than in his *De Anima*. Fear is a mode of disclosure and not simply a psychological state. The primordial consciousness of the world is thus a sentient consciousness—a consciousness of being in the world with respect to an involvement in living relationships in which one "feels at home" in the world or somehow senses that one is a stranger to it. The reality element in the mode of sentient consciousness is the world as an immediately presented life-world. Indissolubly linked with the reality element is the sentient apprehension through involvement and participation. This constitutes the intentional structure of sentient consciousness as man's primitive awareness.

Moral consciousness discloses another mode of presence in the world. The conscious self as a moral self experiences presence in its interdependence with other moral selves who are already there when it appears on the scene. The moral self *finds* itself in a world of interacting moral agents. This is part of the self's situationality. And it is only through the self's relatedness to other selves that it can become fully conscious of its own selfhood. In the mode of moral consciousness we thus witness the concomitant upsurge of the self and other, not as discrete experiences but as dialectical moments within the consciousness of being present in a world of moral selves. Awareness of self and awareness of the other are inseparable. I become a self only by acknowledging others as selves and accepting their acknowledgment of myself as a self. It was a profound insight on the part of Fichte when he defined moral knowledge as acknowledgment and thus freed the lonely monads of Leibnitz from their theoretical isolation. The same point is brilliantly expressed in Martin Buber's "I-Thou" philosophy. The "I" for Buber is always an "I" in the presence of a "Thou." Consciousness of the ego arises only in and through the moral demands of a "Thou." So also Martin Heidegger in his ontology of existence sees the self-other relation as a fundamental and universal determinant of man's being-in-the-world. Human being, he writes, is *essentially* a being with others (*Dasein ist wesenhaft Mitsein*).[1]

The intentionality of moral consciousness, like that of sentient consciousness, is a precognitive intentionality in which the reality element (interacting moral selves) does not admit of the theoretical distinction between subject and object. The encountered self is never an object. Objectivization properly arises only on the level of thematic consciousness, whereby the world becomes an object of theoretical reason and scientific analysis. However, the intentionality of moral consciousness differs from sentient consciousness in that the "intended" world is not simply a field of living relationships but a field of moral preoccupations and concerns. The world of moral consciousness is the sphere of moral activity. This may express itself, as it does in the philosophy of Heidegger, in a personal concern (*Fürsorge*) through which the mutual fulfilment of human projects is realized; or, as in the philosophy of Fichte, in terms of a utilization of the world as material for the execution of moral duties.[2]

Historical consciousness, like that of moral consciousness, involves a consciousness of interacting moral selves, but a new determinant is added—the consciousness of a personal and communal history with its personal and communal memory and hope. The existing self is indelibly historical. It remembers a past, anticipates a future, and decides in the present in light of its past and future. It is the self's historicity which distinguishes the self from an object of nature. Nature is essentially immune to historical becoming. Insofar as nature has a history, it is secondary and derivative. The time of nature as *chronos* or objectively measured time, based on spatial determinants, does not admit of historical projectedness. It is quantitative and reversible as opposed to the time of history which is qualitative and irreversible. Only historical time can give rise to a historical consciousness.

Wilhelm Dilthey, probably more clearly than any previous thinker, saw the significant implications of man's historicity for the problem of knowledge. There are truths which arise only in the context of man's personal and social history. The question concerning the nature of these truths is always asked from within a given historical nexus, and their final relevancy resides in their illumination of the historicity out of which they arise. Indeed, the question is itself conditioned by the historical context. Now it is primarily in historical consciousness that religious knowledge becomes possible. Religious knowledge is historical knowledge. It arises from a personal and social memory of God's decisive action which infuses the moment with existential import and makes of the future a living reality. For religious knowledge the historical past is never simply a chronological past. It is an existential past in which past events continue as repeatable possibilities. It is a past which we carry with us—a past which constitutes our destiny but still remains within the purview of our freedom. It illuminates our present choices made in our historical freedom. This was Kierkegaard's profound insight in his doctrine of contemporaneity. The nineteen hundred years which separate us from the birth and death of Jesus Christ are of a profound indifference. Christ is contemporaneous as a living reality in each decisive action. Thus Kierkegaard is right when he says that *repetition* is the primal category of existence and knowledge and will have to replace the Greek category of knowledge-*recollection*. Historical knowledge, and hence religious knowledge, is based on repetition rather than recollection.

If it is our historicity that makes religious knowledge a human possibility, then our categories of interpretation need to be historical and existential rather than cosmological in character. The world of historical consciousness is not the cosmos of Greek philosophy; nor is it the *res extensa* of Cartesian philosophy. It is a manner or mode of historical relatedness—a *comportement* through which man relates himself authentically or unauthentically to his personal and communal past and future. Religiously, the ethical definition of authentic and unauthentic relatedness turns on the distinction between sin and faith. The unauthenticity of sin involves a sacrifice of one's personal uniqueness to the world in an attitude of *worldliness*. The authenticity of faith involves a triumph over worldliness in such a way that the world is transformed into a new mode of existence, a mode in which past possibilities, understood concretely in light of God's redeeming activity, are appropriated, projected as future possibilities, and preenacted in the present decision. Sin and faith, properly understood, are modes of concrete historical relatedness. They are modes of historical relatedness which either disrupt or knit together man's past, present, and future. Man in his concrete historical existence exists in one or another of these modes. His personal and social history is a history of sin and faith, estrangement and reconciliation, rebellion and love, despair and hope. It is thus that religion provides the context of meaning for the concrete events of our historicity, by virtue of which they are seen not simply as passing states of consciousness but as experiences which manifest a divine purpose. Religious knowledge is knowledge of this divine purpose as it is appropriated in the self's concrete historical and existential encounters. Religious truth is a truth which emerges from history through a process of historical disclosure. It is for this reason that the traditional formula, *veritas est adequatio rei et intellectus*, has limited applicability in defining the nature of religious truth. Indeed, the application of this formula may result in a most vicious distortion of religious truth insofar as it *objectivizes* its reality. Religious truth is *disclosure* rather than *adequation*—a disclosure which occurs in and through the self's personal and social historical becoming.

Thematic consciousness is the consciousness which makes objectivization possible. The world as immediately encountered can become *object*, and consciousness can apprehend itself as *subject*. Knowledge for the thematic consciousness thus becomes a relation between a knowing subject and a known object. The intentionality of thematic consciousness becomes a *theoretical* intentionality which "reaches out" to a determinate object. (To what extent this object is grasped and to what extent it is shaped by consciousness must remain a purely speculative question from the point of view of the thematic consciousness.) All the special sciences presuppose this structure of the thematic consciousness. The world of the special sciences becomes a world of extensiveness and spatial co-ordinates, which readily lends itself to quantitative analysis and experimentation. The scientific world, as extended and spatial, is characterized by regularity and generality and is therefore amenable to measurement. Without a thematic consciousness no scientific world is possible. But this thematization of the world is a relatively late development in the human consciousness, genetically and anthropologically as well as epistemologically. It is a derivative rather than a primitive knowledge and, as such, is rooted in the primordial pretheoretical encounter with the world as disclosed in the sentient and moral consciousness. The subject-object dichotomy is a valid epistemological distinction, but it must be understood as being grounded in a preconceptual awareness of already "having" or being in a world which is genuinely practical in nature. I first encounter my world as that which defines my practical projects. I write with a pen which is initially disclosed as a tool or utensil for the realization of my purpose. It is an *instrument* which I use for writing. Only *later* do I abstract the scientific qualities from its instrumental function and define it as an *object* having a certain extension or occupying a locus in world space and possessing certain determinates of weight, solidity, texture, color, etc. So also my knowledge of other selves is initially an encounter whereby I find myself "with" them in various modes of personal relatedness. They resist or help realize my personal projects, they curtail or fulfil my freedom, they respond in terms of love or hate, they are indifferent or enthusiastic about my various undertakings. Thematic consciousness as a later mode of awareness abstracts from this concrete participation and objectivizes other selves as isolated loci of consciousness which can then properly become objects for scientific and psychological inquiry. In the same manner, society is first disclosed as the field of my social preoccupations—only later does it become an object of theoretical sociological investigation. Any special scientific inquiry is rendered possible only through a thematic consciousness which itself arises out of more primitive and more fundamental modes of awareness.

Finally, there is the datum of aesthetic consciousness. Aesthetic consciousness shares with thematic consciousness its proclivity for abstraction insofar as its intentional object is the formal factor in the experience of aesthetic reality; but it does not know the objectivization which occurs in science. Like all the other modes of consciousness, aesthetic consciousness uncovers a world—a world of harmony and disharmony, uniformity and contrast, proportion and disproportion. The world of the aesthetic consciousness is the world of the beautiful and the ugly. To express this world is the task of art. The artist seeks to depict and create the aesthetic qualities of human experience. The distorted nudes of Picasso reveal the uglification of everyday existence; the *Ninth Symphony* of Beethoven depicts reality as a celestial harmony of joy and beauty.

Existence is never aesthetically neutral. It is colored by aesthetic dispositions. The artist seeks to wrest the form of the aesthetic disposition from its particular manifestation and portray it on different levels of abstraction. Music, for example, dispenses entirely with verbal and concrete imagery; painting utilizes non-verbal concrete imagery; whereas poetry, drama, the short story, and the novel all utilize a concrete imagery which is at the same time verbal. But all levels of art seek to capture various dispositional forms, whether this be the loneliness and alienation expressed by Van Gogh's "Night Café" or the peace and serenity conveyed by Raphael's "Madonna and Child."

These five modes of consciousness which we have delineated constitute man's world of experience, and in their totality they define the horizons of human knowledge. The structural character of human existence is such that it unfolds in differentiated modes of consciousness through which the different kinds of human knowledge become ontic possibilities. Man can apprehend himself and attain knowledge through each of these different modes, but no one mode exhausts the range of human experience. Any restriction of knowledge to one of these modes, such as we find in scientism or logical positivism, results in a falsification of the breadth of the human consciousness. Any adequate theory of experience must remain broad enough to deal adequately with the phenomenon or the facts, as they are given, whether these facts be scientific facts, moral facts, or facts of religious and aesthetic experience. It is for this reason that in the final analysis the problem of knowledge, and the problem of being itself, must be dealt with phenomenologically.

Now, if human experience is differentiated into at least five modes of consciousness, is there a consciousness which unifies the distinguishable modes of consciousness? Is there a unity of knowledge in which the different modes constitute a dialectical moment taken up (à la Hegel) in some unified perspective of reality? Or is the web of human experience so incurably fractured and fragmented that no unified vision is possible? If I understand Karl Jaspers correctly, the latter is the philosophical position which he seeks to maintain and to which he refers as *Existenzerhellung*.[3] This is in no way to imply that Hegel's Absolute Idealism and Jasper's existentialism exhaust the relevant alternatives. One might argue that the problem of the unity of knowledge has its most productive resolution in a doctrine of analogy. And this resolution itself admits of varied formulations. Analogy may be conceived in the Thomistic sense of analogies of attribution and proper proportionality; or it may be conceived in terms of what Dorothy Emmet has called "co-ordinating analogies" through which the different regions of experience are co-ordinated through the analogical extension of a key idea derived from a dominant mode of intellectual, artistic, or religious experience.[4] (The problem which Emmet never successfully solves is the problem of the selection of this key idea which is to provide the basis for the establishment of a set of co-ordinating analogies.)

Whether there is a fundamental unity of knowledge remains problematic from a phenomenological point of view. Phenomenology *as* phenomenology cannot proceed beyond a description of the various modes of consciousness to a unifying perspective—either of a dialectical or analogical variety. But it can and must perform the task of delineating the universal ontological determinants presupposed by the ontic experience in each of the modes. Each mode of consciousness—sentient, moral, historical, thematic, and aesthetic—exhibits its own irreducible means of apprehension and distinctive method of inquiry. Any reduction of the one to the other results in a restriction and eventual falsification of the reach or range of human experience. Any serious ontology of knowledge must therefore seek to set forth a description of human consciousness in which the modal distinctions and their intentional structures are clearly delineated. It is toward this end that the foregoing discussion has sought clarification.

NOTES

1. *Sein und Zeit* (7th ed.; Tübingen: Max Neimeyer Verlag, 1953), p. 120. Also cf. Karl Jaspers' discussion of communication in *Von der Wahrheit*: "Weil der Mensch eigentlich nur ist, indem er er selbst ist, muss er einsam werden; aber einsam wird er erst ganz offen für Kommunikation. Er ist er selbst und eisam zugleich doch nur, insofern er für andere ist. Selbstsein und In-Kommunkation-Sein ist untrennbar" (München: R. Piper & Co. Verlag, 1947), p. 546.

2. For Fichte's concept of the world see his short treatise on *The Vocation of Man*, where he writes: "The world is the object and sphere of my duties, and absolutely nothing more; there is no other world for

me, and no other qualities of my world than what are implied in this;—my whole united capacity, all finite capacity, is insufficient to comprehend any other. Whatever possesses an existence for me, can bring its existence and reality into contact with me only through this relation, and only through this relation do I comprehend it:—for any other existence than this I have no organ whatever" (Chicago: Open Court Publishing Co., 1955), pp. 108-9.

3. In Book II of his *Philosophie* he informs us that because of man's inevitable "shipwreck" (*Scheitern*) in being thrown from one situation to another, any unifying perspective of existence is impossible. "Existenz gewinnt *keine Rundung* als Bild, weder für andere noch für sich selbst; denn der Mensch muss in der Welt *scheitern*" (Heidelberg: Springer-Verlag, 1948), p. 647.

4. *The Nature of Metaphysical Thinking* (London: Macmillan & Co., 1949); see chap. ix in particular.

# 13. FACTUAL KNOWLEDGE

# AND RELIGIOUS CLAIMS

## Paul F. Schmidt

*Paul Schmidt is chairman of the Philosophy Department at the University of New Mexico. In addition to* Religious Knowledge, *he is author of "Truth in Physics," "Models of Scientific Thought," and other articles.*

The second type of knowledge by description that might include religious claims concerns matters of fact. Such factual knowledge, or empirical knowledge as it is also called, is exemplified by the natural, social, and historical sciences as well as by the enormous amount of everyday information. The distinction between formal and empirical knowledge goes back a long way in the history of thought to the Greek philosophers, but it was not until the present century that each was sufficiently well understood for the essential differences between them to be clearly presented. Credit for this clear separation goes to the Logical Positivists. In their early exuberance they propounded some rash analyses of religion and ethics,[1] but these were the signs of fresh insight and novelty, and they cleared the ground for our own analysis. Unknowingly, they pointed a way for us, and their doctrine is a fire of purification.

Our first task is to delineate the subject matter of empirical knowledge and the types of statements found therein. Its subject matter has been variously described as nature, the external world, the space-time order, the phenomenal realm, and sense-datum experience. All of these are dangerous and misleading in different

Reprinted by permission of The Free Press of Glencoe, Inc. (Macmillan) from *Religious Knowledge* (1961), pp. 45-60.

ways. They suggest a dualism of knower and known, a subjectivism of experience, a dematerialization of the world, and a gap between nature and reality. But we can avoid all this by setting down the general procedures that investigators agree upon in these areas. Empirical knowledge deals with events and objects for which operational definitions could be given and, in some cases, with unobservable events and objects that are linked by logical-mathematical relations to operationally defined objects and events. Such operational definitions tell us what investigators do to identify and describe, in terms of observable behavior, some event or object. Is this copper? What is its atomic weight? Is this society polygamous? Did Plato visit Egypt? We answer such questions more or less firmly, without making use of the puzzling metaphysical terms like nature, external world, phenomena, or sense data.

For our purposes, we shall approach the types of statements involved in a system of empirical knowledge with an eye on their relevance to the question of religious knowledge. First, there are the many particular statements about matters of fact, usually the result of observations or some refinements thereof. Second, we find general statements summarizing matters of fact, and abstract statements belonging to hypotheses and theories sometimes involving mention of objects and events that are not observable. Third, there are procedural statements about methods of empirical research, specific and general. And fourth, we have logical and mathematical statements serving as tools for organization and prediction within the sciences.

The structure of systems of empirical knowledge varies somewhat, depending on the degree of development of theories. In history, theory development is at a minimum; in physics it is at a maximum. But we do not find generically different kinds of structures. We find that a theory is made up of general laws specifying the characteristics and relationships of some objects and events in such a manner that when we add some particular statements of matters of fact and some procedural statements, this combined whole yields, by logical or mathematical rules of derivation, other particular statements of matters of fact that can then be put to an observational or experimental test.

The question often arises: from whence the theory? An answer cannot, at the present time, be formulated that sets down a series of steps an investigator can proceed to perform in order to lead to a new theory. Scientific discovery of new theories depends upon the creative imagination of the scientist. On the other hand, the question of when we should accept a theory has quite a definite answer. Scientific justification can be specified in a series of steps giving the experimental procedures for the verification or falsification of a theory. There has been much technical analysis of the procedures of justification (verification, confirmation, hypothetical-deduction, and induction), but the differences of interpretation do not affect our argument.

When are statements accepted or rejected in empirical knowledge? A particular statement is accepted if (1) it follows as a consequence from an accepted theory or if (2) it can be observed directly or by some experimental instruments. It is rejected if its denial is acceptable. It may be neither acceptable nor rejectable. A theory is accepted when a sufficient number of consequences that follow from it can be positively observed, directly or experimentally. It is rejected if some of its consequences are rejected. It is common to say that accepted statements and theories are true or empirically true or factual truths and that rejected statements and theories are false.

True and false are most commonly used in this manner, and no end of confusion has arisen in the history of thought from taking this use as the only use of these terms. Worse yet, this use was incorrectly combined with the uses appropriate to formal knowledge, with the consequence that both types of knowledge failed to receive a proper analysis until this century. This confusion of uses still exists with respect to ethical statements and also for religious claims. When people say ethical or religious claims are true, they simply carry over the use from empirical knowledge, with little understanding of its inappropriateness. The search for a single use of true and false is another of the great ghosts of thought never to be caught, for there is nothing to catch. It would not be possible to take up this search if one understood the proper uses of these terms. It is absolutely essential to use these terms with their proper qualifiers, that is, to see them in their relationship to some type of knowledge.

So far, we have dealt with the subject matter of empirical knowledge, namely, with matters of fact and the theories explaining them; with the structure of such systems; and with the procedures of justification for different types of statements in the structures. Thus, we have met the two conditions for a type of knowledge by description: what it is about and how claims are tested. What are the characteristics of empirical knowledge?

Empirical knowledge gives us *concrete information about, or causal explanations of, matters of fact.* The warrant for this characteristic consists of the enormous body of scientific knowledge and everyday information: physics, chemistry, biology, psychology, sociology, history, and all the many crafts practiced by man. In contrast to formal knowledge, which makes no reference beyond its own symbolic expression, empirical knowledge has reference to matters of fact; it tells us something about the environment we live in. I suppose this is why it has become the model of knowledge for most people.

Second, this information can be *tested.* It is being continually revised by the elimination of some claims, the more precise statement of other claims, and the addition of new information. The possibility of putting such claims to a test distinguishes them from apparently factual claims that cannot be put to such a test. Such apparent factual claims can be found in metaphysics and in most religious systems, and we shall have more to say about this later.

Third, these testing procedures are *public*; they are not restricted to any particular class of persons, seers, medicine men, witch doctors, or enlightened individuals. Anyone can carry out these tests to satisfy himself if he can undergo a period of appropriate training. Such publicity of testing leads to common information for all. Hence, it is not arbitrary. We cannot invent whatever systems of empirical knowledge we like, as we can in formal knowledge.

As a consequence of testability and publicity, the information is *objective.* By objective I do not mean finding out what nature really is. This notion of objectivity is connected with the idea of an omniscient observer, like a deity, but scientists are not omniscient observers. According to our analysis of empirical knowledge, objectivity means that, relative to some chosen frame of reference, the carrying out of appropriate testing procedures by any trained investigator will yield identical empirical descriptions.

The logical character of the testing procedure for accepting theories leads to a very important characteristic of empirical knowledge. Such theories are at best *probable* or *tentative*, never certain or final. Consider their general form: if a theory is given, along with some initial conditions, then certain observable consequences will follow. The consequences are tested by observation or experiment. Is that theory the only possibility? No. Others might entail the same consequences. At best, in empirical knowledge we have a theory, but we never know if it is the only theory. Scientists have sometimes talked and acted otherwise, but in so doing they were turning to other than empirical knowledge. Historically, this logical point was overlooked in the enormous success of modern science, especially that of physics in the eighteenth and nineteenth centuries. Physics was so highly successful that few doubted its certainty. Then came the shocks of the twentieth-century revolutions in physics.

The last characteristic I want to notice is the *changing conception of the world* given to us by scientific information as empirical investigations proceed. We do not arrive at the one conception of the world, whatever that means. Nor can we say that each conception comes closer to this one correct conception, approaching it like an asymptote. For what could be the criterion for such an approach? Wouldn't any criterion assume some way of getting a "sneak peek" at reality in order to measure how close we are getting? But if such a peek is possible, why bother with the inferior kind of knowledge that only approaches it? All we can say is that conceptions change according to their degree of adequacy for dealing with the known data. Each is better than the previous one in its adequacy.

This is, perhaps, a good place to make some remarks about the term "reality" in relation to this analysis. It is commonplace to suppose that the philosopher is concerned with reality, and as regards knowledge, with knowing that reality. Yet if one studies the work of mathematicians and scientists in formal and factual knowledge, respectively, one will find no need to mention "knowing reality." Nor did I need to mention it in my description of these two types of knowledge. Reality was a conception introduced into

Western philosophy by the Greeks, a conception which played an important role but which is now no longer a useful term. Its use now generates philosophical problems instead of clarifying them, as it may have done in the past. Because I make no use of the term "reality," you are not to assume that I deny it, hold it unknowable, or any other such doctrine. We are quite beyond such doctrines in the mid-twentieth century so far as a description of knowledge goes. Religions seem to want to continue using this term, and this suggests that religious language is not to be assimilated to either formal or factual knowledge.

With our list of characteristics of factual knowledge, we are ready to raise the question whether religious claims belong to empirical knowledge. There is no doubt that, traditionally, most religious persons intended some of their religious statements to be factual, to state historical, cosmological, and theological facts about the world. Even today, a large number of people continue to believe that some of their religious statements are factual. To see that this is not the case constitutes a difficult but all-important step forward. Our point-by-point procedure hopes to make this clear. The classic examples of such factual claims in Christianity are the cosmological picture in Genesis, the biological claims about the origin and nature of man, and the astronomical and physical views. Each of these has come into sharp conflict with the development of modern science. Galileo, Darwin, and Copernicus were among the iconoclasts who precipitated these conflicts between science and religion. I shall discuss some features of this conflict in a later chapter. I mention them here as examples of the factual claims of religion.

Factual knowledge is at best probable; religious claims in the factual area have been presented as certain. Such dogmas are to be believed without question; they are often said to be the very center of a faith; to have that faith is to hold those beliefs without question. In science, in contrast, every belief can be questioned and should be held only tentatively. It will be pointed out that religious dogmas have changed in the course of history. Doesn't this show that someone held them open to doubt and question? Isn't this just like our doubt and questioning of scientific statements? I don't think so. There has been change from one dogma to another in religion, but it is a change from one certainty to another, neither of which is held with the tentativeness of factual knowledge. Against this difference, others will point to the many doctrinal interpretations of a given dogma as evidence for the revision and alteration of views parallel to that of scientific knowledge.[2] For example, there are the different doctrinal interpretations of the dogma "that in Jesus Christ God became incarnate."[3] Although these different doctrinal interpretations are open to doubt and, in this way, parallel science in their tentativeness, they fail to parallel science with respect to the characteristics of objectivity and testability. This point we shall treat shortly. Finally, it is said that any really devout person has periods of questioning and doubt in his religious life. Doesn't this parallel the questioning attitude of the scientist? No. The differences are in the psychological attitudes of the persons and in the way the questioning is carried on. For the scientist, the questioning is genuinely open to the possibility of the answer being true or false, and either alternative is a worthwhile result. Furthermore, the questioning is submitted to public, objective tests. For the religious person, it is doubtful whether a negative answer would be adopted or welcomed. In addition, his questioning involves private and subjective methods.

Now let us look more closely at these differences in testing procedures. Empirical knowledge uses testing procedures in which experimentation plays a major role leading to public information. In contrast, religions use testing procedures that make little use of experimentation. It is simply a matter of history that religions have not used experimentation to provide the warrant for their claims. But, someone will say, have they not used observation and experience, and aren't these the forerunners of experimentation? To suppose so is to exploit an ambiguity. There is all the difference in the world between an observation or experience restricted to a limited group of people or to an individual, and an observation or experience that could be had by anyone under conditions that could be fulfilled by anyone.

This ambiguity leads straight to the difference between public and private, objective and subjective. The traditional testing procedures used by religions are revelation, authority of person or text, intuitive insight, mystical insight, and personal consequences ("By their fruits, ye shall know them"). It is clear, to begin with, that none of these test procedures is used by empirical knowledge in the experimental testing of the consequences of a theory. Hence, religious claims are not tested by the procedures of empirical knowledge. These religious procedures have a common difficulty in that two different persons using them often arrive at contradictory or contrary results. Therefore, it is not the case that anyone can employ the procedures to confirm a common result. This is what we mean by public, and the common result achieved is what we call an objective piece of information. It is all too notorious that one religion holds one claim while another holds the opposite, that one mystic apprehends the universe this way and another flatly denies it. Further, it is well known that some people who seriously try to use these methods to gain religious knowledge fail to do so. When the sort of result obtained depends upon who the subjects are that use the procedures, we call the procedures subjective. We see that the religious procedures are of this sort.

A word of warning is perhaps in order now. The fact that we find that religious claims fail to have the characteristics of formal or factual knowledge is no reason to disapprove of religion. This feeling is likely to arise, and care must be taken to point out that this feeling is not justified by the analysis. Actually, our aim is to show that a serious intellectual confusion will occur if religious statements are thought to belong to formal or factual knowledge. We are aiming at a clarification of religious statements. By clearly distinguishing such statements, we can better appreciate just what their function is, and from this we may be able to understand their meaning.

A special word is also in order about the testing procedure of personal consequences. No one can deny that the lives of some persons have been radically and permanently altered as a result of religious experience, and it is supposed that the consequences in human deeds of that altered life attest to the genuineness of the religious experience. It is then claimed that this is parallel to testing the consequences of a theory. Much confusion has come from this gambit. The key difference is that the consequences of a scientific theory follow regardless of whether I believe the theory to be true or commit myself to it, while for the religious view we are required to commit ourselves firmly to it. But how can we critically and dispassionately appraise a view when the first condition for testing it is a commitment which forces us to relinquish our impartial position? Once again, let us refrain from attaching pro-and-con value judgments to these points. Commitment is an important feature of religious language, to be dealt with later. The point here is that the method of consequences in science does not involve commitment, while the method of consequences in religion does depend on commitment.

The last characteristic of empirical knowledge I want to discuss in relation to religion is that it gives us concrete information or causal explanations of matters of fact. Religious claims seem to have this characteristic. God is often conceived as the ultimate explanation, and in a first-cause argument he is conceived as the ultimate cause. Furthermore, there is no end of concrete information presented in sacred texts. We seem to have found a common feature.

But this difficulty emerges: if the religious claim is about a matter of fact that belongs within the area of one of the recognized sciences, then it will have to abide by the tests appropriate to that science; it cannot be accepted on any other basis, lest it forfeit its claim to give empirical knowledge. On the other hand, if it is said that the claim does not belong to any one of the recognized sciences, then we cannot accept it until criteria are presented that delineate the new area of empirical facts to which it belongs and that indicate how it is to be tested publicly. I do not think that this second alternative has been eliminated, nor has it been presented so as to convince anyone. On the former alternative, there remains nothing distinctively religious about the claim, and it is handed over to the appropriate science. These two difficulties show that religious claims do not provide us with concrete information in the same manner as empirical knowledge.

We have now answered, point by point, our question whether religious claims belong to empirical knowledge. The answer is that they do not, although on superficial analysis one might say that they do. Certainly many people have thought and still do think that they do. The major reason for the confusion stems from an older and inadequate understanding of empirical knowledge. Only in the last half century have we come to an adequate understanding of such knowledge. In answering the question, I have had in

222PAUL F. SCHMIDT

mind those religious claims which I called cosmological, theological, and historical. I have not dealt with the other sorts because I do not think people generally suppose them to be making empirical claims; I, at least, do not interpret them as doing so.

There are some contemporary theologians who would admit all of the differences I have pointed out and who would hold that they arise from older and, in their view, antiquated religious views. Several approaches need to be distinguished. First, some would hold that religions make no formal or empirical claims and that if such claims are found in a religion, they should be given over to the relevant science. They are not touched in the least by all that has been maintained so far. Several variants will be encountered: those who take religion to be ethics; others who take it to be restricted to what I have called devotional and purely religious statements. If either of these variants is assumed, it is obvious that the claims are outside the area of empirical or factual knowledge. A second group would hold that religions do make empirical claims and, in so doing, make use of the characteristics of empirical knowledge we have listed. They admit that religious claims are at best probable; that they must be tested by observation and experiment so as to yield results that are public and objective; and that criteria can be given for the delineation of a new area of empirical data. Two efforts of this sort can be distinguished: the eschatological-verification view and the psychological-attitude view. The latter view I shall discuss later, since it involves our discussion of value knowledge in the next chapter.

The eschatological-verification view is presented by Professor Hick in his book *Faith and Knowledge*.[4] He argues that a few basic religious assertions could be verified empirically and are therefore meaningful and possibly true. His example is the claim to survival after death. Now there are serious difficulties that can be raised concerning the meaningfulness or intelligibility of the notion of life after death. Hick is well aware of these problems stemming from the alleged separation of mind from body and of precisely what could be meant by this separation.[5] I think these difficulties are genuine; nevertheless, we can grant Hick the meaningfulness of these notions and still show that they fail to conform to the verification characteristics of empirical knowledge. He says: ". . . the logical peculiarity of the claim is that it is open to confirmation but not to refutation. There can be conclusive evidence for it if it be true, but there cannot be conclusive evidence against it if it be untrue. For if we survive bodily death we shall (presumably) know that we have survived it, but if we do not survive death we shall not know that we have not survived it. The verification situation is thus asymmetrical. However, the religious doctrine is at least open to verification and is accordingly meaningful. Its eschatological prediction assures its status as an assertion."[6]

Elsewhere, Hick explains what he means by verification: "... verification consists in the exclusion of grounds for rational doubt concerning the truth of a proposition."[7] Different types of assertions will involve different grounds for doubt. Hence, we have to be careful to understand the sort of claim being made before we can know what grounds would verify it. In the case of the religious claim concerning survival, these grounds would be certain experiences by the person who survived.

The apparent success of Hick's position comes from trading on several ambiguities in the term "verify," and when these are sorted out his position is logically untenable because it violates one of the meanings of "verify" essential to his argument. In the first ambiguity, one sense of "to verify" means "to utilize the procedures of verification, that is to point out what relevant sorts of data would make the empirical claim acceptable and what other sorts would make it rejectable," or "under what conditions one labels it empirically true or empirically false." In the other sense, "to verify" means "to be acceptable," "to be empirically true," in contrast to being rejectable or falsified or empirically false. Hick shows how the survival claim is verified in the second sense and then goes on to assert that it is verifiable in the first sense. This assertion does not follow, however, and actually violates the meaning of the first sense. He admits, in the long quotation, that there cannot be evidence against the claim and makes a point of this queer feature in his remark about the asymmetry. But if there is no possible evidence against the claim, it is not rejectable, and if it is not rejectable, then it is not a claim made in accordance with verification in the first sense. That first sense requires that, for any claim, we can specify what would make it rejectable. A reading of the lengthy literature of verification makes it clear that this is what is meant. Hick's eschatological verification fails to conform to the meaning of verification in the first sense, and it is this meaning which he has to conform to if his view is to count as a piece of empirical knowledge. The question of what would count to falsify religious claims is still crucial if these claims are put forward as a part of empirical knowledge.

The second ambiguity crucial to his position results from shifting from verification in the sense of private experience to verification in the sense of public experimentation. Hick shows how I might have a positive verification, in my experience, of surviving death, but he fails to show how this private experience could be made public as an observation for others. Yet any careful reading of the literature of verification makes clear that this second sense of public observation is crucial. His talk of verification, therefore, departs considerably from the current use and is thus misleading.

For several thousand years, people have thought that some religious assertions were factual claims. If our analysis is correct, however, this long tradition, still strong in some of our contemporary theologians, is mistaken. Our conclusion stands despite these recent efforts. Religious claims do not belong to factual knowledge. This constitutes, I believe, a tremendous step forward in the understanding of religion and opens the way for a new understanding of religious claims.

NOTES

1. A. J. Ayer, *Language, Truth and Logic* (London: Victor Gollanz, Ltd., 1948).

2. I use this distinction between dogma and doctrine as given by John Hick in *Faith and Knowledge* (Ithaca, N. Y.: Cornell University Press, 1957), pp. 198-99.

3. Ibid., p. 198.

4. Hick, op. cit., pp. 150-63.

5. Cf. a mimeographed paper by Hick, "On the Verification of Re-

ligious Statements," read at a Danforth Seminar, University of Minnesota, June, 1958, p. 7. I refer to this with his permission.

6. *Faith and Knowledge*, p. 150.

7. "On the Verification of Religious Statements," p. 5. A restatement of his position is now available: cf. "Theology and Verification," *Theology Today*, XVII (1960), 12-31.

# 14. ON THE

# "KNOWLEDGE OF GOD"

## Søren Kierkegaard

*Søren Kierkegaard (1813-1855), who regarded himself as a kind of
"Socrates in Christendom," is often viewed as the father of contemporary existentialism. His influential works include* Philosophical Fragments, Either/Or, Fear and Trembling, Concluding Unscientific Postscript, *to name only a few.*

When the question of truth is raised in an objective manner, reflection is directed objectively to the truth, as an object to which the
knower is related. Reflection is not focussed upon the relationship,
however, but upon the question of whether it is the truth to which
the knower is related. If only the object to which he is related is the
truth, the subject is accounted to be in the truth. When the question of the truth is raised subjectively, reflection is directed subjectively, to the nature of the individual's relationship; if only the
mode of this relationship is in the truth, the individual is in the
truth even if he should happen to be thus related to what is not
true.[1] Let us take as an example the knowledge of God. Objectively,
reflection is directed to the problem of whether this object is the
true God; subjectively, reflection is directed to the question whether
the individual is related to a something *in such a manner* that his
relationship is in truth a God-relationship. On which side is the
truth now to be found? Ah, may we not here resort to a mediation,
and say: It is on neither side, but in the mediation of both? Ex-
cellently well said, provided we might have it explained how an

Reprinted by permission of the Princeton University Press from *Concluding Unscientific Postscript*, trans. D.F. Swenson and W. Lowrie, pp. 178-83.
Copyright, 1941, by Princeton University Press. The title is provided by the
editor.

existing individual manages to be in a state of mediation. For to be in a state of mediation is to be finished, while to exist is to become. Nor can an existing individual be in two places at the same time—he cannot be an identity of subject and object. When he is nearest to being in two places at the same time he is in passion; but passion is momentary, and passion is also the highest expression of subjectivity.

The existing individual who chooses to pursue the objective way enters upon the entire approximation-process by which it is proposed to bring God to light objectively. But this is in all eternity impossible, because God is a subject, and therefore exists only for subjectivity in inwardness. The existing individual who chooses the subjective way apprehends instantly the entire dialectical difficulty involved in having to use some time, perhaps a long time, in finding God objectively; and he feels this dialectical difficulty in all its painfulness, because every moment is wasted in which he does not have God.[2] That very instant he has God, not by virtue of any objective deliberation, but by virtue of the infinite passion of inwardness. The objective inquirer, on the other hand, is not embarrassed by such dialectical difficulties as are involved in devoting an entire period of investigation to finding God—since it is possible that the inquirer may die tomorrow; and if he lives he can scarcely regard God as something to be taken along if convenient, since God is precisely that which one takes *a tout prix*, which in the understanding of passion constitutes the true inward relationship to God.

It is at this point, so difficult dialectically, that the way swings off for everyone who knows what it means to think, and to think existentially; which is something very different from sitting at a desk and writing about what one has never done, something very different from writing *de omnibus dubitandum* and at the same time being as credulous existentially as the most sensuous of men. Here is where the way swings off, and the change is marked by the fact that while objective knowledge rambles comfortably on by way of the long road of approximation without being impelled by the urge of passion, subjective knowledge counts every delay a deadly peril, and the decision so infinitely important and so instantly pressing that it is as if the opportunity had already passed.

Now when the problem is to reckon up on which side there is

most truth, whether on the side of one who seeks the true God objectively, and pursues the approximate truth of the God-idea; or on the side of one who, driven by the infinite passion of his need of God, feels an infinite concern for his own relationship to God in truth (and to be at one and the same time on both sides equally, is as we have noted not possible for an existing individual, but is merely the happy delusion of an imaginary I-am-I): the answer cannot be in doubt for anyone who has not been demoralized with the aid of science. If one who lives in the midst of Christendom goes up to the house of God, the house of the true God, with the true conception of God in his knowledge, and prays, but prays in a false spirit; and one who lives in an idolatrous community prays with the entire passion of the infinite, although his eyes rest upon the image of an idol: where is there most truth? The one prays in truth to God though he worships an idol; the other prays falsely to the true God, and hence worships in fact an idol.

When one man investigates objectively the problem of immortality, and another embraces an uncertainty with the passion of the infinite: where is there most truth, and who has the greater certainty? The one has entered upon a never-ending approximation, for the certainty of immortality lies precisely in the subjectivity of the individual; the other is immortal, and fights for his immortality by struggling with the uncertainty. Let us consider Socrates. Nowadays everyone dabbles in a few proofs; some have several such proofs, others fewer. But Socrates! He puts the question objectively in a problematic manner: *if* there is an immortality. He must therefore be accounted a doubter in comparison with one of our modern thinkers with the three proofs? By no means. On this "if" he risks his entire life, he has the courage to meet death, and he has with the passion of the infinite so determined the pattern of his life that it must be found acceptable—*if* there is an immortality. Is any better proof capable of being given for the immortality of the soul? But those who have the three proofs do not at all determine their lives in conformity therewith; if there is an immortality it must feel disgust over their manner of life: can any better refutation be given of the three proofs? The bit of uncertainty that Socrates had, helped him because he himself contributed the passion of the infinite; the three proofs that the others have do not profit them at all, because they are dead to spirit and enthusiasm, and their three proofs, in lieu of proving anything else, prove just this. A young girl may enjoy all the sweetness of love on the basis of what is merely a weak hope that she is beloved, because she rests everything on this weak hope; but many a wedded matron more than once subjected to the strongest expressions of love, has in so far indeed had proofs, but strangely enough has not enjoyed *quod erat demonstrandum*. The Socratic ignorance, which Socrates held fast with the entire passion of his inwardness, was thus an expression for the principle that the eternal truth is related to an existing individual, and that this truth must therefore be a paradox for him as long as he exists; and yet it is possible that there was more truth in the Socratic ignorance as it was in him, than in the entire objective truth of the System, which flirts with what the times demand and accommodates itself to *Privatdocents*.

*The objective accent falls on* WHAT *is said, the subjective accent on* HOW *it is said*. This distinction holds even in the aesthetic realm, and receives definite expression in the principle that what is in itself true may in the mouth of such and such a person become untrue. In these times this distinction is particularly worthy of notice, for if we wish to express in a single sentence the difference between ancient times and our own, we should doubtless have to say: "In ancient times only an individual here and there knew the truth; now all know it, except that the inwardness of its appropriation stands in an inverse relationship to the extent of its dissemination.[3] Aesthetically the contradiction that truth becomes untruth in this or that person's mouth, is best construed comically: In the ethico-religious sphere, accent is again on the "how." But this is not to be understood as referring to demeanor, expression, or the like; rather it refers to the relationship sustained by the existing individual, in his own existence, to the content of his utterance. Objectively the interest is focussed merely on the thought-content, subjectively on the inwardness. At its maximum this inward "how" is the passion of the infinite, and the passion of the infinite is the truth. But the passion of the infinite is precisely subjectivity, and thus subjectivity becomes the truth. Objectively there is no infinite decisiveness, and hence it is objectively in order to annul the difference between good and evil, together with the principle of contradiction, and therewith also the infinite difference between the true and the false. Only in subjectivity is there decisiveness, to seek objectivity is to be in error. It is the passion of the infinite that is the decisive factor and not its content, for its content is precisely itself. In this manner subjectivity and the subjective "how" constitute the truth.

But the "how" which is thus subjectively accentuated precisely because the subject is an existing individual, is also subject to a dialectic with respect to time. In the passionate moment of decision, where the road swings away from objective knowledge, it seems as if the infinite decision were thereby realized. But in the same moment the existing individual finds himself in the temporal order, and the subjective "how" is transformed into a striving, a striving which receives indeed its impulse and a repeated renewal from the decisive passion of the infinite, but is nevertheless a striving.

When subjectivity is the truth, the conceptual determination of the truth must include an expression for the antithesis to objectivity, a memento of the fork in the road where the way swings off; this expression will at the same time serve as an indication of the tension of the subjective inwardness. Here is such a definition of truth: *An objective uncertainty held fast in an appropriation-process of the most passionate inwardness is the truth*, the highest truth attainable for an *existing* individual. At the point where the way swings off (and where this is cannot be specified objectively, since it is a matter of subjectivity), there objective knowledge is placed in abeyance. Thus the subject merely has, objectively, the uncertainty; but it is this which precisely increases the tension of that infinite passion which constitutes his inwardness. The truth is precisely the venture which chooses an objective uncertainty with the passion of the infinite. I contemplate the order of nature in the hope of finding God, and I see omnipotence and wisdom; but I also see much else that disturbs my mind and excites anxiety. The sum of all this is an objective uncertainty. But it is for this very reason that the inwardness becomes as intense as it is, for it embraces this objective uncertainty with the entire passion of the infinite. In the case of a mathematical proposition the objectivity is given, but for this reason the truth of such a proposition is also an indifferent truth.

But the above definition of truth is an equivalent expression for faith. Without risk there is no faith. Faith is precisely the contradiction between the infinite passion of the individual's inwardness and the objective uncertainty. If I am capable of grasping God objectively, I do not believe, but precisely because I cannot do this I must believe. If I wish to preserve myself in faith I must constantly be intent upon holding fast the objective uncertainty, so as to remain out upon the deep, over seventy thousand fathoms of water, still preserving my faith.

In the principle that subjectivity, inwardness, is the truth, there is comprehended the Socratic wisdom, whose everlasting merit it was to have become aware of the essential significance of existence, of the fact that the knower is an existing individual. For this reason Socrates was in the truth by virtue of his ignorance, in the highest sense in which this was possible within paganism. . . .

NOTES

1. The reader will observe that the question here is about essential truth, or about the truth which is essentially related to existence, and that it is precisely for the sake of clarifying it as inwardness or as subjectivity that this contrast is drawn.

2. In this manner God certainly becomes a postulate, but not in the otiose manner in which this word is commonly understood. It becomes clear rather that the only way in which an existing individual comes into relation with God, is when the dialectical contradiction brings his passion to the point of despair, and helps him to embrace God with the "category of despair" (faith). Then the postulate is so far from being arbitrary that it is precisely a life-necessity. It is then not so much that God is a postulate, as that the existing individual's postulation of God is a necessity.

3. *Stages on Life's Way*, Note on p. 426. Though ordinarily not wishing an expression of opinion on the part of reviewers, I might at this point almost desire it, provided such opinions, so far from flattering me, amounted to an assertion of the daring truth that what I say is something that everybody knows, even every child, and that the cultured know infinitely much better. If it only stands fast that everyone knows it, my standpoint is in order, and I shall doubtless make shift to manage with the unity of the comic and the tragic. If there were anyone who did not know it I might perhaps be in danger of being dislodged from my position of equilibrium by the thought that I might be in a position to communicate to someone the needful preliminary knowledge. It is just this which engages my interest so much, this that the cultured are

accustomed to say: that everyone knows what the highest is. This was not the case in paganism, nor in Judaism, nor in the seventeen centuries of Christianity. Hail to the nineteenth century! Everyone knows it. What progress has been made since the time when only a few knew it. To make up for this, perhaps, we must assume that no one nowadays does it.

# 15. THE NATURE OF

# RELIGIOUS PROPOSITIONS

## Paul L. Holmre

Paul Holmer, formerly Professor of Philosophy at the University of Minnesota, is now on the staff of Yale Divinity School. Among his writings are "Kierkegaard and Ethical Theory," "Language and Theology: Some Critical Notes," and Theology and the Scientific Study of Religion.

Are religious propositions cognitive? That the question can be put at all indicates that the vulgar-vernacular language used to describe and explain them no longer seems adequate. Once it would have been quite enough to ask: Of what are they cognitive? For if there is a single and necessary epistemological standpoint, a cognitive ground to which all propositions are referable, then there are conceivably a common sense and common premises for all learning. This is the conviction about cognition which has sustained supernaturalistic philosophies. For any supernaturalism turns out to be a vernacular kind of language and reflection which construes even moral and religious sentences by analogy with those sentences descriptive of nature. And it is because the convictions and beliefs about the possibility of such cognition itself have changed, that the vernacular accounts no longer seem relevant. The issue now is to show how religious propositions can be cognitive at all. Any descriptive philosophic account which takes for granted the possibility of cognitive meaning of religious sentences no longer meets the issue. The issue is now stated in the question: Are religious sentences cognitive?

Reprinted by permission of the Columbia University Press from *The Review of Religion*, Volume 19 (1955), pp. 136-49.

I

Attempts to translate religious sentences into other linguistic-reflective systems are also fraught with difficulties. It has been the claim of some philosophers that there is a unique philosophical standpoint, qualitatively distinct from all other kinds of standpoints. As Kierkegaard noted about Hegel, there are those who contend that philosophy is reflexive, a kind of awareness about awareness, in which trans-empirical reals are to be apprehended. Conceivably, then, there are at least two levels from which sentences are to be understood: first, as the expression of feelings, sensory intuition, imagination, and issuing in poetry, moral judgments, religious literature, and even empirical science; and, secondly, from the reflexive philosophic and truly cognitive standpoint. In this latter kind of understanding, the achievement is among others the translation of religious sentences into an even more abstract linguistic system, and the extent to which they can be thus translated is the extent to which they are true. This is by now a relatively familiar treatment of religious sentences by the philosophically sophisticated. Again, this kind of translation coincides with the vulgar view that there is a single philosophical standpoint, that there is a hidden "nature" and "truth" to which such a vantage point gives cognitive access. Here, also, there is ample ground for doubt, for if philosophy is not the cognition of trans-empirical "reals" but only of the forms and modes of reflection and expression, then nothing whatever is gained by translating religious sentences into philosophical rubrics.

On the other hand, it has been irresponsible thinking which has led many technical philosophers who have been otherwise known for their care and precision to insist, without careful analysis, that all religious sentences are simply nonsensical. Instead of the patient and exacting analysis of religious sentences with that kind of neutralization which the dialectical and linguistic tools of technical philosophy permits, we have seen, instead, a quick dumping of religious sentences to the heap called the meaningless. This is understandable psychologically, when one remembers that the vulgar-vernacular philosophies had so defined the religious sentence that even an acknowledgment of the likelihood of its truth seemed to come close to being a religious act.

Religious faith (or "belief" as it too is called) and cognitive belief have been defined so as to be almost indistinguishable in kind. And especially is this apparent when religious sentences and all others claiming to be cognitive are articulated within the same system of language and thought. It has been easy for anyone who denies the cognitive quality of a religious sentence to move too quickly, and by trading on the analogy between religious belief and cognitive belief, to insist that, if these sentences were meaningless, then there could be no faith or belief. This position is clear enough if one thinks about "believing" a descriptive sentence which purports to be true but yet is nonsensical. And contrariwise, to admit that there might be cognitive significance to a religious sentence seems almost to admit that one is a religious man. But, this is all the more reason why precautions are in order. The long discussion in theological history as well as the constantly shifting focus in philosophy ought to counsel even more care and solicitude than otherwise. And where the passions and enthusiasms of men are so proximate, as they are in religious matters, more care and precision is essential rather than less.

II

An extreme resolution always tempts the student of these matters. There are numerous illustrations, some of them recent, of such extremes. If one argues that religious sentences are cognitive and make truth claims, then the assent to the truth claim is a kind of belief. If the difference between being religious and being non-religious or irreligious can be cognitively described, then, it has often been urged, this difference is statable in terms of the sentences which are denied or asserted. The use to which creeds and other groups of sentences have been put by religious practitioners is a case in point. But, even here, difficulties have been acknowledged. For even the most avid adherents of creeds have known that assent to the truth claim of sentences is not a sufficient personal qualification to make one religious. Furthermore, the differential between persons that makes it easy for some to respond affirmatively to the sentences and others to respond negatively does not seem attributable to the ostensible truth function of the sentence. Therefore, both from the side of a religious interest and from a somewhat more disinterested cognitive side, there have come serious questions. More typically religiously motivated is the question—how do the personal qualities of the religious life stand related to an act of assent to the truth of sentences, whatever their content? And the cognitive interest is paramount in the question—how do we know religious sentences are true?

Beginning on the side of cognition, it is easy enough to insist that religion is not cognitive at all and that being religious is not "believing," at least in any sense analogous to cognitive assent or belief. This kind of analysis saves cognition from the apparent absurdities of religious knowing claims and yet demarcates an area, attitudinal and emotive, for religion. Arguing from the limits of cognition, one then proceeds to exclude cognitive components from religion, arguing that religious sentences are not propositions and are not cognitive but, instead, are expressions of convictions and attitudes. And these latter are not to be confused with the convictions or attitudes present when we say that something or other is true.

Then from the side of religion there comes a somewhat similar rejoinder. Sometimes one must admit that the motives for this kind of rejoinder are engendered by a need to defend religion against its learned despisers, but often too the case is made in order, ostensibly, to keep religious faith distinctively religious. Thus it has been often noted that, if religious faith is only an act of assent to true sentences, then this act of belief does not include many of the most important ingredients of religious living. The insistence upon cognitive religious truth gives maximal significance to the act of its acknowledgment. In order to combat the danger of a kind of intellectualism which might attenuate the stress upon other qualities of the religious life, like love, a sense of sin, etc., religious thinkers also push to the extreme of denying the cognitive component altogether. They then identify religious faith, not with belief (erstwhile cognitive), but rather with trust and confidence and loving. In the latter instance, then, one denies cognition in religious sentences for the sake of faith understood as a quality of a man. In the former instance, one denies the cognition in religious sentences for the sake of the intellectual consistency. But, in both instances, the cognitive status of religious sentences is denied, and the endeavor to describe the subject's religious act of belief by analogy

with cognitive acts is intentionally decried. And to such extremes
have both recent philosophy and also much of recent theology
brought the argument. This is the point towards which kinds of
positivists and some radical fideistic Protestants seem to converge.

But I should like to suggest that, despite the apparent agreement
between two parties otherwise disparate, this position is not as
significant as it might seem. One may concur in the attacks upon
the systematic constructs in which religion has been described without thereby agreeing that all religions are simply non-cognitive. For
to say the latter is to neglect the fact that religious sentences are
cognitive, but in somewhat peculiar ways. To deny that they are
cognitive in familiar ways is pertinent, for most theologians have
been so intent upon saying that they are cognitive, without distinguishing the peculiar sense in which they are so, that criticism
is deserved. Perhaps, too, religiosity is primarily a quality of persons, not of sentences, and perhaps religious faith is not analogous
to cognitive belief; but one can concede these points and still recognize a cognitive content in the religious sentences.

All of this is a token of the confusion that has long been manifest
in the discussions about cognition and belief, reason and faith. Most
philosophers, and certainly theologians, have shared the view that
to admit cognitive components in certain kinds of sentences is to
admit certain behavioral consequents. But there are no necessary
or even probable consequences between the act of admitting the
truth of objective cognitive sentences, whatever they concern, and
other acts and attitudes of a subject.

Theologians frequently speak as if the admission of cognitive
values in an ostensibly religious sentence "necessitates" the religious life, and philosophers seem to be holding in turn that a non-
cognitive attitude (if this is what faith is) "necessitates" that
religious sentences be non-cognitive. All of this reflects the confusion created by those who, in construing religious sentences as
cognitive, also insisted that the cognitive act of believing them was
a religious act of faith. This is an ambiguity closely related in kind
to that noted in other places between the "is" and the "ought." But
in religious theory, principally because the "ought" is so frequently
psychologically described, and also because the transformation of
the personality is so paramount, the confusion has been between
the statement of a truth (the "is") and the consequences that

knowing the truth is supposed to effect (the "ought"). Without noting that the nature of the transition from an objective and disinterested apprehension of true sentences to a subjective quality, called being religious is not itself an implication nor a *natural* movement to be described as a relation of cause to effect, the distinction intrinsic to the peculiarity of religious sentences is thereby blurred.

It is with the intention of drawing these distinctions that the following is written.

Religious sentences are cognitive, but in a manner which begs elucidation. They are cognitive of a possible way of constituting one's life and daily existence. There are truths about actualities and truths about possibilities. As long as men cannot know descriptively and as an actuality the future which does not as yet exist, they only encounter it as a possibility. A future which is conceived or which is conceivable is a possibility. Perhaps it is to the extent that one has fears and anxieties and concern about himself and others that every man also tries to conceive and plan his anticipated existence. The rules for describing and conceiving possibilities are stringent, but do not by themselves limit markedly the range of possibilities. Sentences about a possibility are true or false about it considered as an object to be described. And this is cognitive truth—truth as a quality of a sentence. Such truth presupposes that we agree about the definition of the possibility before describing it. Possibilities have names and are definable. There is a correctness in respect to that which is defined and named, even if one names fictions.

But it must be admitted immediately that such cognitive truth is not peculiarly religious. For to cognize possibilities is a prerogative of all kinds of persons, and it is logically conceivable that the knowledge of a possibility might be entertained irrespective of qualities more personal and idosyncratic. Furthermore, one can dawdle with possibilities as do the world's dreamers, the insane, and children. Of course, it is one thing to entertain possibilities and another thing to know about them. The latter presupposes that they be systematic and coherent, free of ambiguities, clearly articulated and defined. But granted this restriction, there still does not seem to be anything peculiarly religious about such sentences as might be said to describe conceived future possibilities. And it is another question altogether to decide which possibility will, in fact, be the one I shall seek to realize.

One might state the matter in another form: To assent to the truth of a sentence about a possibility, even if it were one describing a Nirvana-kind of existence or the converted life of a Christian, does not mean anything more in respect to the subject than that he admits that the sentence is true of the way of life thus named. Everyone who agreed to this description could, ostensibly, from the truth of the description decide not to choose such a kind of life among the several possibilities which there are. Therefore, the admission of the cognitive truth about possibilities does not seem to involve necessarily anything that religion has tried to describe with the word faithfulness or righteousness.

Therefore, it would seem that, to the degree that religious sentences are about future possibilities, they can be cognitive and true, but that the knowledge of this truth is not intrinsically religious. But to say this much is to omit something very important from consideration, viz., the fact that many sentences called religious are also cognitive in a factual sense. At least they claim to be cognitive factually. And it is the supposed factual reference that has made religious sentences appear to be crypto-scientific and hence occasioned repeated conflicts between science and religion. It is typical of the religious literature of Christianity, Judaism, and Islam to make many factual assertions. It is not my purpose here to suggest that all of them, or even any of them, are true or false. The question of which are true and which false, which are meaningless, etc., has to be decided by empirical investigation, and certainly it is only philosophical naïveté that has credited the idea that all of any group of sentences about matters of fact must be true together or otherwise false together. Both religious apologists and attackers have shared this genial error in the past, thus exciting glee that was incommensurate with either the proofs or the refutations.

But there is a kind of factual claim that is intrinsic to some religious statements. Some religions, and most notably those mentioned above, contend that the future possibility is to be discovered in human history. The history of Israel, taken both as a series of events experienced by Jews and as a narrative about those events, is claimed to be a disclosure also of a possible way of existing. Likewise, the life of a historical man, Jesus, is claimed to be the possibility of a new life. In the latter instance, extremely interesting and difficult things are said; for there are those who say that the possibility was created by his words and language, and others who say that his existence itself is the possibility, even if he had not sketched a new life linguistically. But this is a controversy for theologians—the issue at point is that some religions make cognitive claims about historical events and relate these to the cognitive claims about the possibilities.

Cognitive claims about historical events, even the claims that a man existed or that tribes existed, are hypothetically certain claims. And it is important to remember that sentences used by religious men to assert the factual existence of anyone or any group are probable assertions and subject to the dialectic of all sentences about matters of fact. There is certainly no a priori reason why some sentences about matters of fact are more certain than others. Attempts of religious thinkers to make all the sentences of religious literature both factual and certain led to such absurdities as inspiration and infallibility, both desperate efforts to make secure what could not in fact be made secure.

Once again it must be indicated that the admission of the truth of sentences about matters of fact does not, of itself, produce religiosity. It is most difficult to see that sentences about anything you please in the past can become religious by virtue simply of their truth claim. The admission of a man's existence (or assertion that he existed, was of such an age, height, race, etc.), just as the admission of a people's existence and history seem to be left simply as a cognitive act, best achieved in a state of neutrality and objectivity. Thus, granting that religious sentences are cognitive of either a possibility or an actual existent does not sufficiently distinguish them from other sentences to make them religious, for it is certainly possible to admit the cognitive truth of ostensibly religious sentences without losing the neutrality of the knowing subject, and without becoming a passionately religious man.

But at this point it is well to remember again what the more speculative and braver philosophies (and theologies) attempted. We have admitted two kinds of cognitive truths that are ostensibly to be found in religious propositions, but metaphysical philosophies have proposed a way to connect these two and thus make these cognitive truths more specifically religious, much less neutral and detached. First, however, the setting must be remembered. There were and are today people who report that there was an ancient people called Jews, who did so and so. With more detail we learn that they believed they were chosen and that this made them heavy with the responsibility of being priests to all nations. Thus far we have two kinds of cognition: reports about an existing people and an account of a possible way of living (perhaps also the remark that some of them lived this way, others did not, etc.). Other persons might say there was a man, and that by him a new way of life was preached. Classical philosophies in the service of these claims tried to resolve the two questions: Why should the possibility be here? and, Why should I choose this possibility among others? Classical supernaturalism attempts to give a kind of present tense linguistic description in which God can be understood and described as equally related to past, present, and future. In this present tense language system, the historical events and future possibilities are treated in non-temporal language, and cognitive links are purported to stand forth between otherwise disparate and discontinuous events.

Thus it was and is argued that *because* of God, therefore the possibilities do exist and are to be actualized. Of course, one cannot deny that the kind of cognition which claims to know that sentences about God are true, appears richer and also appears more religious, in virtue of its subject matter, than knowledge of historical events in their historicity and knowledge of possibilities ever can. But this is the question. Attempts to show that one has cognition of God and that sentences about God are meaningful and/or true are vitiated by epistemological considerations. Therefore it seems both more expedient and befittingly modest to let the cognition of religious sentences rest at what it is, viz., claims about historical existence (in some faiths) and claims about possibilities. Therewith, however, it must be admitted that we do not seem to be in the position to show cognitively why any possibility is thus asserted, or that it ought to be asserted, or that it ought to be actualized. We can only begin with the cognitive assertions and test their veracity if we choose, but not include them in any broader cognitive claim which might seem to make cognition itself religious.

But then the question arises as to whether this analysis does justice to the uses given religious sentences. We have admitted that, as cognitive truths (supposing them cognitive and omitting those which cannot be shown to be), there is nothing intrinsically peculiar either about their content nor the act of believing them. There is, in other words, nothing religious in either instance. This is to say that the act of belief in a cognitive sentence is not an act of religious faith. Attempts to enlarge cognition to include a trans-empirical object (God) has the superficial merit of introducing a religious content into the sentence and making the act of believing such a sentence a religious appearing act. In another context I argue that this is theological superstition, and, in any case, it is insupportable on cognitive grounds.

But how can religious faith be distinguished? Religions differ at this point, but let us begin with the most complex first—those religions which make historical claims. Religious faith for such religions does suppose that one believes in a proposition that, e.g., a people or a person did exist. Here there are historical grounds for the belief. The belief is cognitive; its meaning is delineated by the evidence the sentence accounts for. Secondly, all religions seemingly described a possibility—a way of living and of personal being that is at least conceivable, however difficult it may be to actualize. Again, one may believe that the description is true—one may further believe that this possibility is presented in historical concreteness (thus the second is combined with the first). However, neither of these acts of belief by itself nor both together are acts of religious faith, but, depending on the religion, they may be necessary in order that the act of religious faith takes place. (This is an issue that again must be discussed by theologians, for it involves the differentia between religions, most notably those of Christianity and Judaism as over against perhaps some of those of the Orient.)

The peculiarity of the religious act of faith, or belief as it too is sometimes called, is that it requires not simply that I hold certain sentences to be true, but rather that I am becoming the possibility thus described. This latter act is non-cognitive, but probably presupposes the cognitive acts noted above. To become a possibility is to admit an interest, an enthusiasm, a passion for the possibility heretofore only cognitively described. The cognitive act of belief is qualitatively distinct from religious faith, as disinterested apprehension is from interested pursuit. The peculiar difficulties of discussion at this point have been more typical of those religions which involve both a disinterested knowledge and an interested enthusiasm, less typical of those religions which minimize the significance of an historical locus for the occurrence of the possibility. But it seems clarifying, to me at least, to distinguish the cognitive sentences, admitting their religious neutrality whatever their religious use, and then also to separate the cognitive act of belief from the religious act of belief as objectivity is separated from subjectivity, as contemplation is from enthusiasm.

The confusion in religious discourse may be described this way: insisting upon the importance of the cognition of a (religious) possibility, religious faith becomes confused with cognitive belief; insisting upon the non-cognitive aspect of faith, religious sentences mistakenly are assumed to be non-cognitive. Here, instead, a distinction is drawn. Religious sentences are cognitive but are not religious in virtue of this. As cognitive, since sentences describe the possibility of a religious life and believing these sentences is a neutral cognitive act. But becoming religious is a matter of having a non-cognitive enthusiasm and interest in becoming the possibility that can be cognitively described. To translate the sentences into this non-cognitive and passionate context is to put the sentence to a truly religious use. Thus, both cognition and faith can be delineated in relation to the same sentences, the first being nonreligious and dispassionate, the second being religious and passionate. But a possibility which can be objectively known and yet subjectively reduplicated is properly called religious when it is remembered that the stress is upon the latter, the reduplication and becoming, rather than the former, the act of awareness.

IV

All of this is a proposal that cognitive-appearing sentences in religious discourse once again be examined closely. It is being here proposed that a sentence, for example, in which it is asserted that a man is God (and, e.g., all other sentences about an incarnation) be read as, there is or there was (as the case may be) a man who is (or announces) a new possibility, a new way of life. To say this much is to stay within the cognitive. The details about this possibility which contrast it with other possibilities can be added and usually are in more discourse.

This is to assert further, that men do not have knowledge of a divine being who has divine qualities. Religious sentences, including the above, are phrased as if they do. The mode of arguing by analogy, therefore, suggests that the incarnation is a kind of surprise, because it means the juxtaposition of divine qualities and a human being. Whatever justice this may have done to the passions men have felt, this does not do justice when considered from a cognitive standpoint. For *cognitively* men do not encounter a divine being. Men might call certain qualities, with which cognition has to do, divine, and this for various reasons, some of which might be appropriate. But, that these qualities are *known* to be of a divine being is another matter. Here the structure of language seems to have invited the confusion, and many other features of reflective and linguistic usage have sustained it. The cognitive meaning of the God idea is given only by the order of ethical and logical possibilities as this is augmented by long experience of the race. The Hebrews and Christians utilized the first of these (ethical possibilities), certain Greeks the second, and most of Western theology has tried to wed the two into one by insisting the God could be *known* as an actuality, an existing being with attributes. What I am here suggesting is, therefore, only that the cognitive content of religious sentences be admitted to be as limited as it is. To say a man is God or that the world is created by God (to choose another salient example) is to say something cognitive, but, when such sentences are analyzed, they say among other things—this man is (or taught) a kind (to be specified . . .) of possibility or the world and things in it are like gifts—they are given—and can be understood so. It is the qualities of the possibility that are the cognitive grounds for the divinity claim.

The analysis of the sentences of Christian literature into *kerygma* and *didache* made by C. H. Dodd and others, roughly corresponds to the distinctions noted here. The didache sentences, which are defined as moral teaching, are there distinguished from the kerygmatic sentences, which are factual and historical. From a standpoint of an epistemological analysis, however, this distinction is only approximate, for it is characteristic of religious sentences that a declaration of possibility be given within a factual and historical assertion. The didache sentences are specifications of the possibility and identify it in contrast to all other possibilities; furthermore, in the New Testament they enjoin and persuade and stimulate and, therefore, are not simply cognitive but much else besides.

This position here argued does not deny the importance of religious cognition. With rather technical reasons which will be considered in a later paper, it can be shown that the extent of cognitive significance of a religious sentence depends upon the peculiarity and specificness of the possibility it names or describes. That many religious sentences describe only in different modes and words the same possibility may be the case; but that all do so becomes doubtful as one begins to read the religious literature. There are some striking differences among religious and moral teachings. And one must remember, too, that there is no a priori way, nor any ultimate metaphysical intuition from which one can leap into this array of possibilities and decide which is true, which are religious, which are only ethical or non-religious, etc. The fact that the possibility which religious sentences describe is peculiar means that its source in history is a problem. Some religions, at least, do not describe a possibility that is in accord with the wishes of the majority, and this draws attention not only to the question of the source of such possibilities but also gives a clue as to why it has seemed plausible to some to claim that anyone who advances such a possibility might be called unique if not divine.

A related issue has to do with the question of the desirability of this possibility. When persons have argued that religious propositions are emotive or, as Freud did, that they are wish-fulfillments, they seem to have taken for granted that the religious possibility expressed the wish. Interestingly enough, most religious theories, i.e., sentences about religious sentences, have denied this. The declaration of the possibility can be cognitively encountered when it is specifically declared, and this should indicate that a religious sentence is not so individuated as to lack all intersubjective reference. But granted this reference, it is argued further that the possibility thus declared is not possible to do or to be, by which it is meant, I take it, that it is not desirable to all who recognize it cognitively as a possibility.

The fact that a possibility must be cognized before it is significantly realized is also a requirement of some religions—this insistence reflecting the view that, otherwise, the religious possibility might not actually be met, because one's own wish might then be determinative. Such niceties again belong to another kind of analysis, but suffice it to note that religious sentences are not easy to believe in. If they were only wish-fulfillments, it would be a little difficult to understand the stress that has been put upon the cognitive and identifiable character of the religious possibility. And, likewise, if religious faith were only unrestrained subjectivity, then it is difficult also to understand the large stress which has been given to showing that faith is something unexpected—this because it is thought so widely that the reduplication of the qualities of life which such a possibility describes is so difficult a matter.

V

In conclusion it might be said that this paper urges that the endeavor to interpret religious sentences as cognitive of trans-empirical realities be given up. And this for two reasons: one, that there is no epistemological warrant for such kinds of assertions (even if there is an intuition of such realities, this would be an event, an occurrence, but not a warrant for the truth of sentences!); and secondly, that the attempt to use knowledge of a trans-empirical Deity as the ground for the possibility so occurring in a given instance and also as the reason for my pursuit of it—this was also a mistaken argument. It seems more appropriate, therefore, to urge that religious sentences can be cognitive of historical events and, also, that they are the occasion for the cognition of a possibly new and definitive mode of life. But the religious act of faith is not to believe the truth of the description of the possibility nor even the historical claims. Perhaps such an act of belief is a necessary condition for religious faith, but it is not itself religious, for religious faith peculiarly is the passionate and enthusiastic becoming of a possibility. Faith is not belief—cognitive belief—but is instead a non-cognitive translation of a heretofore cognated possibility into the concreteness of one's idiosyncratic character.

This point of view seems to do justice to both the restraints that are induced by ruled reflection and the uses to which religious sentences are in fact put. What this point of view omits is the luxurious claims that there are cognitive truths about God Himself. But in the nature of the case, these are allowable only from God's point of view! And the attempted simulation of a God's cognitive grasp does honor neither to the religious life nor to the proper use of language and reflection.

# 16. THE COGNITIVE FACTOR

# IN RELIGIOUS EXPERIENCE

A SYMPOSIUM

## H. D. Lewis · C. H. Whiteley

H. D. Lewis is Professor of the History and Philosophy of Religion at King's College, University of London. His writings include Morals and the New Theology, Morals and Revelation, and Our Experience of God. He is also editor of Religious Studies, a new journal in the philosophy of religion, and contributor to many other philosophical works.
C. H. Whiteley is Reader in Philosophy at the University of Birmingham. He is author of "The Elements of Meaning" and other scholarly writings.

H. D. LEWIS

A further point about religious experience, which I do not expect to arouse much opposition, is that the main questions to ask about religious experience, most of all at a gathering of philosophers, are the epistemological ones about its validity or cognitive value. It may be possible to say more precise and colourful things at the more descriptive or phenomenological level, and that is the approach to the subject most commonly adopted today by recent writers on the subject, from William James to Monsignor Knox. But that is very unfortunate, partly because the decisive issues, in matters of thought at present, are epistemological ones, and partly because the question of truth is a basic one in religion for the layman and the specialist alike. What most of us want to know initially about religion is whether its claims are true and how they are established.

Reprinted by permission of the Editor of The Aristotelian Society from Proceedings of the Aristotelian Society, Supplementary Volume 29 (1955), pp. 61-64, 75-83, 85-92.

This makes it all the more regrettable that religious and theological writers in general today—there are notable exceptions—should be so extremely evasive about epistemological questions. They are not altogether without excuse, and I may be found to incur a somewhat similar reproach myself in due course; for the cognitive factor in religious experience is peculiarly elusive, as I shall stress. But there can be no justification for the common procedure today of addressing oneself to distinctively epistemological questions, often with a great flourish, and then converting these, in the course of discussing them, into ethical or psychological ones. I have ventured to censure this confusing procedure sharply elsewhere.

It also seems to be a factor of major importance in the decline of religion that men generally have come to despair of settling its claims or even of making them meaningful. There are no doubt many other reasons for the prevailing indifference to religion, notably social ones; and it is well known, in many matters beside religion, that we may believe certain things very firmly without heeding them much. Newman has told us a great deal about this in the celebrated account he gives (in a well known but somewhat neglected work, *The Grammar of Assent*) of the distinction he draws between "real" and "notional" assent. Ideas need to be made vivid for us and made to count for us personally by being related to matters that concern us closely if their full impact is to be felt. There is scope here for much co-operation of the artist, the prophet, the priest and the thinker. We may also bring to mind Hobbes's shrewd observation that although "the power of spirits invisible" is greater than the power of men, the latter is usually much more feared. I think this reflects more than Hobbes's religious scepticism, but when every allowance has been made for the need to enliven our beliefs and bring out the implications of what we profess, it seems evident that the claims of religion are so overwhelming and, in the case of religions such as Christianity, so closely related to social and ethical matters, that no one could easily remain indifferent to them—if only he could be certain they were true.

This brings me to a more controversial point, but one of the soundness and importance of which I have no doubt at all myself. This point is obviously not so evident to other philosophers today as it is to me, for it has been seriously queried in a number of recent philosophical discussions of the subject, to say nothing of similar expressions of opinion in cognate studies and popular writings. I am none-the-less certain that the beginning of wisdom in dealing with religious questions, together with our hope of addressing ourselves effectively to a situation of peculiar interest which confronts us in the relations of religion and culture today, depends on the point to which I now turn.

It is that we cannot expect to give an adequate account of religious experience entirely in terms of the agent who has it or of his relations to his fellow men. The object of religious experience is God, and whatever else we may find it possible to say about God, it is certain that we must think of God as some reality "more than human," as the common phrase goes. Indeed, I am sure we must go further and refuse to identify God with any part of our natural environment or any other finite reality. It is here that the word "spiritual," and even the word "supernatural," are apt to be rather misleading. The former is sometimes used to designate anything which is not strictly material or physical; and, in some cases of this kind, it might easily be rendered by "mental." Others understand by "spiritual realities" such things as the moral law or values or some alleged "purpose in history." "Supernatural," again, may be applied to beings other than men who are without many of our limitations, the dead in after life, for example, or other disembodied spirits superior in power at least to ourselves although not always superior in goodness, some of them being evil spirits. What grounds there may be for believing in such beings does not concern us now, although I shall have one comment to make on the subject shortly. But what I wish especially to stress is that we must think of God as not merely "more than human" or supernatural in the senses noted, but as complete and perfect or absolute in a way which it is not possible for any other finite being to be. The compulsion upon us to believe in God is bound up with His having this perfection, and many of the arguments for and against His existence miss the mark by failing to pay due heed to this particular point or to understand it. The idea of "a finite God," still much canvassed in some quarters, misrepresents religion at almost every point, and most of all perhaps where it seems to provide a solution of outstanding difficulties such as the problem of evil. . . .

How then must the infinite or transcendent nature of God be understood? I shall not say anything very new here. The view I hold is substantially the same as the one we associate mainly at present with the work of the Neo-Thomists, but of which the exponents and followers of St. Thomas cannot claim a strict monopoly. It is a view peculiarly difficult to state, and that is itself a point we need especially to stress, the exhibition of the difficulty being a main achievement of the writers to whom I have referred. One way of stating this difficult point would be to say that nothing can be finally fortuitous except certain acts of choice which modify but do not suspend the continuity we find elsewhere. But the fullness of this conviction cannot be unfolded until it is also seen that the inevitability of the fact of everything being what it is carries us beyond any particular facts of experience or relations between them to an absolute or unconditioned ground or source of the existence of anything other than itself. But because we are bound to be moving here at the limits of intelligibility and cannot rely on processes of thinking similar to those by which we normally make sense of our environment, the formulation of the conviction to which I have alluded can never be satisfactory or given a content similar to other assertions. This does not affect its certainty; I believe it is one of the most certain convictions men have. But to lay hold upon it in reflection and indicate how the necessity we find in things can only be properly appreciated when it is also felt to have a certain "beyondness" which from the nature of the case eludes specification, is also extremely difficult. Perhaps the best advice we can offer here is that of a recent Catholic writer who urges us to go on looking at "what 'being' stands for until it breaks into finite and infinite."[1]

There are many subtle philosophical reflections of this situation, the most obvious of them to my mind being the predicament of those who write about "the grounds of induction." On the one hand they find it hard to provide reasonable grounds for being reasonable without moving in a circle; on the other, they feel that grounds or justification there must somehow be. The world may spring endless surprises upon us and defy our calculations, but nothing would induce us to abandon the attempt to make it meaningful. Nor would this be merely a case of desperate hope or of being conditioned to look for explanations. On the contrary we believe that explanation there must eventually be, and however much sophistication may cause us to doubt this, I submit that it remains at the end an ineradicable conviction that comes to us with a force akin to logical necessity. At the same time there is implied in the compulsion upon us to look for intelligibility in this way the requirement that the intelligibility or meaningfulness of the world derives from more than any meaning we will actually find in it. The guarantee of this meaningfulness must come from outside itself and bring our thoughts beyond its own limits to the recognition of some absolute existence in which reason, and the evaluations that go with it, can find rest beyond its own restlessness and limitations. All our experience posits the transcendent in this way. However far we push our account of any matter there will always confront us a question "Why?" to be asked, a question to which in the last resort no answer is possible although it will always remain significant to ask it. Problems about beginning and end in Space or Time exhibit this situation particularly sharply, but I can hardly consider closely here the various ways we may converge on my present theme.

The view I have outlined used to be presented at one period as "the demand that reality should be a whole." There seems to me to be much to be said for this formulation, subject to certain qualifications the most important of which is that "the whole" should not be understood in the sense of rationalist Neo-Hegelian idealism. It must be a "supra-rational" whole, and this brings me to some further points to be noted here. The movement from finite fact to the transcendent is not an argument in the proper sense, and attempts to prove the existence of God commonly err by neglecting this. That is what makes them open to obvious objections with which we are quite familiar, but critics have also been over-confident and have failed to appreciate subleties which suggest that the sponsors of the arguments had more in mind than their formal expositions show. The "argument from design" deviates most obviously from the truth, although I believe it also reflects imperfectly the notion of intelligibility passing beyond itself; and we can certainly regard design as having importance for religion. To avoid the pitfalls of the traditional proofs, some elect to speak of "an intuition of the being of God." But there is need here also of caution, for the phrase might be taken in the very objectionable sense that we have some unmediated contact with God similar to the direct awareness of other finite minds which some philosophers have, very mistakenly in my opinion, thought to be possible. "Intuition" is also generally used to indicate some apprehension which has a more specific content than the awareness of the transcendent to which I have referred. But with caveats of this sort in mind, we may well use the term "intuition of the being of God" until better terms are found for a movement of thought peculiarly difficult to designate.

The reference to an unmediated contact with God accentuates a further point. For if the transcendent, while being implicit in all operations of thought in the way indicated, must also be so completely beyond the reach of understanding as I have made out, must it not remain for us, in every way other than the intuition of its existence, an absolute mystery? Can we know anything of God other than that He must be—or the minimum which that has already been seen to involve? If we cannot, then it does not seem very appropriate to speak of "religious experience," for whatever else these words mean they certainly imply some more personal intimate relation of ourselves to God than is involved in the formal apprehension of the general dependence of all things upon Him. The person who claims to have had a religious experience thinks of himself as having been "in the presence of God," he declares that God "has laid His hand upon" him, or spoken to him, and that there is light to be gained in the personal communion of men with God which is not available in any other way. It is said that there are times when God is very near and times when He is remote, the individual is "comforted" by the presence of God and, at other times, feels forsaken or abandoned because God has withdrawn His presence. I need not multiply examples. But it is evident that, if we are to speak of religious experience, in the sense of some communion of the individual with God, there is presupposed in this some very particular knowledge of God by which the communion is sustained. There will, no doubt, be many other aspects of the experience and many things which the individual will learn in the course of it about himself or his society or his natural environment. But he learns all this in the context of a communion with God which involves apprehension of God of a much more intimate nature than the formal knowledge that He must exist as an incomprehensible transcendent source of everything else that exists. Is such knowledge possible, and is it proper to regard it, as some religious persons do, as the very core of religion?

It has certainly been held in some religions at times that we do not have the personal communion of the individual with God to which I have just referred, and this teaching has had repercussions on moral and social outlooks as well as on more strictly religious practices, leading to passivity and world renunciation. Others lay claim to experiences in which they become literally one with God or have it revealed to them that they are always so, the seeming distinctness of finite creatures being an illusion. Neither of these latter positions seems to me possible, literal identification with God being the same as complete annihilation. One can well understand how one might seem to lose one's identity in certain forms of mystical experience, and those who report their own experiences in such terms are undoubtedly saying something of the utmost importance for our understanding of religion; but I am equally certain, as I hinted at the start, that they are confused. I am also convinced that there has been much misunderstanding of religious allusions to total extinction of the self, most of all in our study of Eastern religions on which we have only too often imposed our own habits of thought and speech. A further way of dealing with our problem is to seek to extract, by the method of analogy, certain particular truths about God out of the initial intuition of His being and perfection, but I doubt whether this brings any substantial advance, if any at all, on what we originally knew; least of all does it give us the warmth and vitality of faith, as its sponsors are well aware. How then do we stand? Are we to renounce particular knowledge of God, or can we still claim it?

It must be said at once here that almost all religions do make this claim at some point, and the claims to particular knowledge of God made by some religions are very extensive. It is held for example that God answers prayer and that a peculiarly intimate sense of His presence to the individual worshipper is possible and has happened in some very notable ways that have much affected the course of history. There are men who claim to live continuously under the guidance of God. Such claims are not always convincing, and it is well known how prone certain types of religious people are to delude themselves or to adhere stubbornly to fixed ideas whose religious credentials are very doubtful. This is a subject of study in itself. But it is also evident that forms of religion which elicit the highest respect depend on the claim to know some things about God in a very definite way and to have communion with Him on that basis. The transcendent is also immanent, and it is impossible to consider the cognitive problems of religion effectively without a lively sense of the importance of both these terms in it. To say something helpful about this problem, without radical modification of the two terms that make it especially acute, seems to be the main task of religious apologetics at present.

No easement of the problem is possible by mere appeal to authority, whether it be of doctrine, scriptures or church. There is place for authority in religion, a peculiarly important one which goes beyond any part authority normally plays in social existence and the general pursuit of truth. But we certainly cannot rest on mere authority. Even those who attach most importance to it must say something at least about its credentials. Nor do we seem to me in very much better case in respect of a view very much in favour at present among upholders of religion, especially the more intellectual kind, namely that in some fashion we choose to believe or commit ourselves to a faith. There certainly is commitment in religion, but we cannot just opt for a particular faith. To say that we can do so gives very dangerous hostages to fortune, for people may opt for very strange things. Belief is not in fact a matter of choice at all, although we may choose to cultivate belief. Whether there is a duty to do that beyond the duty to put ourselves in the way of the fullest appreciation of the truth is a moot point which I will not attempt to investigate now.

What alternative then have we? Particular knowledge of God religion must have, the more enlightened as much as any. But how is this possible if God is also so remote and so far beyond our comprehension as religion itself, as well as philosophical thought about it, declares Him to be?

It is for this dilemma that we must seek a solution in terms of a special sort of experience. The more we appreciate the peculiar and absolute character of God's transcendence, the more evident does it become, as notable religious writings have recently stressed, that we cannot acquire particular knowledge of God by speculations of our own based on what we find our secular experience to be. We must rather rely on some intrusion into the latter in the form of distinctive religious experiences.

The dominating feature of such experiences, however, must be

the part which is played in them by the initial intuition of the being
of God to which I have already alluded; and here it must be stressed
that although the intuition in question is elusive in the sense indicated already, namely that it is peculiarly difficult to describe it or
to exhibit its content, it is not elusive in the sense of being confined
to a few or to very rare moments of insight or illumination. It does
indeed present a special problem to philosophers, and I believe that
it is a very important part of the task of the philosophy of religion
today to bring out the peculiarity and elusiveness of the conviction
of the existence of God in the way noted above, more especially as
our training and many other features of contemporary culture induce us to look for God in the wrong way. But that does not make
our awareness of God directly the result of philosophical thinking
or a privilege of philosophers. The function of philosophy here is
to refine our thought and its expression, to turn our attention in
the right direction, and to remove obstructions and thwarting presuppositions. The divination of an overwhelming mystery in which
all existence is rooted, not in the sense of a mere failure of normal
explanation but, as stressed above, in the sense of being compelled
to believe in a positive, but wholly incomprehensible, source of all
other reality, is, in my opinion, one which flashes on the minds of
most men in most cultures at some time or another, and it is the
basis of further religious experiences.

For, I submit, it is in the association of this intuition of the being
of God with the outstanding secular features of the situations in
which it occurs to an individual that shape is given to specific religious experiences. It is at this point that I part company, in some
measure at least, from my Thomist friends, for they accord to the
doctrine of analogy a sort of intermediary function between the
awareness of God's existence and revealed truth, and thereby also
extend the gap between natural and revealed theology. I deem
these two to be closely integrated, and I find the integration especially in the way the initial sense of ultimate mystery lends something of its own quality to the secular situations which evoke it.
This does not, as some theologians have assumed, degrade or render
otiose the principles and evaluations of normal secular experience.
On the contrary it lends them a new depth or dimension by taking
them up as essential ingredients in the life of religion. The impact
of the sense of our relation to God upon the matters which present

themselves independently as having the greatest worth in our lives, and especially the occurrence of this in moments of strain and crisis, presents itself moreover with a peculiar insistence and starkness which distinguishes the experience as a whole sharply from other cases of upheaval and excitement, and this, in combination with the enhancement of ordinary insight and evaluation, gives the experience as a whole the force of an intrusion upon our secular existence whose course increasingly induces an association of it with the transcendent reality which is present in a specially insistent way to our minds as a controlling feature of the whole experience. The illumination obtained in such moments may present itself also therefore as a sense of a personal Presence in ways that have close affinity with our relations to one another.

The repercussions of moments of religious insight of this kind upon the remainder of experience is considerable, and in many cases the evidence of the live religious experience can only be found in the persistence of some of its effects, such as a heightening of the moral quality of our conduct. This is what lends pragmatic accounts of religious truth some plausibility. But the evidence cannot be really appropriate unless it is taken in conjunction with direct consideration of properly religious occurrences. Of the course which such occurrences take in the life of individuals or of societies and of the significance they have in relation to one another and to other features of experience, especially through the transmutation of ordinary standards, the clearest indication is found in the accumulated experience of religious societies. To reflect upon this experience and bring out what is most distinctive and significant in it seems to me to be an urgent and outstanding task of religious thought, and in undertaking it we should be careful to examine religious utterances that reflect a warm many-sided experience in relation to the varied complicated factors which constitute that experience in the lives of individuals. Religious doctrines have often taken shape, unfortunately, by systematising religious utterances without due heed to their reference to the experiences they reflect; and this, in combination with the confusions and the corruptions of genuine religion to which I referred earlier, has resulted in many religious notions, taken very often to be beyond question and indispensable to religious living, which it is extremely hard to accept in the sense we would normally give them. I do not say they should be shelved for that reason, but their function and the account we finally give of them need to be examined by taking them in relation to the original experiences they reflect.

## II. C. H. WHITELEY

The expression "religious experience" can be used in a wider or in a narrower sense. In its wide sense it would cover all those experiences men have when they are concerning themselves with a divine being—worshipping him, praying to him, meditating upon him, or endeavouring to please him. In particular, it would include all feelings and attitudes of reverence, fear, trust, love, etc. directed towards God, or one of many gods. In the present context, I do not think this wide sense of the expression is serviceable. For if we are to put religious experiences into a special category, as we might put aesthetic or erotic experiences, and inquire into their properties, we assume that, as experiences, they have a special character or combination of characters which groups them together and marks them off from secular experiences; "the experiences which are properly religious," says Professor Lewis, "are distinctive and specific." Now it seems to me that the great majority of religious experiences, in this wide sense of the expression, have no such character. The fact that an attitude or sentiment is directed towards a divine being does not suffice to give it a distinctive nature. Revering God, fearing God, trusting in God have no special feature which should make us class them together rather than with their respective secular counterparts—revering a wise teacher or the Moral Law, fearing one's parents or the police, trusting the word of a friend or the solvency of a bank. Preachers indeed often use such analogies. Even the love of God, to judge from the language in which it is described, can sometimes be very like the love of a mistress.

Our inquiry will not have much point unless there are certain experiences occurring in religious contexts which are of an exceptional character, distinguishing them from all secular experiences. (Of course, the difference may well be one of degree, admitting many intermediate cases.) I believe that there are such experiences, and I will try to give some indication of what is peculiar about them. Firstly, they seem to be experiences of being laid hold of, gripped, drawn, enveloped, even possessed, by a power of a kind outside the range of the subject's ordinary experience, not therefore to be identified with any normal power of his own personality or his material environment. Something takes hold of him and impresses upon him a conviction, a sentiment, an attitude of mind, a resolve. The influence may come suddenly and unexpectedly, or the subject may struggle for a long time before surrendering to it; but in either case it feels like an alien and unfamilar power. Secondly, these experiences are experiences of conviction, in which it seems to the subject that some truth is revealed to him. He becomes certain of something of which otherwise he would be uncertain, and that in a manner which admits of no doubt at the time, and may indeed dismiss all doubt for the rest of his life. Thirdly, whatever emotions are present in religious experience (wonder, joy, thankfulness, despair) are felt, not necessarily violently, but deeply and intensely. Religious experience is absorbing, it cannot be taken lightly, it engages the whole attention and the whole personality. Fourthly, religious experience is influential. It not only seems at the time to be of great importance, but it has an effect, often a very great effect, on the subsequent thoughts, feelings, attitudes and actions of the subject. It is to experiences of this type, or approximating to it, that I shall refer in speaking of religious experience in this paper; not that I think that the everyday religious sentiments, attitudes and endeavours are unimportant, but I cannot find anything significant to say about them in general, as a class. Religious experiences in this sense are rare. To most men they happen on only a few occasions in a lifetime; and there may well be many men, accounted religious, to whom they never happen. But they are not isolated from the more ordinary religious feelings and actions of those to whom they happen, and they are not to be understood apart from the rest of the religious life.

Religious experience, as I have described it, has as one of its features a conviction that something or other is true. Now the things that men have become convinced of in the course of religious experience are very various, and some of them are very strange. They cannot all be true, because they are not all mutually consistent. And many of them are on other grounds very hard for contemporary thinkers to swallow. At the same time, religious experiences are often extremely satisfying and desirable in themselves, and salutary in their effects on the happiness and good behaviour of those who enjoy them. Consequently, many people are attracted by the hope of detaching the affective and conative elements in religious experience from their cognitive accompaniments, so that men may continue to enjoy the emotional experience and put it to the service of a purely secular way of living. For such people, the cognitive features of religious experience are incidental and irrelevant. What men seek and obtain from religious experience is not information; it is encouragement, consolation, moral balance, mystical rapture. Can we not seek and obtain these things without the encumbrance of metaphysical beliefs, and especially without the belief that these experiences involve any contact with supernatural beings? Can we not have the sort of experience hitherto described as "meeting God" without committing ourselves to the dogma that there is a God to be met? Is this programme feasible?

Professor Lewis thinks that it is not; and while I am open to conviction on this matter, I am strongly inclined to agree with him. Even if all these religious doctrines were in fact false, it would not follow that they were dispensable. Let us suppose, what must sometimes be the case, that the whole benefit a neurotic derives from his visits to a psychiatrist arises from the fact that on the psychiatrist's couch, and nowhere else, he is able to relax and unburden his mind of its anxieties. Then it would be true that he would be equally benefited if the psychiatrist was an ignoramus, or was not listening, or even was not there at all. But it would not be true that he would be equally, or at all, benefited if he *believed* that the psychiatrist was an ignoramus, or not listening, or not there.

A similar difficulty attends the attempt to separate the emotional and moral factors in religious experience from the beliefs which accompany and condition them. At the least, one can say that people are far more likely to have religious experiences if they already hold, or are already familiar with and attracted by, certain theological beliefs. You are much more likely to get a satisfactory response if you cry unto the Lord and put your trust in Him than if you cry unto the subconscious and put your trust in it; and this holds whether it is in fact the Lord or the subconscious that responds. Also, if a man who has had a religious experience is persuaded that his belief in its supernatural source is false, the effect upon his subsequent feelings and behaviour will be greatly diminished if not altogether lost. Something may be achieved by a carefully preserved inconsistency or incoherence of belief. But in general, while an experience taken as a psychological pick-me-up may, like whiskey or dexedrin, induce a mood of cheerfulness to tide one over an awkward patch, still, for a secure and settled adjustment to the whole scheme of things, for a safeguard against the ultimate despair which finds the universe "absurd," there is no adequate substitute for faith in the supernatural.

So I agree that a cognitive factor, namely some sort of awareness of a supernatural being, is integral to religious experience. But I would add some qualifications. The beliefs which lead up to, accompany, and issue from religious experience may be very meagre and very vague. Quite flimsy and hazy notions of some sort of heavenly power attending and guiding men may support vivid and powerful religious experiences. I doubt if there is much correlation between the frequency and intensity of these experiences and the richness and precision, or even the coherence, of theological doctrine. Again, while some sort of awareness of the supernatural is an element in religious experience, there is not one standard form which this awareness always takes. There are wide variations in the reports given as to the nature of the divine beings revealed in these experiences. Some people claim to have apprehended the one God, the All, the Atman, the eternal source of all being. Some have visions or impressions of Jesus, the Virgin Mary, angels, demons, and sundry other divine or supernatural personages figuring in various religious doctrines. Some have only the intimation of a Presence not further identifiable. And some can say nothing as to the source of their experiences. Some prophets and faith-healers (who surely have religious experiences) believe that they work their wonders by the help of the one God to whom they pray; others, by the help of lesser divine or supernatural beings; others (shamans or spiritualists) by the help of the spirits of deceased men; and others again proffer no theory, or a naturalistic theory, of the powers they bring into action. But these differences of attribution do not seem to correspond to any marked difference in the experiences undergone or the powers exercised. It is not, as in the story of Elijah and the priests of Baal, that those who call upon one supernatural being receive a response and those who call upon another do not. Christian, Mohammedan, Hindu, Buddhist mystics give similar accounts of the nature of their mystical experiences, and different accounts of the object of those experiences.

This being so, we can hardly take the cognitive factors in religious experience at their face value, as information about the nature of the supernatural. We are told what the experience appears to the subject to be; we must allow for the possibility that it may appear to be other than it is. In this case the allowance to be made must be substantial. Religious experiences are rare, and therefore unfamiliar; we do not know our way about them as we do about the everyday world, and we do not have the same amount of guidance from other people. Furthermore, the state of mind of a man enjoying a religious experience is one of surrender or transport; it is not one of critical scrutiny. Acute and hard-headed thinkers may have these experiences; but if so, they do not retain during them the cool watchfulness which guarantees accurate observation. The mind opened to supernatural influences, by the suspension of its normal preoccupations and assumptions, is also opened to suggestions from less exalted quarters. There is good reason to believe that such suggestions do influence the form taken by religious experience, that its subjects are apt to perceive and learn what they are expecting to perceive and learn. These expectations will be affected both by their personal desires and by the religious doctrines with which they are familiar. What the subject of religious experience supposes himself to be apprehending cannot be unaffected by what he already believes there is to be apprehended. Now, if the subject's notions of what it is he is apprehending are partly determined by his preconceived notions of what he is likely to apprehend, it would be rash to cite the evidence of religious experience in favour of the doctrines of any particular religious creed, or any particular theory of the nature of God. The part which religious experience plays among the evidences of religion is that of a phenomenon to be explained. Since it has an unusual character, it will need an unusual explanation. The man who says that his religious experiences come from God, and that what he apprehends therein is God, offers an explanation of their extraordinary nature. We are not bound to accept his explanation, though we are bound, in whatever explanation we give, to do justice to those features of his experience which make his explanation plausible.

Professor Lewis is quite explicit as to the explanation he adopts. In his view, the object of religious experience is God, that is, a being infinite, absolute or perfect. But here I suspect he may be doing something which I have just refused to agree to, namely, citing religious experience in favour of a particular theory as to the nature of God. "The idea of a finite God," he says, "misrepresents religion at almost every point." But this can only be maintained if the meaning of "religion" is narrowed in a rather arbitrary fashion. There is indeed in most, if not all, forms of religion, a tendency to believe in one God, whose nature, being infinite or absolute, has nothing in common with the nature of other beings. This belief appeals especially to religious theorists. It is associated with mystical practices, whose aim is to bring the mind of the worshipper into conformity with the divine. There is another equally conspicuous tendency in religion to believe in a plurality of finite divinities, who to some extent share the nature of their worshippers, and therefore can be specially concerned for particular interests and particular persons. This sort of belief accords with the practical rather than the theoretical concerns of men. (The coexistence of a monotheistic theology and a polytheistic cult is noticeable both in Hinduism and in Catholic Christianity.) It is associated with magical practices, whose aim is to appropriate the divine power in the service of human enterprises. One may conjecture, as Lewis does, that the latter tendency has arisen out of the former by an attempt to "incapsulate" the infinite in manageable finite forms. One may equally well conjecture that the former tendency has arisen out of the latter by an attempt to make the concept of divinity satisfy certain demands of the understanding. Both are mere conjectures. What is clear is that actual religions embody both tendencies, and neither has a monopoly of religious experience. If we commit ourselves entirely and rigorously to the notion of an infinite, absolute or perfect God, how much of conventional religious practice, based on the idea of a Heavenly Father who answers prayer and intervenes in human lives, will survive? Much of the writing of Spinoza is aimed at showing that there will not be very much; and there is force in his arguments.

As to the assertion that the infinite God is the object of religious experience, I find here ground for serious perplexity. To say that God is the object of a particular experience is clearly to say more than that the subject of that experience has the conviction that God exists, whether his conviction be reached by rational insight, by a flash of inspiration, or in some other way. It is to assert the presence of God to a given person on a given occasion in a way in which He is not present to other persons and on other occasions. I agree with Lewis that if we are to say anything at all about God beyond that He exists, there must be some experiences in which He is present to men in this special intimate fashion. My difficulty is as to the manner in which an infinite God could be an object of human experience. Are we to suppose that the infinitude or per-fection of God can be *directly* apprehended in the way that one apprehends sensory qualities, or in the way that one apprehends one's own desires and intentions? Is God a datum whose properties one can inspect, as one can note that a sense-datum is oblong or spotted? This idea seems to me desperately unplausible, and I gather that Lewis also rejects it. There remains the alternative that we can be aware of God, as we are aware of other persons, through the manner in which His action affects our experience. As, for instance, from what I hear you say I recognise you as intelligent, as sympathetic or hostile, etc., so I would recognise God for what He is by virtue of modifications of my experience proceeding from Him as your words proceed from you. Religious experience, as I said above, would be a kind of phenomenon to which one could reason-ably assign God as a cause. Now there is no difficulty in supposing that some experiences might be such that we would have to assign them to a supernatural but finite cause. But, even supposing one can properly say of an infinite God, "He is here, and *not* there," "This, and *not* that, is His doing," can one ever say of a given ex-perience that it needs to be assigned to an infinite cause in order to account for it? I am inclined to say that, all human experience being finite, the attribution of any of it to an infinite cause must always go beyond the evidence; that is, that whereas one might derive from religious experience ground for believing in God, one could not derive from it ground for believing in an infinite God.

A few words by way of summary. There are cognitive factors in religious experience: that is, such experiences do contain ostensible knowing of truths and ostensible awareness of supernatural beings. These cognitive claims must be received with great caution; many of the convictions arising out of religious experience must be erroneous (this fact is recognised by regular practitioners of mysticism). We cannot give any description of a divine being which will fit the ostensible object of all or most religious experience. If we wish to maintain that there is one such being who is the real object of all such experiences, that is, that they all involve some more or less confused and distorted awareness of Him, this is a hypothesis to explain the peculiar features of religious experience. In assessing any such explanation, we must consider the total character of the experience. And what is most striking and most distinctive in the total experience seems to me to be not its cognitive elements, but its affective and conative elements. It is distinctive in its manner of feeling; it is distinctive in its power to inspire faith, devotion, peace and strength of mind. What one comes to know from religious experience is chiefly how to live, how to be at peace with oneself and with the universe at large. Whatever power it is that enables men to achieve such serenity of mind, this they call God.

NOTES

1. *The Meaning of Existence.* Pontifex and Trethowan, p. 137.

# 17. ARE RELIGIOUS DOGMAS

# COGNITIVE AND MEANINGFUL?

A SYMPOSIUM

## Raphael Demos · C. J. Ducasse

*Raphael Demos is Professor Emeritus of Philosophy at Harvard University, and has been Visiting Professor of Philosophy at Mc-Gill University, Canada. His publications include the editing of* Plato Selections, *as well as numerous contributions to scholarly periodicals.*
*C. J. Ducasse is an eminent American philosopher. He is author of eight books and over a hundred scholarly articles. A book of essays in his honor, entitled* Current Philosophical Issues, *has been published by Charles C. Thomas, Publisher.*

### I. RAPHAEL DEMOS

Although in this paper I am solely concerned with the cognitive elements of religion, I do not of course assume that cognition is all that is important in religion. In this paper, by religion I will mean chiefly the Christian religion; this is the one I know best by far and it is the one in whose truth I believe. I will first discuss religious belief and then I will explore religious meaning. My study of religious cognition will also involve extended digressions into general epistemology.

We may tentatively distinguish the following systems of belief: common sense, science, animism, religion and philosophy. In this scheme common sense stands to science as animism to religion, the first member of the pair representing a relatively undeveloped ver-

Reprinted by permission of the authors and the University of Pennsylvania Press from *Academic Freedom, Logic and Religion,* Proceedings of American Philosophical Association, Eastern Division, Volume 2 (1953), pp. 71-87, 89-97.

sion of the second. Later on, I will make a similar distinction of philosophical levels.

It is generally taken for granted that the appeal to faith is a uniquely distinguishing feature of religious belief. Certainly religious thinkers do not hesitate to declare that faith is a valid source of belief in religion; thus, the author of the Epistle to the Hebrews speaks of faith as the 'evidence' of things unseen. In this passage faith means belief not resting on the evidence of the senses; but the word has for me a wider meaning; namely, as belief which rests on no evidence whatever, whether empirical or a priori. Of the other systems of belief it is popularly assumed that scientific beliefs rest on empirical evidence exclusively; and that so do those of common sense, although with a lesser degree of firmness. It is also believed that philosophers at any rate *intend* to ground their doctrines rationally, by appealing to experience or to self-evidence, and more vaguely, to intelligent speculation.

Religion seems to stand, then, apart from these other systems, by unashamedly resting its beliefs on faith—standing not only apart from, but behind these systems so to speak; and thus remaining in the rear of the progress of the human mind. Now I will try to show that religion is not alone, but that all the systems of belief I have cited are in the same boat, all floating on the infirm waters of faith. Putting the matter more cautiously, I will say that all the above-mentioned systems of belief rest on ultimate commitments. For instance, why do I, as a man of common sense, believe in the existence of independent physical objects? Because I believe it. Why do I believe that other people exist? Because I believe it. Perhaps for both cases I should add that I believe as I do because other people believe likewise; because these beliefs are part of common sense. (The circle in this 'argument' should be noted). And this is what I call faith.

One reason why in the case of both science and philosophy the element of faith is unnoticed is because the commitments are unconscious. These are, to a considerable extent, commitments as to what is a valid way of knowing. The air of important demonstration in science and philosophy is dissipated as soon as we notice that both make basic assumptions as to what constitutes evidence; for instance as to the meaning and validity of 'experience,' as to the validity of memory, as to the criteria of valid theory—and so forth.

Let me dwell on memory for a moment. Memory, it is agreed, is of the past which, because it is past cannot be given to the mind; thus memory is contrasted with experience—and in a wider sense of 'experience,' with rational intuition of Descartes' sense of the word, when he opposed it to deduction. That science must rely on memory is obvious; we are obliged to remember the evidence of the senses obtained in the past, on which we base our present theories. It is true that most scientific observations are preserved in records; but in order that such records be authentic and not fairy tales, they must at some point be connected with memory. Possibly even so-called report-sentences or protocols depend on a memory of the sensory given; for the latter has a very brief duration and it takes time to write, utter, or even think the protocol sentences.

I submit that reliance on memory is a sheer trust or faith. For, let us agree that there are many good reasons—proofs, if you like —for believing that memory is veridical. I will not go into these reasons, since it does not matter here what they are. But these reasons are not now present in my mind; I only remember them, and in so doing, I am using memory to support memory.

Of course, I may once more and now go through these reasons. So now I know that memory is trustworthy. But so long as I have these reasons present to my mind I cannot engage in remembering. The business of justifying memory is self-defeating. While actually involved in memory, I cannot be also intuiting the reasons which justify it; and, as we have just noted, so long as I am contemplating the reasons, I am unable to engage in remembering. It is as though an instrument invariably disintegrated in the very process of performing its function.

So far as I know, Descartes was the first philosopher to point up the relevance of memory not only for science but for mathematics. He showed that trust in memory was involved in the carrying out of any extended mathematical proof. Descartes realized that the reliance of mathematicians on memory is a matter of sheer trust or faith; he therefore tried to correct the situation by proving the existence of God who, being perfect, will not deceive man in the various faculties with which he endows men—faculties inclusive of memory and our disposition to believe in the existence of physical objects. Nevertheless Descartes, too, is obliged to remember the proofs of God and so must trust the memory which justifies the trust. As distinct from mathematics, science relies on sense-experience. But for science too memory is more important than sense-experience. Immediacy functions in science in a Pickwickian sense; it is remembered immediacy. Both immediacy and inference function as materials for memory. As scientists and as plain men we live in the past.

What of the assumed relevance of sense-data for the purpose of confirming predictions in science? Here we are forced to distinguish between sense-data and images, for images have no confirmatory value. But how distinguish the one from the other? Not surely by the criterion of voluntary control, for there are compulsive images, not subject to the conscious will. Berkeley suggested that sense-data are regular, obeying laws. But surely images obey laws too? Surely a scientist would not deny that there are causes even for images, physiological or psychological or both, even when he cannot point to these causes. Berkeley only evaded the issue when he asserted that sense-data, as distinct from images, obey 'natural' laws; natural laws are simply those laws which sense-data obey and images do not. Thus science is able to verify generalizations by rigorously selecting as data just those elements in experience which do, in principle, verify generalizations in science.

It is said that religious belief in the existence of God rests on faith. But natural science too entails an undemonstrated belief in something like the uniformity of nature—a belief, that is to say, that nature has the kind of structure which justifies our taking its behavior in the past as a clue to its behavior in the future. Thus, not only in their source, but in their content too, the two systems of belief seem to me to be analogous, in that both seem to be beliefs in the existence of something like an order of nature. To be more specific, the belief in God is equivalent to the view that things make 'moral' sense in the universe; that, although there is evil in nature, this evil will somehow be overcome by good. The natural scientist has *his* evil too, which is chance; yet he too believes that somehow there is an explanation for everything that happens.

But to return to the question of justification—I would say that the religious belief is no more of a faith than is the belief that nature is uniform. They are both acts of faith, not only in that they go *beyond* the evidence but in that, at least up to a point, they go *against* the evidence. Job said: "Though he slay me, yet will I trust in him." And the scientists' position may be caricatured by putting these words in his mouth: "I will find an explanation even if it kills me;" more accurately; "I will go on believing that there is an explanation, even though I cannot find one." It may be urged that modern science, in recognizing the so-called Heisenberg principle of uncertainty has correspondingly *limited* the range of the principle of explanation. To this I might answer that there is an analogous phenomenon in modern doctrines of religion in so far as they recognize a limited God. But I prefer to dispute the truth of the above interpretation of the impact of the principle of uncertainty on the principle of explanation. Heisenberg himself views his principle merely as an extension of the doctrine of secondary qualities. He writes:

"According to Democritus, atoms have lost the qualities like colors, taste, etc., they only occupied space, but geometrical assertions about atoms were admissible and required no further analysis. In modern physics, atoms lose this last property, they possess geometrical qualities in no higher degree than color, taste, etc. . . . Only the experiment of an observer forces the atom to indicate *a position*, (italics mine) a color and a quantity of heat." (*Philosophic Problems of Nuclear Physics*, p. 38; see also pp. 105-6).

I have referred earlier to the religious belief that events in nature make "moral" sense. There is here a notion of meaningfulness which requires elucidation. For the scientist, too, as was noted, the universe is meaningful, though in a different sense of the term. Meaningfulness as a religious notion may be approached by its application to conduct. Echoing Kant, we speak today of action being rational (or reasonable) in the sense that it is not self-inconsistent, or not self-defeating. What I have in mind, however, is something different, although it too has connections with Kant, namely with what he was reaching out for when arguing for his postulates. The notion of meaningfulness in religious language is essentially a common sense one and untechnical. We say that life is meaningful when it achieves values in some stable fashion. Mere action and change are meaningless, we say; they must aim at something; and at something worthwhile. But striving without a chance of accomplishment is also deemed meaningless. And ends, once accomplished, must be capable of preservation, for the activity to be meaningful.

This is meaningfulness in living. Now, we say, derivatively, that the real world is meaningful in so far as it makes such accomplishment possible, probable, nay perhaps certain. Religion is the belief that the world is meaningful in this fashion. For such a belief the senses provide no evidence—certainly not any conclusive evidence; and the scientifically-minded see no reason for adopting this belief. Certainly such a belief is founded on faith, but no more so than the scientist's own belief that nature is meaningful in his sense, namely that nature is such that it enables us to make successful predictions and generalizations.

The reader will recall Spinoza's doctrine that God's attributes are infinite. By this Spinoza meant that each attribute is self-contained and complete, never intersecting with another attribute. I wish to say that in some sense both the scientific and the religious accounts are, like Spinoza's attributes, infinite, that is to say, autonomous. Or, to use Prof. Tillich's phrase for theology (*Systematic Theology, I,* p. 8), each system is a circle, in other words a closed system.

Let us, for instance, compare the scientific account of thunder with the magical account. The scientist will of course reject the latter; but he cannot refute it. The animist will introduce, let us say, evidence from a dream; but dream images are irrelevant for the scientist. Each system has its own definition of fact. Each system carries a lantern by which to illuminate the darkness. While what is thereby seen is seen indeed, the lantern itself is not illuminated, or rather the lantern shines both on itself and other things. The lanterns are different, and each is checked by its own light.

It may be thought that science is able to crash into the animistic circle by an appeal to pragmatic considerations. Science 'works.' Our own kind of medical men can cure diseases which the witch-doctors cannot; also we can produce crops as the magician cannot. But the fact is that pragmatism is an appeal to values, and that the values, too, are part of the system. The religious believer, for instance, may say that his values are not material primarily, that what he is concerned with is the salvation of his soul and with blessedness. There are also differences involving factual matters. Where the scientist may claim that his system provides greater satisfaction for life on this earth, the religious believer might retort that he is concerned with what happens to him in the life after death. And for the scientist to say that there is no life after death is to beg the (factual) question.

The formalization of religious belief is theology; the formalization of natural science is naturalism. We may legitimately call both naturalism and theology exhibitions of philsophical thinking, provided we understand that neither goes beyond formalization, that neither attempts to justify its correlative system of belief. They both rest on faith. Thus, in the passage cited earlier Prof. Tillich admits, nay asserts, that he founds his theology on the authority of the Bible. So the naturalistic philosopher accepts all the premises of natural science, and simply formalizes them. His professed rules of evidence are the scientist's rules of evidence. Verification, he says, must be (sense-) empirical; also a concept has a meaning only to the extent that, in principle, it may be verified or falsified by sense-experience. Naturalism may be defined as the theology of natural science. Does the philosopher concerned offer any arguments in support of these views about validation and meaning? Not so far as I know. He simply borrows the practice of the natural scientist and erects it into a formal principle. His meta-scientific statements then are precisely personal declarations of faith, professions of belief, not assertions but expressions of the form 'I believe that $p$.' In both the theologian and the philosopher of the naturalistic school (along with his brother the positivist) we find operating a modified version of St. Augustine's principle "believe in order to understand" (your experience, or the world).

In calling religion and science systems of belief, in describing naturalism and theology as professions of belief, I do not, of course, imply that they are false. Neither do I imply that they are not knowledge; I am only asserting that they are not known to be knowledge. Nor do I regard faith as the last word for either of these systems. Naturalism and theology are unself-criticized philosophies. I will call this level Philosophy A. 'True' philosophy (Philosophy B) begins with the Socratic query: why do I believe as I do?; with the Socratic knowledge, which is knowledge of one's ignorance—the awareness that one's beliefs rest on faith. Then there is Philosophy C, which (in the way of Plato's dialectic) criticizes, modifies or justifies fundamental beliefs; or even adds wider speculations of its own. For myself, I take the basic beliefs of both science and religion to be 'insights'—instances of knowledge, in the sense in which Plato opposed knowledge to opinion.

The question is how I, or anyone else, would be justified in regarding these systems of belief as valid, while at the same time rejecting others. There must be an implicit reference to some fundamental criteria, but if so, would not these criteria constitute but another set of premises, that is to say, of beliefs, and therefore of 'commitments'? Any attempt to justify premises would appear to be a self-defeating task. Perhaps then the very question is a pseudo-question. Thus we might take a position like that indicated by Spinoza's words: "when I am asleep and dreaming I think I am awake; when I am awake, I know that I am awake and that I was dreaming." I have no solution for this most vital problem. But I would strongly insist that any view which regards premise-adopting as arbitrary commitment, as irrational, as relative to person, place, and time is excluded. For such a view itself claims to be non-arbitrary, non-relative and rational.

Is argument in religion of a different sort than in any other field, say science? That there are vital differences between religious and scientific cognition surely is obvious from the fact that considerations which are held as conclusive in religious discussion for the most part make not the slightest impression on the scientist. In so far as their differing basic premises include validating forms of inference, then the respective modes of argument are different. I refer the reader back to what was said about the different senses of meaningfulness in science and in religion.

There is a corresponding difference as to conceptions and categories of description and explanation. A scientist thinks in terms of spatio-temporal conceptions, and of physical events which are determined. An animist or a religious believer thinks of the world in terms of agencies, of persons, of minds; he posits non-temporal, eternal entities; he thinks of agencies which are free and creative; of entities which act purposively, which strive. A physical object is something which can only act here and now, but a mind can reach out of the present into the past through memory; and indeed, can think of, intend, or 'mean' anything anywhere. Thus in religion we encounter the notion of spirit, of something immaterial in that intrinsically it is not limited by spatio-temporal conditions and does not act according to the principle of physical causation.

From the fact that the world (or part of it) is categorized by religion (at least the Christian religion) in *personal* terms, certain consequences follow. In science one event or substance is like another except in so far as its description is different; particulars *qua* particulars don't count. Conversely, in the Christian doctrine, certain historical events and times are vested with special significance. Whereas, in the scientific view, similar substances or events function simply as illustrations of law, in the Christian view, of such two numerically different but descriptively similar entities one may have a special significance which the other may lack. In the scientific view, the particular is nothing more than a carrier of a description or an essence; thus all science is Platonizing. But in the religious view, the individual functions in its uniqueness. Time flows equably but persons observe birthdays, and for Christians, December 25 is Christmas. Now, when particular events are vested with special significance, such events are appropriately termed miracles. They are miraculous because their special significance is inexplicable in terms of their natural properties; in the physical order, they do not differ from other events.

I come now to the problem of religious meaning.

Take such apparently descriptive phrases as the following: God is a Spirit; God is a Person; God is Eternal Life; God is Love; the Lord God Almighty; the Lord Most High; Our Father in Heaven. What is the way to view such representations of God?

(a) It is possible to think of them as literal descriptions of God; this is the position of fundamentalist Christianity. It is not satisfactory because it leads to idolatry: identifying God with what is at best an image of God.

(b) At an other extreme is the view that these are not descriptions at all, but purely mythical or symbolic. By 'symbol' I mean a word whose meaning is exclusively emotive. A symbol does not refer to anything in the object; its function is to arouse appropriate attitudes, feelings and responses.

(c) This view in turn leads to a still more extreme doctrine— that we can know nothing of God's attributes. This is the alternative of nescience. I am rejecting both *b* and *c*. Against the latter, I maintain that we can know God; against the former, that in using attribute-words for God we are referring to properties in the object. Nevertheless I deny the first alternative; I do not think that the descriptions of God are literal.

(d) But if attribute-words in religion are neither literal nor emotive, might they be metaphors? I use this word in the sense of allegory; although a metaphor has emotive overtones like a symbol, I distinguish it from the latter because a metaphor is descriptive. A metaphor may be defined as condensed literal meaning, and when the meaning is spread out, the metaphor evaporates.

Adopting then the view that a metaphor is *potentially* descriptive (literally) as distinguished from what might be called ordinary prose (which is an actual literal description) I would deny that religious attribute-words like 'person' 'love' 'spirit' are metaphors; I take this position because I do not think that the descriptions into which a metaphor could be translated apply to God literally. Religious attribute-words, while descriptive, are not literal; they are, in fact, *analogical*.

To sum up the above diversities of meaning and arranging them in an ascending order:

1. Words with zero meaning, as in nescience.
2. Symbols—terms with emotive meaning only.
3. Metaphors—literal, quasi-descriptive.
4. Analogical terms—descriptive but not literal.
5. 'Prose' terms—both descriptive and literal.

Before defining what I mean by analogical terms, I will explain why I believe that the descriptive terms in religious discourse are not literal. This is not at all because of any assumption on my part that God has no essence, or that, if he has an essence such an essence is intrinsically un-intelligible. God can certainly comprehend his own nature. It is only that man, because of the finite nature of his mind, cannot comprehend God's nature in terms of his (God's) intrinsic properties. Hence man must have recourse to terms of comparison; he can understand God's nature by comparing it with properties which he knows literally. Take the familiar statement that man is (created as) an image of God. Therefore, God can be thought of in the image of man. Moreover, this relation of analogy between God and man is known literally. While, if I say that God is a person in an analogical sense, I am not ascribing the attribute of personality to God in a literal sense, yet I am ascribing literally a certain analogical relation between personality in man and personality in God.

It is sometimes said that although we cannot literally know *what* God is we can literally know *that* God is. The similarity to Kant's doctrine of things-in-themselves is obvious here; there are things in themselves but we cannot literally know what they are. Against Kant's view, the valid question has been raised: "If you cannot know what the noumena are, how can you even know that they are? Surely the reasons preventing you from knowing their essence would operate equally to prevent you from knowing their existence." So with God. The statement that while we can know that God exists, we cannot know what he is, is facile. In fact, just as we can ascribe personality to God analogically only, so do we ascribe existence to God in an analogical—and in no other—sense. In this connection I would like to quote from Prof. Stace's recent and important work *Time and Eternity*. "Religion is the desire to break away from being and existence altogether. . . ." (p. 5.). "The nothingness of God finds expression in other phrases having the same sense. God is Non-Being, Nothing, Emptiness, the Void, the Abyss. Silence and darkness, used as privative terms importing the absence of sound, the absence of light, are also used as metaphors of his Non-Being." (p. 8). Nevertheless Mr. Stace denies that the statement that God is Nothing is equivalent to the statement that there is no God. For the proposition "God does not exist" is false too. (pp. 7, 61). Thus in some sense of existence it is false that God exists, but in another sense it is true that God exists; the former is the literal, the latter the analogical sense. (I am not in any way suggesting that Mr. Stace would accept the interpretation I put on his statements. Nevertheless, as the reader will gather from my later remarks, my debt to his book in this essay is considerable.)

Now for the reasons why an appeal to analogy is necessary. In attempting to describe God, theologians seem compelled to make contradictory statements. Thus God is said to be transcendent, yet also immanent; eternal yet also temporal; personal, yet also impersonal. The Kingdom of Heaven is within us; yet also forever beyond us. Such assertion of contradictory statements superficially suggests that God is intrinsically unintelligible and that theological truth is irrationalistic. Of course, Hegel has made a logic out of anti-logic through his formulation of the dialectic. But Christian theology need not be Hegelian. The descriptions of God cited above are not in fact inconsistent because, to take one example, the sense in which time is denied of God and that in which time is ascribed to God are not the same senses; yet they are not different either; the senses are analogical.

As we know, the mystics have proclaimed that God is ineffable. St. Chrysostom wrote five sermons on the incomprehensibility of God, in which he rises to flights of sublime eloquence. St. Chrysostom quotes St. Paul to show that God is unapproachable as well as inconceivable. Yet St. Paul also writes: "The invisible things of him (of God) from the creation of the world are *clearly seen*, being understood by the things that are made, even his eternal power and Godhead." (*Romans I*, 2). What is the answer to the paradox? The nature of God cannot be known intrinsically; it can be known by comparison with other things. Now, anyone would be rash to contradict the mystics; but in fact, the mystics are inconsistent, like St. Paul. Of course when the mystics assert that God is incomprehensible they do not mean that God is uncognizable. What they mean is that God is cognizable by a mode of cognition which is unique—different from sense-perception and from conception. The real question is whether what is cognized in the mystical mode can be translated into the language of some other mode. And here mystics divide themselves into two groups: those who maintain that the language of the mystic is not translatable into any other, and those who assert that it is. Of the second group are those mystics who regard nature as the manifestation of God ("the heavens declare the glory of God") and who regard natural events as 'symbolic' of divine meanings.

When I say that both Smith and Jones are men, the sense in which I use the term man in the two cases is exactly the same. Thus, as the schoolmen would say, the sense of man in this example is univocal. When I use the word post for the mail and also to designate a pillar I am using the word in two different senses. This is what the schoolmen called the equivocal use of a term. Now I submit that identity of sense and difference of sense do not exhaust the meaning of sense; there is a third alternative, namely that the sense of a term is analogical—neither the same nor different. Some scholastic philosophers have tried to define analogy as part-identity and part-difference. I regard this view as wrong; analogy is an irreducible relation, other than both identity and difference. When religious analogy is misconstrued as difference, we are liable to get the extreme forms of mysticism, merging with the doctrine of nescience. When analogy is misconstrued as identity (that is to say, taken as literally descriptive) we find anthropomorphism. Of course, the doctrine of analogy is taken from Aristotle, although in a modified version.

Compare analogy with likeness. In its ordinary sense (which I will call conceptual likeness) this relation is always reducible, and reducible to identity and difference together. Thus when I say that Smith is like Jones, you can always ask me: in what respect? and I can answer: in intelligence or in height; both Smith and Jones are smart or they are both tall. Here, likeness between two things means that A and B have a common property. Thus conceptual likeness is reducible to identity in a certain respect, and is the same as Aristotle's generic identity—for instance, that men and dogs are both animals. Now analogy is not, at all, that kind of likeness (if likeness it be). It is likeness perhaps in that we are comparing two things; but it is not a likeness which is reducible to the possession of a common property; it is not likeness in this or that 'respect'; it is just likeness. It is reported that Wittgenstein said something as follows: "To propose to think in violation of the law of contradiction is like proposing to play chess without the queen; and that is all one can say about the comparison." Now this would be an instance of analogical likeness: A is to B, as C is to D.

To return to theology: God exists; God has or is a mind; God is a living God; God is love; God has designs and purposes—in all these sentences the attributions must be taken analogically. Thus God loves, but his love is not the sort of thing we mean when we say, man loves; when we ascribe purposiveness to God, we must not be taken to mean that he proceeds by the route of means and ends, as when man acts purposively. Now, these are negative statements; and there have been mystics according to whom the only statements we can make about God are negations. Yet this is half the story; the senses of 'love' and 'design' are analogical. Thus affirmative statements about God are available.

I will now make the further proposal that the concept of analogy is applicable also outside theological thought, and within philosophical discourse. I will consider the remarks by Margaret Macdonald on "The Philosopher's Use of Analogy" (*Logic and Language*, First Series, ed. by Antony Flew, pp. 80-100), especially because they are typical of widely accepted views among members of the school of philosophical analysis. In a very acute discussion, among other things, of Aristotle's concepts of matter and form and of Descartes' famous example of the piece of wax, Miss Macdonald makes the following point. Both Aristotle and Descartes speak of stripping matter of all secondary qualities, and Aristotle of all qualities whatever. Miss Macdonald concedes that they do not mean "that qualities are taken from objects as skins from an onion" (p. 87). Philosophers who use such language have in mind abstraction or intellectual analysis. But her point is precisely that when philosophers use these words, they are using them in a different sense from their ordinary usage—and therefore in a misleading sense. For instance, in its ordinary sense, 'analysis' is an operation by which we decompose a complex object into its parts; and for such an operation we have sensible criteria by which to identify it. But "it is logically impossible to apply any such criteria to the separation of matter from its qualities" (*Ibid*). Again, by Aristotle's own admission matter is that which receives all predicates, and "since nothing which is known can be described except by ascribing predicates, no description or knowledge of matter is possible . . . obviously, therefore, it is logically impossible to apply any sensible criteria whatever for the distinction of material and design. But such criteria are part of what we *mean* by such words; they give the words their use and philosophers who attempt to apply them by analogy without indicating similar criteria, or indeed any sensible criteria whatever are not using an analogy but simply misusing these ordinary words. . . ." (p. 94). And on the next page she states that philosophical 'theories' are not theories at all, because they are not testable as scientific theories are.

May I point out an 'analogy' between Miss Macdonald's argument and Mr. Stace's? For instance, Mr. Stace insists cogently that the religious infinite is wholly different from the conceptual or mathematical infinite. "We must understand that the word 'infinite' in the religious sense, has nothing at all to do with that sense of the word in which it is applied to space, time, and the number series." (*Ibid* p. 47). In the same fashion Mr. Stace argues that when we ascribe love and existence to God, these terms are not used in their ordinary meanings. Nevertheless, Mr. Stace also asserts that the proposition 'God is Not-Being' is not equivalent to the proposition 'There is no God.' In some sense, he agrees, God exists, and also that God is love.

Now, Miss Macdonald's contribution is certainly important as showing that the philosophers' use of such terms as matter, form, abstraction, analysis, is not the same as those of science or common sense. Traditional philosophers, I think, must be convicted of not having been sufficiently aware of these distinctions. What I would dispute however is Miss Macdonald's conclusion that philosophers are giving a new and simply different sense to these words while pretending to use them in the old one; and that so far the philosophers' language is misleading. I would urge, in opposition, that the philosopher's use of these terms has an analogical relation to that of science and common sense. It is noteworthy that Miss Macdonald is herself setting the problem as I would have done: she is raising the question whether the philosopher's use of analogy is justified. She denies that it is justified because—so she implies— analogy involves similarity of criteria. Now by similarity she means what I have called conceptual likeness, possession of a common genus, or identity of sense. But I submit that there is, at any rate, another sort of analogy irreducible to identity 'in respect of x'; and this sort does exist between philosophical, scientific and common sense discourse. By their arguments, members of the school of philosophical analysis have intended to show that philosophical 'theorizing,' or philosophical argument, or philosophical 'rational discourse' is nothing of the sort. My own conclusion from their arguments is just the reverse. It is true that ethical discourse, scientific discourse, theological discourse, philosophical discourse are not rational in the same sense. There is no definition of rationality which applies in the same sense to these various operations. Shall we therefore say that 'rationality' is simply an equivocal word? Yet surely it is not equivocal as the word 'kind' is, when referring both to genus and to willingness to help: I maintain that it is the case both that rationality has not the same meaning, and that it has not a different meaning in these various descriptions.

A case in point is the current controversy about ethical sentences. In the earlier phase of their discussion, analytical philosophers had tended sharply to oppose ethical sentences to scientific and other factual sentences. The meaning of the former, it was then pointed out, is emotive, while the meaning of the latter is empirical. But more recently, without at all blurring this distinction, analytical philosophers have come to agree that there is such a thing as ethical reasoning, no less than scientific reasoning, and that consequently, considerations of validity are no less pertinent in ethical sentences than in those of science. My own interpretation of the fact of both difference and similarity is that ethical discourse is analogous to scientific discourse, and that rationality is an analogous term; so is meaning also; so is meaningfulness.

In conclusion, it is relevant to indicate how similar the contrast between philosophy and science (and common sense) on the one hand is to the contrast between mysticism and conceptual thought on the other. A fundamental objection by the analytical school against traditional philosophers has been that the latter has abused linguistic usage in that they have taken a term with limited meaning and have then applied it to everything. For instance, in every day life, the term existence has a definite limited meaning. We say that men and horses exist but centaurs and hobgoblins do not. But a traditional philosopher uses the same term so as to ask the question whether the whole physical world exists. The objection raised is that the word existence has now been forced into another meaning, or rather it is meaningless because it has been given an absolutely general application which allows of no contrast. For instance —the analyst will ask—what would the nonexistence of the physical world mean? Now, an objection of this sort challenges the very concept of philosophy as it has been traditionally employed; at least *metaphysics* has meant the attempt to make general statements about the totality of things.

And now let us turn to the complaints of the mystics concerning theological-conceptual formulations. I will refer again to Mr. Stace's account of religious knowledge. Mr. Stace asserts that the mystical intuition cannot be given a conceptual expression for the reason that concepts are limited. "It is being this or that which is the disease of things." (p. 5). "The discursive, discriminating, conceptual intellect cannot apprehend the divine." (p. 39) "For, to conceptualize is to divide and relate" (p. 45) . . . "the infinity of God means *that than which there is no other.*" (p. 47) Indeed we know from Spinoza, the philosopher-mystic, that particular modes exist by negation, whereas God exists by inclusion. When, therefore, a Christian of the common garden variety says that God loves man, the mystic accuses him of taking an attribute which in everyday experience has an opposite (love as contrasted with hate) and applying it to God whose attributes admit of no opposites.

I suggest that the respective complaints, on the one hand, of the mystic addressed to the ordinary Christian and, on the other, of the philosophical analyst addressed to the ordinary philosopher, have the same import. Both the mystic and the traditional philosopher employ terms which designate what I may call 'total' properties—properties which have no opposites. The mystic complains that the ordinary Christian takes terms which designate limited properties and then wrongly applies them to God where their application is unlimited. And the philosophical analyst complains that the traditional philosopher takes terms which have only a partial application and applies them in an unlimited fashion.

Now, I believe that the 'ineffabilist' variety of mystic to be wrong. Despite differences I hold that there are analogies between God and human experience. So I would urge that despite differences there are analogies between philosophical discourse and the language of common sense, justifying the transfer of terms from one language to the other. No man is an island, said John Donne. Today, the Christian neo-fundamentalists, with their insistence that God is an absolute 'Other' are trying to place God on an inaccessible island where no influences from common experience might pollute him. So do the philosophical analysts try to isolate traditional philosophy from common sense and science by a kind of quarantine during which after proper therapy it will be purified of all infection. The motives are different but they lead to the same result—isolation. Now, I believe in islands, including Shakespeare's 'scepter'd isle' in which the Oxford School of Analysis is flourishing today. Yet I hope we shall construct causeways from the islands to the mainland, or, at least, establish a ferry service to the continent of common experience; and this may be done by what I have called analogical relations and analogical terms.

The considerations set forth in Professor Demos's paper have to do only with the purportedly cognitive aspect of religion, not with its emotional or pragmatic aspects. Furthermore, the only religion he considers is Christianity, which he tells us is the one he believes to be true. His paper apparently aims to show that the beliefs distinctive of Christianity, and more particularly those about God, are true. The beliefs about God specifically mentioned in the paper are that God exists, has or is a mind, is a living God, is love, is a person, is a spirit, and has designs and purposes.

To show that these beliefs represent knowledge about God, two things would be necessary. One is that the attribute-terms predicated of God in the statements of those beliefs should have some definite meaning, and that we should be told what it is. The other is that evidence should be presented, sufficient to show that the attributes meant by those terms are in fact possessed by God.

As regards the first of these two requisites, philosophical reflection leads Professor Demos to assert (as against the fundamentalists) that those statements about God are *not* true if the attribute-terms predicated in them are taken literally; i.e., are taken in the sense they have when predicated of human beings. He asserts also that the function of the attribute-terms in those statements is not emotive, or at least not solely or essentially emotive, but is descriptive; and hence he rejects the view that God is incomprehensible and unknowable. He maintains, however, that those attribute-terms are not descriptive in the sense in which metaphorical terms are so; for metaphorical terms are capable of being translated into literal terms, and he thinks that the literal terms into which such religious words as "person," "love," "spirit," and the rest could be translated would not apply to God literally. What Professor Demos maintains is that those predicates are descriptive neither literally nor metaphorically but "analogically."

What then is analogical description? Professor Demos says a good many things about analogy, as follows:

(a) That analogy is not analyzable as part-identity and part-difference;

(b) That analogy is not conceptual likeness, which always reduces to possession of a common property;

(c) That "the doctrine of analogy is taken from Aristotle, although in a modified version," which version, however, Professor Demos does not so far as I can find state explicitly but only illustrates, by saying that there is "analogical likeness: A is to B as C is to D" between proposing to think in violation of the law of contradiction, and proposing to play chess without the queen;

(d) That analogy is "an irreducible relation;"

(e) That "it is not likeness in this or that respect," but is "just likeness."

In a portion of his typescript omitted because of space limitations from his paper as printed, he also stated:

(f) That "analogy cannot be analyzed; it is known by being seen, by being recognized immediately;" and

(g) That "there are no definite criteria for deciding whether there is analogy or not."

I must confess that I am unable to extract from these seven statements any conception, consistent with all of them, of what Professor Demos means by "analogy." The ordinary meaning of the term is likeness of relationship; i.e., that the relation between A and B is similar to the relation between C and D. Hence the only terms that can be analogical in this sense are terms that designate relationships. But some at least of the attribute-terms predicated of God, which Professor Demos mentions, are *prima facie* not relational terms at all; and he makes no attempt to show them to be relational. Yet, that ordinary meaning of the term "analogy" seems to be the one he adopts at the place where he illustrates analogy by citing the likeness between proposing to think in violation of the law of contradiction, and proposing to play chess without the queen.

But if this *is* an example of what he means by analogy, then analogy is *not* unanalyzable, and *is* reducible to possession of a generic character; for, in that example, there is a generic character which the two proposals share. It is the paradoxical one that both are proposals to engage in activity of a kind defined specifically as activity in modes *conforming* to all of certain rules, and yet are proposals *not to conform* to some of those rules.

This is the only clear-cut example I can find in Professor Demos's paper of what he means by analogy; and, as we have just seen, this example is analyzable into predication of literal sameness in respect of a generic character. It therefore refutes the very contention it is intended to prove, namely, that, unlike metaphorical predications, analogical predications are *not* so analyzable. The paper thus brings forth no reason to believe that any predications are analogical in a sense other than that of metaphorical. Professor Demos's insistence nonetheless that analogy is unanalyzable, seems explicable only as expression of a deep wish that the attribute-terms which Christian theologians predicate of the God they define should somehow be descriptive, although they are not descriptive either literally or metaphorically. But since *no* meaning for those predicates is actually offered in the paper, belief that God has certain characters, which in fact are specified only by those vacuous predicates, would seem to be itself vacuous.

This does not augur well for the possibility that the statements which apply those predicates to God are cognitive, i.e., represent knowledge. The argument of the part of the paper which appears intended to establish that they are cognitive is not too clear. It seems to be in essence that even those things commonly accounted as the most certainly known are not really known at all but ultimately are matters of pure faith—"faith" being defined (correctly I think) as "belief which rests on no evidence whatever, whether empirical or *a priori*;" for the paper describes as equally "floating on the infirm waters of faith," two systems of belief. One consists of common sense, of science, and of philosophy of science, or more specifically, naturalistic philosophy of science. The other system consists of animism, of religious beliefs, and of theology.

As examples of beliefs belonging to the first group, Professor Demos mentions belief in the validity of memory, belief that independent physical objects exist and that other people exist, belief "as to what constitutes evidence," belief "as to the criteria of valid theory," belief in the uniformity of nature. As belonging to the second group, on the other hand, he cites belief in God; belief—to which he declares the belief in God equivalent—"that things make 'moral' sense in the universe," i.e., that in the universe valuable ends can be attained and preserved; and, belief that certain individual things, events, and persons function in their uniqueness and are "vested with special significance;" such events—for example, the birth of Jesus—being "then appropriately termed miracles" because their special significance "is inexplicable in terms of their natural properties;" whereas "in the scientific view, the particular is nothing more than a carrier of description or an essence."

To dissect exhaustively such truth as there is in these various contentions from what seem to me fatal errors in them would be too lengthy a task for the space at my disposal. I shall therefore be able to call attention only to a few of the graver mistakes I think I see.

(a) To begin with the last item of the second group of beliefs just listed, I submit that the religious view of individual events and persons is mistakenly identified there with what in fact is only the historical view of them. The birth of George Washington on February 22, or indeed that of John Doe on a particular other day, is, as truly as that of Jesus on December 25, a historical and therefore unique event, and one vested (for some persons, many or few,) with special significance of one kind or another. But Washington is not on this account reckoned as divine or even as a saint, nor his birth as a miracle. Hence, that an individual person or event functions to some extent "in its uniqueness" and is "vested with special significance," is not sufficient to confer religious status on either.

Moreover, so far as I can see, the special significance of Jesus and of Washington, however different in kind and magnitude, is, if indeed inexplicable, then inexplicable in both cases only in the sense in which are so the historical repercussions of *any* historical event, which, *qua* historical, are, like the event itself, unique and therefore in some degree novel. Those repercussions are inexplicable in the sense that the inexhaustible detail and specificity of *any* concrete event is never *totally* predictable, even theoretically.

On the other hand, the special significance which any given *past* historical event has turned out to have *is* explicable to some extent in the sense of traceable to causes—to the extent, namely, that the "natural properties" of the event and of its historical context happen to resemble those of other events and of their contexts, that had been observed earlier.

(b) I turn next to Professor Demos's statement that "religion is the belief that the world is meaningful" in the sense that, in it, valuable ends can be attained and preserved; and that "for such a belief the senses provide no evidence."

That the world, up to the present, *has been* such as to make achievement and preservation of valuable ends possible to some extent is, I submit, evidenced by the fact that such achievement and preservation has been observed again and again by each of us. Belief that the world *will continue* to be such is due to the phychological momentum called habit, which automatically extrapolates to the future the regularities or approximate regularities we have observed in the past. As so generated, this belief is no more intrinsically religious than is the belief that tomorrow water will continue to run downhill as usual. Moreover, even if it were religious, it would not be essentially Christian or even theistic, since Buddhism and Jainism, which are non-theistic religions—and indeed, contemporary Humanism, not to mention atheists and agnostics, also hold that belief.

(c) The subject of extrapolation to the future brings me to Professor Demos's most radical contention, namely, that the basic beliefs of science and of the naturalistic or, I assume, of any other philosophy of science are, exactly as much as those of religion, matters of pure faith; that is, rest on no evidence whatever, of any kind; so that there is not the slightest reason to regard them as true rather than as false.

How then, Professor Demos asks, would one be justified in regarding the basic beliefs of both science and religion "as valid, while at the same time rejecting others." For this, he says, it would be necessary to appeal "to some fundamental criteria." But would not *these* likewise be matters of pure faith? Professor Demos declares that he has "no solution for this most vital problem."

The solution, I would suggest, lies in noticing that, in the definition of faith as "belief which rests on no evidence whatever," the term "evidence" enters; and hence that we are entitled to ask what is that thing, called Evidence, upon which that definition tacitly postulates that some beliefs rest, and prescribes that those to be termed "faith" do *not* rest. Either this negation is wholly devoid of meaning, or else some definition of what the term "evidence" is to be taken to mean is implicit in the very notion of faith as defined.

But definitions and defining postulates are neither true nor false and neither believed nor disbelieved, but only respected or disregarded by this or that person. Their status is thus essentially that of rules of a game—a game, in the broad sense, being an activity whose modes one makes conform to certain rules—those, namely, which together define the nature of the particular game concerned. Of course, the rules of a given game—say, chess—are binding only on persons who elect to play that particular game—chess rather than perhaps checkers. But if a person violates them either deliberately or unawares, then in so doing he is in fact playing a different game, which may resemble chess to some extent, but is not chess itself.

Now, there is a game called Pursuit of Knowledge, and the rules which define its nature and differentiate this game from others are those called The Rules of Evidence—specifically, the rules of observational, experimental, inductive, deductive, circumstantial, and testimonial evidence. Nobody is obligated to obey these rules, but whoever flouts them is automatically then playing a different game; and, if he nevertheless continues to employ the words which have meaning only in terms of those rules—words, namely, such as "true," "false," "valid," "fallacious," "proof," "probability," "knowledge," etc.—then the game he is actually playing is that of *cheating at the pursuit of knowledge*; just as purporting to play chess but making the king move two steps at a time instead of only one is not playing chess but cheating at chess. The game of thinking loosely, inconsistently, incongruously, of arguing illogically, and of believing irresponsibly, may be more fun and is certainly easier and far more popular than that of thinking precisely, logically and scientifically, that is, of thinking in the manners that yield knowledge as distinguished from erroneous or groundless beliefs; but it is not the same game. Yet the knowledge-producing game is the one which those unconscious cheaters too intend and purport to be playing. For they too intend their statements to *communicate* their thoughts; intend their arguments to *prove or disprove* something; and intend their assertions to represent *facts*, not fictions or groundless opinions. That is, the rules by which they intend and purport to be playing, but which they are breaking unawares, are those of the game of communication—one of which is that statements shall not be ambiguous; or those of the game of logical inference; or those of the game of ascertaining facts.

Now, Professor Demos's initial and most radical contention was, we noted, that the basic beliefs of science are, like those of religion, matters of pure faith. This contention, however, and all that he rests upon it, is, I submit, disposed of at one sweep by the fact, which the preceding remarks have made clear, that what he calls the basic beliefs of science *are really not beliefs at all*, but are the rules of the game of pursuit of knowledge; and that it is only *within* this game, i.e., in terms of its rules, that the question whether a given belief is erroneous or true, groundless or well-grounded, valid or invalid, has any meaning at all.

This game, however, is the one which the theologian too intends and purports to be playing; but he cheats at it when he takes, as starting point for his inferences of fact, assertions merely *known to be contained in the Bible*, instead of—as the rules of that game require—assertions *known to be true* by observation, whether physical, psychological, sociological, or other. The automatic consequence of such cheating is that the beliefs reached through it put into the hands of the cheater no verifiable power to predict events, nor any verifiable power to control them. This pragmatic difference is not, as Professor Demos asserts, a matter of values, but is a matter of plain fact, independent of such positive or negative values as power of prediction or of control may have. The theologian, of course, claims these powers for his beliefs, but hides from himself and from others his incapacity to substantiate the claim by making the further and equally unsubstantiated claim that his predictions will be verified and the efficacy of his beliefs proved, *in a life after death*. There is thus a radical difference between the scientific and the theological systems of belief. It is that difference which constitutes the first a system of knowledge, but the second a system only of faith, that is, according to Professor Demos's own definition, a system of beliefs "which rests on no evidence whatever." And it is that difference which justifies the characterization of theology—by Michelet, I believe—as "the art of befuddling oneself methodically."

This conclusion must not be thought to ignore the possibility of kinds of experience other than the traditional five species of sensation; for example, perhaps, clairvoyant or telepathic impressions, or the here more directly relevant kind of experience which the mystics report. The mystical experience is sometimes regarded —plausibly, I think—as religious experience *par excellence*, which all other religious experiences but approximate or adumbrate in various degrees.

In paranormal or mystical experiences, however, just as in ordinary sense-experiences, it is essential to distinguish between the experience itself, and what the person who has it takes it to signify. He may, for example, declare that he hears a bell, or that he tastes sugar; whereas the auditory sensation he experiences may in fact be caused not by a bell but by a phonograph and the sweet taste he tastes not by sugar but by saccharin. The distinction between what an experience is, and what it means, applies to the mystical ecstasy also: its literally experienced psychological characters are one thing; and what the experience is taken to signify is quite another thing—for instance, as believed by theistic mystics, that it signifies union with God.

No doubt is possible, I think, that the extraordinary state termed mystical ecstasy has been aspired after and sometimes experienced by certain men and women; that the intrinsic value of this state is found by them far greater than that of any other human experience; and that the traces left by it on those who have experienced it have sometimes infused their subsequent life with notable energy, courage, and devotion to noble work. Moreover, they testify that the experience is not only one of intense bliss, but also one of great insight. Greatness of insight, however, is not necessarily insight into something great. That the feeling of insight, like some other feelings, is capable of being generated, and with great intensity, by subjective physiological or psychological causes, was shown by Wm. James's experiments with the inhaling of nitrous oxide. Other persons who, like the present writer, have repeated the experiment, have likewise sometimes obtained what James called the "anaesthetic revelation," in which great insight is obtained into something; usually, however, into something very trivial, such as the casual words being uttered at the moment by the anaesthetist.

This suggests that consciousness of insight, whether generated thus by drugs or by peculiar psychological exercises, will automatically attach itself to any idea that happens to be occupying attention at the time. In the mystic, the idea which occupies it is virtually certain to be that of *unity*, for all-encompassing love is the feeling the mystic cultivates, and love, like other emotions, tends to generate in the person experiencing it the ideas and beliefs congruous with it; specifically in the case of love, the idea and belief of *unity* between lover and beloved. To this, the feeling of insight or conviction, which is a feature of the mystical as well as of the anaesthetic trance, automatically adheres. And it is this psychological adhesion which the mystic reports as "insight" or "revelation" *that* such unity is a cosmic fact; or, if he happens to be a theist, *that* he has been united with God. For, as Professor Coe has memorably pointed out, the mystic acquires his cosmological or theological ideas in the very same ordinary and observable ways as do other persons. He does not derive them from the mystical experience, but brings them with him to the experience. *They* are what determines whether the beloved object, to which the mystic feels himself united in the ecstasy, is conceived by him impersonally as the whole universe; or on the contrary, personalistically, as some divine being—Jesus, for St. Teresa; or Kali the world-mother, for Ramakrishna; etc.

The actual fact thus is only that when, or in so far as, anybody harbors intense and limitless love, then, or in so far, such love unites him with whatever real or imaginary object he bestows it upon. The mystic trance does not *discover*, but *institutes*, this unity.

# IV. *Justification, Verification, and Falsifiability*

# 18. GODS

## John Wisdom

*John Wisdom, a well-known Cambridge philosopher, is a former
pupil of Wittgenstein. His publications include* Other Minds,
Philosophy and Psycho-Analysis, Paradox and Discovery, *as well
as contributions to periodical literature.*

1. *The existence of God is not an experimental issue in the way it
was.* An atheist or agnostic might say to a theist 'You still think
there are spirits in the trees, nymphs in the streams, a God of the
world.' He might say this because he noticed the theist in time of
drought pray for rain and make a sacrifice and in the morning look
for rain. But disagreement about whether there are gods is now
less of this experimental or betting sort than it used to be. This is
due in part, if not wholly, to our better knowledge of why things
happen as they do.

It is true that even in these days it is seldom that one who believes in God has no hopes or fears which an atheist has not. Few
believers now expect prayer to still the waves, but some think it
makes a difference to people and not merely in ways the atheist
would admit. Of course with people, as opposed to waves and machines, one never knows what they won't do next, so that expecting
prayer to make a difference to them is not so definite a thing as
believing in its mechanical efficacy. Still, just as primitive people
pray in a business-like way for rain so some people still pray for
others with a real feeling of doing something to help. However, in
spite of this persistence of an experimental element in some theistic
belief, it remains true that Elijah's method on Mount Carmel of
settling the matter of what god or gods exist would be far less
appropriate to-day than it was then.

Reprinted by permission of the Editor of The Aristotelian Society from
the *Proceedings of the Aristotelian Society* (1944-1945).

2. *Belief in gods is not merely a matter of expectation of a world to come.* Someone may say 'The fact that a theist no more than an atheist expects prayer to bring down fire from heaven or cure the sick does not mean that there is no difference between them as to the facts, it does not mean that the theist has no expectations different from the atheist's. For very often those who believe in God believe in another world and believe that God is there and that we shall go to that world when we die.'

This is true, but I do not want to consider here expectations as to what one will see and feel after death nor what sort of reasons these logically unique expectations could have. So I want to consider those theists who do not believe in a future life, or rather, I want to consider the differences between atheists and theists in so far as these differences are not a matter of belief in a future life.

3. *What are these differences? And is it that theists are superstitious or that atheists are blind?* A child may wish to sit a while with his father and he may, when he has done what his father dislikes, fear punishment and feel distress at causing vexation, and while his father is alive he may feel sure of help when danger threatens and feel that there is sympathy for him when disaster has come. When his father is dead he will no longer expect punishment or help. Maybe for a moment an old fear will come or a cry for help escape him, but he will at once remember that this is no good now. He may feel that his father is no more until perhaps someone says to him that his father is still alive though he lives now in another world and one so far away that there is no hope of seeing him or hearing his voice again. The child may be told that nevertheless his father can see him and hear all he says. When he has been told this the child will still fear no punishment nor expect any sign of his father, but now, even more than he did when his father was alive, he will feel that his father sees him all the time and will dread distressing him and when he has done something wrong he will feel separated from his father until he has felt sorry for what he has done. Maybe when he himself comes to die he will be like a man who expects to find a friend in the strange country where he is going, but even when this is so, it is by no means all of what makes the difference between a child who believes that his father lives still in another world and one who does not.

Likewise one who believes in God may face death differently

from one who does not, but there is another difference between them besides this. This other difference may still be described as belief in another world, only this belief is not a matter of expecting one thing rather than another here or hereafter, it is not a matter of a world to come but of a world that now is, though beyond our senses.

We are at once reminded of those other unseen worlds which some philosophers 'believe in' and others 'deny,' while non-philosophers unconsciously 'accept' them by using them as models with which to 'get the hang of' the patterns in the flux of experience. We recall the timeless entities whose changeless connections we seek to represent in symbols, and the values which stand firm[1] amidst our flickering satisfaction and remorse, and the physical things which, though not beyond the corruption of moth and rust, are yet more permanent than the shadows they throw upon the screen before our minds. We recall, too, our talk of souls and of what lies in their depths and is manifested to us partially and intermittently in our own feelings and the behaviour of others. The hypothesis of mind, of other human minds and of animal minds, is reasonable because it explains for each of us why certain things behave so cunningly all by themselves unlike even the most ingenious machines. Is the hypothesis of minds in flowers and trees reasonable for like reasons? Is the hypothesis of a world mind reasonable for like reasons—someone who adjusts the blossom to the bees, someone whose presence may at times be felt—in a garden in high summer, in the hills when clouds are gathering, but not, perhaps, in a cholera epidemic?

4. *The question 'Is belief in gods reasonable?' has more than one source*. It is clear now that in order to grasp fully the logic of belief in divine minds we need to examine the logic of belief in animal and human minds. But we cannot do that here and so for the purposes of this discussion about divine minds let us acknowledge the reasonableness of our belief in human minds without troubling ourselves about its logic. The question of the reasonableness of belief in divine minds then becomes a matter of whether there are facts in nature which support claims about divine minds in the way facts in nature support our claims about human minds.

In this way we resolve the force behind the problem of the existence of gods into two components, one metaphysical and the same which prompts the question 'Is there *ever any* behaviour which gives reason to believe in *any* sort of mind?' and one which finds expression in 'Are there other mind-patterns in nature beside the human and animal patterns which we can all easily detect, and are these other mind-patterns super-human?'

Such over-determination of a question syndrome is common. Thus, the puzzling questions 'Do dogs think?', 'Do animals feel?' are partly metaphysical puzzles and partly scientific questions. They are not purely metaphysical; for the reports of scientists about the poor performances of cats in cages and old ladies' stories about the remarkable performances of their pets are not irrelevant. But nor are these questions purely scientific; for the stories never settle them and therefore they have other sources. One other source is the metaphysical source we have already noticed, namely, the difficulty about getting behind an animal's behaviour to its mind, whether it is a non-human animal or a human one.

But there's a third component in the force behind these questions, these disputes have a third source, and it is one which is important in the dispute which finds expression in the words 'I believe in God,' 'I do not.' This source comes out well if we consider the question 'Do flowers feel?' Like the questions about dogs and animals this question about flowers comes partly from the difficulty we sometimes feel over inference from *any* behaviour to thought or feeling and partly from ignorance as to what behaviour is to be found. But these questions, as opposed to a like question about human beings, come also from hesitation as to whether the behaviour in question is *enough* mind-like, that is, is it enough similar to or superior to human behaviour to be called 'mind-proving'? Likewise, even when we are satisfied that human behaviour shows mind and even when we have learned whatever mind-suggesting things there are in nature which are not explained by human and animal minds, we may still ask 'But are these things sufficiently striking to be called a mind-pattern? Can we fairly call them manifestations of a divine being?'

'The question,' someone may say, 'has then become merely a matter of the application of a name. And "What's in a name?"'

5. *But the line between a question of fact and a question or decision as to the application of a name is not so simple as this way of putting things suggests.* The question 'What's in a name?' is

engaging because we are inclined to answer both 'Nothing' and 'Very much.' And this 'Very much' has more than one source. We might have tried to comfort Heloise by saying 'It isn't that Abelard no longer loves you, for this man isn't Abelard;' we might have said to poor Mr. Tebrick in Mr. Garnet's *Lady into Fox* 'But this is no longer Silvia.' But if Mr. Tebrick replied 'Ah, but it is!' this might come not at all from observing facts about the fox which we have not observed, but from noticing facts about the fox which we had missed, although we had in a sense observed all that Mr. Tebrick had observed. It is possible to have before one's eyes all the items of a pattern and still to miss the pattern. Consider the following conversation:

'"And I think Kay and I are pretty happy. We've always been happy."

'Bill lifted up his glass and put it down without drinking.

'"Would you mind saying that again?" he asked.

'"I don't see what's so queer about it. Taken all in all, Kay and I have really been happy."

'"All right," Bill said gently, "Just tell me how you and Kay have been happy."

'Bill had a way of being amused by things which I could not understand.

'"It's a little hard to explain," I said. "It's like taking a lot of numbers that don't look alike and that don't mean anything until you add them all together."

'I stopped, because I hadn't meant to talk to him about Kay and me.

'"Go ahead," Bill said. "What about the numbers." And he began to smile.

'"I don't know why you think it's so funny," I said. "All the things that two people do together, two people like Kay and me, add up to something. There are the kids and the house and the dog and all the people we have known and all the times we've been out to dinner. Of course, Kay and I do quarrel sometimes but when you add it all together, all of it isn't as bad as the parts of it seem. I mean, maybe that's all there is to anybody's life."

'Bill poured himself another drink. He seemed about to say something and checked himself. He kept looking at me.'[2]

Or again, suppose two people are speaking of two characters in a story which both have read[3] or of two friends which both have known, and one says 'Really she hated him,' and the other says 'She didn't, she loved him.' Then the first may have noticed what the other has not although he knows no incident in the lives of the people they are talking about which the other doesn't know too, and the second speaker may say 'She didn't, she loved him' because he hasn't noticed what the first noticed, although he can remember every incident the first can remember. But then again he may say 'She didn't, she loved him' not because he hasn't noticed the patterns in time which the first has noticed but because though he has noticed them he doesn't feel he still needs to emphasize them with 'Really she hated him.' The line between using a name because of how we feel and because of what we have noticed isn't sharp. 'A difference as to the facts,' 'a discovery,' 'a revelation,' these phrases cover many things. Discoveries have been made not only by Christopher Columbus and Pasteur, but also by Tolstoy and Dostoievsky and Freud. Things are revealed to us not only by the scientists with microscopes, but also by the poets, the prophets, and the painters. What is so isn't merely a matter of 'the facts.' For sometimes when there is agreement as to the facts there is still argument as to whether defendant did or did not 'exercise reasonable care,' was or was not 'negligent.'

And though we shall need to emphasize how much 'There is a God' evinces an attitude to the familiar[4] we shall find in the end that it also evinces some recognition of patterns in time easily missed and that, therefore, difference as to there being any gods is in part a difference as to what is so and therefore as to the facts, though not in the simple ways which first occurred to us.

6. *Let us now approach these same points by a different road.*

6.1. *How it is that an explanatory hypothesis, such as the existence of God, may start by being experimental and gradually become something quite different can be seen from the following story:*

Two people return to their long neglected garden and find among the weeds a few of the old plants surprisingly vigorous. One says to the other 'It must be that a gardener has been coming and doing something about these plants.' Upon inquiry they find that no neighbour has ever seen anyone at work in their garden. The first man says to the other 'He must have worked while people slept.'

The other says 'No, someone would have heard him and besides, anybody who cared about the plants would have kept down these weeds.' The first man says 'Look at the way these are arranged. There is purpose and a feeling for beauty here. I believe that some-one comes, someone invisible to mortal eyes. I believe that the more carefully we look the more we shall find confirmation of this.' They examine the garden ever so carefully and sometimes they come on new things suggesting that a gardener comes and some-times they come on things suggesting the contrary and even that a malicious person has been at work. Besides examining the garden carefully they also study what happens to gardens left without attention. Each learns all the other learns about this and about the garden. Consequently, when after all this, one says 'I still believe a gardener comes' while the other says 'I don't' their different words now reflect no difference as to what they have found in the garden, no difference as to what they would find in the garden if they looked further and no difference about how fast untended gardens fall into disorder. At this stage, in this context, the gardener hypothesis has ceased to be experimental, the difference between one who accepts and one who rejects it is now not a matter of the one expecting something the other does not expect. What is the difference between them? The one says 'A gardener comes unseen and unheard. He is manifested only in his works with which we are all familiar,' the other says 'There is no gardener' and with this difference in what they say about the gardener goes a difference in how they feel towards the garden, in spite of the fact that neither expects anything of it which the other does not expect.

But is this the whole difference between them—that the one calls the garden by one name and feels one way towards it, while the other calls it by another name and feels in another way towards it? And if this is what the difference has become then is it any longer appropriate to ask 'Which is right?' or 'Which is reasonable?'

And yet surely such questions *are* appropriate when one person says to another 'You still think the world's a garden and not a wilderness, and that the gardener has not forsaken it' or 'You still think there are nymphs of the streams, a presence in the hills, a spirit of the world.' Perhaps when a man sings 'God's in His heaven' we need not take this as more than an expression of how he feels. But when Bishop Gore or Dr. Joad write about belief in God and young men read them in order to settle their religious doubts the impression is not simply that of persons choosing exclamations with which to face nature and the 'changes and chances of this mortal life.' The disputants speak as if they are concerned with a matter of scientific fact, or of trans-sensual, trans-scientific and metaphysical fact, but still of fact and still a matter about which reasons for and against may be offered, although no scientific reasons in the sense of field surveys for fossils or experiments on delinquents are to the point.

6.2. *Now can an interjection have a logic?* Can the manifestation of an attitude in the utterance of a word, in the application of a name, have a logic? When all the facts are known how can there still be a question of fact? How can there still be a question? Surely as Hume says '. . . after every circumstance, every relation is known, the understanding has no further room to operate.'[5]

6.3. When the madness of these questions leaves us for a moment *we can all easily recollect disputes which though they cannot be settled by experiment are yet disputes in which one party may be right and the other wrong* and in which both parties may offer reasons and the one better reasons than the other. *This may happen in pure and applied mathematics and logic.* Two accountants or two engineers provided with the same data may reach different results and this difference is resolved not by collecting further data but by going over the calculations again. Such differences indeed share with differences as to what will win a race, the honour of being among the most 'settlable' disputes in the language.

6.4. *But it won't do to describe the theistic issue as one settlable by such calculation,* or as one about what can be deduced in this *vertical* fashion from the facts we know. No doubt dispute about God has sometimes, perhaps especially in mediaeval times, been carried on in this fashion. But nowadays it is not and we must look for some other analogy, some other case in which a dispute is settled but not by experiment.

6.5. *In courts of law* it sometimes happens that opposing counsel are agreed as to the facts and are not trying to settle a question of further fact, are not trying to settle whether the man who admittedly had quarrelled with the deceased did or did not murder him, but are concerned with whether Mr. A who admittedly handed his long-trusted clerk signed blank cheques did or did not exercise reasonable care, whether a ledger is or is not a document,[6] whether a certain body was or was not a public authority.

In such cases we notice that the process of argument is not a *chain* of demonstrative reasoning. It is a presenting and representing of those features of the case which *severally co-operate* in favour of the conclusion, in favour of saying what the reasoner wishes said, in favour of calling the situation by the name by which he wishes to call it. The reasons are like the legs of a chair, not the links of a chain. Consequently although the discussion is *a priori* and the steps are not a matter of experience, the procedure resembles scientific argument in that the reasoning is not *vertically* extensive but *horizontally* extensive—it is a matter of the cumulative effect of several independent premises, not of the repeated transformation of one or two. And because the premises are severally inconclusive the process of deciding the issue becomes a matter of weighing the cumulative effect of one group of severally inconclusive items against the cumulative effect of another group of severally inconclusive items, and thus lends itself to description in terms of conflicting 'probabilities.' This encourages the feeling that the issue is one of fact—that it is a matter of guessing from the premises at a further fact, at what is to come. But this is a muddle. *The dispute does not cease to be* a priori *because it is a matter of the cumulative effect of severally inconclusive premises*. The logic of the dispute is not that of a chain of deductive reasoning as in a mathematic calculation. But nor is it a matter of collecting from several inconclusive items of information an expectation as to something further, as when a doctor from a patient's symptoms guesses at what is wrong, or a detective from many clues guesses the criminal. It has its own sort of logic and its own sort of end—the solution of the question at issue is a decision, a ruling by the judge. But it is not an arbitrary decision though the rational connections are neither quite like those in vertical deductions nor like those in inductions in which from many signs we guess at what is to come; and though the decision manifests itself in the application of a name it is no more merely the application of a name than is the pinning on of a medal merely the pinning on of a bit of metal. Whether a lion with stripes is a tiger or a lion is, if you like, merely a matter of the application of a name. Whether Mr. So-and-So of whose conduct we have so complete a record did or did not exercise reasonable care is not merely a matter of the application of a name or, if we choose to say it is, then we must remember that with this name a game is lost and won and a game with very heavy stakes. With the judges' choice of a name for the facts goes an attitude, and the declaration, the ruling, is an exclamation evincing that attitude. But *it is an exclamation which not only has a purpose but also has a logic*, a logic surprisingly like that of 'futile,' 'deplorable,' 'graceful,' 'grand,' 'divine.'

6.6. *Suppose two people are looking at a picture or natural scene.* One says 'Excellent' or 'Beautiful' or 'Divine'; the other says 'I don't see it.' He means he doesn't see the beauty. And this reminds us of how we felt the theist accuse the atheist of blindness and the atheist accuse the theist of seeing what isn't there. And yet surely each sees what the other sees. It isn't that one can see part of the picture which the other can't see. So the difference is in a sense not one as to the facts. And so it cannot be removed by the one disputant discovering to the other what so far he hasn't seen. It isn't that the one sees the picture in a different light and so, as we might say, sees a different picture. Consequently the difference between them cannot be resolved by putting the picture in a different light. And yet surely this is just what can be done in such a case—not by moving the picture but by talk perhaps. To settle a dispute as to whether a piece of music is good or better than another we listen again, with a picture we look again. Someone perhaps points to emphasize certain features and we see it in a different light. Shall we call this 'field work' and 'the last of observation' or shall we call it 'reviewing the premises' and 'the beginning of deduction (horizontal)'?

If in spite of all this we choose to say that a difference as to whether a thing is beautiful is not a factual difference we must be careful to remember that there is a procedure for settling these differences and that this consists not only in reasoning and re-description as in the legal case, but also in a more literal re-setting-before with re-looking or re-listening.

6.7. *And if we say as we did at the beginning that when a difference as to the existence of a God is not one as to future happenings then it is not experimental and therefore not as to the facts, we must not forthwith assume that there is no right and wrong about it*, no rationality or irrationality, no appropriateness or inappropriateness, no procedure which tends to settle it, *nor even that this procedure is in no sense a discovery of new facts*. After all even in science this is not so. Our two gardeners even when they had reached the stage when neither expected any experimental result which the other did not, might yet have continued the dispute, each presenting and re-presenting the features of the garden favouring his hypothesis, that is, fitting his model for describing the accepted fact; each emphasizing the pattern he wishes to emphasize. True, in science, there is seldom or never a pure instance of this sort of dispute, for nearly always with difference of hypothesis goes some difference of expectation as to the facts. But scientists argue about rival hypotheses with a vigour which is not exactly proportioned to difference in expectations of experimental results.

The difference as to whether a God exists involves our feelings more than most scientific disputes and in this respect is more like a difference as to whether there is beauty in a thing.

7. *The Connecting Technique*. Let us consider again the technique used in revealing or proving beauty, in removing a blindness, in inducing an attitude which is lacking, in reducing a reaction that is inappropriate. Besides running over in a special way the features of the picture, tracing the rhythms, making sure that this and that are not only seen but noticed, and their relation to each other—besides all this—there are other things we can do to justify our attitude and alter that of the man who cannot see. For features of the picture may be brought out by setting beside it other pictures; just as the merits of an argument may be brought out, proved, by setting beside it other arguments, in which striking but irrelevant features of the original are changed and relevant features emphasized; just as the merits and demerits of a line of action may be brought out by setting beside it other actions. To use Susan Stebbing's example: Nathan brought out for David certain features of what David had done in the matter of Uriah the Hittite by telling him a story about two sheep-owners. This is the kind of thing we very often do when someone is 'inconsistent' or 'unreasonable.' This is what we do in referring to other cases in law. The paths we need to trace from other cases to the case in question are often numerous and difficult to detect and the person with whom we are discussing the matter may well draw attention to connections

which, while not incompatible with those we have tried to emphasize, are of an opposite inclination. A may have noticed in B subtle
and hidden likenesses to an angel and reveal these to C, while C has
noticed in B subtle and hidden likenesses to a devil which he reveals
to A.

Imagine that a man picks up some flowers that lie half withered
on a table and gently puts them in water. Another man says to him
'You believe flowers feel.' He says this although he knows that the
man who helps the flowers doesn't expect anything of them which
he himself doesn't expect; for he himself expects the flowers to be
'refreshed' and to be easily hurt, injured, I mean, by rough handling, while the man who puts them in water does not expect them
to whisper 'Thank you.' The Sceptic says 'You believe flowers feel'
because something about the way the other man lifts the flowers
and puts them in water suggests an attitude to the flowers which
he feels inappropriate although perhaps he would not feel it inappropriate to butterflies. He feels that this attitude to flowers is
somewhat crazy *just as it is sometimes felt that a lover's attitude is
somewhat crazy even when this is not a matter of his having false
hopes about how the person he is in love with will act.* It is often
said in such cases that reasoning is useless. But the very person who
says this feels that the lover's attitude is crazy, is inappropriate like
some dreads and hatreds, such as some horrors of enclosed places.
And often one who says 'It is useless to reason,' proceeds at once
to reason with the lover, nor is this reasoning always quite without
effect. We may draw the lover's attention to certain things done
by her he is in love with and trace for him a path to these from
things done by others at other times[7] which have disgusted and
infuriated him. And by this means we may weaken his admiration
and confidence, make him feel it unjustified and arouse his suspicion and contempt and make him feel our suspicion and contempt reasonable. It is possible, of course, that he has already
noticed the analogies, the connections, we point out and that he
has accepted them—that is, he has not denied them nor passed
them off. He has recognized them and they have altered his attitude,
altered his love, but he still loves. We then feel that perhaps it is
we who are blind and cannot see what he can see.

8. *Connecting and Disconnecting.* But before we confess ourselves thus inadequate there are other fires his admiration must

pass through. For when a man has an attitude which it seems to us he should not have or lacks one which it seems to us he should have then, not only do we suspect that he is not influenced by connections which we feel should influence him and draw his attention to these, but also we suspect he is influenced by connections which should not influence him and draw his attention to these. It may, for a moment, seem strange that we should draw his attention to connections which we feel should not influence him, and which, since they do influence him, he has in a sense already noticed. But we do—such is our confidence in 'the light of reason.'

Sometimes the power of these connections comes mainly from a man's mismanagement of the language he is using. This is what happens in the Monte Carlo fallacy, where by mismanaging the laws of chance a man passes from noticing that a certain colour or number has not turned up for a long while to an improper confidence that now it soon will turn up. In such cases our showing up of the false connections is a process we call 'explaining a fallacy in reasoning.' To remove fallacies in reasoning we urge a man to call a spade a spade, ask him what he means by 'the State' and having pointed out ambiguities and vaguenesses ask him to reconsider the steps in his argument.

9. *Unspoken Connections. Usually, however, wrongheadedness or wrongheartedness in a situation, blindness to what is there or seeing what is not, does not arise merely from mismanagement of language but is more due to connections which are not mishandled in language, for the reason that they are not put into language at all.* And often these misconnections too, weaken in the light of reason, if only we can guess where they lie and turn it on them. In so far as these connections are not presented in language the process of removing their power is not a process of correcting the mismanagement of language. But it is still akin to such a process; for though it is not a process of setting out fairly what has been set out unfairly, it is a process of setting out fairly what has not been set out at all. And we must remember that the line between connections ill-presented or half-presented in language and connections operative but not presented in language, or only hinted at, is not a sharp one.

Whether or not we call the process of showing up these connections 'reasoning to remove bad unconscious reasoning' or not, it is certain that in order to settle in ourselves what weight we shall attach to someone's confidence or attitude we not only ask him for his reasons but also look for unconscious reasons both good and bad; that is, for reasons which he can't put into words, isn't explicitly aware of, is hardly aware of, isn't aware of at all—perhaps it's long experience which he *doesn't* recall which lets him know a squall is coming, perhaps it's old experience which he *can't* recall which makes the cake in the tea mean so much and makes Odette so fascinating.[8]

I am well aware of the distinction between the question 'What reasons are there for the belief that S is P?' and the question 'What are the sources of beliefs that S is P?' There are cases where investigation of the rationality of a claim which certain persons make is done with very little inquiry into why they say what they do, into the causes of their beliefs. This is so when we have very definite ideas about what is really logically relevant to their claim and what is not. Offered a mathematical theorem we ask for the proof; offered the generalization that parental discord causes crime we ask for the correlation co-efficients. But even in this last case, if we fancy that only the figures are reasons we underestimate the complexity of the logic of our conclusion; and yet it is difficult to describe the other features of the evidence which have weight and there is apt to be disagreement about the weight they should have. In criticizing other conclusions and especially conclusions which are largely the expression of an attitude, we have not only to ascertain what reasons there are for them but also to decide what things are reasons and how much. This latter process of sifting reasons from causes is part of the critical process for every belief, but in some spheres it has been done pretty fully already. In these spheres we don't need to examine the actual processes to belief and distil from them a logic. But in other spheres this remains to be done. Even in science or on the stock exchange or in ordinary life we sometimes hesitate to condemn a belief or a hunch[9] merely because those who believe it cannot offer the sort of reasons we had hoped for. And now suppose Miss Gertrude Stein finds excellent the work of a new artist while we see nothing in it. We nervously recall, perhaps, how pictures by Picasso, which Miss Stein admired and others rejected, later came to be admired by many who gave attention to them, and we wonder whether the case is not a new instance of her perspicacity and our blindness. But if, upon giving all our attention to the work in question, we still do not respond to it, and we notice that the subject matter of the new pictures is perhaps birds in wild places and learn that Miss Stein is a bird-watcher, then we begin to trouble ourselves less about her admiration.

It must not be forgotten that our attempt to show up misconnections in Miss Stein may have an opposite result and reveal to us connections we had missed. Thinking to remove the spell exercised upon his patient by the old stories of the Greeks, the psycho-analyst may himself fall under that spell and find in them what his patient has found and, incidentally, what made the Greeks tell those tales.

10. *Now what happens, what should happen, when we inquire in this way into the reasonableness, the propriety of belief in gods?* The answer is: A double and opposite-phased change. Wordsworth writes:

> '. . . And I have felt
> A presence that disturbs me with the joy
> Of elevated thoughts; a sense sublime
> Of something far more deeply interfused,
> Whose dwelling is the light of setting suns,
> And the round ocean and the living air,
> And the blue sky, and in the mind of man:
> A motion and a spirit, that impels
> All thinking things, all objects of all thought,
> And rolls through all things . . .'[10]

We most of us know this feeling. But is it well placed like the feeling that here is first-rate work, which we sometimes rightly have even before we have fully grasped the picture we are looking at or the book we are reading? Or is it misplaced like the feeling in a house that has long been empty that someone secretly lives there still. Wordsworth's feeling *is* the feeling that the world is haunted, that something watches in the hills and manages the stars. The child feels that the stone tripped him when he stumbled, that the bough struck him when it flew back in his face. He has to learn that the wind isn't buffeting him, that there is not a devil in it, that he was wrong, that his attitude was inappropriate. And as he learns that the wind wasn't hindering him so he also learns it wasn't helping him. But we know how, though he learns, his attitude lingers. It is plain that Wordsworth's feeling is of this family.

Belief in gods, it is true, is often very different from belief that stones are spiteful, the sun kindly. For the gods appear in human form and from the waves and control these things and by so doing reward and punish us. But varied as are the stories of the gods they have a family likeness and we have only to recall them to feel sure of the other main sources which co-operate with animism to produce them.

What are the stories of the gods? What are our feelings when we believe in God? They are feelings of awe before power, dread of the thunderbolts of Zeus, confidence in the everlasting arms, unease beneath the all-seeing eye. They are feelings of guilt and inescapable vengeance, of smothered hate and of a security we can hardly do without. We have only to remind ourselves of these feelings and the stories of the gods and goddesses and heroes in which these feelings find expression, to be reminded of how we felt as children to our parents and the big people of our childhood. Writing of a first telephone call from his grandmother, Proust says: '. . . it was rather that this isolation of the voice was like a symbol, a presentation, a direct consequence of another isolation, that of my grandmother, separated for the first time in my life, from myself. The orders or prohibitions which she addressed to me at every moment in the ordinary course of my life, the tedium of obedience or the fire of rebellion which neutralized the affection that I felt for her were at this moment eliminated. . . . "Granny!" I cried to her . . . but I had beside me only that voice, a phantom, as unpalpable as that which would come to revisit me when my grandmother was dead. "Speak to me!" but then it happened that, left more solitary still, I ceased to catch the sound of her voice. My grandmother could no longer hear me . . . I continued to call her, sounding the empty night, in which I felt that her appeals also must be straying. I was shaken by the same anguish which, in the distant past, I had felt once before, one day when, a little child, in a crowd, I had lost her.'

Giorgio de Chirico, writing of Courbet, says: 'The word yesterday envelops us with its yearning echo, just as, on waking, when the sense of time and the logic of things remain a while confused, the memory of a happy hour we spent the day before may sometimes linger reverberating within us. At times we think of Courbet and his work as we do of our own father's youth.'

When a man's father fails him by death or weakness how much he needs another father, one in the heavens with whom is 'no variableness nor shadow of turning.'

We understood Mr. Kenneth Graham when he wrote of the Golden Age we feel we have lived in under the Olympians. Freud says: 'The ordinary man cannot imagine this Providence in any other form but that of a greatly exalted father, for only such a one could understand the needs of the sons of men, or be softened by their prayers and be placated by the signs of their remorse. The whole thing is so patently infantile, so incongruous with reality. . . .' 'So incongruous with realty'! It cannot be denied.

But here a new aspect of the matter may strike us.[11] For the very facts which make us feel that now we can recognize systems of superhuman, sub-human, elusive, beings for what they are—the persistent projections of infantile phantasies—include facts which make these systems less fantastic. What are these facts? They are patterns in human reactions which are well described by saying that we are as if there were hidden within us powers, persons, not ourselves and stronger than ourselves. That this is so may perhaps be said to have been common knowledge yielded by ordinary observation of people,[12] but we did not know the degree in which this is so until recent study of extraordinary cases in extraordinary conditions had revealed it. I refer, of course, to the study of multiple personalities and the wider studies of psycho-analysts. Even when the results of this work are reported to us that is not the same as tracing the patterns in the details of the cases on which the results are based; and even that is not the same as taking part in the studies oneself. One thing not sufficiently realized is that some of the things shut within us are not bad but good.

Now the gods, good and evil and mixed, have always been mysterious powers outside us rather than within. But they have also been within. It is not a modern theory but an old saying that in each of us a devil sleeps. Eve said: 'The serpent beguiled me.' Helen says to Menelaus:

> '. . . And yet how strange it is!
> I ask not thee; I ask my own sad thought,
> What was there in my heart, that I forgot
> My home and land and all I loved, to fly
> With a strange man? Surely it was not I,
> But Cypris there!'[13]

Elijah found that God was not in the wind, nor in the thunder, but in a still small voice. The kingdom of Heaven is within us, Christ insisted, though usually about the size of a grain of mustard seed, and he prayed that we should become one with the Father in Heaven.

New knowledge made it necessary either to give up saying 'The sun is sinking' or to give the words a new meaning. In many contexts we preferred to stick to the old words and give them a new meaning which was not entirely new but, on the contrary, *practically* the same as the old. The Greeks did not speak of the dangers of repressing instincts but they did speak of the dangers of thwarting Dionysos, of neglecting Cypris for Diana, of forgetting Poseidon for Athena. We have eaten of the fruit of a garden we can't forget though we were never there, a garden we still look for though we can never find it. Maybe we look for too simple a likeness to what we dreamed. Maybe we are not as free as we fancy from the old idea that Heaven is a happy hunting ground, or a city with streets of gold. Lately Mr. Aldous Huxley has recommended our seeking not somewhere beyond the sky or late in time but a timeless state not made of the stuff of this world, which he rejects, picking it into worthless pieces. But this sounds to me still too much a looking for another place, not indeed one filled with sweets but instead so empty that some of us would rather remain in the Lamb or the Elephant, where, as we know, they stop whimpering with another bitter and so far from sneering at all things, hang pictures of winners at Kempton and stars of the 'nineties. Something good we have for each other is freed there, and in some degree and for a while the miasma of time is rolled back without obliging us to deny the present.

The artists who do most for us don't tell us only of fairylands. Proust, Manet, Breughel, even Botticelli and Vermeer show us reality. And yet they give us for a moment exhilaration without anxiety, piece without boredom. And those who, like Freud, work in a different way against that which too often comes over us and forces us into deadness or despair,[14] also deserve critical, patient and courageous attention. For they, too, work to release us from human bondage into human freedom.

Many have tried to find ways of salvation. The reports they bring back are always incomplete and apt to mislead even when they are not in words but in music or paint. But they are by no means useless; and not the worst of them are those which speak of oneness with God. But in so far as we become one with Him He becomes one with us. St. John says he is in us as we love one another.

This love, I suppose, is not benevolence but something that comes of the oneness with one another of which Christ spoke.[15] Sometimes it momentarily gains strength.[16] Hate and the Devil do too. And what is oneness without otherness?

NOTES

1. In another world, Dr. Joad says in the *New Statesman* recently.

2. *H. M. Pulham, Esq.*, p. 320, by John P. Marquand.

3. e.g. Havelock Ellis's autobiography .

4. 'Persuasive Definitions,' *Mind*, July, 1938, by Charles Leslie Stevenson, should be read here. It is very good. [Also in his *Ethics and Language*, Yale, 1945.—Ed.]

5. Hume, *An Enquiry concerning the Principles of Morals*. Appendix I.

6. *The Times*, March 2nd, 1945. Also in *The Times* of June 13th, 1945, contrast the case of Hannah v. Peel with that of the cruiser cut in two by a liner. In the latter case there is not agreement as to the facts. See also the excellent articles by Dr. Glanville L. Williams in the *Law Quarterly Review*, 'Language and the Law,' January, and April 1945, and 'The Doctrine of Repugnancy,' October, 1943, January, 1944, and April, 1944. The author, having set out how arbitrary are many legal decisions, needs now to set out how far from arbitrary they are— if his readers are ready for the next phase in the dialectic process.

7. Thus, like the scientist, the critic is concerned to show up the irrelevance of time and space.

8. Proust: *Swann's Way*, Vol. I, p. 58, Vol. II. Phoenix Edition.

9. Here I think of Mr. Stace's interesting reflections in *Mind*, January, 1945, 'The Problems of Unreasoned Beliefs.'

10. *Tintern Abbey*.

11. I owe to the late Dr. Susan Isaacs the thought of this different aspect of the matter, of this connection between the heavenly Father and 'the good father' spoken of in psychoanalysis.

12. Consider Tolstoy and Dostoievsky—I do not mean, of course, that their observation was ordinary.

13. Euripides: *The Trojan Women*, Gilbert Murray's Translation. Roger Hinks in *Myth and Allegory in Ancient Art* writes (p. 108): 'Personifications made their appearance very early in Greek poetry. . . . It is out of the question to call these terrible beings "abstractions." . . .

They are real daemons to be worshipped and propitiated. . . . These beings we observe correspond to states of mind. The experience of man teaches him that from time to time his composure is invaded and overturned by some power from outside, panic, intoxication, sexual desire.'

'What use to shoot off guns at unicorns?
Where one horn's hit another fierce horn grows.
These beasts are fabulous, and none were born
　　　Of woman who could lay a fable low.'—
　　　　　　　　　　*The Glass Tower*, Nicholas Moore, p. 100.

14. Matthew Arnold: *Summer Night*.
15. St. John xvi. 21.
16. 'The Harvesters' in *The Golden Age*, Kenneth Graham.

# 19. THEOLOGY AND FALSIFICATION

## Antony Flew · R. M. Hare
## Basil Mitchell · I. M. Crombie

*Antony Flew is Professor of Philosophy at University of Keele (previously established as University College of North Stafford-shire.) He is author of* Hume's Philosophy of Belief, *and editor of* Essays in Conceptual Analysis *and two series of* Logic and Language.

*R. M. Hare is Fellow at Balliol College, Oxford University. His publications include* The Language of Morals, Freedom and Reason, *and other contributions to scholarly works.*

*Basil Mitchell is Tutor in Philosophy and Fellow at Keble College, Oxford University. He is editor of* Faith and Logic.

*I. M. Crombie is Lecturer in Philosophy and Webster Fellow at Wadham College, Oxford University. His published works include* An Examination of Plato's Doctrines *and* Plato, the Mid-wife's Apprentice, *among others.*

## A. ANTONY FLEW

Let us begin with a parable. It is a parable developed from a tale told by John Wisdom in his haunting and revelatory article 'Gods.'[1] Once upon a time two explorers came upon a clearing in the jungle. In the clearing were growing many flowers and many weeds. One explorer says, 'Some gardener must tend this plot.' The other disagrees, 'There is no gardener.' So they pitch their tents and set a watch. No gardener is ever seen. 'But perhaps he is an invisible

Reprinted by permission of SCM Press Ltd. from *New Essays in Philosophical Theology* (1955), pp. 96-108, 124-130. Published in the USA by Macmillan.

gardener.' So they set up a barbed-wire fence. They electrify it. They patrol with bloodhounds. (For they remember how H. G. Wells's *The Invisible Man* could be both smelt and touched though he could not be seen.) But no shrieks ever suggest that some intruder has received a shock. No movements of the wire ever betray an invisible climber. The bloodhounds never give cry. Yet still the Believer is not convinced. 'But there is a gardener, invisible, intangible, insensible to electric shocks, a gardener who has no scent and makes no sound, a gardener who comes secretly to look after the garden which he loves.' At last the Sceptic despairs, 'But what remains of your original assertion? Just how does what you call an invisible, intangible, eternally elusive gardener differ from an imaginary gardener or even from no gardener at all?'

In this parable we can see how what starts as an assertion, that something exists or that there is some analogy between certain complexes of phenomena, may be reduced step by step to an altogether different status, to an expression perhaps of a 'picture preference.'[2] The Sceptic says there is no gardener. The Believer says there is a gardener (but invisible, etc.). One man talks about sexual behaviour. Another man prefers to talk of Aphrodite (but knows that there is not really a superhuman person additional to, and somehow responsible for, all sexual phenomena).[3] The process of qualification may be checked at any point before the original assertion is completely withdrawn and something of that first assertion will remain (Tautology). Mr. Wells's invisible man could not, admittedly, be seen, but in all other respects he was a man like the rest of us. But though the process of qualification may be, and of course usually is, checked in time, it is not always judiciously so halted. Someone may dissipate his assertion completely without noticing that he has done so. A fine brash hypothesis may thus be killed by inches, the death by a thousand qualifications.

And in this, it seems to me, lies the peculiar danger, the endemic evil, of theological utterance. Take such utterances as 'God has a plan,' 'God created the world,' 'God loves us as a father loves his children.' They look at first sight very much like assertions, vast cosmological assertions. Of course, this is no sure sign that they either are, or are intended to be, assertions. But let us confine ourselves to the cases where those who utter such sentences intend them to express assertions. (Merely remarking parenthetically that those who intend or interpret such utterances as crypto-commands, expressions of wishes, disguised ejaculations, concealed ethics, or as anything else but assertions, are unlikely to succeed in making them either properly orthodox or practically effective).

Now to assert that such and such is the case is necessarily equivalent to denying that such and such is not the case.[4] Suppose then that we are in doubt as to what someone who gives vent to an utterance is asserting, or suppose that, more radically, we are sceptical as to whether he is really asserting anything at all, one way of trying to understand (or perhaps it will be to expose) his utterance is to attempt to find what he would regard as counting against, or as being incompatible with, its truth. For if the utterance is indeed an assertion, it will necessarily be equivalent to a denial of the negation of that assertion. And anything which would count against the assertion, or which would induce the speaker to withdraw it and to admit that it had been mistaken, must be part of (or the whole of) the meaning of the negation of that assertion. And to know the meaning of the negation of an assertion, is as near as makes no matter, to know the meaning of that assertion.[5] And if there is nothing which a putative assertion denies then there is nothing which it asserts either: and so it is not really an assertion. When the Sceptic in the parable asked the Believer, 'Just how does what you call an invisible, intangible, eternally elusive gardener differ from an imaginary gardener or even from no gardener at all?' he was suggesting that the Believer's earlier statement had been so eroded by qualification that it was no longer an assertion at all.

Now it often seems to people who are not religious as if there was no conceivable event or series of events the occurrence of which would be admitted by sophisticated religious people to be a sufficient reason for conceding 'There wasn't a God after all' or 'God does not really love us then.' Someone tells us that God loves us as a father loves his children. We are reassured. But then we see a child dying of inoperable cancer of the throat. His earthly father is driven frantic in his efforts to help, but his Heavenly Father reveals no obvious sign of concern. Some qualification is made—God's love is 'not a merely human love' or it is 'an inscrutable love,' perhaps— and we realize that such sufferings are quite compatible with the truth of the assertion that 'God loves us as a father (but, of course, . . .).' We are reassured again. But then perhaps we ask:

what is this assurance of God's (appropriately qualified) love worth, what is this apparent guarantee really a guarantee against? Just what would have to happen not merely (morally and wrongly) to tempt but also (logically and rightly) to entitle us to say 'God does not love us' or even 'God does not exist'? I therefore put to the succeeding symposiasts the simple central questions, 'What would have to occur or to have occurred to constitute for you a disproof of the love of, or of the existence of, God?'

## B.* R. M. HARE

I wish to make it clear that I shall not try to defend Christianity in particular, but religion in general—not because I do not believe in Christianity, but because you cannot understand what Christianity is, until you have understood what religion is.

I must begin by confessing that, on the ground marked out by Flew, he seems to me to be completely victorious. I therefore shift my ground by relating another parable. A certain lunatic is convinced that all dons want to murder him. His friends introduce him to all the mildest and most respectable dons that they can find, and after each of them has retired, they say, 'You see, he doesn't really want to murder you; he spoke to you in a most cordial manner; surely you are convinced now?' But the lunatic replies 'Yes, but that was only his diabolical cunning; he's really plotting against me the whole time, like the rest of them; I know it I tell you.' However many kindly dons are produced, the reaction is still the same.

Now we say that such a person is deluded. But what is he deluded about? About the truth or falsity of an assertion? Let us apply Flew's test to him. There is no behaviour of dons that can be enacted which he will accept as counting against his theory; and therefore his theory, on this test, asserts nothing. But it does not follow that there is no difference between what he thinks about dons and what most of us think about them—otherwise we should not call him a lunatic and ourselves sane, and dons would have no reason to feel uneasy about his presence in Oxford.

Let us call that in which we differ from this lunatic, our respective *bliks*. He has an insane *blik* about dons; we have a sane one.

* Some references to intervening discussion have been excised.–Editors.

It is important to realize that we have a sane one, not no *blik* at all; for there must be two sides to any argument—if he has a wrong *blik*, then those who are right about dons must have a right one. Flew has shown that a *blik* does not consist in an assertion or system of them; but nevertheless it is very important to have the right *blik*.

Let us try to imagine what it would be like to have different *bliks* about other things than dons. When I am driving my car, it sometimes occurs to me to wonder whether my movements of the steering-wheel will always continue to be followed by corresponding alterations in the direction of the car. I have never had a steering failure, though I have had skids, which must be similar. Moreover, I know enough about how the steering of my car is made, to know the sort of thing that would have to go wrong for the steering to fail—steel joints would have to part, or steel rods break, or something—but how do I know that this won't happen? The truth is, I don't know; I just have a *blik* about steel and its properties, so that normally I trust the steering of my car; but I find it not at all difficult to imagine what it would be like to lose this *blik* and acquire the opposite one. People would say I was silly about steel; but there would be no mistaking the reality of the difference between our respective *bliks*—for example, I should never go in a motor-car. Yet I should hesitate to say that the difference between us was the difference between contradictory assertions. No amount of safe arrivals or bench-tests will remove my *blik* and restore the normal one; for my *blik* is compatible with any finite number of such tests.

It was Hume who taught us that our whole commerce with the world depends upon our *blik* about the world; and that differences between *bliks* about the world cannot be settled by observation of what happens in the world. That was why, having performed the interesting experiment of doubting the ordinary man's *blik* about the world, and showing that no proof could be given to make us adopt one *blik* rather than another, he turned to backgammon to take his mind off the problem. It seems, indeed, to be impossible even to formulate as an assertion the normal *blik* about the world which makes me put my confidence in the future reliability of steel joints, in the continued ability of the road to support my car, and not gape beneath it revealing nothing below; in the general non-homicidal tendencies of dons; in my own continued well-being (in some sense of that word that I may not now fully understand) if I continue to do what is right according to my lights; in the general likelihood of people like Hitler coming to a bad end. But perhaps a formulation less inadequate than most is to be found in the Psalms: 'The earth is weak and all the inhabiters thereof: I bear up the pillars of it.'

The mistake of the position which Flew selects for attack is to regard this kind of talk as some sort of *explanation*, as scientists are accustomed to use the word. As such, it would obviously be ludicrous. We no longer believe in God as an Atlas—*nous n'avons pas besoin de cette hypothèse*. But it is nevertheless true to say that, as Hume saw, without a *blik* there can be no explanation; for it is by our *bliks* that we decide what is and what is not an explanation. Suppose we believed that everything that happened, happened by pure chance. This would not of course be an assertion; for it is compatible with anything happening or not happening, and so, incidentally, is its contradictory. But if we had this belief, we should not be able to explain or predict or plan anything. Thus, although we should not be *asserting* anything different from those of a more normal belief, there would be a great difference between us; and this is the sort of difference that there is between those who really believe in God and those who really disbelieve in him.

The word 'really' is important, and may excite suspicion. I put it in, because when people have had a good Christian upbringing, as have most of those who now profess not to believe in any sort of religion, it is very hard to discover what they really believe. The reason why they find it so easy to think that they are not religious, is that they have never got into the frame of mind of one who suffers from the doubts to which religion is the answer. Not for them the terrors of the primitive jungle. Having abandoned some of the more picturesque fringes of religion, they think that they have abandoned the whole thing—whereas in fact they still have got, and could not live without, a religion of a comfortably substantial, albeit highly sophisticated, kind, which differs from that of many 'religious people' in little more than this, that 'religious people' like to sing Psalms about theirs—a very natural and proper thing to do. But nevertheless there may be a big difference lying behind—the difference between two people who, though side by side, are walking in different directions. I do not know in what direction Flew is walking; perhaps he does not know either. But we have had some examples recently of various ways in which one can walk away from Christianity, and there are any number of possibilities. After all, man has not changed biologically since primitive times; it is his religion that has changed, and it can easily change again. And if you do not think that such changes make a difference, get acquainted with some Sikhs and some Mussulmans of the same Punjabi stock; you will find them quite different sorts of people.

There is an important difference between Flew's parable and my own which we have not yet noticed. The explorers do not *mind* about their garden; they discuss it with interest, but not with concern. But my lunatic, poor fellow, minds about dons; and I mind about the steering of my car; it often has people in it that I care for. It is because I mind very much about what goes on in the garden in which I find myself, that I am unable to share the explorers' detachment.

## C. BASIL MITCHELL

Flew's article is searching and perceptive, but there is, I think, something odd about his conduct of the theologian's case. The theologian surely would not deny that the fact of pain counts against the assertion that God loves men. This very incompatibility generates the most intractable of theological problems—the problem of evil. So the theologian *does* recognize the fact of pain as counting against Christian doctrine. But it is true that he will not allow it—or anything—to count decisively against it; for he is committed by his faith to trust in God. His attitude is not that of the detached observer, but of the believer.

Perhaps this can be brought out by yet another parable. In time of war in an occupied country, a member of the resistance meets one night a stranger who deeply impresses him. They spend that night together in conversation. The Stranger tells the partisan that he himself is on the side of the resistance—indeed that he is in command of it, and urges the partisan to have faith in him no matter what happens. The partisan is utterly convinced at that meeting of the Stranger's sincerity and constancy and undertakes to trust him.

They never meet in conditions of intimacy again. But sometimes the Stranger is seen helping members of the resistance, and the partisan is grateful and says to his friends, 'He is on our side'.

Sometimes he is seen in the uniform of the police handing over patriots to the occupying power. On these occasions his friends murmur against him: but the partisan still says, 'He is on our side.' He still believes that, in spite of appearances, the Stranger did not deceive him. Sometimes he asks the Stranger for help and receives it. He is then thankful. Sometimes he asks and does not receive it. Then he says, 'The Stranger knows best.' Sometimes his friends, in exasperation, say 'Well, what *would* he have to do for you to admit that you were wrong and that he is not on our side?' But the partisan refuses to answer. He will not consent to put the Stranger to the test. And sometimes his friends complain, 'Well, if *that's* what you mean by his being on our side, the sooner he goes over to the other side the better.'

The partisan of the parable does not allow anything to count decisively against the proposition 'The Stranger is on our side.' This is because he has committed himself to trust the Stranger. But he of course recognizes that the Stranger's ambiguous behaviour *does* count against what he believes about him. It is precisely this situation which constitutes the trial of his faith.

When the partisan asks for help and doesn't get it, what can he do? He can (*a*) conclude that the stranger is not on our side; or (*b*) maintain that he is on our side, but that he has reasons for withholding help.

The first he will refuse to do. How long can he uphold the second position without its becoming just silly?

I don't think one can say in advance. It will depend on the nature of the impression created by the Stranger in the first place. It will depend, too, on the manner in which he takes the Stranger's behaviour. If he blandly dismisses it as of no consequence, as having no bearing upon his belief, it will be assumed that he is thoughtless or insane. And it quite obviously won't do for him to say easily, 'Oh, when used of the Stranger the phrase "is on our side" *means* ambiguous behaviour of this sort.' In that case he would be like the religious man who says blandly of a terrible disaster, 'It is God's will.' No, he will only be regarded as sane and reasonable in his belief, if he experiences in himself the full force of the conflict.

It is here that my parable differs from Hare's. The partisan admits that many things may and do count against his belief: whereas Hare's lunatic who has a *blik* about dons doesn't admit that anything counts against his *blik*. Nothing *can* count against *bliks*. Also the partisan has a reason for having in the first instance committed himself, viz. the character of the Stranger; whereas the lunatic has no reason for his *blik* about dons—because, of course, you can't have reasons for *bliks*.

This means that I agree with Flew that theological utterances must be assertions. The partisan is making an assertion when he says, 'The Stranger is on our side'.

Do I want to say that the partisan's belief about the Stranger is, in any sense, an explanation? I think I do. It explains and makes sense of the Stranger's behaviour: it helps to explain also the resistance movement in the context of which he appears. In each case it differs from the interpretation which the others put upon the same facts.

'God loves men' resembles 'the Stranger is on our side' (and many other significant statements, e.g. historical ones) in not being conclusively falsifiable. They can both be treated in at least three different ways: (1) As provisional hypotheses to be discarded if experience tells against them; (2) As significant articles of faith; (3) As vacuous formulae (expressing, perhaps, a desire for reassurance) to which experience makes no difference and which make no difference to life.

The Christian, once he has committed himself, is precluded by his faith from taking up the first attitude: 'Thou shalt not tempt the Lord thy God.' He is in constant danger, as Flew has observed, of slipping into the third. But he need not; and, if he does, it is a failure in faith as well as in logic.

## D. ANTONY FLEW

It has been a good discussion: and I am glad to have helped to provoke it. But now—at least in *University*\*—it must come to an end: and the Editors of *University* have asked me to make some concluding remarks. Since it is impossible to deal with all the issues

\* The journal in which this discussion first appeared.—Ed.

raised or to comment separately upon each contribution, I will concentrate on Mitchell and Hare, as representative of two very different kinds of response to the challenge made in 'Theology and Falsification'.

The challenge, it will be remembered, ran like this. Some theological utterances seem to, and are intended to, provide explanations or express assertions. Now an assertion, to be an assertion at all, must claim that things stand thus and thus; *and not otherwise.* Similarly an explanation, to be an explanation at all, must explain why this particular thing occurs; *and not something else.* Those last clauses are crucial. And yet sophisticated religious people—or so it seemed to me—are apt to overlook this, and tend to refuse to allow, not merely that anything actually does occur, but that anything conceivably could occur, which would count against their theological assertions and explanations. But in so far as they do this their supposed explanations are actually bogus, and their seeming assertions are really vacuous.

Mitchell's response to this challenge is admirably direct, straightforward, and understanding. He agrees 'that theological utterances must be assertions.' He agrees that if they are to be assertions, there must be something that would count against their truth. He agrees, too, that believers are in constant danger of transforming their would-be assertions into 'vacuous formulae.' But he takes me to task for an oddity in my 'conduct of the theologian's case. The theologian surely would not deny that the fact of pain counts against the assertion that God loves men. This very incompatibility generates the most intractable of theological problems, the problem of evil'. I think he is right. I should have made a distinction between two very different ways of dealing with what looks like evidence against the love of God: the way I stressed was the expedient of qualifying the original assertion; the way the theologian usually takes, at first, is to admit that it looks bad but to insist that there is—there must be—some explanation which will show that, in spite of appearances, there really is a God who loves us. His difficulty, it seems to me, is that he has given God attributes which rule out all possible saving explanations. In Mitchell's parable of the Stranger it is easy for the believer to find plausible excuses for ambiguous behaviour: for the Stranger is a man. But suppose the Stranger is God. We cannot say that he would like to help but cannot: God is omnipotent. We cannot say that he would help if he only knew: God is omniscient. We cannot say that he is not responsible for the wickedness of others: God creates those others. Indeed an omnipotent, omniscient God must be an accessory before (and during) the fact to every human misdeed; as well as being responsible for every non-moral defect in the universe. So, though I entirely concede that Mitchell was absolutely right to insist against me that the theologian's first move is to look for an *explanation*, I still think that in the end, if relentlessly pursued, he will have to resort to the avoiding action of *qualification*. And there lies the danger of that death by a thousand qualifications, which would, I agree, constitute 'a failure in faith as well as in logic.'

Hare's approach is fresh and bold. He confesses that 'on the ground marked out by Flew, he seems to me to be completely victorious.' He therefore introduces the concept of *blik*. But while I think that there is room for some such concept in philosophy, and that philosophers should be grateful to Hare for his invention, I nevertheless want to insist that any attempt to analyse Christian religious utterances as expressions or affirmations of a *blik* rather than as (at least would-be) assertions about the cosmos is fundamentally misguided. *First*, because thus interpreted they would be entirely unorthodox. If Hare's religion really is a *blik*, involving no cosmological assertions about the nature and activities of a supposed personal creator, then surely he is not a Christian at all? *Second*, because thus interpreted, they could scarcely do the job they do. If they were not even intended as assertions then many religious activities would become fraudulent, or merely silly. If 'You ought *because* it is God's will' asserts no more than 'You ought,' then the person who prefers the former phraseology is not really giving a reason, but a fraudulent substitute for one, a dialectical dud cheque. If 'My soul must be immortal *because* God loves his children, etc.' asserts no more than 'My soul must be immortal,' then the man who reassures himself with theological arguments for immortality is being as silly as the man who tries to clear his overdraft by writing his bank a cheque on the same amount. (Of course neither of these utterances would be distinctively Christian: but this discussion never pretended to be so confined.) Religious utterances may indeed express false or even bogus assertions: but I simply do not believe that they are not both intended and interpreted to be or at any rate to presuppose assertions, at least in the context of religious practice; whatever shifts may be demanded, in another context, by the exigencies of theological apologetic.

One final suggestion. The philosophers of religion might well draw upon George Orwell's last appalling nightmare 1984 for the concept of *doublethink*. '*Doublethink* means the power of holding two contradictory beliefs simultaneously, and accepting both of them. The party intellectual knows that he is playing tricks with reality, but by the exercise of *doublethink* he also satisfies himself that reality is not violated' (1984, p. 220). Perhaps religious intellectuals too are sometimes driven to doublethink in order to retain their faith in a loving God in face of the reality of a heartless and indifferent world. But of this more another time, perhaps.


E.* I. M. CROMBIE

. . . . Statements about God, then, are in effect parables, which are referred, by means of the proper name 'God,' out of our experience in a certain direction. We may, if we like, by the process of whittling away, which I have mentioned, try to tell ourselves what part of the meaning of our statements applies reasonably well, what part outrageously badly; but the fact remains that, in one important sense, when we speak about God, we do not know what we mean (that is, we do not know what that which we are talking about is like), and do not need to know, because we accept the images, which we employ, on authority. Because our concern with God is religious and not speculative (it is contemplative in part, but that is another matter), because our need is, not to know what God is like, but to enter into relation with him, the authorized images serve our purpose. They belong to a type of discourse— parable—with which we are familiar, and therefore they have communication value, although in a sense they lack descriptive value.

If this is so, how do we stand with regard to verification and falsification? Must we, to preserve our claim to be making assertions, be prepared to say what would count against them? Let us see how far we can do so. Does anything count against the assertion that God is merciful? Yes, suffering. Does anything count decisively

* Crombie's contribution appeared in connection with the preceding discussion, which first appeared in *University*.—Ed.

against it? No, we reply, because it is true. Could anything count decisively against it? Yes, suffering which was utterly, eternally and irredeemably pointless. Can we then design a crucial experiment? No, because we can never see all of the picture. Two things at least are hidden from us; what goes on in the recesses of the personality of the sufferer, and what shall happen hereafter.

Well, then, the statement that God is merciful is not testable; it is compatible with any and every tract of experience which we are in fact capable of witnessing. It cannot be verified; does this matter?

To answer this, we must make up our minds why the demand for verification or falsification is legitimate. On this large matter I shall be summary and dogmatic, as follows. (1) The demand that a statement of fact should be verifiable is a conflation of two demands (2) The *first* point is that all statements of fact must be verifiable in the sense that there must not exist a *rule of language* which precludes testing the statement. That is to say, the way the statement is to be taken must not be such that to try to test it is to show that you do not understand it. If I say that it is wrong to kill, and you challenge my statement and adduce as evidence against it that thugs and headhunters do so out of religious duty, then you have not understood my statement. My statement was not a statement of fact, but a moral judgment, and your statement that it should be tested by anthropological investigations shows that you did not understand it. But so long as there exists no *logical* (or we might say *interpretational*) ban on looking around for verification, the existence of a *factual* ban on verification does not matter. 'Caesar had mutton before he crossed the Rubicon' cannot in fact be tested, but by trying to devise ways of testing it you do not show that you have not understood it; you are merely wasting your time. (3) The *second* point is that, *for me*, *fully* to understand a statement, I must know what a test of it would be like. If I have no idea how to test whether somebody had mutton, then I do not know what 'having mutton' means. This stipulation is concerned, not with the logical nature of the expression, but with its communication value for me. (4) There are then two stipulations, and they are different. The first is a logical stipulation, and it is to the effect that nothing can be a statement of fact if it is untestable in the sense that the notion of testing it is precluded by correctly inter-

preting it. The second is a communicational stipulation, and it is
to the effect that nobody can fully understand a statement, unless
he has a fair idea how a situation about which it was true would
differ from a situation about which it was false.

Now with regard to these two stipulations, how do religious
utterances fare? With regard to the first, there is no language rule
implicit in a correct understanding of them which precludes putting
them to the test (there may be a rule of faith, but that is another
matter). If a man says, 'How can God be loving, and allow pain?'
he does *not* show that he has misunderstood the statement that
God is loving. There *is* a *prima facie* incompatibility between the
love of God, and pain and suffering. The Christian maintains that
it is *prima facie* only; others maintain that it is not. They may
argue about it, and the issue cannot be decided; but it cannot be
decided, not because (as in the case of e.g. moral or mathematical
judgments) the appeal to facts is *logically* the wrong way of trying
to decide the issue, and shows that you have not understood the
judgment; *but* because, since our experience is limited in the way it
is, we cannot get into position to decide it, any more than we can
get into position to decide what Julius Caesar had for breakfast
before he crossed the Rubicon. For the Christian the operation of
getting into position to decide it is called dying; and, though we
can all do that, we cannot return to report what we find. By this
test, then, religious utterances can be called statements of fact; that
is their *logical* classification.

With regard to the second stipulation, the case is a little complicated, for here we are concerned with communication value, and
there are the two levels, the one on which we remain within the
parable, and the other on which we try to step outside it. Now, on
the first level we know well enough how to test a statement like
'God loves us'; it is, for example, like testing 'My father loves me.'
In fact, of course, since with parents and schoolmasters severity is
notoriously a way of displaying affection, the decisive testing of
such a statement is not easy; but there is a point beyond which it is
foolish to continue to have doubts. Now, within the parable, we
are supposing 'God loves us' to be a statement like 'My father
loves me,' 'God' to be a subject similar to 'My father,' 'God loves
us' being thus related to 'My father loves me' as the latter is related
to 'Aristotle's father loved him.' We do not suppose that we can

actually test 'God loves us,' for reasons already given (any more than we can test the one about Aristotle); but the communication value of the statement whose subject is 'God' is derived from the communication value of the same statement with a different proper name as subject. If we try to step outside the parable, then we must admit that we do not know what the situation about which our parable is being told is like; we should only know if we could know God, and know even as also we have been known; see, that is, the unfolding of the divine purposes in their entirety. Such ignorance is what we ought to expect. We do not know how what we call the divine wrath differs from the divine mercy (because we do not know how they respectively resemble human wrath and mercy); but we do know how what *we mean* when we talk about the wrath of God differs from what *we mean* when we talk about his mercy, because then we are within the parable, talking within the framework of admitted ignorance, in language which we accept because we trust its source. We know what is meant *in* the parable, when the father of the Prodigal sees him coming a great way off and runs to meet him, and we can therefore think in terms of this image. We know that we are here promised that whenever we come to ourselves and return to God, he will come to meet us. This is enough to encourage us to return, and to make us alert to catch the signs of the divine response; but it does not lead us to presume to an understanding of the mind and heart of God. In talking we remain within the parable, and so our statements communicate; we do not know how the parable applies, but we believe that it does apply, and that we shall one day see how. (Some even believe, perhaps rightly, that in our earthly condition we may by direct illumination of our minds be enabled to know progressively more about the realities to which our parables apply, and in consequence about the manner of their application).

Much of what I have said agrees very closely with what the atheist says about religious belief, except that I have tried to make it sound better. The atheist alleges that the religious man supposes himself to know what he means by his statements only because, until challenged, he interprets them anthropomorphically; when challenged, however, he retreats rapidly backwards towards complete agnosticism. I agree with this, with two provisos. The first is that the religious man does not suppose himself to know what he means by his statements (for what religious man supposes himself to be the Holy Ghost?); he knows what his statements mean within the parable, and believes that they are the right statements to use. (Theology is not a science; it is a sort of art of enlightened ignorance.) The second proviso is that the agnosticism is not complete; for the Christian, under attack, falls back not in any direction, but in one direction; he falls back upon the person of Christ, and the concrete realities of the Christian life.

Let us consider this for a moment with regard to the divine love. I could be attacked in this sort of way:—'You have contended,' my opponent might argue, 'that when we say that God loves us the communication value of the statement is determined by the communication value of a similar statement about a human subject; and that we know the statement to be the right statement, but cannot know *how* it is the right statement, that is, what the divine love is like. But this will not do. Loving is an activity with two poles, the lover and the loved. We may not know the lover, in the case of God, but we *are*, and therefore *must know*, the loved. Now, to say that the image or parable of human love is the right image to use about God must imply that there is some similarity or analogy between human and divine love. Father's love may be superficially very unlike mother's, but, unless there is some similarity of structure between them, we cannot use the same word of both. But we cannot believe that there is any similarity between the love of God and human love, unless we can detect some similarity between being loved by God and being loved by man. But if being loved by God is what we experience all the time, then it is not like being loved by man; it is like being let down right and left. And in the face of so great a discrepancy, we cannot believe that God loves us, if that is supposed to be in any sense a statement of sober fact.'

I cannot attempt to answer this objection; it involves the whole problem of religion. But there is something I want to say about it, which is that the Christian does not attempt to evade it either by helter-skelter flight, or by impudent bluff. He has his prepared positions on to which he retreats; and he knows that if these positions are taken, then he must surrender. He does not believe that they can be taken, but that is another matter. There are three main fortresses behind which he goes. For, *first*, he looks for the resurrection of the dead, and the life of the world to come; he believes, that is, that we do not see all of the picture, and that the parts which we do not see are precisely the parts which determine the design of the whole. He admits that if this hope be vain then we are of all men the most miserable. *Second*, he claims that he sees in Christ the verification, and to some extent also the specification, of the divine love. That is to say, he finds in Christ not only convincing evidence of God's concern for us, but also what sort of love the divine love is, what sort of benefits God is concerned to give us. He sees that, on the New Testament scale of values, it is better for a man to lose the whole world if he can thereby save his soul (which means his relationship to God); and that for that hope it is reasonable to sacrifice all that he has, and to undergo the death of the body and the mortification of the spirit. *Third*, he claims that in the religious life, of others, if not as yet in his own, the divine love may be encountered, that the promise 'I will not fail thee nor forsake thee' is, if rightly understood, confirmed there. If, of course, this promise is interpreted as involving immunity from bodily suffering, it will be refuted; but no reader of the New Testament has any right so to interpret it. It is less glaringly, but as decisively, wrong to interpret it as involving immunity from spiritual suffering; for in the New Testament only the undergoing of death (which means the abdication of control over one's destiny) can be the beginning of life. What then does it promise? It promises that to the man who begins on the way of the Christian life, on the way that is of seeking life through death, of seeking relationship with God through the abdication of the self-sovereignty claimed by Adam, that to him the fight will be hard but not impossible, progress often indiscernible, but real, progress which is towards the paring away of self-hood, and which is therefore often given through defeat and humiliation, but a defeat and humiliation which are not final, which leave it possible to continue. This is the extra-parental nurture of religious belief of which I spoke earlier, and it is the third of the prepared positions on to which the Christian retreats, claiming that the image and reflection of the love of God may be seen not only hereafter, not only in Christ, but also, if dimly, in the concrete process of living the Christian life.

One final word. Religion has indeed its problems; but it is useless to consider them outside their religious context. Seen as a whole religion makes rough sense, though it does not make limpidity.

NOTES

1. *P.A.S.*, 1944-5, reprinted as Ch. X of *Logic and Language*, Vol. I (Blackwell, 1951), and in his *Philosophy and Psychoanalysis* (Blackwell, 1953).

2. Cf. J. Wisdom, 'Other Minds,' *Mind*, 1940; reprinted in his *Other Minds* (Blackwell, 1952).

3. Cf. Lucretius, *De Rerum Natura*, II, 655-60,

> Hic siquis mare Neptunum Cereremque vocare
> Constituet fruges et Bacchi nomine abuti
> Mavolat quam laticis proprium proferre vocamen
> Concedamus ut hic terrarum dictitet orbem
> Esse deum matrem dum vera re tamen ipse
> Religione animum turpi contingere parcat.

4. For those who prefer symbolism: $p \equiv \sim \sim p$.

5. For by simply negating $\sim p$ we get $p$: $\sim \sim p \equiv p$.

# 20. AN EMPIRICIST'S VIEW OF THE

## NATURE OF RELIGIOUS BELIEF

### R. B. Braithwaite

*R. B. Braithwaite is Knightbridge Professor of Moral Philosophy at Cambridge University. He is author of* Scientific Explanation *and many articles on epistemology, ethics, and religion.*

The meaning of any statement, then, will be taken as being given by the way it is used. The kernel for an empiricist of the problem of the nature of religious belief is to explain, in empirical terms, how a religious statement is used by a man who asserts it in order to express his religious conviction.

Since I shall argue that the primary element in this use is that the religious assertion is used as a moral assertion, I must first consider how moral assertions are used. According to the view developed by various moral philosophers since the impossibility of regarding moral statements as verifiable propositions was recognized, a moral assertion is used to express an *attitude* of the man making the assertion. It is not used to assert the proposition that he has the attitude—a verifiable psychological proposition; it is used to show forth or evince his attitude. The attitude is concerned with the action which he asserts to be right or to be his duty, or the state of affairs which he asserts to be good; it is a highly complex state, and contains elements to which various degrees of importance have been attached by moral philosophers who have tried to work out an 'ethics without propositions.' One element in the attitude is a feeling of approval towards the action; this element was taken

Reprinted by permission of Cambridge University Press from *An Empiricist's View of the Nature of Religious Belief* (1955), pp. 11-28, 29-35, by R. B. Braithwaite.

as the fundamental one in the first attempts, and views of ethics without propositions are frequently lumped together as 'emotive' theories of ethics. But discussion of the subject during the last twenty years has made it clear, I think, that no emotion or feeling of approval is fundamental to the use of moral assertions; it may be the case that the moral asserter has some specific feeling directed on to the course of action said to be right, but this is not the most important element in his 'pro-attitude' towards the course of action: what is primary is his intention to perform the action when the occasion for it arises.

The form of ethics without propositions which I shall adopt is therefore a conative rather than an emotive theory: it makes the primary use of a moral assertion that of expressing the intention of the asserter to act in a particular sort of way specified in the assertion. A utilitarian, for example, in asserting that he ought to act so as to maximize happiness, is thereby declaring his intention to act, to the best of his ability, in accordance with the policy of utilitarianism: he is not asserting any proposition, or necessarily evincing any feeling of approval; he is subscribing to a policy of action. There will doubtless be empirical propositions which he may give as reasons for his adherence to the policy (e.g. that happiness is what all, or what most people, desire), and his having the intention will include his understanding what is meant by pursuing the policy, another empirically verifiable proposition. But there will be no specifically moral proposition which he will be asserting when he declares his intention to pursue the policy. This account is fully in accord with the spirit of empiricism, for whether or not a man has the intention of pursuing a particular behaviour policy can be empirically tested, both by observing what he does and by hearing what he replies when he is questioned about his intentions.

Not all expressions of intentions will be moral assertions: for the notion of morality to be applicable it is necessary either that the policy of action intended by the asserter should be a general policy (e.g. the policy of utilitarianism) or that it should be subsumable under a general policy which the asserter intends to follow and which he would give as the reason for his more specific intention. There are difficulties and vaguenesses in the notion of a general policy of action, but these need not concern us here. All that we require is that, when a man asserts that he ought to do so-and-so, he is using the assertion to declare that he resolves, to the best of his ability, to do so-and-so. And he will not necessarily be insincere in his assertion if he suspects, at the time of making it, that he will not have the strength of character to carry out his resolution.

The advantage this account of moral assertions has over all others, emotive non-propositional ones as well as cognitive propositional ones, is that it alone enables a satisfactory answer to be given to the question: What is the reason for my doing what I think I ought to do? The answer it gives is that, since my thinking that I ought to do the action is my intention to do it if possible, the reason why I do the action is simply that I intend to do it, if possible. On every other ethical view there will be a mysterious gap to be filled somehow between the moral judgment and the intention to act in accordance with it: there is no such gap if the primary use of a moral assertion is to declare such an intention.

Let us now consider what light this way of regarding moral assertions throws upon assertions of religious conviction. The idealist philosopher McTaggart described religion as 'an emotion resting on a conviction of a harmony between ourselves and the universe at large,'[1] and many educated people at the present time would agree with him. If religion is essentially concerned with emotion, it is natural to explain the use of religious assertions on the lines of the original emotive theory of ethics and to regard them as primarily evincing religious feelings or emotions. The assertion, for example, that God is our Heavenly Father will be taken to express the asserter's feeling secure in the same way as he would feel secure in his father's presence. But explanations of religion in terms of feeling, and of religious assertions as expressions of such feelings, are usually propounded by people who stand outside any religious system; they rarely satisfy those who speak from inside. Few religious men would be prepared to admit that their religion was a matter merely of feeling: feelings—of joy, of consolation, of being at one with the universe—may enter into their religion, but to evince such feelings is certainly not the primary use of their religious assertions.

This objection, however, does not seem to me to apply to treating religious assertions in the conative way in which recent moral philosophers have treated moral statements—as being primarily declarations of adherence to a policy of action, declarations of commitment to a way of life. That the way of life led by the believer is highly relevant to the sincerity of his religious conviction has been insisted upon by all the moral religions, above all, perhaps, by Christianity. 'By their fruits ye shall know them.' The view which I put forward for your consideration is that the intention of a Christian to follow a Christian way of life is not only the criterion for the sincerity of his belief in the assertions of Christianity; it is the criterion for the meaningfulness of his assertions. Just as the meaning of a moral assertion is given by its use in expressing the asserter's intention to act, so far as in him lies, in accordance with the moral principle involved, so the meaning of a religious assertion is given by its use in expressing the asserter's intention to follow a specified policy of behaviour. To say that it is belief in the dogmas of religion which is the cause of the believer's intending to behave as he does is to put the cart before the horse: it is the intention to behave which constitutes what is known as religious conviction.

But this assimilation of religious to moral assertions lays itself open to an immediate objection. When a moral assertion is taken as declaring the intention of following a policy, the form of the assertion itself makes it clear what the policy is with which the assertion is concerned. For a man to assert that a certain policy ought to be pursued, which on this view is for him to declare his intention of pursuing the policy, presupposes his understanding what it would be like for him to pursue the policy in question. I cannot resolve not to tell a lie without knowing what a lie is. But if a religious assertion is the declaration of an intention to carry out a certain policy, what policy does it specify? The religious statement itself will not explicitly refer to a policy, as does a moral statement; how then can the asserter of the statement know what is the policy concerned, and how can he intend to carry out a policy if he does not know what the policy is? I cannot intend to do something I know not what.

The reply to this criticism is that, if a religious assertion is regarded as representative of a large number of assertions of the same religious system, the body of assertions of which the particular one is a representative specimen is taken by the asserter as implicitly specifying a particular way of life. It is no more necessary for an empiricist philosopher to explain the use of a religious statement taken in isolation from other religious statements than it is for him to give a meaning to a scientific hypothesis in isolation from other scientific hypotheses. We understand scientific hypotheses, and the terms that occur in them, by virtue of the relation of the whole system of hypotheses to empirically observable facts; and it is the whole system of hypotheses, not one hypothesis in isolation, that is tested for its truth-value against experience. So there are good precedents, in the empiricist way of thinking, for considering a system of religious assertions as a whole, and for examining the way in which the whole system is used.

If we do this the fact that a system of religious assertions has a moral function can hardly be denied. For to deny it would require any passage from the assertion of a religious system to a policy of action to be mediated by a moral assertion. I cannot pass from asserting a fact, of whatever sort, to intending to perform an action, without having the hypothetical intention to intend to do the action if I assert the fact. This holds however widely fact is understood—whether as an empirical fact or as a non-empirical fact about goodness or reality. Just as the intention-to-act view of moral assertions is the only view that requires no reason for my doing what I assert to be my duty, so the similar view of religious assertions is the only one which connects them to ways of life without requiring an additional premiss. Unless a Christian's assertion that God is love (*agape*)—which I take to epitomize the assertions of the Christian religion—be taken to declare his intention to follow an agapeistic way of life, he could be asked what is the connexion between the assertion and the intention, between Christian belief and Christian practice. And this question can always be asked if religious assertions are separated from conduct. Unless religious principles are moral principles, it makes no sense to speak of putting them into practice.

The way to find out what are the intentions embodied in a set of religious assertions, and hence what is the meaning of the assertions, is by discovering what principles of conduct the asserter takes the assertions to involve. These may be ascertained both by asking him questions and by seeing how he behaves, each test being supplemental to the other. If what is wanted is not the meaning of the religious assertions made by a particular man but what the set of assertions would mean were they to be made by anyone of the same religion (which I will call their *typical* meaning), all that can be done is to specify the form of behaviour which is in accordance with what one takes to be the fundamental moral principles of the religion in question. Since different people will take different views as to what these fundamental moral principles are, the typical meaning of religious assertions will be different for different people. I myself take the typical meaning of the body of Christian assertions as being given by their proclaiming intentions to follow an agapeistic way of life, and for a description of this way of life—a description in general and metaphorical terms, but an empirical description nevertheless—I should quote most of the Thirteenth Chapter of I Corinthians. Others may think that the Christian way of life should be described somewhat differently, and will therefore take the typical meaning of the assertions of Christianity to correspond to their different view of its fundamental moral teaching.

My contention then is that the primary use of religious assertions is to announce allegiance to a set of moral principles: without such allegiance there is no 'true religion.' This is borne out by all the accounts of what happens when an unbeliever becomes converted to a religion. The conversion is not only a change in the propositions believed—indeed there may be no specifically intellectual change at all; it is a change in the state of will. An excellent instance is C. S. Lewis's recently published account of his conversion from an idealist metaphysic—'a religion [as he says] that cost nothing'—to a theism where he faced (and he quotes George Mac-Donald's phrase) 'something to be neither more nor less nor other than *done.*' There was no intellectual change, for (as he says) 'there had long been an ethic (theoretically) attached to my Idealism': it was the recognition that he had to do something about it, that 'an attempt at complete virtue must be made.'[2] His conversion was a re-orientation of the will.

In assimilating religious assertions to moral assertions I do not wish to deny that there are any important differences. One is the fact already noticed that usually the behaviour policy intended is not specified by one religious assertion in isolation. Another difference is that the fundamental moral teaching of the religion is frequently given, not in abstract terms, but by means of concrete examples—of how to behave, for instance, if one meets a man set upon by thieves on the road to Jericho. A resolution to behave like the good Samaritan does not, in itself, specify the behaviour to be resolved upon in quite different circumstances. However, absence of explicitly recognized general principles does not prevent a man from acting in accordance with such principles; it only makes it more difficult for a questioner to discover upon what principles he is acting. And the difficulty is not only one way round. If moral principles are stated in the most general form, as most moral philosophers have wished to state them, they tend to become so far removed from particular courses of conduct that it is difficult, if not impossible, to give them any precise content. It may be hard to find out what exactly is involved in the imitation of Christ; but it is not very easy to discover what exactly is meant by the pursuit of Aristotle's *eudaemonia* or of Mill's *happiness*. The tests for what it is to live agapeistically are as empirical as are those for living in quest of happiness; but in each case the tests can best be expounded in terms of examples of particular situations.

A more important difference between religious and purely moral principles is that, in the higher religions at least, the conduct preached by the religion concerns not only external but also internal behaviour. The conversion involved in accepting a religion is a conversion, not only of the will, but of the heart. Christianity requires not only that you should behave towards your neighbour as if you loved him as yourself: it requires that you should love him as yourself. And though I have no doubt that the Christian concept of *agape* refers partly to external behaviour—the agapeistic behaviour for which there are external criteria—yet being filled with *agape* includes more than behaving agapeistically externally: it also includes an agapeistic frame of mind. I have said that I cannot regard the expression of a feeling of any sort as the primary element in religious assertion; but this does not imply that intention to feel in a certain way is not a primary element, nor that it cannot be used to discriminate religious declarations of policy from declarations which are merely moral. Those who say that Confucianism is a code of morals and not, properly speaking, a religion are, I think, making this discrimination.

The resolution proclaimed by a religious assertion may then be taken as referring to inner life as well as to outward conduct. And the superiority of religious conviction over the mere adoption of a

moral code in securing conformity to the code arises from a religious
conviction changing what the religious man wants. It may be hard
enough to love your enemy, but once you have succeeded in doing
so it is easy to behave lovingly towards him. But if you continue
to hate him, it requires a heroic perseverance continually to behave
as if you loved him. Resolutions to feel, even if they are only partly
fulfilled, are powerful reinforcements of resolutions to act.

But though these qualifications may be adequate for distinguishing religious assertions from purely moral ones, they are not sufficient to discriminate between assertions belonging to one religious
system and those belonging to another system in the case in which
the behaviour policies, both of inner life and of outward conduct,
inculcated by the two systems are identical. For instance, I have said
that I take the fundamental moral teaching of Christianity to be
the preaching of an agapeistic way of life. But a Jew or a Buddhist
may, with considerable plausibility, maintain that the fundamental
moral teaching of his religion is to recommend exactly the same
way of life. How then can religious assertions be distinguished into
those which are Christian, those which are Jewish, those which are
Buddhist, by the policies of life which they respectively recommend
if, on examination, these policies turn out to be the same?

Many Christians will, no doubt, behave in a specifically Christian
manner in that they will follow ritual practices which are Christian
and neither Jewish nor Buddhist. But though following certain
practices may well be the proper test for membership of a particular
religious society, a church, not even the most ecclesiastically-
minded Christian will regard participation in a ritual as the fundamental characteristic of a Christian way of life. There must be some
more important difference between an agapeistically policied
Christian and an agapeistically policied Jew than that the former
attends a church and the latter a synagogue.

The really important difference, I think, is to be found in the
fact that the intentions to pursue the behaviour policies, which may
be the same for different religions, are associated with thinking of
different *stories* (or sets of stories). By a story I shall here mean a
proposition or set of propositions which are straightforwardly empirical propositions capable of empirical test and which are thought
of by the religious man in connexion with his resolution to follow

the way of life advocated by his religion. On the assumption that the ways of life advocated by Christianity and by Buddhism are essentially the same, it will be the fact that the intention to follow this way of life is associated in the mind of a Christian with thinking of one set of stories (the Christian stories) while it is associated in the mind of a Buddhist with thinking of another set of stories (the Buddhist stories) which enables a Christian assertion to be distinguished from a Buddhist one.

A religious assertion will, therefore, have a propositional element which is lacking in a purely moral assertion, in that it will refer to a story as well as to an intention. The reference to the story is not an assertion of the story taken as a matter of empirical fact: it is a telling of the story, or an alluding to the story, in the way in which one can tell, or allude to, the story of a novel with which one is acquainted. To assert the whole set of assertions of the Christian religion is both to tell the Christian doctrinal story and to confess allegiance to the Christian way of life.

The story, I have said, is a set of empirical propositions, and the language expressing the story is given a meaning by the standard method of understanding how the story-statements can be verified. The empirical story-statements will vary from Christian to Christian; the doctrines of Christianity are capable of different empirical interpretations, and Christians will differ in the interpretations they put upon the doctrines. But the interpretations will all be in terms of empirical propositions. Take, for example, the doctrine of Justification by means of the Atonement. Matthew Arnold imagined it in terms of

> . . . a sort of infinitely magnified and improved Lord Shaftesbury, with a race of vile offenders to deal with, whom his natural goodness would incline him to let off, only his sense of justice will not allow it; then a younger Lord Shaftesbury, on the scale of his father and very dear to him, who might live in grandeur and splendour if he liked, but who prefers to leave his home, to go and live among the race of offenders, and to be put to an ignominious death, on condition that his merits shall be counted against their demerits, and that his father's goodness shall be restrained no longer from taking effect, but any offender shall be admitted to the benefit of it on simply pleading the satisfaction made by the son;—and then, finally, a third Lord Shaftesbury, still on the same high scale, who keeps very much in the background, and

works in a very occult manner, but very efficaciously nevertheless, and who is busy in applying everywhere the benefits of the son's satisfaction and the father's goodness.[3]

Arnold's 'parable of the three Lord Shaftesburys' got him into a lot of trouble: he was 'indignantly censured' (as he says) for wounding 'the feelings of the religious community by turning into ridicule an august doctrine, the object of their solemn faith.'[4] But there is no other account of the Anselmian doctrine of the Atonement that I have read which puts it in so morally favourable a light. Be that as it may, the only way in which the doctrine can be understood verificationally is in terms of human beings—mythological beings, it may be, who never existed, but who nevertheless would have been empirically observable had they existed.

For it is not necessary, on my view, for the asserter of a religious assertion to believe in the truth of the story involved in the assertions: what is necessary is that the story should be entertained in thought, i.e. that the statement of the story should be understood as having a meaning. I have secured this by requiring that the story should consist of empirical propositions. Educated Christians of the present day who attach importance to the doctrine of the Atonement certainly do not believe an empirically testable story in Matthew Arnold's or any other form. But it is the fact that entertainment in thought of this and other Christian stories forms the context in which Christian resolutions are made which serves to distinguish Christian assertions from those made by adherents of another religion, or of no religion.

What I am calling a *story* Matthew Arnold called a *parable* and a *fairy-tale*. Other terms which might be used are *allegory*, *fable*, *tale*, *myth*. I have chosen the word 'story' as being the most neutral term, implying neither that the story is believed nor that it is disbelieved. The Christian stories include straightforward historical statements about the life and death of Jesus of Nazareth; a Christian (unless he accepts the unplausible Christ-myth theory) will naturally believe some or all of these. Stories about the beginning of the world and of the Last Judgment as facts of past or of future history are believed by many unsophisticated Christians. But my contention is that belief in the truth of the Christian stories is not the proper criterion for deciding whether or not an assertion is a Christian one. A man is not, I think, a professing Christian unless he both proposes to live according to Christian moral principles and associates his intention with thinking of Christian stories; but he need not believe that the empirical propositions presented by the stories correspond to empirical fact.

But if the religious stories need not be believed, what function do they fulfil in the complex state of mind and behaviour known as having a religious belief? How is entertaining the story related to resolving to pursue a certain way of life? My answer is that the relation is a psychological and causal one. It is an empirical psychological fact that many people find it easier to resolve upon and to carry through a course of action which is contrary to their natural inclinations if this policy is associated in their minds with certain stories. And in many people the psychological link is not appreciably weakened by the fact that the story associated with the behaviour policy is not believed. Next to the Bible and the Prayer Book the most influential work in English Christian religious life has been a book whose stories are frankly recognized as fictitious—Bunyan's *Pilgrim's Progress*; and some of the most influential works in setting the moral tone of my generation were the novels of Dostoevsky. It is completely untrue, as a matter of psychological fact, to think that the only intellectual considerations which affect action are beliefs: it is *all* the thoughts of a man that determine his behaviour; and these include his phantasies, imaginations, ideas of what he would wish to be and do, as well as the propositions which he believes to be true. . . .

. . . My contention that the propositional element in religious assertions consists of stories interpreted as straightforwardly empirical propositions which are not, generally speaking, believed to be true has the great advantage of imposing no restriction whatever upon the empirical interpretation which can be put upon the stories. The religious man may interpret the stories in the way which assists him best in carrying out the behaviour policies of his religion. He can, for example, think of the three persons of the Trinity in visual terms, as did the great Christian painters, or as talking to one another, as in the poems of St. John of the Cross. And since he need not believe the stories he can interpret them in ways which are not consistent with one another. It is disastrous for anyone to try to believe empirical propositions which are mutually inconsistent, for the courses of action appropriate to inconsistent beliefs are not compatible. The needs of practical life require that the body of believed propositions should be purged of inconsistency. But there is no action which is appropriate to thinking of a proposition without believing it; thinking of it may, as I have said, produce a state of mind in which it is easier to carry out a particular course of action, but the connexion is causal: there is no intrinsic connexion between the thought and the action. Indeed a story may provide better support for a long range policy of action if it contains inconsistencies. The Christian set of stories, for example, contains both a pantheistic sub-set of stories in which everything is a part of God and a dualistic Manichaean sub-set of stories well represented by St. Ignatius Loyola's allegory of a conflict between the forces of righteousness under the banner of Christ and the forces of darkness under Lucifer's banner. And the Marxist religion's set of stories contains both stories about an inevitable perfect society and stories about a class war. In the case of both religions the first sub-set of stories provides confidence, the second spurs to action.

There is one story common to all the moral theistic religions which has proved of great psychological value in enabling religious men to persevere in carrying out their religious behaviour policies— the story that in so doing they are doing the will of God. And here it may look as if there is an intrinsic connexion between the story and the policy of conduct. But even when the story is literally believed, when it is believed that there is a magnified Lord Shaftesbury who commands or desires the carrying out of the behaviour policy, that in itself is no reason for carrying out the policy: it is necessary also to have the intention of doing what the magnified Lord Shaftesbury commands or desires. But the intention to do what a person commands or desires, irrespective of what this command or desire may be, is no part of a higher religion; it is when the religious man finds that what the magnified Lord Shaftesbury commands or desires accords with his own moral judgement that he decides to obey or to accede to it. But this is no new decision, for his own moral judgement is a decision to carry out a behaviour policy; all that is happening is that he is describing his old decision in a new way. In religious conviction the resolution to follow a way of life is primary; it is not derived from believing, still less from thinking of, any empirical story. The story may psychologically support the resolution, but it does not logically justify it.

In this lecture I have been sparing in my use of the term 'religious belief' (although it occurs in the title), preferring instead to speak of religious assertions and of religious conviction. This was because for me the fundamental problem is that of the meaning of statements used to make religious assertions, and I have accordingly taken my task to be that of explaining the use of such assertions, in accordance with the principle that meaning is to be found by ascertaining use. In disentangling the elements of this use I have discovered nothing which can be called 'belief' in the senses of this word applicable either to an empirical or to a logically necessary proposition. A religious assertion, for me, is the assertion of an intention to carry out a certain behaviour policy, subsumable under a sufficiently general principle to be a moral one, together with the implicit or explicit statement, but not the assertion, of certain stories. Neither the assertion of the intention nor the reference to the stories includes belief in its ordinary senses. But in avoiding the term 'belief' I have had to widen the term 'assertion,' since I do not pretend that either the behaviour policy intended or the stories entertained are adequately specified by the sentences used in making isolated religious assertions. So assertion has been extended to include elements not explicitly expressed in the verbal form of the assertion. If we drop the linguistic expression of the assertion altogether the remainder is what may be called religious belief. Like moral belief, it is not a species of ordinary belief, of belief in a proposition. A moral belief is an intention to behave in a certain way: a religious belief is an intention to behave in a certain way (a moral belief) together with the entertainment of certain stories associated with the intention in the mind of the believer. This solution of the problem of religious belief seems to me to do justice both to the empiricist's demand that meaning must be tied to empirical use and to the religious man's claim for his religious beliefs to be taken seriously.

Seriously, it will be retorted, but not objectively. If a man's religion is all a matter of following the way of life he sets before himself and of strengthening his determination to follow it by imagining exemplary fairy-tales, it is purely subjective: his religion is all in terms of his own private ideals and of his own private imaginations. How can he even try to convert others to his religion if there is nothing objective to convert them to? How can he argue in its defence if there is no religious proposition which he believes, nothing which he takes to be the fundamental truth about the universe? And is it of any public interest what mental techniques he uses to bolster up his will? Discussion about religion must be more than the exchange of autobiographies.

But we are all social animals; we are all members one of another. What is profitable to one man in helping him to persevere in the way of life he has decided upon may well be profitable to another man who is trying to follow a similar way of life; and to pass on information that might prove useful would be approved by almost every morality. The autobiography of one man may well have an influence upon the life of another, if their basic wants are similar.

But suppose that these are dissimilar, and that the two men propose to conduct their lives on quite different fundamental principles. Can there be any reasonable discussion between them? This is the problem that has faced the many moral philosophers recently who have been forced, by their examination of the nature of thinking, into holding non-propositional theories of ethics. All I will here say is that to hold that the adoption of a set of moral principles is a matter of the personal decision to live according to these principles does not imply that beliefs as to what are the practical consequences of following such principles are not relevant to the decision. An intention, it is true, cannot be logically based upon anything except another intention. But in considering what conduct to intend to practise, it is highly relevant whether or not the consequences of practising that conduct are such as one would intend to secure. As R. M. Hare has well said, an ultimate decision to accept a way of life, 'far from being arbitrary, . . . would be the most well-founded of decisions, because it would be based upon a consideration of everything upon which it could possibly be founded.'[5] And in this consideration there is a place for every kind of rational argument.

Whatever may be the case with other religions Christianity has always been a personal religion demanding personal commitment to a personal way of life. In the words of another Oxford philosopher, 'the questions "What shall I do?" and "What moral principles should I adopt?" must be answered by each man for himself.'[6] Nowell-Smith takes this as part of the meaning of morality: whether or not this is so, I am certain that it is of the very essence of the Christian religion.

NOTES

1. J. M. E. McTaggart, *Some Dogmas of Religion* (1906), p. 3.
2. C. S. Lewis, *Surprised by Joy* (1955), pp. 198, 212-13.
3. Matthew Arnold, *Literature and Dogma* (1873), pp. 306-7.
4. Matthew Arnold, *God and the Bible* (1875), pp. 18-19.
5. R. M. Hare, *The Language of Morals* (1952), p. 69.
6. P. H. Nowell-Smith, *Ethics* (1954), p. 320.

# 21. MOTIVES, RATIONALES,

# AND RELIGIOUS BELIEFS

## *Diogenes Allen*

*Diogenes Allen has been a member of the Philosophy Department at York University in Toronto, Canada. In 1967 he became Associate Professor of Philosophy at Princeton Theological Seminary. Dr. Allen is author of "Christianity's Stake in Metaphysics,"* Theology Today *(July, 1967) among other writings.*

PART I

In the literature about the Christian religion, there is a recurrent picture of the way religious beliefs are asserted, which may be characterized in the following way. Religious convictions are a matter of faith, but there is a certain amount of evidence for them. People may or may not come to make affirmations through a knowledge of this evidence, but there must be some evidence for religious affirmations, otherwise to assert them would be to act blindly or irrationally. In the examination of the evidence for religious affirmations, how religious people do in fact make religious affirmations is in the last analysis irrelevant because the evidence for the affirmations is the real or *ultimate* basis for them and for people's belief in them. Biographical reasons—how one comes to have faith and to remain in faith—are not the basic ground for the assertion of religious beliefs. The story of Augustine's trials in becoming a Christian as recorded in his *Confessions*, for example, is edifying, inspiring, and may even be a factor in converting some people to Christianity, but it is only Augustine's way of coming to the faith. It is not proper to cite it as a basis for Christian beliefs.

Reprinted by permission of the editor from the *American Philosophical Quarterly*, Volume 3, Number 2 (1966), pp. 111-119.

It is my conviction that biographical reasons are, on the contrary, a proper basis for the affirmation of Christian beliefs. The motives one has for one's adherence to religious beliefs are not grounds which warrant other kinds of assertions, but they are a basis for the assertion of religious beliefs. To believe on the basis of one's motives is not to act arbitrarily, blindly, or without any reason.

Moreover, as far as religious beliefs are concerned, there are no reasons which are more ultimate or more basic than motives. This is the kind of basis which is appropriate to them.

I therefore argue that: (1) the response of faith to the Christian religion may be a rational and adequate basis for the affirmation of religious beliefs, and (2) there are no reasons which are more ultimate or basic than biographical ones.[1]

## 1. CAN MOTIVES BE REASONS FOR BELIEFS?

Faith is not put forward by me as a reason or ground for affirming and adhering to religious beliefs because of a consideration of the degree to which it *counts toward establishing the truth* of religious truth-claims. From the standpoint of a consideration of the degree to which the satisfactions gained in the response of faith count toward showing the truth of religious beliefs, faith is a very weak ground (if one at all) for showing the truth of a truth-claim. Nonetheless, in the response of faith a person's needs are so fulfilled that, *unless there are specific reasons which count decisively against the truth of religious truth-claims*, a person can rationally, on the ground of his response of faith and the nourishment thereby gained, adhere to these truth-claims as true. The response of faith can, without being based or undergirded by any other reason, be an adequate basis for a rational adherence to religious beliefs as true.

There are two kinds of reply to the question: Why do you adhere to Christian truth-claims? (1) I adhere to them because they awaken faith and fulfill my needs. (2) I adhere to them because there are reasons which show or count significantly toward showing that Christian beliefs are true. Each is of a different logical status. The latter is a reason in the sense of giving grounds for the truth of the beliefs. The former is a reason in the sense of being a person's *motive* for adhering to religious truth-claims. That one has faith and needs fulfilled by religious truth-claims does not count toward showing that they are true. It is a biographical fact about how an individual adheres to religious truth-claims.

Now it is possible that an individual's actual reason for adhering to religious truth-claims is: (1) a reason or reasons which count toward showing that the truth-claims are true, *and* (2) that religious truth-claims arouse faith in him and meet his needs.[2] On the other hand, I wish to consider the case in which an individual's actual reason for adhering to religious truth-claims may be *only* that they arouse faith in him and satisfy his needs.

I wish to show that such a motive is capable of being a basis or ground for an adherence to religious truth-claims[3] without the necessity of a person relying on any reasons which count toward *establishing the truth* of religious truth-claims. In other words, faith is not *merely* a biographical fact, but it is a motive that can be an adequate basis for making religious truth-claims. I do not deny that faith is a logically different kind of basis or ground from one that consists of reasons that count toward establishing the truth of religious truth-claims. I only seek to show that faith can be a sufficient reason or ground for adhering to truth-claims, and that religious truth-claims are not in need of another logically different kind of reason to have a basis for being adhered to.

I shall call reasons which count toward establishing the truth of religious beliefs "rationales." Such reasons can be cited by an individual as his actual reason for his adherence to religious beliefs, but they *need* not be cited by another individual who adheres to religious truth-claims. *If* faith is an individual's *actual* reason for adhering to religious truth-claims, then rationales are to him *possible* bases; ones which *some one* may rely upon for his adherence to religious truth-claims, but not *his actual* basis.[4]

## 2. CHALLENGES AND REBUTTALS

An instance of an adherence to religious truth-claims by faith will be considered to show that motives may be a ground for affirming religious truth-claims without the need of rationales, and that such a motive does not rest on rebuttals to "challenges" to the truth of religious beliefs.[5]

Let us say that the way a person comes to believe in religious truth-claims is by exposure to the Christian community.[6] He goes to Sunday School, he attends worship services and hears preaching, he is taught certain things about God and Jesus, he reads or hears Scripture read, he sees the way professing Christians behave, talk, and react to various circumstances, he observes and perhaps receives sacraments, he takes part in prayers. In short, he receives "training" in Christianity and he finds that he himself (either suddenly or gradually) can affirm some of the things that Christians affirm. He believes in God; he can pray; his behavior is also similar to that which Christians exhibit and similar at least in some degree to the behavior of Jesus. This pattern does not seem to me to be a bizarre or an unusual one, but roughly suggests the way many people do in fact become Christians.

I wish to argue that a person could legitimately cite *only* this training and its consequences as the reason why he is a Christian: "I am a Christian because through the Christian community I have come to have faith." This would be a reason in the sense of a motive, the way he has taken which leads to his profession of faith in God. This might be the *only* reason a person has for his adherence to religious truth-claims. At the core of this motive would be the fact that he finds himself a man with faith; all the training would be the setting and medium of this awakened faith.[7]

Why would one who finds himself by this path spiritually nourished and capable of worshipping and believing in God need to give another kind of reason for his affirmation of religious beliefs? That is, a reason which is not the *actual* reason why he makes affirmations, but a reason which counts toward establishing the truth of religious beliefs and thus showing on that basis that it is justifiable for one to adhere to religious beliefs. Why is it believed necessary to give rationales for one's beliefs?

It might be said that it is necessary to cite rationales for religious beliefs because, as truth-claims, something which counts toward establishing their truth must be cited for them to be affirmed. Otherwise, a belief is held blindly or irrationally. Just because you believe is not good enough. Thus rationales must be given to show that it is justifiable to adhere to religious truth-claims, even if some individuals may believe them by faith.

My reply to this line of argument is as follows: A belief that has developed in the context of the Christian community is not a belief with absolutely no grounds and hence is not a blind or irrational belief. The grounds are that a man has come to have faith in response to the witness of the Christian community and in the condition of faith he finds his soul nourished. By praying, by reading the Scriptures, by fellowship with other Christians, he finds his life is beginning to conform to what Paul described as the new life. This nourishment is his ground for believing religious truth-claims.[8] The very response of faith itself (which includes receiving nourishment) is a ground for adhering to religious beliefs as true. . . .

Let us consider the case where challenges arise. It is possible that a person has received as part of his "training" in a Christian community some views which he later finds seriously challenged. He may have been taught, for example, any one or several of the following: a particular view of Scripture, such as that it is to be regarded as infallible on every subject with which it deals; that religion and morality are so closely related that moral living without religion is impossible; that miracles and prophecy prove the truth of the Bible; that God's existence can be proved by the very existence of the world and also by its particular arrangement; that Christianity is a world view superior to any other; that there is an entity called the soul; that there are demons. It is possible that some of these items would be mixed in as part of his motive for being a Christian, i.e., as part of that to which he reacts with faith.

The truth of all of these items has of course been questioned. A person who becomes acquainted with a challenge or challenges could become upset, find it difficult to pray and worship, and come to believe that his religion is seriously in jeopardy. He could come to wonder whether he is able to rely upon his response of faith and he might seek a way to counter or mitigate the challenge(s) so he could believe that his faith, that he is in communion with God, is sound.

There are at least two different ways to meet challenges. One is to seek to find reasons to continue to hold to the items challenged which were taught as part of the training in a Christian community and to which he responds with faith. Another way to respond to challenges is to revise the character of the items (e.g., revise one's view of the nature of Scripture) or to consider the affirmation of some of the items as not an essential part of one's religion. These may of course be combined.

Another kind of challenge is not one that arises from doubts regarding beliefs or views learned as part of one's training, but "external" challenges such as a philosophic view which claims that religious language is meaningless. Here again one might believe that he must respond to this challenge in order to believe that his faith that he is in communion with God is not an illusion.

With both internal and external challenges, the point to be made, however it is made, is that what has been put forward does not rightly prevent one from having the belief that he has communion with God.

Now it is very tempting to say that part of the reason for affirming a religious belief or professing religion is the reason which has been used to rebut a challenge. And in one sense it is true. It is a reason for believing a religious belief or in a religion. But it is a reason in the sense of turning back a claim that would make profession of Christianity *absurd*. The actual and decisive reason for belief is still that a man finds himself believing, responding with faith to religious truth-claims. This reason has not been displaced. The reply to a challenge need not be part of the motive leading to faith. It may be cited to show that it is permissible for him to continue to believe that his response of faith is an adequate reason for faith. Someone believes because he has found himself to be a man of faith; and a rebuttal enables him to show that he may continue to believe.

Now a rebuttal, although it permits him to show that he may continue to rely on his motives, is not related to his motives as their foundation or warrant. It does not underlie them. To establish this point it is necessary to recall that a person who is not in the condition of doubt or confronted with a challenge does not need to have any rationale. He need not have any reasons to justify his situation as a man with faith other than that he finds himself with faith.

Shall we say, however, that this person really does need rebuttals, that he presupposes rebuttals, even if he does not know it, since challenges do exist even if he is not aware of the challenges? If we say yes, then it follows that no one ever has a religious commitment which is "really" solidly founded. For no matter how many challenges one is aware of, and however many rebuttals one has, one never is sure of having enough, since new challenges may appear. Every challenge as it materializes would reveal a gap in one's motives as a basis of affirming religious beliefs that existed all the time.

Moreover, to say rebuttals are a basis for motives suggests that there is an invisible foundation of rebuttals which emerges bit by bit as challenges arise and are rebutted; and rebuttals are the *real* ground of religious affirmations, rather than the actual way a person makes affirmations. For they establish all that is necessary to prevent it to be absurd to affirm religious truth-claims.

But challenges do not reveal gaps in motives; motives are not the sort of things which have "gaps" revealed by challenges and filled by rebuttals. In the special case we are considering, the training through which one has found that one could affirm certain things and act in certain ways is the *achievement of a goal*. One has succeeded in reaching a certain place; one has faith; one is being nourished. A challenge does not reveal that one has not attained this goal. Challenges that arise cause doubts about the truth of one's faith, but they do not reveal that the faith one has is not based upon finding oneself responding with faith and being nourished in a Christian community. Challenges do not exist as "holes" within a motive which one comes to discover; therefore rebuttals do not plug holes in a motive. *Rebuttals come and go with challenges.* Their function is to be employed to deal with challenges to the truth of religious beliefs which are affirmed by faith. They are not a permanent fixture, an invisible foundation for faith which we uncover bit by bit.

If rebuttals were an "invisible" support for a motive, then in the case of a person who is not troubled with doubt or aware of challenges, we would have to say that such a person had no basis at all for his religious beliefs. A response of faith in the context of a Christian community would be ruled out as a ground for religious beliefs. From the perspective of a "deeper" level, we would have to say that it is not a ground at all.

Now it is not being claimed that rebuttals do not have a function and cannot be described as reasons for believing. Rebuttals function *alongside* motives. For a person who believes does not believe because there are rebuttals, but because he finds himself responding with faith. Rebuttals endorse this achievement when it is challenged; they are not the hidden but true road to the achievement. . . .

### 4. CONCLUSION TO PART I

I have shown a sense in which the response of faith is a reason or ground for affirming truth-claims. For it can be a reasonable basis for the affirmation of truth-claims, as long as there are no decisive reasons which count against their truth. It is a different kind of ground or reason for making truth-claims from one that establishes their truth. Moreover, the rebuttals to reasons which count against the truth of religious truth-claims are not a support on which faith rests. They are not the *actual* basis or ground for asserting religious truth-claims, even though they "neutralize" reasons which count against their truth and which could prevent a rational affirmation of them unless they are in principle capable of being "neutralized." The *actual* reason religious truth-claims are affirmed in the case we are considering is that they awaken faith and in that condition they give a person nourishment and fulfillment. Rebuttals may be used without becoming part of the actual reason or actual basis of the affirmation of religious beliefs.

Motives, then, may be a reason for affirming and adhering to religious truth-claims. Reasons which count toward establishing their truth do not need to be given for one to assert religious truth-claims rationally. A person does not need to have such a reason or ground in order to give his adherence to Christianity or to an article of that religion rationally. He may respond directly to the claims of the gospel without logically depending on a case which seeks to establish its truth. He may by means of his motives find an adequate ground to affirm it. . . .

## PART II

### 1. NOT ALL MOTIVES ARE GROUNDS

The position that faith is a sound ground for adhering to truth-claims does not commit us to the view that *all* motives are grounds

for truth-claims. I do not suppose that the satisfaction of *any* need
can be a sound basis for adhering to a truth-claim. It is possible to
distinguish between those motives which are not grounds and those
motives which are grounds. One reason it is thought that faith is
not a ground (in the sense I have argued for) is the result of the
failure to distinguish between those motives which are only sources
and those motives which are sources *and* grounds for adhering to
truth-claims.

. . . But I believe that among sources for believing a truth-claim,
we can distinguish between those motives which are *merely* sources
and those which are sources *and* grounds for adhering to truth-
claims (even though they do not count toward showing the truth
of the truth-claims). The basis of this distinction between motives
is whether or not it is the truth of a truth-claim which satisfies needs
and thus motivates a person to assert (or adhere to) the truth-
claim.

## 2. THE BIZARRENESS TEST: DISTINGUISHING BETWEEN MOTIVES

I do not deny that unworthy motives, such as an inordinate desire
for attention, and irrelevant motives, such as a fear of chickens, may
be involved in one's acceptance of Christianity. However, unlike
the illustration concerning Gertrude Stein, we do not have just one
person with a love for bird watching which might be the cause of a
wrong judgment regarding a painter's work. We have many different kinds of people with many different "eccentricities" who become Christians. This variety leads me to think that unworthy
motives and eccentricities, which are indeed irrelevant as grounds
*in any sense* for a truth-claim, are not the only factors which enter
into an acceptance of Christianity and may not even be the important ones. There may be more general causes for people responding with faith. It may be because as human beings people have
needs which the Christian religion touches upon and by satisfying
them awakens faith.

I intend here, however, to argue that, although the *worth* of
some paintings is *irrelevant* to satisfying an interest in bird watching, *whether the belief* that there is a redeeming God *is true* or not

*is relevant* to the satisfaction of human beings who feel sinful and who aspire to goodness. One can distinguish between motives for whose satisfaction the truth of a truth-claim (*what it claims is the case*) does matter and motives for whose satisfaction this does not matter. One can often judge whether the relation between a need and its satisfaction is bizarre or proper. The *quality* of a picture does not satisfy the bird watching fancy of Gertrude Stein; that it has birds for its *subject matter* satisfies that fancy. The claim that a picture is good is not what satisfies the fancy, but that it has birds as its subject matter. Thus the relation between the bird watching fancy (the motive or source of the claim) and the claim that a picture is good is a bizarre one: it is not the claim that satisfies the need; and whether the claim is true or not does not matter to the satisfaction of the need.

The same is true of the desire for attention or a fear of chickens and an adherence to religious truth-claims. But a yearning to be righteous and the claim that there is a God who redeems is not a bizarre relationship. It is *the truth-claim* which satisfies the need (what it claims is the case) and whether the truth-claim is true or not matters to the person who adheres to it because of his need. This allows us to distinguish it from motives whose relation to the making of a truth-claim is bizarre.

The distinction I am drawing between motives can be seen if we take the above cases, and in each instance postulate that the person who makes the judgment is shown the source of his judgment. It would not be surprising to find a person who judged a picture to be good to give up this judgment if he were reminded that the subject matter was birds and that he had a fancy for bird watching. Likewise, it would not be surprising for one who had judged Christianity to be true to withdraw the judgment were he reminded that he had an inordinate desire to be important and that Christianity made him feel important. But if we tell one who believes in God as a redeemer that he has an inordinate desire to be cleansed a reply to this effect would not be a surprising one: "Of course, that is what I've been telling you all along; I am impure and God cleanses me." In this case the reminder of the source of the judgment does not have the tendency to cause one to consider withdrawing the judgment. In the first case one can readily see that a bird watching fancy should not be a criterion for judging the quality of a painting. The same can be said about a fear of chickens and the truth of Christianity. The desire to feel important may be considered an unworthy desire or may be praised as one of the roots of ambition. But an inordinate desire to feel important is one of the things condemned by Christianity. It cannot be sanctioned as a basis for affirming Christian beliefs. Whereas in the last case, an inordinate desire to be cleansed neither is contrary to the Christian faith nor irrelevant to an evaluation of its truth; for one of the things Christianity teaches is the forgiveness of sins.

That religious truth-claims satisfy a yearning to be righteous, can therefore be a ground for adhering to them. For it is *because of what they claim is true* that the needs are satisfied. Were the relation between the beliefs and the needs bizarre, then the satisfaction could not be a basis for adhering to the beliefs. It would be something else which satisfied the needs, not what the beliefs themselves claimed was true.[9]

I am not arguing that faith is a ground in the sense of being a reason that counts toward establishing that something is true. I am defending the idea that the source for believing may be a ground for believing a truth-claim because one receives satisfaction of certain needs from what the truth-claim says is the case. The above discussion shows that the truth of religious truth-claims matters to one who responds to them because of *some* motives but not to a response caused by *other* motives. In other words, we may distinguish between those motives which can be a ground for adhering to truth-claims from those which are not. The distinction is made on the basis of whether the truth of the truth-claims matters to the needs which motivate their assertion. It is what religious truth-claims claim is true that satisfies some needs. Thus the response of faith can be one's *source* for believing and also one's *ground* for believing truth-claims. As long as the sources for believing are motives which can be satisfied only by what religious truth-claims claim is the case, they can be a *ground* for asserting truth-claims. For as we have seen, as long as there is nothing which counts decisively against their truth, they can be affirmed and asserted because they awaken faith, and nourish or fulfill needs. Not any motives which are sources for believing something will be a ground which makes it legitimate for a truth-claim to be asserted, but only ones whose relation to what the truth-claims claim is the case is proper and not bizarre.

## 3. CONCLUSION TO PART II

I am not objecting to rationales—reasons which count toward establishing the truth of religious beliefs. I have tried to show that there are two kinds of grounds for adhering to religious truth-claims, and the response of faith can be a basis for affirming religious truth-claims. My intention has been to show that faith is a *kind* of ground because there is the danger that it may be thought that Christianity affirmed without a sound rationale is completely lacking in grounds of any kind.

### NOTES

1. This does not mean that reasoned arguments and historical evidence have no place in Christianity. On the contrary they do have a place, and in this study some of the uses of reasoned arguments and historical evidence in religion are pointed out. For example, reasoned arguments may be used to rebut a claim that a religious belief is not true or is doubtful, to remove barriers and misunderstandings which prevent one from coming to an affirmation of them, and they may be used in our attempts to conceive of God and of His relation to the universe. Historical evidence may be used to help determine what is orthodox when we are faced with rival interpretations of a Christian belief. Notwithstanding this qualification, it is still the case that religious commitment, which includes the affirmation of beliefs, is not fundamentally based on reasoned arguments nor on historical evidence.

2. This seems to be the case with G. K. Chesterton. In a passage he considers the question: suppose that Christian doctrines contain some truth. Why not take the truths and leave the doctrines? ". . . Why cannot you simply allow for human weakness without believing in the Fall?" (*Orthodoxy: A Personal Philosophy* [reprint of 1st ed. of 1908; London and Glasgow, 1961], p. 141.) He gives some reasons in reply to this question and then concludes, "I have now said enough to show . . . that I have in the ordinary arena of apologetics, a ground of belief. . . . But I will not pretend that this curt discussion is my real reason for accepting Christianity . . . I have another far more solid and central ground for submitting to it as a faith. . . . And that is this: that the

Christian Church in its practical relation to my soul is a living teacher, not a dead one." (P. 153).

3. To claim that a proposition, X, is true, may mean: (1) there are reasons which show that X is true. It can also mean: (2) that one affirms and adheres to the truth-claim. To affirm and adhere to something which is a truth-claim, one is *claiming* that what is affirmed and adhered to is true. I want to show that one can rationally affirm and adhere to a religious belief *as true*, without basing one's adherence to religious beliefs on the ground that there are reasons which count toward establishing their truth.

4. The term "rationale" is not used with any intention of suggesting that a rationale is a "rationalization." Moreover, even if one were to be able to show that, for example, to do metaphysics is to be engaged in rationalization, as W. F. Zuurdeeg apparently claims, this would not *ipso facto* show that a particular metaphysical view or system is false, nor remove the necessity for an examination of the "evidence" for the view or system. Willem F. Zuurdeeg, *An Analytic Philosophy of Religion* (Nashville, Tenn., 1959), chap. IV, esp. pp. 137-138.

5. It is important to remember that the basis described is not the *only* possible kind of basis individuals may actually have for their religious commitment. This must be kept in mind, since in the following pages I speak of the motive of faith as the *actual* basis of adhering to religious truth-claims, whereas an individual may have another kind of ground for his adherence to Christian truth-claims.

6. This expression includes reference to a local congregation, Christians of other congregations and denominations, Christians in the past of whom one can learn, and Christian literature. The amount of exposure may vary as well.

7. I do not mean to imply that "faith is without content," as if training and faith are separated. I simply wish to stress that "finding oneself with faith" is the consequence of the training.

8. In saying that the response of faith *in this context* is itself a ground of faith, I am alluding to the fact that there is a great deal of internal criticism of the practices and beliefs of Christianity by theologians, Biblical critics, and Church historians. Some of the ways this is done are described below. By internal criticism the practices and beliefs that are presented to people for adoption are carefully "screened" to prevent aberations, superstitions, and fantasies. Thus it is possible for a belief to be ruled out and given up because (say) by historical research it is found to be "unorthodox" even though it is part of that to which one previously responded to with faith, and even if it itself may satisfy certain needs. That practices and beliefs are "screened" means that I am not saying that *anything* to which one responds with faith has a sufficient ground to be affirmed. This fact does not, however, mean that faith is itself not the reason religious beliefs are affirmed: for it is the nourishment one receives that is the actual reason one affirms beliefs and

this is a sufficient reason, unless something specifically counts significantly against its truth.

9. This indicates that whether or not God exists matters to a person who affirms religious beliefs. For if the claim that *God* cleanses and redeems is not what satisfies the need for righteousness, then the relation of the truth-claim to the need is bizarre.

# 22. THEOLOGY AND VERIFICATION

## John Hick

*John Hick, formerly Professor of Christian Philosophy at Prince-*
*ton Theological Seminary, is Lecturer in the Philosophy of Re-*
*ligion at Cambridge University. Among his writings are* Faith
and Knowledge, Philosophy of Religion, *and* Evil and the God
of Love.

To ask "Is the existence of God verifiable?" is to pose a question
which is too imprecise to be capable of being answered.[1] There are
many different concepts of God, and it may be that statements
employing some of them are open to verification or falsification
while statements employing others of them are not. Again, the
notion of verifying is itself by no means perfectly clear and fixed;
and it may be that on some views of the nature of verification the
existence of God is verifiable, whereas on other views it is not.

Instead of seeking to compile a list of the various different concepts of God and the various possible senses of "verify," I wish to
argue with regard to one particular concept of deity, namely the
Christian concept, that divine existence is in principle verifiable;
and as the first stage of this argument I must indicate what I mean
by "verifiable."

I

The central core of the concept of verification, I suggest, is the
removal of ignorance or uncertainty concerning the truth of some
proposition. That $p$ is verified (whether $p$ embodies a theory, hypothesis, prediction, or straightforward assertion) means that something happens which makes it clear that $p$ is true. A question is

Reprinted by permission of the author and editor from *Theology Today*,
Volume 17 (1960), pp. 12-31.

settled so that there is no longer room for rational doubt concerning it. The way in which grounds for rational doubt are excluded varies, of course, with the subject matter. But the general feature common to all cases of verification is the ascertaining of truth by the removal of grounds for rational doubt. Where such grounds are removed, we rightly speak of verification having taken place.

To characterize verification in this way is to raise the question whether the notion of verification is purely logical or is both logical and psychological. Is the statement that *p* is verified simply the statement that a certain state of affairs exists (or has existed), or is it the statement also that someone is aware that this state of affairs exists (or has existed) and notes that its existence establishes the truth of *p*? A geologist predicts that the earth's surface will be covered with ice in 15 million years time. Suppose that in 15 million years time the earth's surface *is* covered with ice, but that in the meantime the human race has perished, so that no one is left to observe the event or to draw any conclusion concerning the accuracy of the geologist's prediction. Do we now wish to say that his prediction has been verified, or shall we deny that it has been verified, on the ground that there is no one left to do the verifying?

The range of "verify" and its cognates is sufficiently wide to permit us to speak in either way. But the only sort of verification of theological propositions which is likely to interest us is one in which human beings participate. We may therefore, for our present purpose, treat verification as a logico-psychological rather than as a purely logical concept. I suggest, then, that "verify" be construed as a verb which has its primary uses in the active voice: I verify, you verify, we verify, they verify, or have verified. The impersonal passive, it is verified, now becomes logically secondary. To say that *p* has been verified is to say that (at least) someone has verified it, often with the implication that his or their report to this effect is generally accepted. But it is impossible, on this usage, for *p* to have been verified without someone having verified it. "Verification" is thus primarily the name for an event which takes place in human consciousness.[2] It refers to an experience, the experience of ascertaining that a given proposition or set of propositions is true. To this extent verification is a psychological notion. But of course it is also a logical notion. For needless to say, not *any* experience is rightly called an experience of verifying *p*. Both logical and psychological conditions must be fulfilled in order for verification to have taken place. In this respect, "verify" is like "know." Knowing is an experience which someone has or undergoes, or perhaps a dispositional state in which someone is, and it cannot take place without someone having or undergoing it or being in it; but not by any means every experience which people have, or every dispositional state in which they are, is rightly called knowing.

With regard to this logico-psychological concept of verification, such questions as the following arise. When A, but nobody else, has ascertained that $p$ is true, can $p$ be said to have been verified; or is it required that others also have undergone the same ascertainment? How public, in other words, must verification be? Is it necessary that $p$ could in principle be verified by anyone, without restriction, even though perhaps only A has in fact verified it? If so, what is meant here by "in principle"; does it signify, for example, that $p$ must be verifiable by anyone who performs a certain operation; and does it imply that to do this is within everyone's power?

These questions cannot, I believe, be given any general answer applicable to all instances of the exclusion of rational doubt. The answers must be derived in each case from an investigation of the particular subject matter. It will be the object of subsequent sections of this article to undertake such an investigation concerning the Christian concept of God.

Verification is often construed as the verification of a prediction. However, verification, as the exclusion of grounds for rational doubt, does not necessarily consist in the proving correct of a prediction; a verifying experience does not always need to have been predicted in order to have the effect of excluding rational doubt. But when we are interested in the verifiability of propositions as the criterion for their having factual meaning, the notion of prediction becomes central. If a proposition contains or entails predictions which can be verified or falsified, its character as an assertion (though not of course its character as a true assertion) is thereby guaranteed.

Such predictions may be and often are conditional. For example, statements about the features on the dark side of the moon are rendered meaningful by the conditional predictions which they entail to the effect that if an observer comes to be in such a position in space, he will make such-and-such observations. It would in fact be more accurate to say that the prediction is always conditional, but that sometimes the conditions are so obvious and so likely to be fulfilled in any case that they require no special mention, while sometimes they require for their fulfillment some unusual expedition or operation. A prediction, for example, that the sun will rise within twenty-four hours is intended unconditionally, at least as concerns conditions to be fulfilled by the observer; he is not required by the terms of the prediction to perform any special operation. Even in this case, however, there is an implied negative condition that he shall not put himself in a situation (such as immuring himself in the depths of a coal mine) from which a sunrise would not be perceptible. Other predictions, however, are explicitly conditional. In these cases it is true for any particular individual that in order to verify the statement in question he must go through some specified course of action. The prediction is to the effect that if you conduct such an experiment you will obtain such a result; for example, if you go into the next room you will have such-and-such visual experiences, and if you then touch the table which you see you will have such-and-such tactual experiences, and so on. The content of the "if" clause is of course always determined by the particular subject matter. The logic of "table" determines what you must do to verify statements about tables; the logic of "molecule" determines what you must do to verify statements about molecules; and the logic of "God" determines what you must do to verify statements about God.

In those cases in which the individual who is to verify a proposition must himself first perform some operation, it clearly cannot follow from the circumstances that the proposition is true that everybody has in fact verified it, or that everybody will at some future time verify it. For whether or not any particular person performs the requisite operation is a contingent matter.

II

What is the relation between verification and falsification? We are all familiar today with the phrase, "theology and falsification." A. G. N. Flew and others,[3] taking their cue from John Wisdom,[4] have raised instead of the question, "What possible experiences would verify 'God exists'?" the matching question, "What possible experiences would falsify 'God exists'? What conceivable state of affairs would be incompatible with the existence of God?" In posing the question in this way it was apparently assumed that verification and falsification are symmetrically related, and that the latter is apt to be the more accessible of the two.

In the most common cases, certainly, verification and falsification are symmetrically related. The logically simplest case of verification is provided by the crucial instance. Here it is integral to a given hypothesis that if, in specified circumstances, A occurs, the hypothesis is thereby shown to be true, whereas if B occurs the hypothesis is thereby shown to be false. Verification and falsification are also symmetrically related in the testing of such a proposition as "There is a table in the next room." The verifying experiences in this case are experiences of seeing and touching, predictions of which are entailed by the proposition in question, under the proviso that one goes into the next room; and the absence of such experiences in those circumstances serves to falsify the proposition.

But it would be rash to assume, on this basis, that verification and falsification must always be related in this symmetrical fashion. They do not necessarily stand to one another as do the two sides of a coin, so that once the coin is spun it must fall on one side or the other. There are cases in which verification and falsification each correspond to a side on a different coin, so that one can fail to verify without this failure constituting falsification.

Consider, for example, the proposition that "there are three successive sevens in the decimal determination of $\pi$." So far as the value of $\pi$ has been worked out, it does not contain a series of three sevens, but it will always be true that such a series may occur at a point not yet reached in anyone's calculations. Accordingly, the proposition may one day be verified, if it is true, but can never be falsified, if it is false.

The hypothesis of continued conscious existence after bodily death provides an instance of a different kind of such asymmetry, and one which has a direct bearing upon the theistic problem. This hypothesis has built into it a prediction that one will after the date of one's bodily death have conscious experiences, including the experience of remembering that death. This is a prediction which will be verified in one's own experience if it is true, but which cannot be falsified if it is false. That is to say, it can be false, but *that* it is false can never be a fact which anyone has experientially verified.

But this circumstance does not undermine the meaningfulness of the hypothesis, since it is also such that if it be true, it will be known to be true.

It is important to remember that we do not speak of verifying logically necessary truths, but only propositions concerning matters of fact. Accordingly verification is not to be identified with the concept of logical certification or proof. The exclusion of rational doubt concerning some matter of fact is not equivalent to the exclusion of the logical possibility of error or illusion. For truths concerning fact are not logically necessary. Their contrary is never self-contradictory. But at the same time the bare logical possibility of error does not constitute ground for rational doubt as to the veracity of our experience. If it did, no empirical proposition could ever be verified, and indeed the notion of empirical verification would be without use and therefore without sense. What we rightly seek, when we desire the verification of a factual proposition, is not a demonstration of the logical impossibility of the proposition being false (for this would be a self-contradictory demand), but such weight of evidence as suffices, in the type of case in question, to exclude rational doubt.

III

These features of the concept of verification—that verification consists in the exclusion of grounds for rational doubt concerning the truth of some proposition; that this means its exclusion from particular minds; that the nature of the experience which serves to exclude grounds for rational doubt depends upon the particular subject matter; that verification is often related to predictions and that such predictions are often conditional; that verification and falsification may be asymmetrically related; and finally, that the verification of a factual proposition is not equivalent to logical certification—are all relevant to the verification of the central religious claim, "God exists." I wish now to apply these discriminations to the notion of eschatological verification, which has been briefly employed by Ian Crombie in his contribution to *New Essays in Philosophical Theology*,[5] and by myself in *Faith and Knowledge*.[6] This suggestion has on each occasion been greeted with disapproval by both philosophers and theologians. I am, however, still of the

opinion that the notion of eschatological verification is sound; and
further, that no viable alternative to it has been offered to establish
the factual character of theism.

The strength of the notion of eschatological verification is that it
is not an *ad hoc* invention but is based upon an actually operative
religious concept of God. In the language of the Christian faith, the
word "God" stands at the center of a system of terms, such as Spirit,
grace, Logos, incarnation, Kingdom of God, and many more; and
the distinctly Christian conception of God can only be fully grasped
in its connection with these related terms.[7] It belongs to a complex
of notions which together constitute a picture of the universe in
which we live, of man's place therein, of a comprehensive divine
purpose interacting with human purposes, and of the general nature
of the eventual fulfillment of that divine purpose. This Christian
picture of the universe, entailing as it does certain distinctive expectations concerning the future, is a very different picture from any
that can be accepted by one who does not believe that the God of
the New Testament exists. Further, these differences are such as
to show themselves in human experience. The possibility of experiential confirmation is thus built into the Christian concept of
God; and the notion of eschatological verification seeks to relate this
fact to the logical problem of meaning.

Let me first give a general indication of this suggestion, by repeating a parable which I have related elsewhere,[8] and then try to make
it more precise and eligible for discussion. Here, first, is the parable.

Two men are travelling together along a road. One of them
believes that it leads to a Celestial City, the other that it leads nowhere; but since this is the only road there is, both must travel it.
Neither has been this way before, and therefore neither is able to
say what they will find around each next corner. During their
journey they meet both with moments of refreshment and delight,
and with moments of hardship and danger. All the time one of
them thinks of his journey as a pilgrimage to the Celestial City and
interprets the pleasant parts as encouragements and the obstacles
as trials of his purpose and lessons in endurance, prepared by the
king of that city and designed to make of him a worthy citizen of
the place when at last he arrives there. The other, however, believes none of this and sees their journey as an unavoidable and aim-
less ramble. Since he has no choice in the matter, he enjoys the

good and endures the bad. But for him there is no Celestial City to be reached, no all-encompassing purpose ordaining their journey; only the road itself and the luck of the road in good weather and in bad.

During the course of the journey the issue between them is not an experimental one. They do not entertain different expectations about the coming details of the road, but only about its ultimate destination. And yet when they do turn the last corner it will be apparent that one of them has been right all the time and the other wrong. Thus although the issue between them has not been experimental, it has nevertheless from the start been a real issue. They have not merely felt differently about the road; for one was feeling appropriately and the other inappropriately in relation to the actual state of affairs. Their opposed interpretations of the road constituted genuinely rival assertions, though assertions whose assertion-status has the peculiar characteristic of being guaranteed retrospectively by a future crux.

This parable has of course (like all parables) strict limitations. It is designed to make only one point: that Christian doctrine postulates an ultimate unambiguous state of existence *in patria* as well as our present ambiguous existence *in via*. There is a state of having arrived as well as a state of journeying, an eternal heavenly life as well as an earthly pilgrimage. The alleged future experience of this state cannot, of course, be appealed to as evidence for theism as a present interpretation of our experience; but it does suffice to render the choice between theism and atheism a real and not a merely empty or verbal choice. And although this does not affect the logic of the situation, it should be added that the alternative interpretations are more than theoretical, for they render different practical plans and policies appropriate now.

The universe as envisaged by the theist, then, differs as a totality from the universe as envisaged by the atheist. This difference does not, however, from our present standpoint within the universe, involve a difference in the objective content of each or even any of its passing moments. The theist and the atheist do not (or need not) expect different events to occur in the successive details of the temporal process. They do not (or need not) entertain divergent expectations of the course of history viewed from within. But the theist does and the atheist does not expect that when history is completed it will be seen to have led to a particular end-state and to have fulfilled a specific purpose, namely that of creating "children of God."

The idea of an eschatological verification of theism can make sense, however, only if the logically prior idea of continued personal existence after death is intelligible. A desultory debate on this topic has been going on for several years in some of the philosophical periodicals. C. I. Lewis has contended that the hypothesis of immortality "is an hypothesis about our own future experience. And our understanding of what would verify it has no lack of clarity."[9] And Morris Schlick agreed, adding, "We must conclude that immortality, in the sense defined [i.e. 'survival after death,' rather than 'never-ending life'], should not be regarded as a 'metaphysical problem,' but is an empirical hypothesis, because it possesses logical verifiability. It could be verified by following the prescription: 'Wait until you die!' "[10] However, others have challenged this conclusion, either on the ground that the phrase "surviving death" is self-contradictory in ordinary language or, more substantially, on the ground that the traditional distinction between soul and body cannot be sustained.[11] I should like to address myself to this latter view. The only self of which we know, it is said, is the empirical self, the walking, talking, acting, sleeping individual who lives, it may be, for some sixty to eighty years and then dies. Mental events and mental characteristics are analyzed into the modes of behavior and behavioral dispositions of this empirical self. The human being is described as an organism capable of acting in the "high-level" ways which we characterize as intelligent, thoughtful, humorous, calculating, and the like. The concept of mind or soul is thus not the concept of a "ghost in the machine" (to use Gilbert Ryle's loaded phrase[12]), but of the more flexible and sophisticated ways in which human beings behave and have it in them to behave. On this view there is no room for the notion of soul in distinction from body; and if there is no soul in distinction from body, there can be no question of the soul surviving the death of the body. Against this philosophical background the specifically Christian (and also Jewish) belief in the resurrection of the flesh, or body, in contrast to the Hellenic notion of the survival of a disembodied soul, might be expected to have attracted more attention than it has. For it is consonant with the conception of man as an indissoluble psychophysical unity, and yet it also offers the possibility of an empirical meaning for the idea of "life after death."

Paul is the chief Biblical expositor of the idea of the resurrection of the body.[13] His view, as I understand it, is this. When someone has died he is, apart from any special divine action, extinct. A human being is by nature mortal and subject to annihilation by death. But in fact God, by an act of sovereign power, either sometimes or always resurrects or (better) reconstitutes or recreates him —not, however, as the identical physical organism that he was before death, but as a *soma pneumatikon*, ("spiritual body") embodying the dispositional characteristics and memory traces of the deceased physical organism, and inhabiting an environment with which the *soma pneumatikon* is continuous as the *ante-mortem* body was continuous with our present world. In discussing this notion we may well abandon the word "spiritual," as lacking today any precise established usage, and speak of "resurrection bodies" and of "the resurrection world." The principal questions to be asked concern the relation between the physical world and the resurrection world, and the criteria of personal identity which are operating when it is alleged that a certain inhabitant of the resurrection world is the same person as an individual who once inhabited this world. The first of these questions turns out on investigation to be the more difficult of the two, and I shall take the easier one first.

Let me sketch a very odd possibility (concerning which, however, I wish to emphasize not so much its oddness as its possibility!), and then see how far it can be stretched in the direction of the notion of the resurrection body. In the process of stretching it will become even more odd than it was before; but my aim will be to show that, however odd, it remains within the bounds of the logically possible. This progression will be presented in three pictures, arranged in a self-explanatory order.

First picture: Suppose that at some learned gathering in this country one of the company were suddenly and inexplicably to disappear, and that at the same moment an exact replica of him were suddenly and inexplicably to appear at some comparable meeting in Australia. The person who appears in Australia is exactly similar, as to both bodily and mental characteristics, with the person who disappears in America. There is continuity of memory, complete similarity of bodily features, including even fingerprints, hair and eye coloration and stomach contents, and also of beliefs, habits, and mental propensities. In fact there is everything that would lead us to identify the one who appeared with the one who disappeared, except continuity of occupancy of space. We may suppose, for example, that a deputation of the colleagues of the man who disappeared fly to Australia to interview the replica of him which is reported there, and find that he is in all respects but one exactly as though he had travelled from say, Princeton to Melbourne, by conventional means. The only difference is that he describes how, as he was sitting listening to Dr. Z reading a paper, on blinking his eyes he suddenly found himself sitting in a different room listening to a different paper by an Australian scholar. He asks his colleagues how the meeting had gone after he ceased to be there, and what they had made of his disappearance, and so on. He clearly thinks of himself as the one who was present with them at their meeting in the United States. I suggest that faced with all these circumstances his colleagues would soon, if not immediately, find themselves thinking of him and treating him as the individual who had so inexplicably disappeared from their midst. We should be extending our normal use of "same person" in a way which the postulated facts would both demand and justify if we said that the one who appears in Australia is the same person as the one who disappears in America. The factors inclining us to identify them would far outweigh the factors disinclining us to do this. We should have no reasonable alternative but to extend our usage of "the same person" to cover the strange new case.

Second picture: Now let us suppose that the event in America is not a sudden and inexplicable disappearance, but indeed not a disappearance at all, but a sudden death. Only, at the moment when the individual dies, a replica of him as he was at the moment before his death, complete with memory up to that instant, appears in Australia. Even with the corpse on our hands, it would still, I suggest, be an extension of "same person" required and warranted by the postulated facts, to say that the same person who died has been miraculously recreated in Australia. The case would be considerably odder than in the previous picture, because of the existence of the corpse in America contemporaneously with the existence of the living person in Australia. But I submit that, although the oddness of this circumstance may be stated as strongly as you please, and can indeed hardly be overstated, yet it does not exceed the bounds of the logically possible. Once again we must imagine some of the deceased's colleagues going to Australia to interview the person who has suddenly appeared there. He would perfectly remember them and their meeting, be interested in what had happened, and be as amazed and dumbfounded about it as anyone else; and he would perhaps be worried about the possible legal complications if he should return to America to claim his property; and so on. Once again, I believe, they would soon find themselves thinking of him and treating him as the same person as the dead Princetonian. Once again the factors inclining us to say that the one who died and the one who appeared are the same person would outweigh the factors inclining us to say that they are different people. Once again we should have to extend our usage of "the same person" to cover this new case.

Third picture: My third supposal is that the replica, complete with memory, etc. appears, not in Australia, but as a resurrection replica in a different world altogether, a resurrection world inhabited by resurrected persons. This world occupies its own space, distinct from the space with which we are now familiar. That is to say, an object in the resurrection world is not situated at any distance or in any direction from an object in our present world, although each object in either world is spatially related to each other object in the same world.

Mr. X, then, dies. A Mr. X replica, complete with the set of memory traces which Mr. X had at the last moment before his death, comes into existence. It is composed of other material than physical matter, and is located in a resurrection world which does not stand in any spatial relationship with the physical world. Let us leave out of consideration St. Paul's hint that the resurrection body may be as unlike the physical body as is a full grain of wheat from the wheat seed, and consider the simpler picture in which the resurrection body has the same shape as the physical body.[14]

In these circumstances, how does Mr. X know that he has been resurrected or recreated? He remembers dying; or rather he remembers being on what he took to be his death-bed, and becoming progressively weaker until, presumably, he lost consciousness. But how does he know that (to put it Irishly) his "dying" proved fatal; and that he did not, after losing consciousness, begin to recover strength, and has now simply waked up?

The picture is readily enough elaborated to answer this question. Mr. X meets and recognizes a number of relatives and friends and historical personages whom he knows to have died; and from the fact of their presence, and also from their testimony that he has only just now appeared in their world, he is convinced that he has died. Evidences of this kind could mount up to the point at which they are quite as strong as the evidence which, in pictures one and two, convince the individual in question that he has been miraculously translated to Australia. Resurrected persons would be individually no more in doubt about their own identity than we are now, and would be able to identify one another in the same kind of ways, and with a like degree of assurance, as we do now.

If it be granted that resurrected persons might be able to arrive at a rationally founded conviction that their existence is *postmortem*, how could they know that the world in which they find themselves is in a different space from that in which their physical bodies were? How could such a one know that he is not in a like situation with the person in picture number two, who dies in America and appears as a full-blooded replica in Australia, leaving his corpse in the U. S. A.—except that now the replica is situated, not in Australia, but on a planet of some other star?

It is of course conceivable that the space of the resurrection world should have properties which are manifestly incompatible with its being a region of physical space. But on the other hand, it is not of the essence of the notion of a resurrection world that its space should have properties different from those of physical space. And supposing it not to have different properties, it is not evident that a resurrected individual could learn from any direct observations that he was not on a planet of some sun which is at so great a distance from our own sun that the stellar scenery visible from it is quite unlike that which we can now see. The grounds that a resurrected person would have for believing that he is in a different space from physical space (supposing there to be no discernible difference in spatial properties) would be the same as the grounds that any of us may have now for believing this concerning resurrected individuals. These grounds are indirect and consist in all those considerations (*e.g.*, Luke 16:26) which lead most of those who consider the question to reject as absurd the possibility of, for example, radio communication or rocket travel between earth and heaven.

v

In the present context my only concern is to claim that this doctrine of the divine creation of bodies, composed of a material other than that of physical matter, which bodies are endowed with sufficient correspondence of characteristics with our present bodies, and sufficient continuity of memory with our present consciousness, for us to speak of the same person being raised up again to life in a new environment, is not self-contradictory. If, then, it cannot be ruled out *ab initio* as meaningless, we may go on to consider whether and how it is related to the possible verification of Christian theism.

So far I have argued that a survival prediction such as is contained in the *corpus* of Christian belief is in principle subject to future verification. But this does not take the argument by any means as far as it must go if it is to succeed. For survival, simply as such, would not serve to verify theism. It would not necessarily be a state of affairs which is manifestly incompatible with the nonexistence of God. It might be taken just as a surprising natural fact. The atheist, in his resurrection body, and able to remember his life on earth, might say that the universe has turned out to be more complex, and perhaps more to be approved of, than he had realized. But the mere fact of survival, with a new body in a new environment, would not demonstrate to him that there is a God. It is fully compatible with the notion of survival that the life to come be, so far as the theistic problem is concerned, essentially a continuation of the present life, and religiously no less ambiguous. And in this event, survival after bodily death would not in the least constitute a final verification of theistic faith.

I shall not spend time in trying to draw a picture of a resurrection existence which would merely prolong the religious ambiguity of our present life. The important question, for our purpose, is not whether one can conceive of after-life experiences which would *not* verify theism (and in point of fact one can fairly easily conceive them), but whether one can conceive of after-life experiences which *would* serve to verify theism.

I think that we can. In trying to do so I shall not appeal to the traditional doctrine, which figures especially in Catholic and mystical theology, of the Beatific Vision of God. The difficulty presented by this doctrine is not so much that of deciding whether there are grounds for believing it, as of deciding what it means. I shall not, however, elaborate this difficulty, but pass directly to the investigation of a different and, as it seems to me, more intelligible possibility. This is the possibility not of a direct vision of God, whatever that might mean, but of a *situation* which points unambiguously to the existence of a loving God. This would be a situation which, so far as its religious significance is concerned, contrasts in a certain important respect with our present situation. Our present situation is one which in some ways seems to confirm and in other ways to contradict the truth of theism. Some events around us suggest the presence of an unseen benevolent intelligence and others suggest that no such intelligence is at work. Our situation is religiously ambiguous. But in order for us to be aware of this fact we must already have some idea, however vague, of what it would be for our situation to be not ambiguous, but on the contrary wholly evidential of God. I therefore want to try to make clearer this presupposed concept of a religiously unambiguous situation.

There are, I suggest, two possible developments of our experience such that, if they occurred in conjunction with one another (whether in this life or in another life to come), they would assure us beyond rational doubt of the reality of God, as conceived in the Christian faith. These are, *first*, an experience of the fulfillment of God's purpose for ourselves, as this has been disclosed in the Christian revelation; in conjunction, *second*, with an experience of communion with God as he has revealed himself in the person of Christ.

The divine purpose for human life, as this is depicted in the New Testament documents, is the bringing of the human person, in society with his fellows, to enjoy a certain valuable quality of personal life, the content of which is given in the character of Christ— which quality of life (*i.e.* life in relationship with God, described in the Fourth Gospel as eternal life) is said to be the proper destiny of human nature and the source of man's final self-fulfillment and happiness. The verification situation with regard to such a fulfillment is asymmetrical. On the one hand, so long as the divine purpose remains unfulfilled, we cannot know that it never will be fulfilled in the future; hence no final falsification is possible of the claim that this fulfillment will occur—unless, of course, the prediction contains a specific time clause which, in Christian teaching, it does not. But on the other hand, if and when the divine pupose *is* fulfilled in our own experience, we must be able to recognize and rejoice in that fulfillment. For the fulfillment would not be for us the promised fulfillment without our own conscious participation in it.

It is important to note that one can say this much without being cognizant in advance of the concrete form which such fulfillment will take. The before-and-after situation is analogous to that of a small child looking forward to adult life and then, having grown to adulthood, looking back upon childhood. The child possesses and can use correctly in various contexts the concept of "being grown-up," although he does not know, concretely, what it is like to be grown-up. But when he reaches adulthood he is nevertheless able to know that he has reached it; he is able to recognize the experience of living a grown-up life even though he did not know in advance just what to expect. For his understanding of adult maturity grows as he himself matures. Something similar may be supposed to happen in the case of the fulfillment of the divine purpose for human life. That fulfillment may be as far removed from our present condition as is mature adulthood from the mind of a little child; nevertheless, we possess already a comparatively vague notion of this final fulfillment, and as we move towards it our concept will itself become more adequate; and if and when we finally reach that fulfillment, the problem of recognizing it will have disappeared in the process.

The other feature that must, I suggest, be present in a state of affairs that would verify theism, is that the fulfillment of God's purpose be apprehended *as* the fulfillment of God's purpose and not simply as a natural state of affairs. To this end it must be accompanied by an experience of communion with God as he has made himself known to men in Christ.

The specifically Christian clause, "as he has made himself known to men in Christ," is essential, for it provides a solution to the problem of recognition in the awareness of God. Several writers have pointed out the logical difficulty involved in any claim to have encountered God.[15] How could one know that it was *God* whom one had encountered? God is described in Christian theology in terms of various absolute qualities, such as omnipotence, omnipresence, perfect goodness, infinite love, etc., which cannot as such be observed by us, as can their finite analogues, limited power, local presence, finite goodness, and human love. One can recognize that a being whom one "encounters" has a given finite degree of power, but how does one recognize that he has *un*limited power? How does one observe that an encountered being is *omni*present? How does one perceive that his goodness and love, which one can perhaps see to exceed any human goodness and love, are actually infinite? Such qualities cannot be given in human experience. One might claim, then, to have encountered a Being whom one presumes, or trusts, or hopes to be God; but one cannot claim to have encountered a Being whom one recognized to be the infinite, almighty, eternal Creator.

This difficulty is met in Christianity by the doctrine of the Incarnation—although this was not among the considerations which led to the formulation of that doctrine. The idea of incarnation provides answers to the two related questions: "How do we know that God has certain absolute qualities which, by their very nature, transcend human experience?" and "How can there be an eschatological verification of theism which is based upon a recognition of the presence of God in his Kingdom?"

In Christianity God is known as "the God and Father of our Lord Jesus Christ."[16] God is the Being about whom Jesus taught; the Being in relation to whom Jesus lived, and into a relationship with whom he brought his disciples; the Being whose *agape* toward men was seen on earth in the life of Jesus. In short, God is the transcendent Creator who has revealed himself in Christ. Now Jesus' teaching about the Father is a part of that self-disclosure, and it is from this teaching (together with that of the prophets who preceded him) that the Christian knowledge of God's transcendent being is derived. Only God himself knows his own infinite nature; and our human belief about that nature is based upon his self-revelation to men in Christ. As Karl Barth expresses it, "Jesus Christ is the knowability of God."[17] Our beliefs about God's infinite being are not capable of observational verification, being beyond the scope of human experience, but they are susceptible of indirect verification by the removal of rational doubt concerning the authority of Christ. An experience of the reign of the Son in the Kingdom of the Father would confirm that authority, and therewith, indirectly, the validity of Jesus' teaching concerning the character of God in his infinite transcendent nature.

The further question as to how an eschatological experience of the Kingdom of God could be known to be such has already been answered by implication. It is God's union with man in Christ that makes possible man's recognition of the fulfillment of God's purpose for man as being indeed the fulfillment of God's purpose for him. The presence of Christ in his Kingdom marks this as being beyond doubt the Kingdom of the God and Father of the Lord Jesus Christ.

It is true that even the experience of the realization of the promised Kingdom of God, with Christ reigning as Lord of the New Aeon, would not constitute a logical certification of his claims nor, accordingly, of the reality of God. But this will not seem remarkable to any philosopher in the empiricist tradition, who knows that it is only a confusion to demand that a factual proposition be an analytic truth. A set of expectations based upon faith in the historic Jesus as the incarnation of God, and in his teaching as being divinely authoritative, could be so fully confirmed in *post-mortem* experience as to leave no grounds for rational doubt as to the validity of that faith.

VI

There remains of course the problem (which falls to the New Testament scholar rather than to the philosopher) whether Christian tradition, and in particular the New Testament, provides a sufficiently authentic "picture" of the mind and character of Christ to make such recognition possible. I cannot here attempt to enter into the vast field of Biblical criticism, and shall confine myself to the logical point, which only emphasizes the importance of the historical question, that a verification of theism made possible by the

Incarnation is dependent upon the Christian's having a genuine contact with the person of Christ, even though this is mediated through the life and tradition of the Church.

One further point remains to be considered. When we ask the question, *"To whom* is theism verified?" one is initially inclined to assume that the answer must be, "To everyone." We are inclined to assume that, as in my parable of the journey, the believer must be confirmed in his belief, and the unbeliever converted from his unbelief. But this assumption is neither demanded by the nature of verification nor by any means unequivocally supported by our Christian sources.

We have already noted that a verifiable prediction may be conditional. "There is a table in the next room" entails conditional predictions of the form: if someone goes into the next room he will see, etc. But no one is compelled to go into the next room. Now it may be that the predictions concerning human experience which are entailed by the proposition that God exists are conditional predictions and that no one is compelled to fulfill those conditions. Indeed we stress in much of our theology that the manner of the divine self-disclosure to men is such that our human status as free and responsible beings is respected, and an awareness of God never is forced upon us. It may then be a condition of *post-mortem* verification that we be already in some degree conscious of God by an uncompelled response to his modes of revelation in this world. It may be that such a voluntary consciousness of God is an essential element in the fulfillment of the divine purpose for human nature, so that the verification of theism which consists in an experience of the final fulfillment of that purpose can only be experienced by those who have already entered upon an awareness of God by the religious mode of apperception which we call faith.

If this be so, it has the consequence that only the theistic believer can find the vindication of his belief. This circumstance would not of course set any restriction upon who can become a believer, but it would involve that while theistic faith can be verified—found by one who holds it to be beyond rational doubt—yet it cannot be proved to the nonbeliever. Such an asymmetry would connect with that strain of New Testament teaching which speaks of a division of mankind even in the world to come.

Having noted this possibility I will only express my personal opinion that the logic of the New Testament as a whole, though admittedly not always its explicit content, leads to a belief in ultimate universal salvation. However, my concern here is not to seek to establish the religious facts, but rather to establish that there are such things as religious facts, and in particular that the existence or nonexistence of the God of the New Testament is a matter of fact, and claims as such eventual experiential verification.

NOTES

1. In this article I assume that an indicative sentence expresses a factual assertion if and only if the state in which the universe would be if the putative assertion could correctly be said to be true differs in some experienceable way from the state in which the universe would be if the putative assertion could correctly be said to be false, all aspects of the universe other than that referred to in the putative assertion being the same in either case. This criterion acknowledges the important core of truth in the logical positivist verification principle. "Experienceable" in the above formulation means, in the case of alleged subjective or private facts (*e.g.*, pains, dreams, after-images, etc.), "experienceable by the subject in question" and, in the case of alleged objective or public facts, "capable in principle of being experienced by anyone." My contention is going to be that "God exists" asserts a matter of objective fact.

2. This suggestion is closely related to Carnap's insistence that, in contrast to "true," "confirmed" is time-dependent. To say that a statement is confirmed, or verified, is to say that it has been confirmed at a particular time—and, I would add, by a particular person. See Rudolf Carnap, "Truth and Confirmation," Feigl and Sellars, *Readings in Philosophical Analysis*, 1949, pp. 119 f.

3. A. G. N. Flew, editor, *New Essays in Philosophical Theology*, 1955, Chapter VI.

4. "Gods," *Proceedings of the Aristotelian Society*, 1944-45. Reprinted in A. G. N. Flew, editor, *Logic and Language*, First Series, 1951, and in John Wisdom, *Philosophy and Psycho-Analysis*, 1953.

5. Op. cit., p. 126.

6. Cornell University Press, 1957, pp. 150-62.

7. Its clear recognition of this fact, with regard not only to Christianity but to any religion is one of the valuable features of Ninian Smart's *Reasons and Faiths* (1958). He remarks, for example, that "the claim that God exists can only be understood by reference to many, if not all, other propositions in the doctrinal scheme from which it is extrapolated" (p. 12).

8. *Faith and Knowledge*, pp. 150 f.

9. "Experience and Meaning," *Philosophical Review*, 1934, re-

printed in Feigl and Sellars, *Readings in Philosophical Analysis*, 1949,
p. 142.

10. "Meaning and Verification," *Philosophical Review*, 1936, reprinted in Feigl and Sellars, op. cit., p. 160.

11. E.g. A. G. N. Flew, "Death," *New Essays in Philosophical Theology*; "Can a Man Witness his own Funeral?" *Hibbert Journal*, 1956.

12. *The Concept of Mind*, 1949, which contains an important ex-
position of the interpretation of "mental" qualities as characteristics of
behavior.

13. I Cor. 15.

14. As would seem to be assumed, for example, by Irenaeus (*Ad-
versus Haereses*, Bk. II, Ch. 34, Sec. 1).

15. For example, H. W. Hepburn, *Christianity and Paradox*, 1958,
pp. 56 f.

16. II Cor. 11:31.

17. *Church Dogmatics*, Vol. II, Pt. I, p. 150.